Sacred Books of the Buddhists, Vol. III.

DIALOGUES OF THE BUDDHA
PART II

SACRED BOOKS OF THE BUDDHISTS

TRANSLATED

BY VARIOUS ORIENTAL SCHOLARS

AND EDITED BY

T. W. RHYS DAVIDS
LL.D., Ph.D., D.Sc., F.B.A.
FORMERLY PROFESSOR OF COMPARATIVE RELIGION
AT THE UNIVERSITY OF MANCHESTER

PUBLISHED UNDER THE PATRONAGE OF
HIS MAJESTY THE KING OF SIAM

VOL. III

Published by
THE PALI TEXT SOCIETY, LONDON

Distributed by
ROUTLEDGE & KEGAN PAUL LTD.
LONDON, HENLEY AND BOSTON
1977

DIALOGUES OF THE BUDDHA

FOURTH EDITION

TRANSLATED FROM THE PALI
OF THE DÍGHA NIKÂYA

BY

T. W. AND C. A. F. RHYS DAVIDS

PART II

First Published 1910
Second Edition 1938
Third Edition 1952
Fourth Edition 1959
Fourth Edition reprinted 1972
Fourth Edition reprinted 1977

ISBN 0 7100 8630 X

© Pali Text Society

Printed in Great Britain by
Unwin Brothers Limited, The Gresham Press, Old Woking, Surrey

CONTENTS.

INTRODUCTORY NOTE

THE growing demand for translations of the Pali canon has encouraged the Pali Text Society, which manages the Sacred Books of the Buddhists Series, to bring out a new edition of the important second volume of the *Dialogues of the Buddha*. The original edition of 1910 has now been out of print for fifteen years or so ; and before it had been published for as long as eighteen months, practically the whole of the second edition was destroyed during the war of 1939-45. It has been impossible to find a copy of this second edition, and the present edition is therefore a reprint of the 1910 edition. But it includes the Preface Mrs. Rhys Davids wrote for the second edition, and which she then published in a slightly revised form in her *Wayfarer's Words*, vol. III, p. 963-972 (Messrs. Luzac & Co., 1942). Although possessing a proof copy of the former, we have decided that it would be more in accordance with her wishes to reprint here the version in *Wayfarer's Words*, containing as it does her own revision of what she had already written.

Her Preface has as its principal object the correction of " much error (as well as much knowledge) disseminated by the first edition " (*Wayfarer's Words*, III, p. 962). After studying it, it will be found quite easy to substitute in this reprint of the original edition the alterations she would have made, but did not for reasons she gives, as well as those she did in fact make in the now virtually lost, but not greatly revised, second edition of 1938.

I. B. HORNER

1951

PREFACE TO THE SECOND EDITION

DOES one but hold on long enough in this span of human way-faring, one may be here to see even the translation of a Buddhist text sold out, with the gentle demand for it not yet exhausted. So has this work, after 28 years, attained to a second edition. By the process called ' off-set ', emendations are difficult and costly. And there are no funds. Hence I have made only such as were most desirable, leaving in much which I should have wished to see expressed otherwise, both in my husband's work and in my own, were this more thoroughly a ' new ' edition.

A word first to make clear our partnership in both this and the third (and last) volume, the first being wholly his work (publish-ed 1899). He ceased from his labours here in 1922, soon after the completion of these Dialogues. From the beginning of this century he had undertaken engrossing work as holding the new, the first Chair in a British University for the comparative study of religion, a task, at the present stage of research, fitter for half a dozen men than for one. Concentration on work in any one religious tradition had become impossible. It was only when Estlin Carpenter suggested that I should join in aiding the completion of the Dialogues that we both with good will started to do this. Of this second volume Rh. D. had already, in 1881, published Suttantas XVI and XVII in *Sacred Books of the East*, XI. All the rest I translated, he revising my work, inserting many of the footnotes and contributing all the Introductions save that to the Mahā-Nidāna Suttanta, which is my work.

Another eleven years passed before the remaining volume was issued. Funds had to be raised, and our generous patron no longer sat on Siam's throne. My husband was ageing, his health waning, and the accursed war came down. Siam's later monarch however, paid the printer, and the Dialogues achieved comple-tion in 1921. Introductions to XXXI-XXXIII I wrote and all the translation.

In this edition it is mainly my own work that I have revised. Not a little in my partner's work needed revision, but there was not only expense, but the wish in me not to barge in on what was in a way a ' classic '. Moreover his footnotes, where a rendering seemed to him make-shift, often guard the reader. In all this there is matter in the history of research it may be well to keep in view.

Here I will briefly notice certain prominent renderings I have left unaltered, and also three of vital importance which I have altered.

(1) I have only altered Max-Mullerian transliteration (a system now generally discarded) where cerebrals were involved. To write *K* for C, *G* for J, etc., has proved for the general reader, ay, for the general writer too misleading to be left in. Further, I have let stand the circumflex for the long ā ; also the less correct crude form of -i for -in, e.g. in Vipassin, and the crude form of -a in Gotama, etc. I never could share the partiality of some German and Asiatic scholars for the nominative in -o for general use. Such a phrase as ' he told Ānado ' is too unpleasant a shock —as were one to say ' amo tu '.

(2) I have let stand the use of ' god ' for ' deva ', but I do not find either ' god ' or ' angel ' historically fitting. In early Buddhism (as a consequence of the accepted Immanence) Vedic gods *had become friendly mortals*, living close by and given, in friendly good will, to talk with the ' man-who-saw ' and heard. Immanence had driven out, save for the many-folk, the notions of worship, prayer, ritual, intermediacy. Nor were devas always ' messengers ' (angels) from a Highest. Nor do I like *devatā*, the abstract, as ' fairy ' ; this I have changed to ' being ' or ' spirit '.

(3) I have left in ' brethren ' for *bhikkhu, bhikkhave*, etc. Unwillingly, but cf. footnote, 1st ed., p. 81. I have not the objection to ' monk ' Rh. D. there shows, nor have I found Buddhists objecting. We should not, because of convenience and tradition, force in ' brethren '. The Pali for ' brother ' could have been used, had it seemed meet ; it never was used.

(4) I have left in his ' intoxications ' and my ' intoxicants ' for ' āsavā '. We have no good word for spreading, absorbed, liquid bane. ' Canker ' is on the whole best, yet it is too ' dry '. Drugs, taints, poisons have also served.

(5) I have let *viññāṇa* be rendered by ' cognition ', or by ' consciousness ', albeit the older meaning : ' man-as -surviving ' or ' soul ' is in the main truer. But not in all Suttas. We see, in Majjhima 38, how this older meaning of a persisting principle, referred to as ' speaker, experiencer ', is being hounded out, to be replaced by a meaning virtually identical with that of the other two varieties of cognition : *saññā, vedanā*, as merely the mental outcrop of sensation. *Viññāṇa*, in the Indian tradition, could connote both meanings ; we have no such Janus-word.

(6) I have let ' rapture ' in Jhāna stand for *samādhi* (lit. ' concentration '), although it goes too far, is too near Chalmers' ' ecstasy ', which also goes too far. The only ' rapture ' about *samādhi* is the ' rapt ' quality of hyper-attention. As ' rapture ' it is too easily confused with *pīti*, or emotional rapture, which in *samādhi* had to be suppressed.

(7) I have let the usual ' wobbling ' in translation stand, when it is *bhava* that has to be rendered. Thus (p. 131) the last two lines : ' craving for future life—renewed existence—no more

birth ' show a triple use of the one word *bhava*, thus : ' then is the craving for becoming rooted out—that which leads to becoming is faded out—there is no more becoming '. No one reading the former translation gets any idea of the sinister change which had come over this word. No one unhelped would recognize it as the joyous word on p. 267, when the king sends polite greeting : ' May good fortune (*bhava*) attend the honourable Jotipāla.' (The Commentary strongly supports this rendering). In original Buddhism ' becoming ' is given as the reason why men needed Gotama's message, as one which could promote that ' good fortune ' in the spiritual growth of the man. It had come, in monasticism, to mean the dreadful persistence of life both as ' rebirth ' and as ' re-worlded '. However, the translator, with his triple variant for the one Pali word, gets there, so far as the monastic outlook goes, and so I leave it.

(8) Then there is the great word, of all words hardest fitly to translate : Dhamma. This is quite inaccurately rendered ' Truth ': Had the Buddhist speaker wished to say ' Truth ', he had three strong words at hand : *sacca, bhūta, tathatā.* But no one regrets more than I that Rh. D. and I did not hammer out more often our renderings together. Till near his end I was too much just pupil ; let alone that we were both more or less akin to the Sutta Nipāta rhinoceros :

eko care khaggavisānakappo

My own view of that day I somewhat guard in a footnote (p. 29) by adducing the term ' Norm '. But Dhamma wants a better word than what is a ' good average '. Gotama's many brahmin fellow-workers will have had in mind the Upanishadic term *antaryāmin.* Yet will this not have sufficed for Dhamma, object from the first of the Leader's avowed worship. This was more ; it was inner incentive, urger, not merely restraining force. There was in Dhamma the push of conscience as well as its check. Hence possibly it is why *antaryāmin* did not get taken over by them, as for a while did *amrta.*

But *dhamma* had also got the wider looser meaning of 'religion'; for this no other word was current (save perhaps *suddhi*). Take an instance from our volume III, p. 37 : ' What is this *dhamma* wherein you train your disciples, so that they win comfort and acknowledge inclination as the beginning of the training, *ajjhāsayam ādibrahmacariyam*?' How is not a stronger word, like ' will ', wanted here. For us religion here fits better than any other term. If the reader will bear in mind this wider meaning of *dhamma*, and let ' Truth ' convey this, Rh. D. will not have misled him. Anyway it is better than the rendering ' Law '.

Here a brief codicil. On p. 38 I have once more altered in a formula three epithets, usually applied to *dhamma*, and have let them apply, implicitly as in the Pali, to the life of the ' wayfarer '

(*tathāgata*). If *dhamma* means ' religion ', these epithets :
' beginning, middle, end ' have no fit place. Nor have they if we
call *dhamma* ' Truth '. Nor can the three fit the later meaning,
now general among Southern Buddhists, of *dhamma* as a code of
teaching, for, when this mission-charge was made to the first
disciples, there was not yet any such code of oral teaching. Ob-
viously, for me, the epithets apply to man's span of present life,
here or elsewhere : *dhamma* as ' lovely at the beginning, middle,
end.'

(9) A not unimportant matter is the leaving in, on p. 82 ff.,
of ' prosper ' for growth (*vuddhi*). In the text we find *vuddhi*
opposed to ' decay ' (*parihāni*) : ' just growth is to be expected,
not decay.' ' Prosper ' is not in itself incorrect, but for me it is
vital to remember, that not only here, at the end of his long mission, but at its very beginning, the inspiring message ran :
' Men are decaying ; as learners of (this) *dhamma* they will grow '
(lit. ' become '). The great Man-lover is here shown keeping
faith with the message from the Unseen from first to last. By the
literal rendering ' growth ' the reader can see this, as with
' prosper ' he cannot.

This brings me to the three emendations I have made in our
work, made because it is vital to an improved grasp of the teaching of original Buddhism that they should replace our own
pioneer renderings, through which that grasp has been and still
is crippled.

(10) The first is on pp. 29-32. Here, in translating, I had
docilely followed Oldenberg's rendering in *Vinaya Texts* (S.B.E.)
—these pages being his work, not Rh. D's—and also K. E.
Neumann's (p. 268 of his *Majjhima Nikāya*, 1917). A rendering
I repeated, alas ! knowing no better then, in *Kindred Sayings*,
I, pp. 173ff., 1917. These scholars judged that the word giving
the better state for men who would hear Gotama teach meant
just ' will be ', not " will become ', or ' grow '. But this word
' will be ' or ' become ' is opposed to ' decaying,' thus indicating
no mere future happening, but a causal process, an evolution, and
hence had we all been more discerning, we should have seen that
more was wanted than just a ' will be '. We had before us
contexts in both Upanishads and Pitakas, where *bhavissanti*
(and other *bhu* inflections) clearly meant more than just a copula,
or bare future state. The more pregnant meaning of ' will
become ' gives a hitherto buried consecutive force to the Hesitation scene and to its immediate sequel, as I have repeatedly
pointed out.[1]

(11) The second corrected context is no less important. It is
on p. 108 ; a very solemn, very emphatic parting charge. Rh.
D.'s rendering is echoed by R.O. Franke's, which is yet more

---

[1] Cf. esp. my *To Become or not to Become*, 1937.

free. But that is not the worst. Both entirely ignored the religious import, in Gotama's day, of the word *attā* (*ātmā*), import by
which the accepted teaching of Immanence brought into the
word 'self', or 'spirit', Deity Itself. 'Lamps . . . refuge
unto yourselves' may be good modern English tradition, but it
was not Indian religious idiom of 500 B.C. And when our translators render similar compounds of *ātmā* in the Upanishads, their
procedure is very different. Then it is 'Lamp of the Self, refuge
of the Self', or at least similar usage of this word. Why not
this usage here also ?

Buddhists and lapsed Christians have lapped up this apparent
call to be depending on the actual average self, quite overlooking
that, in the Pali scriptures, the believer is usually told to take as
refuge, not himself, not the two of the injunction : ' live as they
that have the *attā*, that have *dhamma* as lamp, as refuge, and no
other ', but a *trinity* of lamps or refuges. And he cannot have it
both ways. But I am here not mainly concerned with incon-
sistencies. It is for me most vital, I repeat, if we are to grip
rightly the Founder's teaching, that we reject the atheistic or
antitheistic presentation of it which, true enough of degenerate
Hinayāna, is here thrust upon him who was the Child of a teaching of Immanence, the Child of an uplift in man—man as being,
immanently and in germ, the Highest, the Peak of the Immortal
(*t' amat' agge*)—an outlook unrivalled then and since in religious
culture. I do not suppose we shall ever get the word 'self'
to raise us religiously as it raised India. We have seen grow up,
since Johnson's Dictionary registered our language, the meaning
in self and unselfish of ' egoism ', ' altruism '. But long before it,
St. Catherine of Genoa had taught Immanence with a personal
pronoun. ' My Me is God . . . by a process of transformation '.
For her perhaps *ipse, stessa*, did not mean the ugly thing they
now do, yet she chose well. And I think that if our translators
had consistently used ' spirit ', not ' self ', that rather absurd
perversion by our translators of the pathetic farewell had never
been made. But we started our Indian culture with research
into grammar, and only then moved on into religion, taking with
us the *grammatical ātmā*, when we, richer here than India, had
the better alternatives of ' spirit ' and ' soul ', India having the
one word.

(12) The third alternative is of but one word, yet it is hardly
less important than the others. On p. 33, where the Hesitation
scene, true it may be of Gotama only, is told as true or earlier
Buddhas, we see the Teacher-to-be, for whom doubt has now
been dispelled, making glad response to the inspiring deva, whom
psychically he has seen and heard. So glad was this for early
compilers that it had been lifted into poetry :
Opened for man the portals of the Undying !
Man, as learning that he was essentially, not just a being, but

a becoming, was herein to be shown how he had a very guarantee to winning the ' immortal peak ' of Becoming, the very culmination of life (cf. p. 109). This glorious destiny for man conceived as essentially divine reverberates through the early Upanishads and was echoed by the Sakyan missioners.

But for the after-men the vision faded out. Life was to be realized—so far as man, his vision turned earthwards could see—not as an ever more and more, but as something to be got rid of. And for the virtually positive term *amata*, they substituted the actually negative term *nirvāna*. So we get the Commentary telling us, that the ' portals ' are ' *nibbāna* reckoned as *amata* ', and the translators, alas ! following it, choosing (possibly for aesthetic reasons) the more musical exegetic term, and turning from a word belonging, as that term did not, to the best religious teaching *when ' Buddhism ' was born.* Late in time I have restored the 'undying' of the text, where *nirvāna* had been put.

Senior and junior translators, we may, in this volume leave an impression of ' self-lit self-supported ' confidence that is misleading. Nay, none have been more mindful of difficulties. And I regret that, in the translation transferred from *S.B.E.* XI, for my husband's general preface no room was found, since in it are words of modesty and historical sagacity. Thus he wrote : ' with very great diffidence I yet maintain, that the discovery of early Buddhism . . . has turned the flank, so to speak, of most of the existing literature on Buddhism '. After a lapse of sixty years I venture to think, that we can only now go on to achieve the flank-turning. Only now can we, with regard to the refrains and emphases in the Pitakas, endorse with confidence the truth in his special and later Introduction, in this volume, to No. XVI (p. 77). Namely, that these records may be considered authentic enough, but only in the one way in which any such record can be considered authentic, that is, as evidence of beliefs, of values, held *at the date at which it was composed*.

NOTE. I regret that, in the foregoing I did not list my cited reading of *t'amat'agge* : ' The peak of the Highest ' as a fourth alteration. In preparing the volume for reprint, it had broken in on me, that Buddhaghosa's interpretation (p. 109 fn.) was fantastic, and of the worsened outlook of degenerate values. " Darkness " (*tamas*) plays here no part. The *t'* is the emphatic *ta* ; the *agge* is Magadhese nominative (lingering here and there in the Canon) ; and *amata* it was that the New Gospel *professed to be revealing*. The compound, coupled with the pregnant *bhavissanti*, as ' will become ' shows this very grand old man (yet ever young) closing his long work with the very words with which he had begun. But so far philologians have shaken sapient heads at me !

C. A. F. RHYS DAVIDS

1941

MAHÂPADÂNA SUTTANTA.

WE find in this tract the root of that Bîrana-weed which, growing up along with the rest of Buddhism, went on spreading so luxuriantly that it gradually covered up much that was of value in the earlier teaching, and finally led to the downfall, in its home in India, of the ancient faith. The doctrine of the Bodhisatta, of the Wisdom-Being, drove out the doctrine of the Aryan Path. A gorgeous hierarchy of mythological wonder-workers filled men's minds, and the older system of self-training and self-control became forgotten.

Even at its first appearance here the weed is not attractive. The craving for edification is more manifest in it than the desire for truth. We have legends of six forerunners of the historical Buddha, each constructed with wearisome iteration, in imitation of the then accepted beliefs as to the life of Gotama. So exactly do these six legends follow one pattern that it has been possible, without the omission of any detail, to arrange them in parallel columns.

The main motive of this parallelism is revealed in the constantly repeated refrain Ayam ettha dhammatâ: 'That, in such a case, is the rule,' the Norm, the natural order of things, according to the reign of law in the moral and physical world. Precisely the same idea is emphasized in the doctrine of dependent origination, the Paṭicca-samuppâda, placed here in the mouth of Vipassi, the most ancient of these six teachers of old. The fact that it is so placed shows that the early Buddhists, when our Suttanta was composed, believed this doctrine to have been pre-Buddhistic.

It is probable that all the great religious teachers of antiquity appealed, in support of their views, to the wise men of still older times. It is so recorded of most of them; and where it is not recorded, as in the cases of Lao Tsü and Zarathustra, that is probably due to the meagreness of the extant records. In every country where the level of intelligence was sufficient to produce a great leader of men in matters of religion, it was sufficient also to bear in remembrance the names at least, and a vague notion as to some of the doctrines, of former, if perhaps less successful and famous, reformers.

But a Wisdom-Being, appearing from aeon to aeon under similar circumstances to propound a similar faith! This is an exclusively Indian conception; in Indian literature it is mainly Buddhist; and in Buddhist literature its first appearance is in documents of the date of our Suttanta. Did the Buddha himself know anything of this theory? Possibly not. The theory of a number of successive Buddhas presupposes the conception of a Buddha as a different and more exalted personage than an Arahant. Now in our oldest documents these two conceptions are still in a state of fusion. The word Buddha does not occur in its later, special, technical sense. It occurs often enough in ambiguous phrases, where it may be translated by 'Converted One, Awakened One.' Thus at Sutta Nipâta 48 it is said, of Gotama, 'The Awakened One (Buddho) came to Râjagaha'; but the time referred to is some years before he had become a Buddha in the later technical sense. And at Sutta Nipâta 167 it is said: 'Let us ask Gotama, the awakened one who has passed beyond anger and fear'; but the very same adjectives are used at Itivuttaka, No. 68, of any ordinary Arahant. So the phrases used to describe the mental crises in Gotama's career are invariably precisely the same as those used under similar circumstances of his disciples; and this holds good both of his going forth, and of his victory and attainment of Nirvana under the Tree of Wisdom. Further than that, in long descriptions of Gotama—such for instance as that in Sutta Nipâta, verses 153 to 167—all the epithets used are found elsewhere applied to one or other of his disciples. The teacher never called himself a Buddha (as distinct from an Arahant). When addressed as Buddha, or spoken of as such, by his followers, it is always doubtful whether anything more is meant than an enlightened Arahant.

It is needless to state that this does not in the least imply any sense of equality between the teacher and his disciples. The very oldest documents represent the difference as immeasurable; but as a difference of degree, not of kind. The question is as to the manner of the growth and hardening of this sense of difference; and as to the consequent gradual change in the connotation of words.

In the episode of the events between the Wisdom Tree and the First Discourse, in which—for the first time perhaps—we twice have the epithet Sammâsambuddha[1], it is in a similar way associated both times on equal terms with Arahâ. So

---

[1] Majjhima I, 171; Vinaya I, 8, 9; Kathâ Vatthu 289; compare Divy. 393; Mahâvastu III, 326; Jâtaka II, 284.

the word Bodhisatta has gradually changed its meaning and implication. First used of Gotama between the Going Forth and the Nirvana, it is then used of him from the moment of conception ; then of all the Buddhas from conception to Arahantship ; then of those beings on earth—men or animals—who were eventually to become Buddhas ; then of gods ; and finally it became a sort of degree in theology, and was used as a term of respect for any learned and able Mahâyânist doctor.

The word Apadâna, used in the title of this Suttanta for the legend or life-story of a Buddha, is also used as a title of a book in the supplementary Nikâya. There it has come generally to mean the legend or life-story of an Arahant, male or female, though the older connotation is also found. In later books it is never used, I think, for the legend of a Buddha. The full title may mean the Story of the Great Ones—that is the Seven Buddhas—or the Great (the important) Story—that is the Story of the Dhamma, and its bearers and promulgators. The last is probably what is meant, as in the corresponding title of the Mahâvastu.

[XIV. MAHÂPADÂNA SUTTANTA.

THE SUBLIME STORY.]

1. [1] Thus have I heard. The Exalted One was once staying at Sâvatthi, in Anâtha Pindika's pleasaunce in the Jeta Wood, at the Kareri-tree cottage [1]. Now among many bhikkhus who had returned from their alms-tour and were assembled, sitting together after their meal, in the pavilion in the Kareri grounds [2], a religious conversation bearing on previous births arose, to the effect that thus and thus were previous births [3].

2. And the Exalted One, with clear and Heavenly Ear surpassing the hearing of men, overheard this conversation among the bhikkhus [4]. And arising from

---

[1] Kareri, according to Childers, is *Capparis trifoliata*. The Cy. states that this tree which stood by the entrance to the cottage was a Varuna-tree, suggestive, if true, of the superseded tree-cult into which Varuna-worship had declined. See Rhys Davids's 'Buddhist India,' p. 235; Jât. IV, 8. There were four principal buildings in the Jeta Wood: the cottage or chamber in question, the Kosamba-tree cottage, a perfumed chamber, and the fir-tree house (sala*l*a = sarala-ghara). According to the commentator each cost 100,000 [? kahâpanas] to build, but the ancient bas-relief on the Bharahat Tope shows clearly cottages, and apparently cottages of only one room each. In § 12 below this cottage is called a vihâra; and the latter word, in the ancient texts, always means a single room or lodging-place. Anâtha-pindika had built the first three, King Pasenadi the last.

[2] Mâ*l*o. Buddhaghosa describes this as a nisîdana-sâlâ, or sitting-room, built near the cottage. At the time when this Suttanta was composed it meant a thatched roof supported by wooden pillars. There were no walls to it.

[3] According to the Cy. only religious teachers, religious disciples, Pacceka-Buddhas, and the Saviour Buddhas could recall their own or other previous lives, and, of the first, only those who taught Karma. Except the memories of the great Buddhas, which have no limit whatever, a limit is given in the case of each of these classes, past which they could not recall. This systematizing of a popular belief seems to indicate that, when Buddhaghosa lived, no claim to such transcendent memory was actually made among his contemporaries.

[4] Buddhaghosa distinguishes between the 'omniscient knowledge' by which the Buddha realizes the drift of the talk in the Brahmajâla

his seat he came to the pavilion in the Kareri grounds,
and took his seat on the mat spread out for him. And
when he had sat down he said to the brethren :—
'What is the talk on which you are engaged sitting
here, and what is the subject of conversation between
you?' [And they told him all.]

3. [2] Then he said :—' Do you not wish, brethren,
to hear some religious talk on the subject of former
lives?'

'Now is the time, O Exalted One, now is the time,
O Welcome One, for the Exalted One to give us a
religious discourse on the subject of former lives.
When the brethren have heard it from the Exalted
One they will bear it in mind.'

'Wherefore then, brethren, hearken well to me, and
I will speak.'

'So be it, lord,' replied the brethren. And the
Exalted One said :—

4. 'It is now ninety-one aeons ago, brethren, since
Vipassi, the Exalted One, Arahant, Buddha Supreme,
arose in the world. It is now thirty-one aeons ago,
brethren, since Sikhi, the Exalted One, Arahant,
Buddha Supreme, arose in the world. It was in that
same thirty-first aeon, brethren, that Vessabhu, the
Exalted One, Arahant, Buddha Supreme, arose in the
world. It was in this present auspicious aeon, brethren,
that Kakusandha, the Exalted One, Arahant, Buddha
Supreme, arosè in the world. It was in this auspicious
aeon, brethren, that Konâgamana, the Exalted One,
Arahant, Buddha Supreme, arose in the world. It was
in this auspicious aeon, brethren, that Kassapa, the
Exalted One, Arahant, Buddha Supreme, arose in
the world. It is in this auspicious aeon, brethren,
that now I, an Arahant, Buddha Supreme, have arisen
in the world.'

5-12. [And in like manner the rest of the statements
in the following table are given in similar paragraphs.]

Suttanta ('Dialogues,' I, 2), and the divine hearing, as by a finer sense,
operating here.

		Kappa, Aeon.	Jâti, Social rank.	Gotta, Family.	Length of life at that epoch.	Tree under which he became enlightened.
					Years	
1.	Vipassi	91st from now	Noble	Kondañña	80000	Pâṭali
2.	Sikhi	31st from now	do.	do.	70000	Puṇḍarîka
3.	Vessabhu	do.	do.	do.	60000	Sâla
4.	Kakusandha	In this aeon	Brahmin	Kassapa	40000	Sirîsa
5.	Konâgamana	do.	do.	do.	30000	Udumbara
6.	Kassapa	do.	do.	do.	20000	Nigrodha
7.	Gotama	do.	Noble	Gotama	100	Assattha

13. [8] Now not long after he had gone out, this talk arose among the brethren :—'How wonderful a thing, brethren, and how strange is the great genius, the master mind of the Tathâgata, that he should remember the Buddhas of old, who attained final completion, who cut off obstacles, who cut down barriers, who have ended the cycle, who have escaped from all sorrow—that he should remember of these that such was their rank, such were their personal names, such were their family names, such the span of their lives, such their pair of disciples, and such the number of the congregations of their disciples, telling us :—" Of such was the birth of those Exalted Ones, such were their names, and their clans; such were their morals, their doctrines, their wisdom ; thus did they live, and thus they gained emancipation." Now, what think you, brother? Has this principle of truth been clearly discerned by the Tathâgata, so that by his discernment of it he remembers [all those facts] about the Buddhas of the past? Or have gods revealed this matter to the Tathâgata, so that thereby he remembers?'

Names of two chief disciples.	Number of Arahants present at assemblies.	Name of usual attendant Bhikkhu.	Father.	Mother.	Birth-place.
Khanda Tissa	68 lacs 100000 80000	Asoka	Bandhumâ	Bandhumatî	Bandhumatî
Abhibhu Sambhava	100000 80000 70000	Khemaṅkura	Aruna	Pabhâvatî	Pabhâvatî
Sona Uttara	80000 70000 60000	Upasannaka	Suppatîta	Yasavatî	Anopama
Vidhûra Sañjîva	40000	Buddhija	Aggidatta	Visâkhâ	Khemavatî
Bhiyyosa Uttara	30000	Sotthija	Yaññadatta	Uttarâ	Sobhavatî
Tissa Bhâradvâja	20000	Sabbamitta	Brahmadatta	Dhanavatî	Bârânasî
Sâriputta Moggallâna	1250	Ânanda	Suddhodana	Mâyâ	Kapilavatthu

14. [9] Now such was the trend of the talk that was going on among the brethren when the Exalted One, rousing himself at eventide from meditation, went to the pavilion in the Kareri grounds, and took his seat on the mat spread out for him. And when he had sat down, he said to the brethren :—' What is the talk on which you are engaged, brethren, as ye sit here, and what was the subject of conversation between you?' [And they told him all.]

15. [10] 'It is through his clear discernment of a principle of the truth, brethren, that the Tathâgata is able to remember [all those facts about the Buddhas of old[1]]. And gods also have revealed these matters to him, enabling him to remember [all those things]. Do ye not wish, brethren, to hear yet further religious discourse bearing on former lives?'

[11] 'Now, O Exalted One, is the time, now, O Welcome One, is the time! Whatsoever the Exalted

---

[1] In the text is a full repetition of the reminiscence given in § 13.

One may tell us further bearing on former lives, the brethren will listen to it and bear it in mind.'

'Wherefore, brethren, hearken and attend well, and I will speak.'

'So be it, lord,' replied the brethren.   The Exalted One said :—

16. 'I have told you, brethren, when Vipassi, the Exalted One, Arahant, Buddha Supreme, arose in the world, into what rank and family he was born, how long he lived, where he became a Buddha, the names of his leading disciples, the number of his disciples, the name of his ministering bhikkhu, of his father, his mother, and of their place of residence[1].

17. [12] 'Now Vipassi, brethren, when, as Bodhisat, he ceased to belong to the hosts of the heaven of Delight, descended into his mother's womb mindful and self-possessed[2].   That, in such a case, is the rule[3].

---

[1] The text repeats verbatim all that was said above of Vipassi.

[2] This and following paragraphs (to § 30 inclusive) recur in the Acchariyabbhutadhamma Sutta (M. III, pp. 119–24).   The notes appended by Dr. Neumann to his translation of that Sutta, giving parallels from Christian archaeology, are of great interest. (*Reden Gotamo Buddho's* Majjhimanikâyo, III, pp. 253 ff.)   How the Birth-legend had developed in the fifth century A. D. may be seen in the Nidânakathâ, translated in Rhys Davids's 'Buddhist Birth Stories,' pp. 62 ff.

This state of mind in Rule the first, according to a voluminous comment by Buddhaghosa, refers more to the termination of the Bodhisat's life in the Tusita heaven, than to any miraculous embryonic commencement.   He is depicted as being fully aware, with his angelic neighbours, of the imminent culminating career awaiting him, and to have selected country, region, town, father and mother, on the eve of his 'fall' from heaven.   He is further said to be conscious that he was *quâ* god deceased :—' Thus fallen (or deceased) he knows 'I fall.' But he is not aware of his cuti-cittaṁ, or dying thought.   As to when there is awareness of re-conception, the Buddhist fathers were not agreed.   But they admit that, in its content, the dawning idea was either the first, or the fifth of the eight types of 'good thought' enumerated in Dhamma-Sangani (pp. 1, 39 of the translation).   But we learn, under § 21, that there was no consciousness by way of the five senses before birth.

[3] Dhammatâ, i.e. says the Cy. in the nature, or order of things. The five old-world order of things is the Order of Karma, of the

'It is the rule, brethren, that, when the Bodhisat
ceases to belong to the hosts of the heaven of Delight,
and enters a mother's womb, there is made manifest
throughout the universe—including the worlds above
of the gods, the Mâras and the Brahmâs, and the world
below with its recluses and brahmins, its princes and
peoples—an infinite and splendid radiance, passing the
glory of the gods.   Even in those spaces which are
between the worlds, baseless [1], murky and dark, and
where even moon and sun, so wondrous and mighty,
cannot prevail to give light, even there is made manifest this infinite and splendid radiance, passing the
glory of the gods.   And those beings who happen to
be existing there [2], perceiving each other by that
radiance, say :—" Verily there be other beings living
here!"   And the ten thousand worlds of the universe
tremble and shudder and quake.   And that this infinite
splendid radiance is made manifest in the world, passing the glory of the gods—that, in such a case, is the
rule.

17ª. 'It is the rule, brethren, that, when the Bodhisat
is descending into a mother's womb, four sons of the
gods go toward the four quarters to protect him, saying :—" Let no one, be he human, or non-human, or
whatsoever he be, work harm to the Bodhisat or to the
mother of the Bodhisat!"   That, in such a case, is the
rule.

18. 'It is the rule, brethren, that, when the Bodhisat
is descending into a mother's womb, the mother of
the Bodhisat is a woman virtuous through her own
nature :—averse from taking life, averse from taking
what is not given, averse from unchastity, averse from

Seasons, of Life-germs, of Mind, and of the Dhamma.   The last
named is here implicated.

[1] Asaṁvutâ. Cy.—not supported from beneath.

[2] In the Great Inter-world Hell.   They would be undergoing
purgatory for karma of grievous offences against parents and the
religious world, and of cruelty to animals.   Very long in body and
with bats' nails, they were condemned to crawl up the Cakkavâla rock,
till finding no food, they turned back and fell into the river of brine
flowing round the world. Cy.

lying speech, averse from indulgence in strong drinks. That, in such a case, is the rule.

19. [13] 'It is the rule, brethren, that, when the Bodhisat is descending into a mother's womb, that mother has no mind for indulgence in the pleasures of sense with men, and is incapable of transgression with any man whatever who may be enamoured of her. That, in such a case, is the rule.

20. 'It is the rule, brethren, that, when the Bodhisat is descending into a mother's womb, that mother is living in the enjoyment yielded by the five senses, is addicted to it, possessed of it, surrounded by it.   That, in such a case, is the rule.

21. 'It is the rule, brethren, that, when the Bodhisat is descending into a mother's womb, no ailment whatsoever befalls that mother; at ease is she and unafflicted in body; and within her womb she sees the Bodhisat complete in the endowment of all his organs and his limbs.   Just as if, brethren, there were a beautiful cat's-eye gem[1], of purest water, octangular, cut with supreme skill, translucent and flawless, excellent in every way.   And through it were strung a thread, blue or orange, red, white, or yellow.   If a man who had eyes to see were to take it into his hand, he would clearly perceive how the one was strung on the other. Even so, brethren, when the Bodhisat is descending into a mother's womb, no ailment whatever befalls that mother; at ease is she and unaffected in body; and within her womb she sees the Bodhisat complete in the endowment of all his organs and his limbs.   That, in such a case, is the rule.

22. [14] 'It is the rule, brethren, that, on the seventh day after the birth of a Bodhisat, the mother of the

---

[1] This simile, occurring in a similar connexion in M. III, 121, is elsewhere ('Dialogues,' I, 87; M. II, 17) applied to self-knowledge, i. e. of one's body and mind and their interdependence.   The point of the simile is not the perfection of the jewel, but the clarity of vision.   The myth of the visible embryo recurs in mediaeval Christian art.   See Neumann, op. cit.; and 'Buddhist Birth Stories,' p. 65 *n*.

Bodhisat dies, and rises again in the heaven of Delight.
That, in such a case, is the rule.

23. 'It is the rule, brethren, that, whereas other
women bring forth after bearing either nine or ten
months[1], the mother of a Bodhisat brings not forth
till she has borne the child ten months. That, in such
a case, is the rule.

24. 'It is the rule, brethren, that, whereas other
women bring forth sitting or reclining, the mother of
a Bodhisat brings forth not so, but standing. That, in
such a case, is the rule.'

25. 'It is the rule, brethren, that, when a Bodhisat
issues from his mother's womb, gods receive him first,
afterwards men[2]. That, in such a case, is the rule.

26. 'It is the rule, brethren, that, when a Bodhisat
issues from his mother's womb, and has not yet touched
the earth, for four sons of the gods to receive him, and
present him to the mother, saying :—" Rejoice, lady, for
Mighty is the son that is born to thee!" That, in such
a case, is the rule.

27. 'It is the rule, brethren, that, when a Bodhisat
issues from his mother's womb, he comes forth stainless, undefiled by watery matter, undefiled by mucus,
undefiled by blood, undefiled by any uncleanness whatever, pure, spotless. Just as if, brethren, a jewel were
laid down on Benares muslin; the jewel is not stained
by the muslin, nor is the muslin stained by it; and why
is that? Because of the purity of both. Even so,
brethren, is it at the birth of a Bodhisat. That, in such
a case, is the rule.

28. [15] 'It is the rule, brethren, that, when a Bodhisat issues from his mother's womb, two showers of

---

[1] The Cy. holds that these disjunctives may be understood to
include a term of from seven to twelve months. Seven months'
embryos, it adds, live, but cannot endure heat or cold; eight months'
babes do not live—a midwife tradition that, we fancy, is still current
here and now.

[2] Cf. the account of the birth of Gotama, ' Buddhist Birth Stories,'
p. 66, and of the *four*, not *three*, adoring kings in some early Christian
bas-reliefs, Neumann, op. cit.

water appear from the sky, one of cold, the other of warm water, wherewith they do the needful bathing of the Bodhisat and of his mother. That, in such a case, is the rule.

29. 'It is the rule, brethren, that, when a Bodhisat has come to birth, he stands firm on both feet and, with his face to the north, takes seven strides, the while a white canopy is held over him [1], and, looking around on every side, he utters as with the voice of a bull:—"Chief am I in the world, Eldest am I in the world, Foremost am I in the world! This is the last birth! There is now no more coming to be [2]!" That, in such a case, is the rule.

30. 'It is the rule, brethren, that, when a Bodhisat issues from his mother's womb, there is made manifest throughout the universe—including the worlds above of the gods, the Mâras and the Brahmâs, and the world below with its recluses and brahmins, its princes and peoples,—an infinite and splendid radiance passing the glory of the gods. Even in those spaces which are between the worlds, baseless, murky and dark, and where even moon and sun, so wondrous and mighty, cannot prevail to give light, even there is manifest this infinite and splendid radiance, passing the glory of the gods. And those beings who happen to be existing there, perceiving each other by that radiance, say:— "Verily there be other beings living here!" And the ten thousand worlds of the universe tremble and shudder and quake. And this infinite and splendid

---

[1] As an emblem of sovereignty, says the Cy., in which case the emblem is usually named, not its bearers. But these were devatâ, angels or fairies or gods.

[2] Each action of the babe had for the later Buddhists its symbolical meaning. Standing on the earth meant obtaining the Four Iddhipâdas. Facing the north meant the spiritual conquest of multitudes. The seven strides were the Seven Bojjhangas. The canopy was the umbrella of emancipation. Looking around meant unveiled knowledge. The bull-cry meant the irrevocable turning of the wheel of the Truth or Law. The 'lion-roar' of 'the last birth' meant the arahantship he would attain in this life.

radiance is made manifest in the world, passing the glory of the gods.   This, in such a case, is the rule.'

31. [16] 'When the boy Vipassi, brethren, was born, they brought word to Bandhuman the râja saying :— " A son, my lord, is born to you! May it please you to see him?"   Now when Bandhuman the râja had seen the babe, he sent for the brahmin soothsayers[1], saying :— " Let the reverend brahmin soothsayers see the child." Then, brethren, when the brahmin soothsayers had seen the child, they said to Bandhuman the râja :— " Rejoice, lord, for one of the Mighty Ones is born thy son!   Fortune is thine, my lord, good fortune is thine, in that in thy family such a son has come to birth! For this babe, my lord, is endowed with the thirty-two marks of the Great Man ; and to one so endowed two careers lie open, and none other.   If he live the life of the House, he becomes Lord of the Wheel[2], a righteous Lord of the Right[3], ruler of the four quarters, con-queror, guardian of the people's good, owner of the Seven Treasures. His do those seven treasures become, to wit, the Wheel treasure, the Elephant treasure, the Horse treasure, the Gem treasure, the Woman treasure, the Steward treasure, the Eldest Son treasure making seven[4].   More than a thousand sons will be his, heroes, vigorous of frame, crushers of the hosts of the enemy. He, when he has conquered this earth to its ocean bounds, is established not by the scourge, not by the sword, but by righteousness.   But if such a boy go forth from the life of the House into the Homeless state[5], he becomes an Arahant, a Buddha Supreme, rolling back the veil from the world.

---

[1] Literally, mark-men, or augurs.   See 'Dialogues,' I, 16, *n*. 1.
[2] Turner of the Wheel, the now well-known Indian symbol of empire.
[3] Dhamma-râjâ.
[4] For details of each of these see below in the Mahâ-Sudassana Suttanta, No. XVII.
[5] This vigorous and picturesque idiom—agârasmâ anagâriyaṁ pabbajati—has been here and elsewhere rendered as literally as possible.

32. '"And what, my lord, are the thirty-two marks of the 'Great Man[1],' wherewith endowed this child hath two careers open to him, and only two :—that of the Lord of the Wheel . . . that of Buddha Supreme?

[17] '" This babe, my lord, has feet with level tread[2]. That this is so counts to him as one of the marks of a Great Man.

'" On the soles of the babe's feet wheels appear with a thousand spokes, with tyre and hub, in every way complete. That this is so counts to him as one of the marks of a Great Man.

'" This babe has projecting heels[3],
He is long in the fingers and long in the toes[4],
Soft and tender in hands and feet,
With hands and feet like a net[5].
His ankles are like rounded shells[6];
His legs are like an antelope's[7].
Standing and without bending he can touch and rub his knees with either hand.
His male organs are concealed in a sheath.
His complexion is like bronze, the colour of gold.
[18] His skin is so delicately smooth that no dust cleaves to his body[8].

---

[1] Given also at M. II, 136, 137. Comp. the note above Vol. I, p. 110. The whole theory is pre-Buddhistic.

[2] Suppaṭṭhita-pâdo: literally, 'well-planted feet.' The traditional meaning is, that the whole under-surface touched the ground at once. The Great Man was 'flat-footed,' and did not toe or heel the ground in walking.

[3] If the foot of a 'Great Man' be measured in four parts, two are taken up by the sole and toes, one is under the leg, and one is the heel projecting rearward.

[4] And all four, fingers and toes, are of equal length, like a monkey's. Cy.

[5] Like a lattice, says the Cy., and explains this to mean that there is no 'webbing' between fingers and toes, but that these are set in right lines, like the meshes of a net.

[6] Ensuring the maximum of flexibility. Cy. This is desirable in sitting cross-legged.

[7] With protuberant well-modelled joints, like an ear of rice or barley. Cy.

[8] Hence the Buddhas only wash as an example to their followers. Cy.

The down on it grows in single hairs, one to each pore,

The small hairs on his body turn upward, every hair of it, blue-black in colour like eye-paint, in little curling rings, curling to the right.

' " This babe has a frame divinely straight [1].

He has the seven convex surfaces [2].

The front half of his body is like a lion's [3].

There is no furrow between his shoulders [4].

His proportions have the symmetry of the banyan-tree [5] :—The length of his body is equal to the compass of his arms, and the compass of his arms is equal to his height.

His bust is equally rounded [6].

His taste is supremely acute [7].

His jaw is as a lion's [8].

He has forty teeth [9],

Regular teeth.

Continuous,

The eye-teeth very lustrous. His tongue is very long [10].

---

[1] He will not stoop, nor lean backward, as if catching at the stars, nor have a crooked spine, but tower up symmetrically like a golden tower-gate in a city of the gods. Cy.

[2] The backs of the four limbs, the shoulders and the trunk are well fleshed. Cy.

[3] i.e. proportionately broad and full.

[4] Citantaraṁso, lit. he has the shoulder-interval filled up. The Cy. explains, the two sides of the back have no depression in the middle, nor look separated, but from the small of the back upwards the fleshy covering is as a level golden slab.

[5] Literally, he has the banyan circumference. It was believed that a banyan always measured the same, like the diameter of a circle, in height as in width.

[6] Samavattakkhandho. According to the Cy. the exterior of the whole vocal apparatus is here meant, rather than the trunk or shoulders only.

[7] Rasaggasaggi.

[8] That is, with the lower jaw relatively fuller than the upper. Cy.

[9] That is, the Great Man at a more adult stage has eight more than the normal thirty-two. How the learned brahmins saw these signs in the babe is not explained.

[10] See 'Dialogues,' I, 131.

He has a divine voice like the karavîka-bird's [1].

His eyes are intensely blue [2],

He has the eyelashes of a cow [3].

Between the eyebrows appears a hairy mole, white and like soft cotton down.

His [19] head is like a royal turban [4].

This too counts to him as one of the marks of a Great Man [5].

33. '" Endowed, my lord, as is this babe with these two-and-thirty marks of the Great Man, two careers and none other are open to him . . ." [as above, § 31] . . .

'Thereupon Bandhuman the râja, brethren, let the brahmin soothsayers be invested with new robes and gratified their every desire.

34. 'And Bandhuman the râja, brethren, engaged nurses for the babe Vipassi. Some suckled him, some washed him, some nursed him, some carried him about on their hip. And a white canopy was held over him day and night, for it was commanded :—" Let not cold or heat or straws or dust or dew annoy him !" And the boy Vipassi, brethren, became the darling and the beloved of the people, [20] even as a blue or red or white lotus is dear to and beloved of all, so that he was literally carried about from lap to lap [6].

35. 'And when the boy Vipassi was born, brethren, he had a lovely voice, well modulated and sweet and

---

[1] According to Childers, the Indian cuckoo. The Great Man's voice is very clear and pure-toned, neither worn nor broken nor harsh. Cy. Yoga-culture is to-day held to yield, as one result, a pleasant musical voice.

[2] Like flax-blossom. Cy. Perhaps a tradition of Aryan origin.

[3] Completely surrounding the eyes, thick like a black cow's; bright and soft like a new-born red calf's. Cy.

[4] U*n*hîsa-sîso. This expression, says the Cy., refers to the fullness either of the forehead or of the cranium. In either case the rounded highly-developed appearance is meant, giving to the unadorned head the decorative dignified effect of a crested turban, and the smooth symmetry of a water-bubble.

[5] In the text this refrain occurs after the naming of each mark.

[6] Literally by hip to hip; women passing him from arm to arm, men from one shoulder to another, explains the Cy.

charming, just as the voice of the karavika-bird in the mountains of Himâlaya is lovely and sweetly modulated and charming [1].

36. 'And when the boy Vipassi was born, brethren, there was manifested in him the Heavenly Eye born of the result of his karma [2], by the which verily he could see as far as a league by day and eke by night.

37. 'And when the boy Vipassi was born, brethren, he looked forward with unblinking eyes, like the gods in the heaven of Delight. Now it was because of this, people exclaiming "Vipassi, Vipassi"—a Seer, a Seer! —that this became his name [3]. And again, brethren, while Bandhuman râja was sitting as judge, he would take the boy on his hip and so lay down the law as to the cases arising till verily the boy, thus [21] seated on his father's hip, and continually considering, would also determine the points of the matter according to justice [4]. Then at the thought "It is the babe who is judging cases aright" ever more and more did that word "a Seer, a Seer" become used as his name.

38. 'Now Bandhuman râja, brethren, had three palaces built for the boy Vipassi, one for the rains, one for the winter and one for the summer, and he had them fitted with every kind of gratification for the five senses. Thus it came to pass that Vipassi spent

---

[1] The Cy. relates of the bird that it sings a flute-like song after pecking at honey and mangoes, and that the song exercises a sort of Orpheus-spell over every beast that hears it. Asandhimittâ, the consort of Asoka, was converted by it. She had inquired of the Order, if it were known what the Buddha's voice was like; and on its being compared to the karavîka's song, wished to hear that. Asoka sent for one, which would not sing in its cage, till a mirror was placed by it. Fancying it saw a kinsman, it sang, throwing every one into ecstasies, and so exalting the queen's idea of the Buddha's voice, that she attained 'the fruit of sotâpatti.'

[2] That is, not by special practice, but as the result of action in former births, as with the fairies' power of vision. Cy.

[3] Vipassî refers rather to the inward vision of the seer. Vipassanâ is insight or intuition.

[4] Namely by giving signs of dissatisfaction when a decision was wrong.

the four months of the rainy season in the rains-palace, ministered to by bands of female musicians [1]; and not once did he come down (from the upper terrace) into the mansion.'

Here endeth the Birth chapter.

II.

1. 'Now the young lord Vipassi, brethren, when many years, many centuries, many thousands of years had passed by [2], bade his charioteer make ready the state carriages, saying :—"Get ready the carriages, good charioteer, and let us go through the park to inspect the pleasaunce." "Yea, my lord," replied the charioteer, and harnessed the state carriages and sent word to Vipassi :—"The carriages are ready, my lord; do now what you deem to be fit." Then Vipassi mounted a state carriage, and drove out in state into the park.

2. 'Now the young lord Vipassi saw, brethren, as he was driving to the park, [22] an aged man as bent as a roof gable, decrepit, leaning on a staff, tottering as he walked, afflicted and long past his prime. And seeing him Vipassi said :—"That man, good charioteer, what has he done, that his hair is not like that of other men, nor his body?"

'"He is what is called an aged man, my lord."

---

[1] Nippurisehi turiyehi. Both words are ambiguous. Childers, following B. R., who follow Wilson, renders turiya by musical instrument. It is very doubtful whether it ever means that. Music, or orchestra, seems to be required in such passages as I have noted. Nippurisa (only found as yet in this connexion) may be non-human (that is, fairy), or not male. See D. II, 171; M. I, 571; A. I, 145; Vin. I, 15; II, 180; J. I, 58, and Senart's note at Mahâvastu III, 486. The alternative rendering would therefore be 'fairy music.' But the commentator evidently takes the words in the meaning given above.

[2] The legendary age of humans at the time of Vipassi was 80,000 years, so that we may reckon 1000 of his years as one of ours. When this legend is afterwards related of Gotama Buddha (in the Nidânakathâ), he is said to have reached his majority (sixteen years) when the drives begin.

' " But why is he called aged ? "

' " He is called aged, my lord, because he has not much longer to live."

' " But then, good charioteer, am I too subject to old age, one who has not got past old age ? "

' " You, my lord, and we too, we all are of a kind to grow old, we have not got past old age."

' " Why then, good charioteer, enough of the park for to-day ! Drive me back hence to my rooms [1]."

' " Yea, my lord," answered the charioteer, and drove him báck. And he, brethren, going to his rooms sat brooding sorrowful and depressed, thinking :—" Shame then verily be upon this thing called birth, since to one born old age shows itself like that ! "

3. ' Thereupon Bandhuman râja, brethren, sent for the charioteer and asked him :—" Well, good charioteer, did the boy take pleasure in the park ? was he pleased with it ? "

' " No, my lord, he was not."

' " What then did he see on his drive ? "

[23] ' [And the charioteer told the râja all.]

4. ' Then the râja, brethren, thought thus :—" We must not have Vipassi declining to rule. We must not have him going forth from the House into the Homeless state. We must not let what the brahmin soothsayers spoke of come true."

' So, that these things might not come to pass, he let the youth be still more surrounded by sensuous pleasures. And thus Vipassi continued to live amidst the pleasures of sense.

5. ' Now after many years, many centuries, many thousands of years had passed by, the young lord Vipassi, brethren, again bade his charioteer make ready, and drove forth as once before [2].

6. [24] ' And Vipassi, brethren, saw as he was driving

---

[1] Antepuraṁ, or harem. Tradition adds that he ' dismissed his womenfolk, and sat alone in his bedchamber, pierced in heart by this first dart.'

[2] Text repeats in full as in § 1.

to the park, a sick man, suffering and very ill, fallen
and weltering in his own water, by some being lifted
up, by others being dressed. Seeing this, Vipassi asked,
" That man, good charioteer, what has he done that
his eyes are not like others' eyes, nor his voice like the
voice of other men ? "

'" He is what is called ill, my lord."

'" But what is meant by ' ill ' ? "

'" It means, my lord, that he will hardly recover from
his illness."

'" But am I too then, good charioteer, subject to
fall ill; have not I got out of reach of illness ? "

'" You, my lord, and we too, we all are subject to fall
ill, we have not got beyond the reach of illness."

'" Why then, good charioteer, enough of the park
for to-day! Drive me back hence to my rooms."
" Yea, my lord," answered the charioteer, and drove
him back. And he, brethren, going to his rooms sat
brooding sorrowful and depressed, thinking :—" Shame
then verily be upon this thing called birth, since to
one born decay shows itself like that, disease shows
itself like that."

7. 'Thereupon Bandhuman râja, brethren, sent for the
charioteer and asked him :—" Well, good charioteer,
did the young lord take pleasure in the park and was
he pleased with it ? "

'" No, my lord, he was not."

'" What did he see then on his drive ? "

'[And the charioteer told the râja all.]

8. [25] 'Then the râja, brethren, thought thus :—
" We must not have Vipassi declining to rule; we
must not have him going forth from the House to
the Homeless state ; we must not let what the brahmin
soothsayers spoke of come true."

'So, that these things might not come to pass, he
let the young man be still more abundantly surrounded
by sensuous pleasures. And thus Vipassi continued to
live amidst the pleasures of sense.

9. ' Now once again after many years . . . the young
lord Vipassi . . . drove forth. .

10. 'And he saw, brethren, as he was driving to the park, a great concourse of people clad in garments of different colours constructing a funeral pyre. And seeing them he asked his charioteer :—" Why now are all those people come together in garments of different colours, and making that pile ? "

[26] '" It is because some one, my lord, has ended his days."

'" Then drive the carriage close to him who has ended his days."

'" Yea, my lord," answered the charioteer, and did so. And Vipassi saw the corpse of him who had ended his days and asked :—" What, good charioteer, is ending one's days ? "

'" It means, my lord, that neither mother, nor father, nor other kinsfolk will see him any more, nor will he ever again see them."

'" But am I too then subject to death, have I not got beyond the reach of death ? Will neither the râja, nor the ranee, nor any other of my kin see me more, or I ever again see them ? "

'" You, my lord and we too, we all are subject to death, we have not passed beyond the reach of death. Neither the râja, nor the ranee, nor any other of your kin would see you any more, nor would you ever again see them."

'" Why then, good charioteer, enough of the park for to-day! Drive me back hence to my rooms."

'" Yea, my lord," replied the charioteer, and drove him back.

'And he, brethren, going to his rooms, sat brooding sorrowful and depressed, thinking :—" Shame then verily be upon this thing called birth, since to one born the decay of life, since disease, since death shows itself like that ! "

11–12. 'Thereupon Bandhuman râja, brethren, [questioned the charioteer as before [27], and as before let Vipassi be still more surrounded by sensuous enjoyments]. And thus Vipassi continued to live amidst the pleasures of sense.

13. [28] 'Now once again after many years . . . the lord Vipassi . . . drove forth.

14. 'And he saw, brethren, as he was driving to the park, a shaven-headed man, a Wanderer, wearing the yellow robe. And seeing him he asked the charioteer :—" That man, good charioteer, what has he done, that his head is unlike other men's heads and his clothes too are unlike those of others ? "

'" That is what they call a Wanderer, because, my lord, he is one who has gone forth."

'"What is that, to have gone forth ? "

'" To have gone forth, my lord, means being thorough in the religious life, thorough in the peaceful life, thorough in good actions, thorough in meritorious conduct, thorough in harmlessness, thorough in kindness to all creatures."

'" Excellent indeed [29], friend charioteer, is what they call a Wanderer, since so thorough is his conduct in all those respects. Wherefore drive up to that forthgone man."

'" Yea, my lord," replied the charioteer, and drove up to the Wanderer. Then Vipassi addressed him, saying :—" You, master, what have you done that your head is not as other men's heads, nor your clothes as those of other men ? "

'" I, my lord, am one who has gone forth."

'" What, master, does that mean ? "

'" It means, my lord, being thorough in the religious life, thorough in the peaceful life, thorough in good actions, thorough in meritorious conduct, thorough in harmlessness, thorough in kindness to all creatures."

'" Excellently indeed, master, are you said to have gone forth, since so thorough is your conduct in all those respects."

15. 'Then the lord Vipassi, brethren, bade his charioteer, saying :—" Come then, good charioteer, do you take the carriage and drive it hence back to my rooms. But I will even here cut off my hair, and don the yellow robe, and go forth from the House into the Homeless state."

'"Yea, my lord," replied the charioteer, and drove back. But the lord Vipassi, there and then, cutting off his hair and donning the yellow robe, went forth from the House into the Homeless state.

16. 'Now at Bandhumatî, brethren, the râja's seat, a great number of persons—some eighty-four thousand souls[1]—heard of what lord Vipassi had done, [30] and thought:—"Surely this is no ordinary religious rule, this is no common going forth, in that the lord Vipassi himself has had his head shaved and has donned the yellow robe and has gone forth from the House into the Homeless state. If the lord Vipassi has done this, why then should not we also?" And they all had their heads shaved, and donned the yellow robes, and in imitation of Vipassi the Bodhisat they went forth from the House into the Homeless state. So Vipassi the Bodhisat went on his rounds through the villages, towns, and cities accompanied by that multitude.

17. 'Now there arose, brethren, in the mind of Vipassi the Bodhisat, when he was meditating in seclusion, the following consideration:—"That indeed is not suitable for me that I should live beset. 'Twere better were I to dwell alone, far from the crowd!"

'So after a time he dwelt alone, away from the crowd. These eighty-four thousand Wanderers went one way, and Vipassi the Bodhisat went another way.

18. 'Now there arose, brethren, in the mind of Vipassi the Bodhisat, when he had gone to his place[2], and was meditating in seclusion, the following consideration:—"Verily this world has fallen upon trouble; one is born, and grows old, and dies, and falls from one state, and springs up in another."

---

[1] Pâna, 'living creatures.' The number is the usual idiom for a multitude, no more pretending to accuracy than our 'a thousand thanks.'

[2] Vâsupagato. The commentary explains this as meaning 'when seated under his Wisdom-Tree.' But the word in the text is quite vague; and it is only the later tradition which thought it edifying to limit all such deep questions as the one discussed in the following sections to one time and place.

[31] ' " And from this suffering, moreover, no one knows of any way of escape, even from decay and death. O when shall a way of escape from this suffering be made known, from decay and from death ! "

' Then to Vipassi the Bodhisat, brethren, this thought occurred :—"What now being present, is decay and dying also present ; what conditions decay and dying ?" Then, brethren, from attention to the cause[1] arose the conviction through reason :—"Where birth is, there is decay and dying ; birth is the condition of decay and dying."

' Then to Vipassi the Bodhisat, brethren, this occurred :—"What now being present, is birth also present ; what conditions birth ?" Then, brethren, from attention to the cause arose the conviction through reason :—"When becoming is, birth also is present ; becoming is the condition of birth."

' Then to Vipassi the Bodhisat, brethren, this occurred :—"What now being present, is becoming also present ; what conditions becoming ?" Then, brethren, from attention to the cause arose the conviction through reason :—"Where grasping[2] is, there is becoming ; grasping is the condition of becoming."

---

[1] Yoniso manasikârâ. The Cy. paraphrases thus that interesting idiom : ' i.e. from attention to expedients (upâya, that is, expedients in analysis, comp. S. II, 17 ; III, 135 ; III, 53 ; III, 161 ; A. V, 111), from attention to the course [of things] (patha); the attention of one who is attending to impermanence and the rest [dukkha, anattâ] *as such*; the attention of one who is observing the continuity, that is to say the rising and passing away, of the phenomena in question under either their positive or negative aspect.' There is here no attempt to substitute, as an equivalent for yoni, a term for origin or basis—nidâna, e.g. or mûla. The observation that is yoniso appears to Buddhaghosa to be of causation viewed as phenomenal only, as process of invariable antecedent and consequent, with application of the methods of induction known since J. S. Mill as the Methods of Agreement and Difference.

[2] The translating of upâdânam must always be inadequate ; we having no word to fill its dual sense of something-to-hand, *Stoff*, fuel, and a laying hold of something. If 'data,' which is etymologically akin, had chanced to be danda, there would have been an approximation in implication. That the term, in the commentarial tradition,

'Then to Vipassi the Bodhisat, brethren, this occurred :—"What now being present, is grasping also present; what conditions grasping?" Then, brethren, from attention to the cause arose the conviction through reason :—"Where craving is, there is grasping; craving is the condition of grasping."

'Then to Vipassi the Bodhisat, brethren, this occurred :—" What now being present, is craving also present; what conditions craving?" Then, brethren, from attention to the cause arose the conviction through reason :—"Where feeling is, there is craving; feeling is the condition of craving."

'Then to Vipassi the Bodhisat, brethren, this occurred :—"What now being present, is feeling also present; what conditions feeling?" Then, brethren, from attention to the cause arose the conviction through reason :—[32] "Where contact is, there is feeling; contact is the condition of feeling."

'Then to Vipassi the Bodhisat, brethren, this occurred :—" What now being present, is contact also present; what conditions contact?" Then, brethren, from attention to the cause arose the conviction through reason :—"Where is the sixfold field, there is contact; the sixfold field is the condition of contact[1]."

'Then to Vipassi the Bodhisat, brethren, this occurred :—" What now being present, is the sixfold field also present; what conditions the sixfold field?" Then, brethren, from attention to the cause arose the conviction through reason :—"Where name-and-form is, there is the sixfold field; name-and-form is the condition of the sixfold field[2]."

'Then to Vipassi the Bodhisat, brethren, this occurred :—" What now being present, is name-and-form also present; what conditions name-and-form?"

---

held this active force is clear from anupâdâya, 'void of grasping, being paraphrased by agahetvâ, not having laid hold of. See also 'Psychological Ethics,' p. 322, *n.* 1; 'Asl.' pp. 385, 450.

[1] The sixfold field is the sphere of action of the six senses; that is, our five senses, and the representative faculty.

[2] *Name-and-form* is what we should call mind and body.

Then, brethren, from attention to the cause arose the conviction through reason:—" Where cognition is there is name-and-form; cognition is the condition of name-and-form[1]."

' Then to Vipassi the Bodhisat, brethren, this occurred :—" What now being present, is cognition also present; what conditions cognition? " Then, brethren, from attention to the cause arose the conviction through reason :—" Where name-and-form is, there is cognition; name-and-form conditions cognition."

19. ' Then to Vipassi the Bodhisat, brethren, this occurred :—" Cognition turns back from name-and-form; it goes not beyond. Only as follows can one be born or grow old or die or fall from one condition or reappear in another; that is, in that cognition is conditioned by name-and-form, and name-and-form by cognition[2], the sixfold field by name-and-form, contact by the sixfold field, feeling by contact, [33] craving by feeling, grasping by craving, becoming by grasping, birth by becoming, decay and dying by birth, and so too grief, lamentation, ill, sorrow and despair come to pass. Such is the coming to be of this entire body of Ill."

' "Coming to be, coming to be!"—at that thought, brethren, there arose to Vipassi the Bodhisat a vision into things not called before to mind, and knowledge arose, reason arose, wisdom arose, light arose.

---

[1] The Cy. here inquires into the omission of the two ultimate links in the ' Chain of Causation' that are given in most of the passages where the formula occurs—notably in the Nidâna Saṁyutta and in the Majjhima Nikâya (I, pp. 49–52, 261, &c.); also in Dh. S., p. 348, and Vibh., pp. 135 ff. It judges that, whereas avijjâ and saṅkhârâ relate to existence *prior* to that in which the remainder of the terms from viññâ-*n*aṁ to jarâmara*n*aṁ, for any given individual, hold true, Vipassi's vipassanâ was confining itself to any given *present* life. Mr. Loveday, in his essay on the ' Chain,' also came to the conclusion that, to apply the links in succession to any individual life, ' ignorance ' and ' the saṅkhâras ' must be referred to prior existence. (J. A. O. S., 1894.)

[2] In S. II, 114 their independence is compared to two sheaves of reeds leaning one against the other. Elsewhere—in definitions of nâma-rupa*m*—nâma is sometimes made to include viññâ*n*aṁ, Dh. S., pp. 341, 342, sometimes not, M. I, 53; Vibh. 136.

20. 'Then to Vipassi the Bodhisat, brethren, this occurred:—"What now being absent, is decay and dying also absent; by the ceasing of what does decay and dying cease?" Then, brethren, from attention to the cause arose the conviction through reason:— "Where birth is absent, decay and dying are absent; when birth ceases, decay and dying cease ... Where becoming is absent, birth is absent; when becoming ceases, birth ceases ... Where grasping is absent, becoming is absent; when grasping ceases, becoming ceases ... Where craving is absent, grasping is absent; when craving ceases, grasping ceases ... [34] Where feeling is absent, craving is absent; when feeling ceases, craving ceases ... Where contact is absent, feeling is absent; when contact ceases, feeling ceases ... Where the sixfold field is absent, contact is absent; when the sixfold field ceases, contact ceases ... Where name-and-form is absent, the sixfold field is absent; when name-and-form ceases, the sixfold field ceases ... Where cognition is absent, name-and-form is absent; when cognition ceases, name-and-form ceases ... Where name-and-form is absent, cognition is absent; when name-and-form ceases, cognition ceases."

21. 'Then to Vipassi the Bodhisat, brethren, this occurred:—" Lo! I have won to this, [35] the Way to enlightenment through insight[1]. And it is this, that from name-and-form ceasing, cognition ceases, and conversely; that from name-and-form ceasing, the sixfold field ceases; from the sixfold field ceasing, contact ceases; from contact ceasing, feeling ceases; from feeling ceasing, craving ceases; from craving ceasing, grasping ceases; from grasping ceasing, becoming ceases; from becoming ceasing, birth ceases; from birth ceasing, decay and dying, grief, lamentation, ill, sorrow and despair cease. Such is the ceasing of this entire body of Ill."

---

[1] Literally 'the Vipassanâ Way to insight.' As this is not a stock phrase in this connexion it doubtless contains a play on the name Vipassi.

' " Ceasing to be, ceasing to be ! "—at that thought,
brethren, there arose to Vipassi the Bodhisat a vision
into things not called before to mind, and knowledge
arose, reason arose, wisdom arose, light arose.

22. 'Thereafter, brethren, Vipassi the Bodhisat
dwelt in the discernment of the rising and passing
away of the five groups [of individual life] depending
on grasping [1] :—" Such is form, such is the coming to
be of form, such is its passing away ; such is feeling,
such is the coming to be of feeling, such is its passing
away ; such is perception, such is its coming to be,
such is its passing away ; such are the syntheses, such
is their coming to be, such is their passing away ;
such is cognition, such is its coming to be, such is its
passing away."

'And for him, abiding in the discernment of the
rising and passing away of the five groups depending
on grasping, not long was it before his heart, void of
grasping, was set free from the " Intoxicants [2]." '

Here endeth the Second Portion for recitation.

---

[1] That is, the new individual, divisible into five constituent parts,
called into being by the grasping attitude maintained during the
previous life. Khandho, group, is rendered by ' body ' in § 19—
' whole body of Ill '—and, in both connexions, is always paraphrased
by râsi, or heap. Buddhist Pluralism turned away from unifying
concepts, and chose to picture organic processes under aggregates.
The concept is not so atomistic as we might think, the ' heap '
referring to past and potential repetition of process.

[2] This is the standing phrase for the attainment, not of Buddha-
hood, but of Arahantship. Nevertheless Vipassî is henceforth called
a Buddha. Compare what is said above, p. 2. On the Âsavas, here
rendered Intoxicants, see above, Vol. I, pp. 92, 93. The Jain use
of the term is referred to by Bhandarkar, ' Report, &c.,' p. 100.
Other Pâli references are J. IV, 222, 3 and A. I, 124, 7, which confirm
the suggested connotation of a poisonous, intoxicating drug.

III.

1. 'Then to Vipassi the Exalted One, Arahant, Buddha Supreme, brethren, this occurred [1] :—"What if I were now to teach the Truth [2]."

'Then to him, brethren, this occurred [3] :—[36] " I have penetrated this Truth, deep, hard to perceive, hard to understand, calm, sublime, no mere dialectic [4], subtle, intelligible only to the wise. But this is a race devoting itself to the things to which it clings, devoted thereto, delighting therein. And for a race devoting itself to the things to which it clings, devoted thereto, delighting therein, this were a matter hard to perceive, to wit, that this is conditioned by that, and all that happens is by way of cause [5]. This too were a matter hard to discern :—The tranquillization of all the

---

[1] The following episode occurs also in Vinaya I, 4 (translated in Vin. Texts, I, 84–8), and M. I, 167–9 (translated by Dr. Neumann, 'Reden G. Buddho's, Mittlere Sammlung,' I, pp. 268 ff.), and S. I, 137–41.

[2] Dhamma, more literally the Norm. On this difficult but all-pervading term see Rh. D. 'American Lectures,' pp. 2, 38, and 'Buddhist India,' 292–4.

[3] In the eighth week, says the Cy., after his attainment of Buddha-hood, the intervening weeks having been spent in places corresponding to those where Gotama Buddha is alleged, in the Nidânakathâ, to have spent them. Rh. D. 'Buddhist Birth Stories,' pp. 105–9. But there is nothing in the text to confirm this.

[4] See 'Dialogues,' I, 26 :—'not to be grasped by mere logic'— atakkâvacaro. 'Only by ñânani'—knowledge, insight—adds the Cy. Takka, meaning fundamentally thinking, is perhaps too much honoured, in the meaning it had come to bear, by being rendered 'logic.' In the Takka-jâtaka, e. g. where the soubriquet 'takka-pandita,' date-sage, is considered by Mr. Chalmers to imply a word-play on date and logic, the pundit's occupation is said to be foretelling 'what were lucky and unlucky seasons' to villagers for pay. Such low crafts, however, are not classed as takka in the 'Moralities' list of Dialogues, I, pp. 16 ff. And it is very possible that 'takka' con-veyed, to the religious mind of that day, much the same that so-called 'mere logic' or 'sophistry' does at the present time.

[5] Idapaccayatâ paṭiccasamuppâdo :—more literally, that con-ditionedness, genesis by way of cause. The second term implies the universal law, the first is its application to any given case.

activities of life[1], the renunciation of all substrata
of rebirth, the destruction of craving, the death of
passion, quietude of heart, Nirvana.   And if I were
now to teach the Truth, and other men did not acknowledge it to me, that would be wearisome to me, that
would be hurtful to me."

2. 'And then verily, brethren, to Vipassi the Exalted
One, Arahant, Buddha Supreme were revealed on the
spur of the moment[2] these verses unheard of before:—

" This that through many toils I've won—
Enough! why should I make it known?
By folk with lust and hate consumed
Not this the Truth that can be grasped!
Against the stream of common thought,
Deep, subtle, difficult, delicate,
Unseen 'twill be by passion's slaves
Cloaked in the murk of ignorance[3]."

'In these words, brethren, pondering over the
matter, did the heart of Vipassi incline to be averse
from exertion and not to preach the Truth.   Thereupon to one of the Great Brahmâs[4], when he became
aware in thought of the thoughts of Vipassi, [37] this
occurred:—" Alas! the world will perish! Utterly
alas! will the world perish, now that the heart of
Vipassi the Exalted One, Arahant, Buddha Supreme,
inclines to be averse from exertion and not towards
preaching the Truth!"

---

[1] i.e. of the sankhâras of actions, speech and thoughts. 'When
Nirvana is reached,' says the Cy., 'all their diffusions are calmed. So
too all cravings are destroyed, all evil passions are quenched, all
suffering ceases.' For Buddhaghosa, Vipassi's 'Truth' is the calm
and detachment of the intellectually and ethically free man.

[2] Anacchariyâ, i.e. anu-acchar-iyâ, instantaneous; analogous
to the Greek ἀνὰ χρόνον, and similar to the later ἐν ἀτόμῳ of the New
Testament (1 Cor. xv. 52). The expression is frequently used of
the Buddha's similes.

[3] Ignorance, not explicit in the text, is usually symbolized by darkness—tamokkhandho—and is so referred to in the Cy.

[4] 'Although merely referred to,' says the Cy., 'as one among them,
he is to be understood as the chief Great-Brahmâ in this universe.'
But the title of Sahampati, given in the Vinaya and Majjhima versions,
seems to be a later gloss.

3. 'Then, brethren, did that Great Brahmâ, like a
strong man stretching his bent arm out, or drawing
back his outstretched arm, vanish from the Brahma
world and appear before Vipassi.   And the Great
Brahmâ, brethren, draping his outer robe over one
shoulder and stooping his right knee to the ground,
raised his joined hands towards Vipassi the Exalted
One, the Arahant, the Buddha Supreme and said :—
" Lord ! may the Exalted One preach the Truth ! May
the Welcome One preach the Truth !   There are
beings whose eyes are hardly dimmed by dust, they
are perishing from not hearing the Truth ; they will
come to be knowers of the Truth."

4. 'At these words, brethren, Vipassi the Exalted
One, Arahant, Buddha Supreme, spoke thus to the
Great Brahmâ :—" To me too, O Brahmâ, did it
occur :—' What if I now were to preach the Truth ?
But I judged that the world was not fit for it, would
not acknowledge it; and that that would be wearisome
for me, hurtful for me ' . . . [38] And so, O Brahmâ,
pondering over the matter, my heart inclined to be
averse from exertion, and not towards preaching the
Truth."

5. 'But this Great Brahmâ, brethren, addressed
Vipassi a second time . . .

6. ' . . . and again a third time, saying :—" Lord ! let
the Exalted One preach the Truth !   Let the Welcome
One preach the Truth !   There are beings whose eyes
are but hardly dimmed with dust; they are perishing
from not hearing the Truth ; they will come to be
knowers of the Truth ! "

'Then, brethren, when Vipassi the Exalted One,
Arahant, Buddha Supreme, became aware of the en-
treaty of the Brahmâ, because of his pitifulness towards
all beings, he looked down over the world with a
Buddha's Eye [1].   And so looking, brethren, he saw
beings whose eyes were nearly free from dust,

---

[1] On the super-normal sense of a Buddha, one of his ten balas
or powers, see ' Vibhanga,' p. 340.

and beings whose eyes were much dimmed with dust, beings sharp of sense and blunted in sense, beings of good and of evil disposition, beings docile and indocile, some among them discerning the danger in rebirth and in other worlds, and the danger in wrong doing. As in a pond of blue, or red, or white lotuses, some lotus-plants born in the water grow up in the water, do not emerge from the water, but thrive sunken beneath; and other lotus-plants, born in the water and grown up in the water, reach to the level; while other lotus-plants born in the water and grown up in the water, stand thrusting themselves above the water, undrenched by it; [39] even so, brethren, did Vipassi the Exalted One, Arahant, Buddha Supreme, look down over the world with a Buddha's Eye, and see beings whose eyes were nearly free from dust, and beings whose eyes were dim with dust, beings sharp of sense and blunted in sense, beings of good and of evil disposition, beings docile and indocile, and some among them discerning the danger in rebirth in other worlds, and the danger in wrong doing.

7. 'Thereupon that Great Brahmâ, brethren, when he became aware in thought of the thoughts of Vipassi, spoke to him in verse[1] :—

"As on a crag, on crest of mountain standing,
    A man might watch the people far below,
E'en so do thou, O Wisdom fair, ascending,
    O Seer of all, the terraced heights of Truth,
Look down, from grief released, upon the nations
    Sunken in grief, oppressed with birth and age.
Arise, thou Hero! Conqueror in the battle!
    Thou freed from debt! Lord of the pilgrim band!
Walk the world o'er, sublime and blessed Teacher[2]!
    Teach us the Truth; there are who'll understand."

---

[1] The following verses and the response are otherwise arranged in the Vinaya and Majjhima versions, in the former immediately following the deity's petition, in the latter immediately following the lotus simile.

[2] In the text simply, O Exalted (or Blessed) One;—practically the only expression not literally reproduced.

'Thereupon, brethren, Vipassi, the Exalted One, Arahant, Buddha Supreme, made response in verse to that great Brahmâ :—

"Wide opened are the portals to Nirvana[1]!
   Let those that hear renounce their empty faith[2]!
Despairing of the weary task, O Brahmâ,
   I spake not of this doctrine, sweet and good, to men."

'Then, brethren, that Great Brahmâ thinking :—"Verily I am the one by whom an opening has been given for the preaching of the Truth by Vipassi the Exalted One, the Arahant, the Buddha Supreme," [40] bowed down before Vipassi, and passing round him by the left vanished away.

8. 'Then to Vipassi, brethren, the Exalted One, Arahant, Buddha Supreme, this occurred :—" To whom now should I first preach the Truth? Who will quickly understand this doctrine?" And he thought:—"There is Khanda a râja's son, and Tissa, the chaplain's son, both dwelling at Bandhumatî. They are learned, open-minded and wise, and for long have had but little dust in their eyes. If I were now to teach the Truth first to them, they would quickly understand it." Thereupon, brethren, did Vipassi, like a strong man stretching his bent arm out, or drawing back his outstretched arm, vanish from the Wisdom Tree and appear in the Sanctuary, in the deer-park at Bandhumatî[3].

9. 'And Vipassi, brethren, bade the park-keeper, saying :—" Ho you, good park-keeper, go into Ban-

---

[1] Amatassa dvârâ; literally the doors of ambrosia. On this term see Appendix I. Cf. also M. I, 227 :—amatadvâram. 'Wide-flung the living gate, the safe (road) leading to Nirvana.'

[2] Pamuñcantu saddham. The expression is ambiguous. Oldenberg, 'Vinaya Texts,' I, 88, renders it 'Let them send forth faith to meet it.' We think it means let them give up their faith in rites, and gods, and ceremonies, with especial references to the offerings to the dead. Comp. R. O. Franke in Z. D. M. G., 1909, p. 7.

[3] Tradition apparently identified this with Isipatana, the deer-park, in Gotama Buddha's time, at Benares, and attributed the name Khema to the park as having been given as a deer-preserve, or refuge. Cy.

dhumatî and tell Kha*nd*a the râja's son, and Tissa
the chaplain's son, that :—Vipassi, the Exalted One,
Arahant, Buddha Supreme, has arrived at Bandhumatî
and abides in the Khema deer-park. He wishes to
see you." " Ay, my lord," replied the park-keeper,
and went to Bandhumatî and gave this message to
Kha*nd*a and Tissa.

10. [41] 'Then they, ordering out their state carriages,
mounted, and drove out from Bandhumatî to the deer-
park. As far as there was a road they drove, and then
alighting went on foot into the presence of Vipassi.
And being come they saluted Vipassi, the Exalted One,
Arahant, Buddha Supreme, and seated themselves
beside him.

11. 'To them Vipassi discoursed in due order[1];
that is to say, he gave them illustrative talk on generosity, on right conduct, on heaven, on the danger,
the vanity and the defilement of lusts, on the
advantages of renunciation. When the Exalted One
saw that they had become prepared, softened, un-
prejudiced, upraised and believing in heart, then he
proclaimed that Truth which the Buddhas alone have
won; that is to say, the doctrine of Sorrow, of its
origin, of its cessation, and the Path. And just as a
clean cloth, from which all stain has been washed
away, will readily take the dye, just even so did
Kha*nd*a and Tissa obtain, even while sitting there,
the pure and stainless Eye for the Truth, and they
knew :—" Whatsoever has a beginning, in that is also
inherent the necessity of passing away."

12. 'Then they having seen the Truth, won the
Truth, understood the Truth, sounded the depths of
Truth, having crossed the waters of doubt and put
away perplexity, having gained full confidence and
become dependent on none other for the teaching of
the Master, addressed Vipassi, the Exalted One,
Arahant, Buddha Supreme, and said :—
'" Most excellent, lord, most excellent, lord! Just

[1] Cf. 'Dialogues,' I, p. 135.

as if a man were to set up that which has been thrown
down, or were to reveal that which has been hidden
away, or were to point out the right road to him who
has gone astray, or were to bring a light into the
darkness so that those who had eyes could see external
forms,—even so has the truth been made known in
many a figure by the Exalted One. We here, lord,
betake ourselves to the Exalted One [42] as our guide,
and to the Truth. May we be suffered to go forth
from the world under the Exalted One, may we be
suffered to obtain ordination."

13. 'And so, brethren, Khanda the râja's son and
Tissa the chaplain's son obtained retreat and ordination under Vipassi, the Exalted One, Arahant, Buddha
Supreme. Them did Vipassi instruct, arouse, incite
and gladden with religious discourse, making clear the
danger, the vanity and the corruption of component
things, and the advantage in Nirvana. And they thus
instructed, aroused, incited and gladdened by his
discourse, their hearts ere long, being void of grasping,
were set free from the Intoxicants.

14. 'Now a great multitude, brethren, of the inhabitants of Bandhumatî—some 84,000 souls—heard
that Vipassi, the Exalted One, Arahant, Buddha
Supreme, had come to Bandhumatî and was staying
at the Sanctuary (Khema), in the deer-preserve; and
how Khanda the râja's son and Tissa the chaplain's
son, had actually at his instigation shaved their heads
and put on the yellow robe, and had gone forth from
the House into the Homeless state. And hearing it
they thought:—"Surely this is no ordinary religious
rule, this is no common going forth, in that the râja's
son and the chaplain's son have had their heads
shaved, have donned the yellow robe and gone forth
from the House into the Homeless state. Khanda and
Tissa have indeed done this; why then should not we?"

'So all that multitude came out from Bandhumatî
to see Vipassi, the Exalted One, Arahant, Buddha
Supreme, and when they were in his presence they
saluted him and sat down by him.

15. [**43**] 'And to them Vipassi discoursed, even as he had discoursed to Kha*nd*a and Tissa. . . .

16. 'And they too as those . . . who have gained full confidence and become dependent on none other for the teaching of the Master, addressed Vipassi even as Kha*nd*a and Tissa had done, asking that they might obtain ordination.

17. 'And so, brethren, those 84,000 souls obtained retreat and ordination under Vipassi the Exalted One, Arahant, Buddha Supreme. Them did Vipassi instruct, arouse, incite and gladden with religious discourse, [**44**] making clear the danger, the vanity and the corruption of component things, and the advantages in Nirvana. They thus instructed, aroused, incited and gladdened by his discourse, their hearts ere long, being void of grasping, were set free from the Intoxicants.

18. 'Now a great multitude, brethren, of recluses—some 84,000—heard from the former multitude of Vipassi's visitation. And they, too, went out from Bandhumatî to see him.

19. 'And to them did Vipassi likewise discourse, and it happened even so with them.

20, 21. [**45**] '. . . and their hearts too ere long were set free from the Intoxicants.

22. 'Now at that time, brethren, a vast company of bhikkhus[1] was staying at Bandhumatî. And to Vipassi the Exalted One, Arahant, Buddha Supreme, as he meditated in solitude, this idea arose in his mind :—
"There is now a vast company of bhikkhus dwelling at Bandhumatî. What if I were now to grant leave to the bhikkhus and say :—'Fare ye forth, brethren, on the mission that is for the good of the many, for the happiness of the many, to take compassion on the world, to work profit and good and happiness to gods and men. Go not singly; go in pairs; teach ye, brethren, [**46**] the Truth, lovely in its origin, lovely in

---

[1] A*tth*a-sa*tth*i*m* sata-sahassa*m* — 6,800,000—is the literal figure given. See p. 39.

its progress, lovely in its consummation, both in the
spirit and in the letter, proclaim ye the higher life in
all its fullness and in all its purity.   Beings there are
whose eyes are hardly dimmed with dust, perishing
because they hear not the Truth.   Moreover after
every six years have passed come ye to Bandhumatî,
the royal residence, there to recite the summary of the
Rules of the Order[1].'"

23. 'Now one of the Great Brahmâs, brethren, when
he became aware in thought of the thoughts of Vipassi,
like a strong man stretching his bent arm out, or drawing back his outstretched arm, vanished from the
Brahma-world and appeared in the presence of Vipassi
the Exalted One, Arahant, Buddha Supreme.   Then,
draping his outer robe over one shoulder, he raised his
joined hands towards the Exalted One, saying:—
"Even so, O Exalted One! Even so, O Welcome One! Let the Exalted One thus grant leave
to this great company of bhikkhus, as he has a
mind to do . . . Moreover we too, lord, will do even
as the bhikkhus after every six years have passed;
we will come to Bandhumatî there to recite the Pâtimokkha."

'Thus, brethren, spake that Great Brahmâ.   And
bowing down before the Exalted One, he passed round
by the left, and forthwith disappeared.

24, 25. [47] 'Then Vipassi, brethren, arose towards
eventide from his meditations and told the bhikkhus
[of what he had deliberated and of the visitation of the
Great Brahmâ].

26. [48] '"I grant ye leave, brethren! Fare ye forth
on the mission that is for the good of the many, for
the happiness of the many, to take compassion on the
world and to work profit and good and happiness to
gods and men.   Go not singly but in pairs; teach ye,

---

[1] Pâtimokkha, literally the Disburdenment. The text as we have
it (translated in 'Vinaya Texts,' Vol. I) dates only from the times of
early Buddhism, and it is not likely that this technical name used as
the title was much older.

brethren, the Truth, lovely in its origin, lovely in its
progress, lovely in its consummation, both in the spirit
and in the letter ; proclaim ye the higher life in all its
fullness and in all its purity.   Beings there are whose
eyes are hardly dimmed with dust, perishing because
they hear not the Truth ; they will become knowers of
the Truth.   Moreover, brethren, after every six years
have passed come ye to Bandhumatî, there to recite
the Pâtimokkha."

'Then those bhikkhus, brethren, for the most part on
that very day, set forth on their mission among the
people.

27. 'Now at that time, brethren, there was a very
great number of religious dwellings in Jambudîpa—
some 84,000. As one year was drawing to a close
the angels proclaimed the news :—" Ho, friends ! one
year is ending ; now five years remain. At the end of
five years we have to go to Bandhumatî to recite the
Pâtimokkha."

'And [this they did at the close of each remaining
year, proclaiming] at the end of the sixth year :—" Ho,
friends ! The six years are at an end. Now is the
time for us to go to Bandhumatî to recite the Pâtimokkha."   Then, brethren, those bhikkhus, some by
their own magic power, some by the magic power of
the gods, on that very day came to Bandhumatî to
recite the Pâtimokkha.

28. [49] 'Then verily, brethren, did Vipassi, the
Exalted One, Arahant, Buddha Supreme, thus rehearse
a Pâtimokkha :—

" How may ye best the flesh subdue ?
Be patient, brethren, be forbearing.
What is the highest, what the best ?
Nirvana, brethren, say the Buddhas.
For he's no Wanderer who harms
His fellow man ; he's no recluse
Who works his neighbour injury.

Work ye no evil ; give yourselves to good ;
Cleanse ye your hearts,—so runs the Buddhas' word.

Blame not, strike not, restrain self in the Law,
With temperance eat, lonely seek rest and sleep,
Given to thoughts sublime,—so runs the Buddhas'
    word [1]."

29. [50] 'At one time I, brethren, was dwelling at
Ukka*tth*â, in the Delectable Wood, beneath a giant
sâl tree. Now to me as I meditated in solitude this
idea arose in my mind:—" There is but one abode of
beings easily accessible that I have not dwelt in for
a very long time, and that is among the gods of the
Pure Mansions [2]. What if I were now to repair
thither ? Then, brethren, as a strong man stretching
his bent arm out, or drawing back his outstretched
arm, so did I vanish from beneath the giant sâl tree in
the Delectable Wood at Ukka*tth*â and appear among
the gods of the Aviha heaven. In that group of gods,
brethren, several thousands of them came up to me,
and saluting me, stood by and spake thus :—

' " Friend, it is now ninety-one aeons since Vipassi the
Exalted One, Arahant, Buddha Supreme, arose in the
world. Vipassi, friend, was of the noble class and was
born in a noble family. Vipassi, friend, was by family
a Kondañña. . . . The span of life in his time, friend,
was 80,000 years. He attained enlightenment, friend,
under a trumpet-flower tree. His chief disciples, friend,
were a pair named Kha*nd*a and Tissa. [51] He had,
friend, three companies of disciples, sixty-eight lacs,
one lac, and eighty thousand in number. His special
attendant, friend, was named Asoka. His father was
the râja Bandhuman, whose ranee, Bandhumatî, was
his mother, and whose seat was the town of Bandhu-

---

[1] These verses, except lines 8 and 9, have been included in the
Dhammapada 184–6.

[2] The Suddhâvâsâ devâ comprise the five highest spheres of
celestials in the so-called Rûpa loka, i.e. the universe of Form, the five
being named successively in the text. Beyond these five heavens were
yet four spheres of the Formless. The following paragraphs develop
the assertion on p. 7 : ' And gods also have revealed these matters to
him.' . . .

matî.   His leaving the world, his becoming a recluse,
his travail, his enlightenment, his setting the Wheel of
Truth a-rolling, were each on such and such wise.
And we being of those who have lived the holy life
under Vipassi our Exalted One, and purged the lusts
of the flesh, have been reborn here."

30. 'And again, brethren, in that group of gods,
several thousands of them . . .[1].   And again, brethren,
several hundreds of them came up to me, and saluted,
and stood on one side, and said :—" Friend! in this
fortunate aeon the Exalted One has now arisen in the
world as an Arahant, Buddha Supreme.   The Exalted
One, friend, is of noble birth, born in a clan of nobles,
in a family with Gotama for surname.   Small, friend,
is the span of life in the Exalted One's time, [52] brief
and soon past; he who is longlived lives a hundred
years more or less.   The Exalted One, friend, became
a Buddha under an aspen tree.   He has, friend, two
chief disciples, Sâriputta and Moggallâna, a glorious
pair.   He has had one assembly, friend, of disciples,
1250 in number, and in this company all are arahants.
He has for attendant, friend, for chief attendant, one
named Ânanda.   His father, friend, is the râja Suddho-
dana, whose wife Mâyâ is his mother, and whose seat
is the town of Kapilavatthu.   His leaving the world,
his becoming a recluse, his travail, his enlightenment,
his setting the Wheel of Truth a-rolling, were each on
such and such wise.   And we, friend, being of those
who lived the holy life under our Exalted One, and
purged the lusts of the flesh, have been reborn
here."

31, 32. 'Thereafter, brethren, I resorted, not only
to the Aviha gods, but also to the home of the Cool
gods ; and so, including both the Aviha gods and the

---

[1] The text here is greatly abbreviated. It is intended that numbers of the gods claim to have been, in a previous birth, the followers
of each successive Buddha; and § 29 is to be understood, in full, for
each Buddha. The full text is given, as usual, for the first and last
cases only.

Cool gods[1], I came to the home of the Fair gods[2]. Then on, including thus the Aviha and Cool and Fair gods, I came to the home of the Wellseeing gods.[3] And yet on, including thus Aviha and Cool and Fair and Wellseeing gods, till I came to the home of the Senior gods.   [And in each of these heavens numbers of the gods accosted me and told me of their previous birth under Vipassi and the following Buddhas down to the present one, myself.]

33. [53] 'Thus, brethren, through his clear discernment of that principle of the Truth, is the Tathâgata able to remember the Buddhas of old, who attained final completion, who cut off obstacles, who cut down barriers, who have ended the cycle, who have escaped from all sorrow,—so that he can remember as to their birth, their names, their families, [54] the span of life usual in their time, their pair of disciples, and their congregations of disciples, and can say:—"Of such was the birth of those Exalted Ones, such were their names, their families, such were their morals, their doctrines, their wisdom; how they lived and how they gained emancipation."'

Thus spake the Exalted One.   And the brethren, pleased at heart, rejoiced at the word of the Exalted One.

---

[1] The Cy. interprets as active:—na kañci sattam tapentîti—they torment no one.
[2] Paraphrased as 'lovely to look at, beautiful, charming.'
[3] Paraphrased as 'because they see vividly the beautiful vision of the former.'

INTRODUCTION

TO THE

MAHÂ-NIDÂNA-SUTTANTA.

THE doctrine of Paṭicca-samuppâda—that all dhammâ (phenomena physical and mental) are paṭiccasamuppannâ (happen by way of cause) finds in the following Suttanta the fullest exposition accorded to it throughout the Piṭakas. It is true that for some reason (cf. p. 26, *n.* 1) the Dîghabhâṇakas (recorders of the Dîgha-Nikâya) excluded the first two of the Twelve Nidânas—avijjâ, sankhârâ—and that, in the Paccayâkâra-vibhanga of the Abhidhamma, the formula is reiterated and analysed with greater variety of presentation. But in the present instance the doctrinal contents are more fully worked out. There is another feature in this Dîgha exposition which seems to us of no little significance.

But before discussing this feature, we would point to yet another factor in the statement of the chain of the Nidânas which does not find a place in the Nidâna-Suttanta. This is the schematized, or abstract formula of the whole sequence, showing the logic of it without the contents—'That being thus, this comes to be, from the coming to be of that, this arises. That being absent, this does not happen, from the cessation of that, this ceases.' (M. II, 32.) In the other Nikâyas the scheme usually precedes the full formula, and in one case where the principle of the latter is called 'the Dhamma,' *supersedes* the formula. It is on all fours with the modern formulation of the law of causation—'That every event is the result or sequel of some previous event, or events, without which it could not have happened, and which, being present, it must take place.'

The significant feature is this:—although the formula, as expounded in this Suttanta, ends in the usual way—'Such is the uprising of this whole body of Ill'—the burden of the Dialogue is in no way directly concerned with Ill, pain or sorrow. . In certain other passages, on the other hand, where the Nidâna-chain occurs, dukkha occupies the foreground. Thus in A. I, 177, the formula of the Paṭicca-samuppâda is rehearsed to explain the Aryan Truth of the uprising of Ill.

In M. I, 190 the context of the formula is an exhortation by Sâriputta on the primary importance of a right attitude towards, and understanding of, the nature and causes of Ill, so that the brethren may meet persecutions—ills not due to their own ill deeds—with fortitude and serenity. In the Nidâna-Samyutta of the Samyutta-Nikâya, all the contexts of the formula known to the compilers are grouped together. Of the ninety-three brief Suttas of which this division consists, only one-sixth of those in which the formula occurs, have Dukkha (or its opposite) for their subject. A *slightly* larger *proportion* of the Suttas (16) are so many statements upholding the truth of the evolution of phenomena by way of natural causation. That any being exists absolutely and eternally is at the same time denied. And that any being ever perishes absolutely is equally denied. Of the remaining Suttas, four, in which Loka, the world of sense-perception, is substituted in the Paṭicca-samuppâda for Dukkha, belong virtually to the foregoing sixteen. Seven are concerned with rebirth, eight are ethical exhortations to destroy Craving, and *thirty-six* emphasize the importance of mastering the *principle* of the Paṭicca-samuppâda. That holds the key to insight ; to understand it is therefore the test of true knowledge and sound doctrine. This too is the point in Samyutta V, 387-9, where the formula again occurs. Once more, in the very strongly emphasized rehearsal of the formula in the 'Great Taṇhâ-sankhaya-Sutta' of M. I, 256, the doctrine there inculcated is not in any way hedonistic, sentimental or, directly, moral. It has nothing to say about Dukkha. It is a repudiation of the belief in any permanent, transmigrating intelligent principle (viññâṇa) in man, and the affirmation of the contrary view—that viññâṇa is a contingent phenomenon, a happening by way of cause and effect, something that 'becomes' and dies away.

Dukkha, on the other hand, and the causes of it—'evam ... samudayo'—holds, in nearly every case, the last word in this notable formula. And according to the Buddhist records, as told in the preceding Suttanta, the fact and sequence of those causes dawn ever on the mind of every Buddha in response to the anguished questionings of his mind brooding over the misery of the world, and of the infinite living and dying in it.

Hence in trying to account adequately for the profound significance and high importance attached by the founders of Buddhism to the doctrine of the Paṭicca-samuppâda, we need to keep in view this dual aspect of it—that it is a way of explaining phenomena, and that the most interesting phenomenon to be explained is that of Dukkha[1]. The latter standpoint is that of man as recipient or percipient, the former, that of man as intellective or interpreting.

Now if to this twofold aspect we add that of man as reacting, by will and deed, to his impressions and his interpretations, and take the Buddha's doctrine of the Eightfold Paṭh, as the corresponding formula, we have not only the whole of Early Buddhism in a nutshell, but also just those points concerning which we find the most emphatic affirmations of Dhamma as Dhamma ascribed to Gotama—

'Both in the past and now do I set forth *just this*:—" dukkha and the cessation of dukkha[2]."

' Let us put aside questions of the Beginning and the End. I will teach you the Dhamma:—That being thus, this comes to be. From the coming to be of that, this arises. That being absent, this does not happen. From the cessation of that, this ceases[3].

'There is a Middle Path ... discovered by the Tathâgata (discovered by none but a Tathâgata, S. V, 14) . . . this Aryan Eightfold Path . . .[4].' This Path, my friend, *is* the religious life (brahmacariya)[5].'

These three central tenets are put, by our earliest and best authorities, in these or other words, into the mouth of Gotama himself at the very outset of his career, in his first sermon, as the doctrine of the Four Aryan or Noble Truths. And the Paṭicca-samuppâda, with its positive formula of uprising (Samudaya), and its negative formula of passing away (Nirodha), covers the ground staked out by the second and third of these Truths. It is frequently quoted in this connexion[6], and its importance in the Dhamma is thereby made the more evident.

But the reason for that importance only becomes clear, when we look away from the dukkha to which the formula is

---

[1] It is regrettable that later Buddhist teaching, yielding to this fact of 'interest,' obscured the great causal principle taught by Gotama, through the simile of a wheel, so as to include the vaṭṭa, or round of Saṁsâra. A ladder or stairway (nisseṇi), like that used to illustrate the way to see Brahmâ (' Dialogues,' I, 308, Tevijja-Sutta), would have been more appropriate.

[2] M. I, 140.

[3] Ib. II, 32. Cf. ib. I, 190, where Sâriputta says—' The Exalted One has said, that he who sees the Paṭicca-samuppâda, sees the Dhamma, and he who sees the Dhamma sees the Paṭicca-samuppâda.'

[4] Vin. I, 10.   [5] S. V, 15.

[6] e.g. S. II, 14–16, 28, 29, 57–9, 108, 109, 129–31, A. I, 177.

so often applied, away too from the antecedents of dukkha, and consider all that is implied in the Pa*t*icca-samuppâda by way of method and *Weltanschauung*.

If we persist in viewing either Dukkha or its causes as the ' secret ' of the doctrine, we might omit the formula altogether, since the nature and cause and effect of each nidâna is fully taught in each Nikâya. Nor is the order of sequence the main tenet. Frequent liberties are taken in the Canon with both order and number of nidânas [1]. Nor finally could the arrangement of antecedents and consequences in an iterated rigmarole (convenient for oral transmission) appeal with the runic force of a Shibboleth to a movement of thought like that of Buddhism, any more than would the similarly arranged fragment of formula contained in the Sânkhya Kârikâ have appealed, as such, to the followers of that school. No reformers who so carefully purged their literature of all the ' eulalic ' reiterations of Om! Hari! and the rest, that so throng the pages of the Upanishads, would care a brass farthing for any ' accumulative jingle' accounting for things after the fashion of the widely spread pre-historic folk-rune, ' The cat began to kill the rat, the rat began to gnaw the rope,' &c. . . . ' *and so* the old woman got home that night.' Evam etassa, &c.

It was not the fact of Dukkha, nor the fairly obvious conditions of birth and so on, leading up to it, that come as a revelation to each Buddha, beneath his Bo-tree. It was the process of samudaya and nirodha as a natural and universal law. ' Coming to pass! Coming to pass! At that thought there arose in me a Vision into things not called before to mind, and knowledge arose, insight, wisdom, light arose [2].' Not uncaused and casually, nor by the fiat of Îçvara—Indra, Soma, Varu*n*a, Brahmâ [3]—did events happen, painful or otherwise; not as Job and the Psalmist taught—' God distributeth sorrows in his anger.' For ' God is a righteous judge, and God is angry every day [4].' Events came impelled by preceding conditions, causes that man could by intelligence and good will, study and govern, suspend or intensify [5].

---

[1] e. g. this Suttanta omits the first two. In ' Dialogues,' I, p. 53 (Brahmajâla S.), the first five are omitted, so also in S. II, 92. S. II, 101, instead of the usual order of the twelve nidânas, gives 3, 4, 2, 11, 12 only, and in this order. In M. I, 191, a *different* group of antecedents are said to have dukkha as their consequence—desire, attachment, indulgence, lusting after.

[2] See above, p. 26.   [3] See ' Dialogues,' I, p. 310.

[4] Job xxi. 17, Ps. vii. 2.

[5] Cf. herewith Prof. Oltramare's ' La Formule bouddhique des douze

Thus Buddhaghosa, in explaining the name Pa*t*icca-samuppâda[1], points out that it *excludes* all theories of absolutism,
nihilism, chance, irregular causation[2], and indeterminism[3].
And of such theories, it is concerning the implied rejection
of the first two that he is most explicit. Namely, that there
is no persistent ego reaping results in one life sown as causes
in a previous life, and that it is not a different, an alien ego
either, which reaps. The latter person (attabhâva) is the
resultant, the creature, the 'evolute' of the former. Thus
faithfully was the tradition of the Pi*t*akas preserved, wherein
the view of viññâ*n*a as a persistent ego was categorically
contradicted in the words anekapariyâyena pa*t*icca-
samuppanna (causally evolved in various ways). M. I, 256.

Let it be remembered that the 'immanent' absolutism
opposed by Buddhism was chiefly the Brahmanic theosophy.
According to this, the âtman of the individual was not so
much an efflux of the World-Âtman, as was the latter immanent in, and identified with, each man-soul. 'In the
beginning this world was only Soul, in the shape of a man
. . . world-guardian, world-lord, this that is My Soul[5].' 'My
Soul' was therefore, in that theosophy, the personal First

causes' (Genève, 1909), which we have had the good fortune to read
before going to press. 'Le Bouddha a voulu apprendre . . . que la
misère ne vient point à l'homme de quelque agent externe échappant
à sa prise, et qu'elle n'est pas non plus inhérente à une substance
immuable, ce qui la rendrait elle-même incurable. . . . Le Pratityasa-
mutpâda est une tentative d'expliquer la qualité de la vie, sans
qu'interviennent ni la notion d'âme, ni la notion de Dieu,' &c. And
yet to these luminous remarks he prefixes the statement, that the
Buddha certainly did not wish to affirm any formula of universal
causality, since that theory *n'intéresse que l'homme*. To us it seems
that precisely for this reason it would be the object of the quest of him
men called the Naruttama, the Aggapuggala—the supreme Man—who
combined 'philosophical curiosity' or rather, insight, with the practical
bent of a saviour of men.

[1] Visuddhi-Magga, ch. xvii.
[2] Visama-hetu-vâdo. Warren translates this 'heresy of existences due to an over-ruling power.' Buddhism did virtually reject an
Issara, but scarcely in such terms as those above.
[3] Vasavattivâdo. Warren has 'self-determining existences.'
[4] Cf. H. Oldenberg, 'Buddha' (London, 1882). 'Where there is
no being, but only becoming, it is not substance, but only a law, which
can be recognized as the first and the last.' The significance of the
Pa*t*icca-samuppâda as the discerning of such a law has found adequate
emphasis in this scholar's work.
[5] B*r*had. Up. I, 4. 1; Kaush. Up. III, 8.

Cause and Final Cause. And hence the Pa*t*icca-samuppâda of Buddhism was as decided a negation of all teleology as was the theorem of Demokritus and his master Leukippus, that 'nothing happens by chance, but everything through a cause and of necessity [1].'

Had the fates been kinder to the writings of the Atomist of Abdera, had the 'teleological reaction' not been led by two men of such extraordinary genius as Plato and Aristotle, it is conceivable that the whole philosophy, not to say the Dhamma, of the West, might have flowed along a channel in which the influence of the *mikros* and the *megas Diakosmos* might have brought both that philosophy and that Dhamma more nearly parallel to the informing principle of the Pa*t*icca-samuppâda. As it happened, Europe learned from Athens compromise and comprehensiveness, learned to believe in a universe governed partly by necessity and partly by chance, learned to combine belief in unchanging natural law with belief in first and final causes.

And so gradually has the realm of regular, causal sequence encroached upon that of the casual and the arbitrary, that on no period in the intellectual development of Europe can we place our finger and say :—Here the concept of a universe governed, as to its every movement and happening, by natural causation, was brought home to the minds of men,—to the mind of one man. There is nothing resembling the intellectual earthquake caused half a century ago by that extension of the law of causation : the theory of evolution. Or was there some such milestone of rational development reached, when Demokritus formulated the philosophy of Atomism, and won renown as a great prophet and teacher of mankind ?

In the history of Indian thought, on the other hand, we can point to such an epoch-making crisis, we can discern the significance of the law of universal causation breaking in on a great mind with a flash of intuition. The law, we read, stands as fundamental, whether Tathâgatas have arisen or not. But the Tathâgata penetrates and masters it, and delivers the knowledge thereof to the world [2].

---

[1] Lange, 'History of Materialism,' I, ch. 1. Demokritus flourished apparently about half a century after the Buddha's death. See also Vis. Magga XVII : 'the wheel of becoming is without known beginning, lacking both maker (kârako) . . . such as Brahmâ . . . and percipient (vadako) "I." For each consequent proceeds by reason of its antecedent.'

[2] S. II, 25.

No such crisis of thought is patent in the literature of the Brahmins, though that literature extends over practically the whole era of Indian culture. Those Upanishads which are ranked as the oldest show a naïf animism: those ranked later reveal thought attained to relative maturity[1]. But there is no evidence of a transition causing a mental upheaval. In the seventy-two stanzas of the Sânkhya Kârikâ, again, 25 per cent. contain some consciously generalized affirmation respecting cause and effect. The abstract causal concept shows as a well-matured instrument of metaphysical thought. Throughout the Yoga Sûtra too we find allusions to causality as an abstract idea[2]. It is only in the Buddhist Nikâyas that we come up against the actual effort itself of the human mind to get at a more scientific view of world-order,—an effort which is marked with the freshness and vigour of a new fetch of intellectual expansion, and the importance and gravity of which is affirmed with the utmost emphasis, both in the earliest records and in the orthodox literature of ten centuries later.

The significance of the Piṭakas, as the vehicle of this evolutionary cry of travail and new birth, is not minimized by the objection, that a gospel promulgated by laymen (Khattiyas), and preached to the man in the street, would naturally regard, as truths new and wonderful, axioms which, to the more esoteric, philosophical schools of the day, were the commonplaces of dialectical metaphysic. For we have shown that, in the one case where such a school has preserved its ancient literature, we find books of pre-causational and post-causational thought, but nothing indicating that the conviction of a law of universal natural causation was taking birth. The aphorisms, constituting the oldest existing survivals of Yoga and Sânkhya thought, reveal no inner evolution of philosophic progress, and no traces of early animistic culture such as appear in certain of the Upanishads. Most of the Jain literature still awaits it editor, but we have Dr. Jacobi's learned authority for it, that, in spite of an atomistic theory of some interest, its philosophy was crude, animistic and mere 'common

---

[1] Cf. Aitareyya Up. 'The Âtman deliberated: I will send forth worlds—he then formed the person . . . he brooded over him, and . . . a mouth burst forth like an egg'—with Çvetâsvatara Up. 'Should time, or nature, or necessity, or chance, or the elements, or the Person be considered as *the cause* ?'

[2] In one passage (IV, 11), the statement takes the *form* of the negative part of the Buddhist formula. 'As the saṅkhâras are collected by cause, effect, substratum, and support, therefore *through the absence of these, there is an absence of the saṅkhâras.*'

sense.' It is not likely therefore that the Angas which are still inedited will reveal any conception of causation possessing deep philosophical insight. Hence all early Indian literature, for which any such insight is claimed, except that of Buddhism, either shows both the child-like and the more adult stages of thought without the (supremely interesting) transitional stage, or else it has preserved only its more adult records, or else it never had any but adult records to show, i. e. it is later literature only.

Now in the history of philosophy, whether its concepts be sought in the cell and the academy of the originating seer, or in the reaction to his influence in thoughtful and earnest minds, nothing is more illuminating either for chronology or for interpretation, than to catch the intelligence in the act of ascending to a fresh vantage-point in its interpretation of the world—

> . . . dhammamayaṁ, Sumedha.
> pâsâdaṁ āruyha, Samantacakkhu . . .
> avekkhassu ! [1]

And since no auspicious day amid Egyptian or trans-Aegean ruins has brought back to us Leukippus or Demokritus, the Buddhist Piṭakas, by presenting this evolutionary moment, possess a unique interest for the historian of human ideas, not only in India, but in the entire world of culture.

---

[1] See preceding Suttanta, p. 39 of the text.

XV. MAHÂ-NIDÂNA-SUTTANTA.

(THE GREAT DISCOURSE ON CAUSATION.)

1. [55] Thus have I heard. The Exalted One was once dwelling among the Kurus [1]. Now a township of that country is named Kammâssadamma. And the venerable Ânanda came to where the Exalted One was, bowed in salutation before him, and took a seat on one side. And so seated he said to the Exalted One :— ' Wonderful, lord, and marvellous it is, that whereas this doctrine of events as arising from causes is so deep and looks so deep [2], to me it seems as clear as clear can be!'

'Say not so, Ânanda, say not so! Deep is this doctrine of events as arising from causes, and it looks deep too. It is through not understanding this doctrine, through not penetrating it, that this generation [3] has become a tangled skein, a matted ball of thread [4], like

---

[1] The Kurus occupied the country of which Indraprastha, close to the modern Delhi, was the capital. See Rh. D. 'Buddhist India,' p. 27.

[2] Water, muses the Cy., may be shallow and look deep like a pool black with the rotten leaves beneath the surface; it may be deep and look shallow, like the jewel-like translucence of Ganges water; it may be and look shallow, like the contents of a basin; it may be and look deep, like the ocean at the foot of Mount Sineru. But this doctrine is ever and only deep both in substance and appearance.

[3] The Greek γέννημα of the Gospels has much the same vague meaning as pajâ—offspring, here rendered ' generation.'

[4] A more literal rendering than Warren's picturesque 'entangled warp . . . ensnarled web.' The similes are drawn from weaving cloth and making nets. The tangle is due to bad workmanship or the teeth of mice; the matting, to grease (kañjiyasuttaṁ), the ball resembling a bird's nest. Both similes are to illustrate the confused state of the popular mind, lost in fallacies of opinion, prejudice and superstition e. g. among the sixty-two heresies of the first Suttanta (Vol. I). Cy.

to munja-grass and rushes[1], unable to overpass the doom of the Waste[2], the Woeful Way, the Downfall, the Constant Round [of transmigration][3].

2. 'If you, Ânanda, were asked :—" Is old age and death due to a particular cause?" you should say :— " It is." And to the question :—" From what cause is old age and death?" you should say :—" Birth is the cause of old age and death."

'If you, Ânanda, were asked :—" Is birth due to a particular cause?" [56] you should say :—" It is." And to the question :—" From what cause is birth?" you should say :—" Becoming[4] is the cause of birth."

'If you, Ânanda, were asked :—" Is becoming due to a particular cause"? you should say :—" It is." And to the question :—" From what cause is becoming?" you should say : " Grasping is the cause of becoming."

'If you, Ânanda, were asked :—" Is grasping due to a particular cause?" you should say :—" It is." And to the question :—" From what cause is grasping?" you should say :—" Craving is the cause of grasping?"

'If you, Ânanda, were asked : " Is craving due to a particular cause?" you should say :—" It is." And to the question :—" From what cause is craving?" you should say :—" Sensation is the cause of craving."

'If you, Ânanda, were asked :—" Is sensation due to a particular cause?" you should say :—" It is." And to the question :—" From what cause is sensation?" you should say :—" Contact is the cause of sensation."

---

[1] When these are withering and cut in autumn, if gathered up in sheaves wherever they fall, it becomes difficult to extricate stalk from stalk and lay them in parallel order. (Cy.)

[2] Apâya. For the concrete meaning see above, Vol. I, p. 125. In the secondary sense the word is often—quite wrongly, rendered 'hell.' There is no hell, i. e. no existence of *unending* torment, in Indian thought.

[3] These four terms all refer to a change for the worse in rebirth, i.e. to one or other of the four infra-human grades of existence—purgatory, animal kingdom, shades or ghosts, and asuras or fallen angels.

[4] The Cy. is at no pains to explain here the staple terms in the chain of causation, the author having expounded them after his fashion in the Visuddhi Magga.

'If you, Ânanda, were asked :—" Is contact due to a particular cause ?" you should say :—" It is." And to the question :—" From what cause is contact ?" you should say :—" Name-and-form is the cause of contact."

'If you, Ânanda, were asked :—" Is name-and-form due to a particular cause ?" you should say :—" It is." And to the question :—" From what cause is name-and-form ?" you should say :—" Cognition is the cause of name-and-form."

3. 'Thus then is it, Ânanda, that cognition, with name-and-form as its cause; name-and-form, with cognition as its cause; contact, with name-and-form as its cause; sensation with contact as its cause; craving, with sensation as its cause; grasping, with craving as its cause; becoming, with grasping as its cause; birth, with becoming as its cause; old age and death, with birth as its cause; grief, lamentation, ill, sorrow and despair, all come into being. [57] Such is the coming to pass of this whole body of Ill.

4. 'I have said that birth is the cause of old age and death. Now in what way that is so, Ânanda, is to be understood after this manner. Were there no birth of any sort or kind whatever of any one anywhere —that is to say, of gods to godhood, of Gandharvas [1] after their kind, of Yakshas after their kind, of goblins [2] after their kind, of humans to humanity, of quadrupeds to the animal kingdom, of birds to winged things, or of insects to the insect-world—were there no birth after the several kind of every one of these classes of beings, then, there being no birth whatever, would there, owing to this cessation of birth, be any appearance of old age and death ?'

'There would not, lord.'

'Wherefore, Ânanda, just that is the ground, that

---

[1] The Cy., following S. III, 250, speaks of these beings as fairies residing in the perfumes given out by roots and other parts of trees and flowers, saying nothing of their 'celestial musicianship' (see Hardy, 'Manual of Buddhism,' 43), or of Sakka as their king (see Jât. VI, 260).

[2] Bhûtâ.

is the basis, that is the genesis, that is the cause of old age and death, to wit, birth.

5. 'I have said that becoming[1] is the cause of birth. Now in what way that is so, Ânanda, is to be understood after this manner. Were there no becoming of any sort or kind whatever of any one anywhere, that is to say, no coming to be of any sentient, formed, or formless being[2], then there being no becoming whatever, would there, owing to this cessation of becoming, be any appearance of birth ?'

'There would not, lord.'

'Wherefore, Ânanda, just that is the ground, that is the basis, the genesis, the cause of birth, to wit, becoming.

6. 'I have said that grasping[3] is the cause of becoming. Now in what way that is so, Ânanda, is to be understood after this manner. Were there no grasping of any sort or kind whatever by any one at anything—[58] that is to say, no grasping at the things of sense, no grasping through speculative opinions, no grasping after mere rule and ritual, no grasping through theories of soul—then there being no grasping

---

[1] Tattha bhavatîti bhavo. 'Here bhavo means one becomes' (so the Vis. Mag. opens its comment)—not atthi, one is. Burnouf, Oldenberg, Warren all choose 'existence.' Winternitz ('Religions-geschichtliches Lesebuch,' p. 236) has *Dasein*. But the mobile, plastic, evolutionary thing, ever in progress, that life appears as conceived by the Indian, fits ills in the more rigid Western metaphysic of Being. As Buddhist sponsors, possibly also as philosophers, we lost much when we dropped *weorthan* for *becumen*, and may envy our German colleagues with their *Werden* (see Mrs. Rh. D. in 'Buddhism,' March, 1904, pp. 389, 390; Rangoon). Moreover, according to the Vibhanga (p. 137) the bhava which is the cause of birth is not only uppattibhavo,—the becoming which is 'coming into sentient being' of some sort—but also kammabhavo, or the generating of effective actions, effective in good or bad results, or in result which is 'beyond good and bad,' viz. meritorious activity, demeritorious activity, and 'unmoved' or 'static activity' (âneñjabhi-sankhâro). 'Existence' fits here still worse.

[2] These three exhausted, for the Buddhist, the living universe. See Dh. S., §§ 1281–6 (Trans., p. 334).

[3] Upâdâna. See preceding Suttanta, II, 18, and the note there.

whatever, would there, owing to this cessation of grasping, be any appearance of becoming?'

'There would not, lord.'

'Wherefore, Ânanda, just that is the ground, the basis, the genesis, the cause of becoming, to wit, grasping.

7. 'I have said that craving[1] is the cause of grasping. Now in what way that is so, Ânanda, is to be understood after this manner. Were there no craving of any sort or kind whatever by any one for anything—that is to say, no craving for sights, sounds, odours, tastes, tangibles or ideas—then there being no craving whatever, would there, owing to this cessation of craving, be any appearance of grasping?'

'There would not, lord.'

'Wherefore, Ânanda, just that is the ground, that is the basis, the genesis, the cause of grasping, to wit, craving.

8. 'I have said that sensation[2] is the cause of craving. Now in what way that is so, Ânanda, is to be understood after this manner. Were there no sensation of any sort or kind whatever in any one for anything, that is to say, no sensations born of impressions received by way of sight, hearing, smell, taste, touch, or imagination,—then there being no sensation whatever, would there, owing to this cessation of sensation, be any appearance of craving?'

---

[1] Taṇhâ. Usually translated 'thirst,' but not used to express *physical* thirst in the Piṭakas. Dr. Neumann sometimes uses the equivalent (to craving)—*Begier*. Winternitz has *Gier*.

[2] Vedanâ, which is usually, in the Piṭakas, resolved into feeling, pleasurable, painful, neutral, is here explained in terms of sense-reaction to contact. Now the term 'feeling,' in its widest psychological meaning (namely, as consisting essentially in our *being affected* or *acted upon*), is able to bear this connotation as well as the more emotional aspect. But since we have the alternative term 'sensation,' since Buddhaghosa himself emphasizes the different aspect: dvârato vedanâ vuttâ ('the vedanâ mentioned refers to sense,' Vis. Mag.), —and since other translators are unanimous in using 'sensation,' this rendering is followed here. In Sum. Vil., Buddhaghosa characterizes the term in this passage as vipâka-vedanâ, 'resultant vedanâ.'

'There would not, lord.'

'Wherefore, Ânanda, just that is the ground, the basis, the genesis, the cause of craving, to wit, sensation.'

9. 'Thus it is, Ânanda, that craving [1] comes into being because of sensation, pursuit because of craving, gain because of pursuit, decision [2] because of gain, desire and passion [3] because of decision, tenacity because of desire and passion, possession because of tenacity, avarice [4] because of possession, watch and ward because of avarice, [59] and many a bad and wicked state of things arising from keeping watch and ward over possessions :—blows and wounds, strife, contradiction and retort, quarrelling [5], slander and lies.

10. 'I have said that many a bad and wicked state of things arising from keeping watch and ward over possessions, blows and wounds, quarrelling and the like, come into being. Now in what way that is so, Ânanda, is to be understood after this manner. Were there no watch and ward of any sort or kind whatever by any one over anything, then there being no watch and ward whatever, would there, owing to this cessation of watch and ward, be any coming into being of those many bad and wicked states of things ?

'There would not, lord.'

'Wherefore, Ânanda, just that is the ground, the

---

[1] This and the nine following sections constitute a digression in the exposition of the chain which is thus explained by the Cy. Craving may be considered under two aspects :—There is the primordial craving which is the root or base of transmigration (va*t*ta-mûla-bhûtâ purima-ta*n*hâ), and there is craving as manifested in conduct (samudâcâra-ta*n*hâ). The former, with the remaining links, is now put aside, 'as if one were putting a clamorous person out of the road, hitting him on the back and seizing his hair.' And the latter is discussed under the twofold subdivision of craving in the quest, and craving in the found quarry—seeking and gloating over.

[2] Vinicchayo, explained as deciding what to do with one's gains.

[3] Chandarâgo. From these selfish considerations volitions both weak and strong arise. Chando is weak passion (or lust, râgo).

[4] Macchariya*m*; the not suffering others to share.

[5] On tuva*m*tuva*m*, see E. Müller, 'Pali Grammar,' p. 38.

basis, the genesis, the cause of blows and wounds, of strife, contradiction and retort, of quarrelling, slander and lies, to wit, the guarding of property.

11. 'I have said that watch and ward is because of avarice. Now in what way that is so, Ânanda, is to be understood after this manner. Were there no avarice of any sort or kind whatever in any one about anything, then there being no avarice whatever, would there, owing to this cessation of avarice, be any appearance of watch and ward?'

'There would not, lord.'

'Wherefore, Ânanda, just that is the ground, the basis, the genesis, the cause of watch and ward, to wit, avarice.

12. 'I have said that avarice is because of possession. Now in what way that is so, Ânanda, is to be understood after this manner. [60] Were there no possession of any sort or kind whatever by any one of anything, then there being no possessing whatever, would there, owing to this cessation of possession, be any appearance of avarice?'

'There would not, lord.'

'Wherefore, Ânanda, just that is the ground, the basis, the genesis, the cause of avarice, to wit, possession.

13. 'I have said that tenacity is the cause of possession. Now in what way that is so, Ânanda, is to be understood after this manner. Were there no tenacity of any sort or kind whatever shown by any one with respect to anything, then there being no tenacity whatever, would there, owing to this cessation of tenacity, be any appearance of possession?'

'There would not, lord.'

'Wherefore, Ânanda, just that is the ground, the basis, the genesis, the cause of possession, to wit, tenacity.

14. 'I have said that tenacity is because of desire and passion. Now in what way that is so, Ânanda, is to be understood after this manner. Were there no passion or desire of any sort or kind whatever in any

one for anything, then there being no passion or desire
whatever, would there, owing to this cessation of
passion and desire, be any appearance of tenacity?'

'There would not, lord.'

'Wherefore, Ânanda, just that is the ground, the
basis, the genesis, the cause of tenacity, to wit, desire
and passion.

15. 'I have said that passion and desire is because
of decision. Now in what way that is so, Ânanda, is
to be understood after this manner. Were there no
purpose of any sort or kind whatever devised by any
one for anything, then there being no purpose whatever, would there, owing to this cessation of purpose,
be any appearance of passion and desire?'

[61] 'There would not, lord.'

'Wherefore, Ânanda, just that is the ground, the
basis, the genesis, the cause of passion and desire, to
wit, decision.

16. 'I have said that decision is because of gain.
Now in what way that is so, Ânanda, is to be understood after this manner. Were there no gain of any
sort or kind whatever by any one of anything, then,
there being no gain whatever, would there, owing to
this cessation of gain, be any appearance of decision?'

'There would not, lord.'

'Wherefore, Ânanda, just that is the ground, the
basis, the genesis, the cause of decision, to wit, gain.

17. 'I have said that gain is because of pursuit.
Now in what way that is so, Ânanda, is to be understood after this manner. Were there no pursuit of any
sort or kind whatever by any one after anything, then
there being no pursuit whatever, would there, owing
to this cessation of pursuit, be any appearance of
gain?'

'There would not, lord.'

'Wherefore, Ânanda, just that is the ground, the
basis, the genesis, the cause of gain, to wit, pursuit.

18. 'I have said that pursuit is because of craving.
Now in what way that is so, Ânanda, is to be understood after this manner. Were there no craving of

any sort or kind whatever by any one for anything,—
that is to say, the lust of the flesh, the lust of life
eternal and the lust of the life that now is [1]—then,
there being no craving whatever, would there, owing
to this cessation of craving, be any appearance of
pursuit ?'

'There would not, lord.'

'Wherefore, Ânanda, just that is the ground, the
basis, the genesis, the cause of pursuit, to wit, craving.

'So now, Ânanda, these two aspects [of craving]
from being dual become united through the sensation
[which conditions them] [2].'

19. [62] 'I have said that contact is the cause of
sensation. Now in what way that is so, Ânanda, is to
be understood after this manner. Were there no contact of any sort or kind whatever between any one and
anything whatever,—that is to say, no reaction [3] of
sight, hearing, smell, taste, touch or imagination—
then, there being no contact whatever, would there,
owing to this cessation of contact, be any appearance
of sensation ?

'There would not, lord.'

'Wherefore, Ânanda, just that is the ground, the
basis, the genesis, the cause of sensation, to wit,
contact.

20. 'I have said that name-and-form is the cause of
contact. Now in what way that is so, Ânanda, is to
be understood after this manner. Those modes,
features, characters, exponents, by which the aggregate called 'name' manifests itself,—if all these were
absent, would there be any manifestation of a corre-

---

[1] See Rh. D. 'Buddhist Suttas,' p. 148, n. 4. On the three kinds
the Cy. remarks, that the first, kâmataṇhâ, means craving for the five
classes of sense-objects, the second is the passion characterizing
Eternalism; the third, that characterizing Nihilism (see 'Dialogues,' I,
pp. 27, 46).
[2] 'These two aspects' (dhammâ), i.e. according to the Cy., the
two aspects of craving specified above, p. 55, n. 1.
[3] Samphasso.

sponding verbal impression in the aggregate called [bodily] form?[1]'

'There would not, lord.'

'Those modes, features, characters, exponents, by which the aggregate called [bodily] form manifests itself—if all these were absent, would there be any manifestation of an impression of sense-reaction[2] in the aggregate called name?'

'There would not, lord.'

'And if all those modes, &c., of both kinds were absent, would there be any manifestation of either verbal or sensory impression?'

'There would not, lord.'

'So that, if all those moods, &c., by which name-and-form manifests itself were absent, there would be no manifestation of contact?'

'There would not, lord.'

'Wherefore, Ânanda, just that is the ground, the basis, the genesis, the cause of contact[3], to wit, name-and-form.

---

[1] Rûpakâye adhivacanasamphasso. This and its complement the paṭighasamphasso in 'name' (rendered 'impression of sense-reaction') occur in the Vibhanga, p. 6, as two modes of saññâ, or perception, the former being described as refined, subtle, delicate, the latter as gross, coarse, thick. If the psychological comments of Buddhaghosa on these two expressions in the Sammoha-Vinodanî and the Sumangala Vilâsinî be a correct guide to the Buddha's utterance, then the passage under consideration reveals what would now be called a psycho-physiological standpoint of much interest. The 'modes ... exponents' of 'name' are not physical expressions, but the processes of subjective consciousness,—feelings, perceptions, &c. The consciousness, bent back upon itself—piṭṭhivaṭṭakâ hutvâ—refoulée sur soi-même—gives the name to what it finds. The modes, &c., of 'form' are the modes of sensation, by which 'form manifests itself' to the mind,—'at the mind-door,' as the Cy. has it.

[2] See Dh. S., translation, p. 172, n. 1, 183, n. 1.

[3] i.e. of this twofold contact, as the Cy. points out, of mental object with mind-activity or mind, and of sense-object with sense-organ. Cf. Dh. S., §§ 3–5, and translation, p. 5, n. 2. The former mode of contact is there called ceto-samphasso, manoviññâṇadhâtu-samphasso.

The Cy. sums up the relation between nâmarûpa and phasso as follows :—In the channels of the five senses, sight, hearing, &c., by

21. ' I have said that cognition is the cause of name-and form [63]. Now in what way that is so, Ânanda, is to be understood after this manner. Were cognition not to descend[1] into the mother's womb, would name-and-form become constituted therein[2]?'

' It would not, lord.'

' Were cognition, after having descended[1] into the mother's womb, to become extinct, would name-and-form come to birth in this state of being?'

' It would not, lord.'

' Were cognition to be extirpated from one yet young,

---

means of visual and other objects, are the ' form,' while the [other four] skandhas, brought into relation therewith, are the ' name.' Thus in a fivefold way is name-and-form the cause of contact. Moreover in the channel of the sixth sense (mano, ideation) its physical basis,— the heart—as well as such corporeal form as becomes its mental object, constitute ' form,' while the related states of consciousness induced, as well as such incorporeal form as becomes its mental object, constitute incorporeal form. Thus in saying that name-and-form is the cause of contact, we must also include contact that is mental (i.e. of ideas). Name-and-form is therefore in many ways the cause of contact. (On the heart, see Dh. S., translation, p. lxxviii; Pras. Up. III, 1, 5.)

[1] The animistic implication adhering to this term (okkamissatha; ava, down + √kram, stride) would of course have no significance for Buddhist doctrine. Accordingly it is, in the Cy., paraphrased as follows :—' having entered, *so to speak*, and staying (vattamânam=the Latin idiom, *versatum est*), by means of conception, were not to keep going on.' The contradictory term, vokkamissatha, ' become extinct,' rendered by Warren ' go away again,' is paraphrased nirujjhissatha, and only signifies that the advent is in some way annulled. There is no conception of cognition, as a unity, descending from outside into the womb like a ball into a bag. At Samyutta V, 283 we are told of happiness descending on a man, and at Mil. 299 of drowsiness descending into or on to a man. So okkantikâ pîti is a standing expression for a particular sort of joy. In each of these cases the bliss, or drowsiness, or joy is supposed to develop from within ; and so also here of cognition.

[2] Samucchissatha, derived by Dr. Konow (J. P. T. S., 1908) from sam + √murch, to thicken, and by him and Warren rendered ' to be consolidated.' So also Oldenberg ' Buddha[5],' p. 259; and Windisch, ' Buddha's Geburt,' p. 39. The Cy. has kalalâdi-bhâvena ... missibhûtam hutvâ, ' become mixed with the embryo in its different stages.'

youth or maiden, would name-and-form attain to growth, development, expansion ? '

It would not, lord.'

'Wherefore, Ânanda, just that is the ground, the basis, the genesis, the cause of name-and-form, to wit, cognition.

22. 'I have said that name-and-form is the cause of cognition.   Now in what way that is so, Ânanda, is to be understood after this manner.   Were cognition to gain no foothold in name-and-form, would there then, in the coming years, be manifested that concatenation of birth, old age, death and the uprising of Ill ? '

'There would not, lord.'

'Wherefore, Ânanda, just that is the ground, the basis, the genesis, the cause of cognition, to wit, name-and-form.

'In so far only, Ânanda, can one be born, or grow old, or die, or dissolve, or reappear, in so far only is there any process [1] of verbal expression, in so far only is there any process of explanation, in so far only is there any process of manifestation, in so far only is there any sphere of knowledge, in so far only do we go round the round of life [64] up to our appearance amid the conditions of this world [2]—in as far as this is, to wit, name-and-form together with cognition.'

---

23. 'Now with declarations concerning the soul, Ânanda, how many such declarations are there [3] ?

---

[1] Patho, literally, course, path.

[2] Itthatta*m* paññâpanâya, lit. for the making manifest thus-ness.   Warren's rendering :—'And it is all that is reborn to appear in the present shape,'—is beside the point, as well as free.   Barely stated, the summary amounts to this :—'Only through cognition, language and bodily form do we live and express ourselves.'   The little paragraph contains a great part of modern psychology in the germ-state.

[3] The doctrine of origin by way of cause having now been set forth, the following is, according to the Cy., an illustration of how 'this generation has become a tangled skein,' &c., as asserted above (§ 1).   These different impressions as to the nature of the attâ

Either the soul is declared to have form and to be
minute, in the words :—" My soul has form and is
minute."   Or the soul is declared to have form and to
be boundless, in the words :—" My soul has form and
is boundless."   Or the soul is declared to be formless
and minute, in the words :—" My soul is formless and
minute."   Or the soul is declared to be formless and
boundless, in the words :—" My soul is formless and
boundless."

24. 'And in each case, Ânanda, he who makes the
declaration, makes it with regard either to the present
life, or to the next life, or else his idea is :—" My soul
not being like that, I will refashion it into that likeness."   That being so, Ânanda, we have said enough
about the case of one who is given to the theories that
the soul has form and is minute, . . . has form and is
boundless, and so on.

[65] 'In so many ways, Ânanda, are declarations
made concerning the soul.

25. 'And in how many ways, Ânanda, when no
declaration concerning the soul is made [1], is such de-
claring refrained from ?   Either the soul is not declared
to have form and to be minute, in the aforesaid formula,
or the soul is not declared to have form and to be
boundless, in the aforesaid formula, or the soul is not
declared to be formless and minute, in the aforesaid
formula, or the soul is not declared to be formless and
boundless, in the aforesaid formula.

(âtman), soul, or mannikin, are, according to the Cy., deductions
from Jhâna experience.   For instance, in the first 'declaration,' 'he
who, on gazing at a particular kasina' (one of ten kinds of objects
for inducing meditative rapture); 'gets hold of an after-image where
there is no expansion (avaddhitam), and of a consciousness that " it is
the soul," declares that it, the soul, has form and is minute '—and so on.
Comp. on the whole exposition above Vol. I, pp. 45 foll.
  [1] 'Who are they,' asks the Cy., 'who refrain ?   All ariya-puggalâ
—noble-minded persons, learned persons :—those who know the
Three Piṭakas (by heart), or two, or one, or even only one of the
Nikâyas, and can discourse thereon, and are of alert insight.   These
take the kasinas for what they are, and, for them, the constituents
of mind (the four khandhas) are such and no more.'

26. 'And in each case, Ânanda, he who refrains from making the declaration, does not make it with regard either to the present life, or to the next life, nor is it his idea :—" My soul not being like that, I will refashion it into that likeness."   [66] That being so, Ânanda, we have said enough about the case of those who are not given to theories respecting the form and dimensions of the soul.

'In so many ways, Ânanda, is there a refraining from declarations concerning the soul.'

27. 'And under how many aspects, Ânanda, is the soul regarded?   The soul is regarded[1] either as feeling, in the words :—" My soul is feeling "—or the opposite, in the words :—" Nay, my soul is not feeling, my soul is not sentient " ; or again :—" Nay, my soul *is* not feeling, nor is it non-sentient ; my soul *has* feelings, it has the property of sentience."   Under such aspects as these is the soul regarded.

28. 'Herein, Ânanda, to him who affirms :—" My soul is feeling "—answer should thus be made :—" My friend, feeling is of three kinds.   There is happy feeling, painful feeling, neutral feeling.   Of these three feelings, look you, which do you consider your soul is ? "

'When you feel a happy feeling, Ânanda, you do not feel a painful feeling, or a neutral feeling ; you feel just a happy feeling.   And when you feel a painful feeling, you do not feel a happy feeling, or a neutral feeling, but just a painful feeling.   And when you feel a neutral feeling, you do not then feel a happy feeling or a painful feeling ; you feel just a neutral feeling.

---

[1] These three forms of the 'individuality-heresy' amount to an interesting and metaphysically more discriminating statement of the oft-quoted theories identifying the soul or mannikin with one or other of the five Khandhas. (See Vin. I, 13 ('Vin. Texts,' I, 100); M. I, 138, 300; S. III, 66; IV, 34, &c.)   According to the Cy., the second assertion is the identification with the body (rûpakkhandha-vatthukâ), which is usually placed first ; the third assertion includes identification of the soul with the other three Khandhas—with, let us say, thinking and volition.

29. 'Moreover, Ânanda, happy feeling is impermanent, a product [1], the result of a cause or causes, liable
to perish [67], to pass away, to become extinct, to
cease. So too is painful feeling. So too is neutral
feeling. If when experiencing a happy feeling one
thinks :—" This is my soul,"—when that same happy
feeling ceases, one will also think :—" My soul has departed." So too when the feeling is painful, or neutral.
Thus he who says :—" My soul is feeling,"—regards, as
his soul, something which, in this present life, is impermanent, is blended of happiness and pain, and is liable
to begin and to end. Wherefore, Ânanda, it follows
that this aspect :—" My soul is feeling "—does not
commend itself.

30. ' Herein again, Ânanda, to him who affirms :—
" Nay, my soul is not feeling, my soul is not sentient,"
—answer should thus be made :—" My friend, where
there is no feeling of anything, can you there say:—' I
am ' ? " '

' You cannot, lord [2].'

' Wherefore, Ânanda, it follows that this aspect :—
" Nay, my soul is not feeling, my soul is not sentient,"
—does not commend itself.

31. ' Herein again, Ânanda, to him who affirms :—
" Nay, my soul *is* not feeling, nor is it non-sentient ; my
soul has feelings, it has the property of sentience,"—
answer should thus be made :—" My friend, were feeling of every sort or kind to cease absolutely, then there
being, owing to the cessation thereof, no feeling whatever, could one then say :—' I myself am ' ? " '

' No, lord, one could not.'

---

[1] Sankhata, con-fected, composite, the resultant of conditions.
The soul, according to the then current animism, was considered to
be unique, not a product, not causally modifiable through temporal
or spatial conditions. The commentary explains sankhata as 'that
which, having through such and such causes (lit. doings) come together, is made.

[2] All the MSS. agree in putting this answer in the mouth of
Ânanda, instead of in that of the soul-theorist. And it would be quite
like him to rush in, in this way, with his opinion. And so also
below.

'Wherefore, Ânanda, it follows that this aspect:—
"Nay, my soul is not feeling, nor is it non-sentient ; my
soul has feelings, it has the property of sentience,"—
does not commend itself.

32. [68] 'Now when a brother, Ânanda, does not
regard soul under these aspects,—either as feeling, or
as non-sentient, or as having feeling,—then he, thus
refraining from such views, grasps at nothing whatever
in the world; and not grasping he trembles not ; and
trembling not, he by himself attains to perfect peace.[1]
And he knows that birth is at an end, that the higher
life has been fulfilled, that what had to be done had
been accomplished, and that after this present world
there is no beyond!

'And of such a brother, Ânanda, whose heart is
thus set free, if any one should say :—" His creed
is that an Arahant[2] goes on after death"—that
were absurd. Or: "His creed is that an Arahant
does not go on . . . does, and yet does not, go on . . .
neither goes on nor goes not on after death"—all
that were absurd. Why is that ? Because, Ânanda,
whatever verbal expression there is and whatever
system of verbal expression, whatever explanation
there may be, and whatever system of explanation,
whatever communication is possible and whatever
system of communication, whatever knowledge there
is and whatever sphere of knowledge, whatever
round of life and how far the round is traversed,—
by mastery over all this that brother is set free.
But to say, of a brother who has been so set free

---

[1] Parinibbâyati. Usually rendered 'he attains complete Nirvana'
or 'attains Parinirvâna,' or even 'enters Nirvana.' The term is
applied to the death of an Arahant, but it is also used to express
perfected tranquillity, as in the case of a horse (M. I, 446), or of
a man (M. I, 251 ; S. III, 54). Tradition, as represented by the Cy.,
did not associate the hour of death with the term, for it says, 'Having
thus completely parinibbâna-ed (by extinguishing all evil) he goes
on to reflect, "Birth is at an end,"' &c.

[2] Tathâgata; perhaps it merely means 'mortal.' See M. I, 542.

by insight :—" He knows not, he sees not "—that were
absurd ! ¹'

___

33. 'There are seven resting-places for Cognition ²,
Ânanda, and two Spheres ³.   Which are the seven ?
[69] 'There are beings differing in body and differing in intelligence ⁴, for instance, human beings and
certain of the gods and some of those in purgatory.
This is the first resting-place for Cognition.

'There are beings differing in body but of uniform
intelligence, for instance, the gods of the Brahma-
heaven who are there reborn by means of the First
[Jhâna]⁵. This is the second resting-place for Cognition.

'There are beings uniform in body and differing in
intelligence, for instance, the Luminous Gods ⁶.   This
is the third resting-place for Cognition.

___

¹ The argument in this paragraph seems to have appealed in
a special degree to the early Buddhists, for it has been made the basis
of a whole Suttanta, the Jâliya (which is itself repeated, occurring first
as part of the Mahâli, and then again separately). The main point
there emphasized is that the converted man will have gone so far
beyond them that all such questions will have ceased to interest him.
The two other Suttantas have been translated in full in Vol. I; but
see especially pp. 200—5.

² The Sangîti Suttanta (' Dialogues,' III) and A. IV, 39, 40 also
name seven.   S. III, 54 gives only four.

³ The Pâli thus rendered is *th*iti and âyatana*m* respectively.
The Cy. paraphrases the first by ' this is an equivalent for a setting-up
(pati*tth*âna) of viññâ*n*a.' Pati*tth*âna*m* is the affording of a standing-
place, resting-place, *locus standi*, or foothold for. *Th*iti again is the
term for the central, static moment in any process, contrasting with two
others in the same category, viz. inception and dying-out. ' Rest' is
not satisfactory, but no English term suggests itself which exactly
meets the requirement.   For ' sphere' the paraphrase is simply :—
' nivâsana*tth*âna*m*,' dwelling-place, . . . ' These are included to
exhaust [the contents] of the Cycle (sa*m*sâra), for the Cycle goes not
on merely by way of viññâ*n*a-resting places.'

⁴ No two human beings, says the Cy., are ever exactly alike ; even
in twins that are undistinguishable in likeness of appearance and complexion, there will be some difference in look, speech, gait or carriage.

⁵ Cf. Dh. S., §§ 160 ff., 266 ff.; transl., pp. lxxxvii–ix, 43 ff.,
72 ff.

⁶ Ranking sixth in the heavens of Rûpabrahmaloka.

'There are beings uniform in body and of uniform intelligence, for instance, the All-Lustrous Gods [1]. This is the fourth resting-place for Cognition.

'There are beings who, by having passed wholly beyond all consciousness of form, by the dying out of the consciousness of sense-reaction, by having turned the attention away from any consciousness of the manifold, and become conscious only of "space as infinite," are dwellers in the realm of infinite space [2]. This is the fifth resting-place for Cognition.

'There are beings who, by having passed wholly beyond the realm of infinite space, and become conscious only of "cognition as infinite," are dwellers in the realm of infinite cognition. This is the sixth resting-place for Cognition.

'There are beings who, by having passed wholly beyond the realm of infinite cognition, and become conscious only that "there is nothing whatever," are dwellers in the realm of nothingness. This is the seventh resting-place for Cognition.

'The Sphere of beings without consciousness [3].

'Next to that, the Sphere of beings who neither have consciousness nor yet have it not [4].

34. 'Now there, Ânanda—in that first resting-place for Cognition, of differing bodies and differing intelligences,—to wit, human beings and certain of the gods and certain of those in purgatory—think you that he who both knows what that state is, and how it comes to be, and how it passes away,—knows too the pleasures of it, and the miseries [5] of it, and the way of

---

[1] Ranking ninth in the same.

[2] The Cy. refers the inquirer to the Vis. Mag. for further comment. Cf. next Suttanta, and Dh. S., §§ 265–8; trans., pp. 71–5.

[3] Saññâ, perhaps awareness would be a better rendering.

[4] The Cy. here includes cognition with awareness, the extreme tenuity or refinement (sukhumattam) of both being in this sphere such that it is as a zero point between presence and absence of either. See passage last cited in previous note.

[5] Or the peril of it (âdînavo), i. e. the thought of its impermanence, changeableness, &c. Cy.

escape from it,—think you that it were fitting for such
an one to take delight in it?[1]'

[70] ' Nay, lord.'

' And in those other six resting-places for Cognition,
and in those two Spheres,—think you that he who both
knows them for what they are, how they come to be,
and how they pass away, knows too the pleasures of
them, and the miseries of them, and the way of escape
from them,—think you that it were fitting for such an
one to take delight in them?'

' Nay, lord.'

' But, Ânanda, when once a brother has understood
as they really are the coming to be and the passing
away, the pleasures and the miseries of, and the way
of escape from, these seven resting-places for Cognition,
and these two Spheres, that brother, by being purged
of grasping, becomes free. And then, Ânanda, he is
called Freed-by-Reason[2].'

35. ' Now these, Ânanda, are the eight stages of
Deliverance[3]. Which are they?

---

[1] This standpoint of insight into the limitations of all sentient
experience when estimated according to its emotional or hedonistic
values is claimed by the Buddha as a monopoly of his own doctrine,
distinguishing it from other ethical systems. See his graphic exposition
in the Great Suttanta on the Body of Ill; and the passages quoted
under Yathâbhûtam in the Samyutta Index (vol. vi).

[2] Paññâ vimutto, i.e. says the Cy. 'emancipated without the aid
of the following eight grades of deliverance'—by native insight. So
PP. 14, 73. Here, as throughout, when paññâ is rendered by
'reason,' it is but a pis-aller. Paññâ is really intellect as conversant
with, engaged upon, general truths, and thus comes out as approximately Kant's Vernunft, and Reason as distinct from Understanding,
a distinction very general in English and European philosophy. See
Dh. S., transl., p. 17, n. 2. By 'emancipated' the Cy. understands
'having effected the non-perpetuity (in rebirths) of name and form.'

[3] Vimokhâ. See the following Suttanta, p. 111 of the text; A.
IV, 306, 349; Dh. S., §§ 248–50; transl., pp. 63–5. Buddhaghosa's
comments on the last citation are approximately the same as those on
the first three stages here given. Here, too, he explains Release as
deliverance from adverse conditions, so that the attention is sustained
with all the detachment and confidence felt by the little child borne on
his father's hip, his limbs dangling, and no need felt to clutch. In the

'Having one's self external form, one sees [these] forms. This is the first stage.

'Unaware of one's own external form, one sees forms external to one's self. This is the second stage.

[71] '"Lovely!"—with this thought one becomes intent. This is the third stage.

'Passing wholly beyond[1] perceptions of form, all perceptions of sense-reaction dying away, heedless of all perceptions of the manifold, conscious of space as infinite, one enters into and abides in the sphere of space regarded as infinite. This is the fourth stage.

'Passing wholly beyond the sphere of space regarded as infinite, conscious of reason as infinite, one enters into and abides in the sphere of cognition regarded as infinite. This is the fifth stage.

'Passing wholly beyond the sphere of reason re-garded as infinite, conscious of there being nothing whatever, one enters into and abides in the sphere of nothingness. This is the sixth stage.

'Passing wholly beyond the sphere of nothingness, one enters into and abides in the sphere of "neither-consciousness-nor-unconsciousness." This is the seventh stage.

'Passing wholly beyond the sphere of "neither-ideation-nor-non-ideation," one enters into and abides

---

first stage, Jhâna is induced by intense concentration on the *colour* of some bodily feature. In the second, the kasina is an object external to one's body. In the third, consciousness of an uprising glamour (around or superseding the kasina) of perfectly pure colour or lustre is meant. The *aesthetic* suffusion was held to quicken the sense of emancipation from *morally* adverse conditions analogously to that perception of ethical rapture induced by the Four Divine or Sublime Moods, described in the Mahâ Sudassana Suttanta. The Pațisambhidâmagga is again referred to by the Cy., viz. II, p. 39, in this connexion. The curious thing is that in reply to the question, 'How is there release thus :—" How lovely it is—with this thought he becomes intent?"'—the reply is simply and solely the Formula of the Four Sublime Moods.

[1] The 4th–7th stages were afterwards known as the Four Âruppa Jhânas, or the four Jhânas to be cultivated for attaining to the Form-less Heavens (see Dh. S., §§ 265 ff.).

in a state of suspended perception and feeling. This is the eighth stage.

'These, Ânanda, are the eight stages of Deliverance.

36. 'Now when once a brother, Ânanda, has mastered these eight stages of Deliverance in order, and has also mastered them in reverse order, and again, in both orders consecutively, so that he is able to lose himself in, as well as to emerge from, any one of them, whenever he chooses, wherever he chooses, and for as long as he chooses—when too, by rooting out the Taints, he enters into and abides in that emancipation of heart, that emancipation of the intellect which he by himself, here in this present world, has come to know and realize—then such a brother, Ânanda, is called "Free-in-both-ways[1]." And, Ânanda, any other Freedom-in-both-ways higher and loftier than this Freedom-in-both-ways there is not!'

Thus spake the Exalted One. Glad at heart the Venerable Ânanda delighted in his words.

Here endeth the MAHÂ-NIDÂNA-SUTTANTA.

---

[1] Ubhato-bhâga-vimutto, i.e. freed both by Reason and also by the intellectual discipline of the Eight Stages. According to a scholastic elaboration of the term, emanating from the Giri-vihâra of the great Loha-pâsâda (or Brazen Palace), 'both ways' meant the Four Jhânas and the Âruppa-jhânas. How this can be reconciled with this paragraph—confirmed by PP. 14 and 73 and by M. I, 477–8—is not stated. 'Taints' are the Four Âsavas, rendered 'Intoxicants' above, p. 28, n. 2.

INTRODUCTION

TO THE

BOOK OF THE GREAT DECEASE.

THE general conclusions we have to draw as to the gradual growth of the various books in the Buddhist canon have been stated in Chapter X of 'Buddhist India.' To work out the details of it will be greatly facilitated by tabular statements of the differences and resemblances found in the various books, whether in matters of form or of ideas. The following table gives a list of all such passages in this book as have, so far, been traced elsewhere. Others will, no doubt, be discovered; but those here given will throw some light on the method of construction followed in the book. Only parallel passages are given, passages in which some other book has at least a paragraph or more couched in identical, or almost identical, words.

A glance at column three, giving the pages of the text, shows a remarkable result. There are ninety-six pages of Pâli text, beginning on p. 72. With a few gaps—pp. 92, 3; 113–15; 117–21; 130–3; 137–40; 148–50; 153; 158–60; 164–7 (nine in number)—the whole text is found, in nearly identical words, elsewhere. The gaps, filled with matter found only in the Book of the Great Decease, amount altogether to about 32 or 33 pages, that is to about one-third of the whole. That proportion would be reduced if we were to include passages of similar tendency, or passages of shorter length.

Secondly; the parallel passages are found, without exception, in those books which belong to the oldest portion of the canon. In 'Buddhist India,' p. 188, there is a table showing, in groups, the probable relative order in time of the Buddhist literature down to the time of Asoka.

All these passages belong to the two earliest groups; all are found in books included in groups 4–6; not one occurs in any of the books included in the later groups—groups 7, 8, 9, and 10. So far as it goes, therefore, the present table is in harmony with the order suggested in the table referred to.

Thirdly; the slight differences, the more important of which

BOOK OF THE GREAT DECEASE.				OTHER OLD PÂLI BOOKS.
1	Chap. I	§§ 1–10	pp. 72–80	A. IV, 16–24
2		16, 17	81–83	D. XXVIII and S. V, 159–161
3		20–34	84–89	Ud. VIII, 6 and Vin. I, 226
4	II	2, 3	90, 91	S. V, 431; Vin. I, 231 and Netti 166
5		12, 13	94, 95	S. IV, 211
6		14–19	95–98	Vin. I, 231–233 [1]
7		22–26	98–101	S. V, 152–154, § 26, ib. 164, 5
8	III	1–20	102–109	A. IV, 308–313
9		1–10	102–107	S. V, 259–263 and Ud. VI, 1
10		21–23	109, 110	A. IV, 30 (nearly = M. I, 72)
11		24–32	110, 111	A.IV, 305 and 348; M.II, 13, 14
12		33	111, 112	D. II, 70, 71; A. IV, 306 and 349
13		43	116	Quoted KV. 559
14	IV	2, 3	122, 123	A.II, 1, 2 and A.IV, 105 (quoted KV. 115) [2]
15		7–11	123–126	A. II, 167–170
16		13–25	126–129	Ud. VIII, 5
17		39–43	134–136	Ud. VIII, 5
18	V	11	141, 142	D. II, 161
19		12	142, 143	A. II, 245, 6
20		15	144	S. V, 16 (nearly)
21		16	145, 146	A. II, 132
22		17, 18	146, 147	D. II, 169, 170
23		27	151	Quoted KV. 601
24		28	152	D.I, 176; M.I, 391, 494; S.II, 21; Vin. I, 69, 71
25	VI	5	154, 5	A. II, 79, 80
26		7–10	155–158	S. I, 157–159 [3]
27		9	156	A. IV, 410 ff.
28		10	157	Th. I, 905, 1046; A. I, 236
29		17	161	D. II, 141, 2
30		19–20	162, 163	Vin. II, 284, 5 [4]
31		27	167 (end of text)	

[1] Differs as to *locus in quo.*
[2] Differs as to application.
[3] Differs as to order of sentences.
[4] Differs as to order of sentences.

are noted in the table, are very suggestive. No. 26 is the episode of the stanzas uttered at the moment of the Buddha's death. The Saṃyutta gives it in the Brahma-Saṃyutta because the first verse is attributed to Brahmâ. The last two verses are there put into the mouths of Ânanda and Anuruddha respectively, perhaps because Anuruddha's verse forms a more fitting conclusion. In the Dîgha Ânanda's comes last, either in deprecation of Ânanda (which is scarcely probable), or for the reason given in the note to the translation.

In No. 14 we have four lines of verse, and the prose introductory to them, ascribed in the Dîgha to the Buddha, ascribed in the Anguttara to a former teacher whose story is there told by the Buddha. That previous teacher, though not a Buddha, is highly praised in the story; the epithet applied to him in the verses (satthâ) is quite in the right place in that connexion; and the verses when spoken by the Buddha of another teacher, are quite appropriate. On the other hand, when put as the Dîgha puts them, into the mouth of the Buddha as spoken of himself, they are not in the best of taste, and sound forced. There can, I think, be no doubt but that the application of these verses to Sunetta the Teacher was the original one, and that the little poem was only later applied to the Buddha himself. But it does not follow in the least that the Anguttara is older than the Dîgha. For, as is shown by the references in the table, the Anguttara itself contains, in an earlier part of the work, the later application of these verses. There it gives the episode, word for word, as it occurs in the Dîgha. The two passages cannot be of the same age. It is not possible that the same story was told originally of two different people. But the two collections (Nikâyas) may very well have been put together, from older materials of varying age, at the same time.

No. 30 is the episode of the explosion of ill-will on the part of Subhadda. There is a slight but very suggestive difference here between the two texts, one found in our Suttanta the other in the Pañcasatika Khandaka of the Vinaya. For convenience of comparison the two versions of this episode are here reprinted side by side.

DÎGHA.	VINAYA.
Now at that time the venerable Mahâ Kassapa was journeying along the high road from Pâvâ to Kusinârâ with a great company of the brethren, with about five hundred of the brethren. And	Now the venerable Mahâ Kassapa addressed the Bhikkhus and said: 'Once I was journeying along the high road from Pâvâ to Kusinârâ with a great company of the brethren, with about five

the venerable Mahâ Kassapa left the high road, and sat himself down at the foot of a certain tree.

Just at that time a certain ascetic who had picked up a Mandârava flower in Kusinârâ was coming along the high road to Pâvâ. Now the venerable Mahâ Kassapa saw the ascetic coming in the distance, and on seeing him he said to that ascetic: ' O friend! surely thou knowest our Master?'

' Yea, friend! I know him. This day the Sama*n*a Gotama has been dead a week. That is how I obtained this Mandârava flower.'

On that of those of the brethren who not yet free from the passions, some stretched out their arms and wept, and some fell headlong on the ground, and some reeled to and fro in anguish at the thought: ' Too soon has the Exalted One died! Too soon has the Happy One passed away! Too soon has the Light gone out in the world!' But those of the brethren who were free from the passions (the Arahants) bore their grief self-possessed and composed at the thought: ' Impermanent are all component things! How is it possible that (they should not be dissolved?).'

Now at that time a brother named Subhadda, who had been received into the Order in his old age, was seated in that company. And Subhadda, the recruit in his old age, said to those brethren: ' Enough, Sirs! Weep not, neither lament! We are well rid of the great Sama*n*a. We used to be annoyed by being told: "This beseems you, this beseems you not." But now we shall be able

hundred of the brethren. And I left the high road and sat myself down at the foot of a certain tree.

Just at that time a certain ascetic who had picked up a Mandârava flower in Kusinârâ was coming along the high road to Pâvâ. Now I saw that ascetic coming in the distance, and on seeing him I said to that ascetic: ' O friend! surely thou knowest our Master?'

' Yea, friend! I know him. This day the Sama*n*a Gotama has been dead a week. That is how I obtained this Mandârava flower.'

On that, Sirs, of those of the brethren who were not yet free from the passions, some stretched out their arms and wept, and some fell headlong on the ground, and some reeled to and fro in anguish at the thought: ' Too soon has the Exalted One died! Too soon has the Happy One passed away! Too soon has the Light gone out in the world!' But those of the brethren who were free from the passions (the Arahants) bore their grief self-possessed and composed at the thought: ' Impermanent are all component things! How is it possible that (they should not be dissolved?).'

Then I, Sirs, spoke thus to the Bhikkhus: ' Enough, my brethren, weep not, neither lament! Has not the Exalted One, Sirs, formerly declared this, that it is in the very nature of all things near and dear to us that we must divide ourselves from them, leave them, sever ourselves from them. How, then, can this be possible—whereas anything what-ever born, brought into being,

to do whatever we like ; and what we do not like, that we shall not do !'

But the venerable Mahâ Kassapa exhorted the brethren : 'Enough, my brethren ! Weep not, neither lament ! Has not the Exalted One formerly declared this, that it is in the very nature of all things near and dear unto us that we must divide ourselves from them, leave them, sever ourselves from them ? How then, brethren, can this be possible—whereas anything whatever born, brought into being, and organized contains within itself the inherent necessity of dissolution — how then can this be possible that such a being should not be dissolved ? No such condition can exist !'

and organized contains within itself the inherent necessity of dissolution — how then can this be possible that such a being should not be dissolved ? No such condition can exist !'

Now at that time, Sirs, a brother named Subhadda, who had been received into the Order in his old age, was seated in that company. And Subhadda, Sirs, the recruit in his old age, said to those brethren : 'Enough, Sirs ! Weep not, neither lament ! We are well rid of the great Samana. We used to be annoyed by being told : "This beseems you, this beseems you not." But now we shall be able to do whatever we like ; and what we do not like that we shall not do.'

A glance at the above columns shows that the two texts are identical except in two particulars. The Dîgha gives the episode in narrative form, whereas the Vinaya puts it into the mouth of Kassapa himself. And secondly, whereas the Dîgha puts Kassapa's speech *after* the outburst of Subhadda, the Vinaya puts it before—that is, the last two paragraphs in the Dîgha are transposed in the Vinaya.

Professor Oldenberg, who was the first to point out (more than thirty years ago)[1] the parallelism between the two texts, acutely suggests that the change is due to the position occupied by this episode in the Vinaya. It is there used as introduction to the account of the Council at Râjagaha held, according to the tradition, to counteract such sentiments as were expressed in Subhadda's outburst. It was considered more appropriate, therefore, that *in that connexion*, Subhadda's words should come last, to lead up to what follows. The whole of the story is accordingly taken from our Suttanta. But the last paragraphs are transposed, and the whole is put into the mouth of Kassapa, on whose advice the Council is stated to have been convened.

This seems a very probable explanation of the transposition, and of the existence of two slightly different accounts of the

---

[1] Introduction to the Vinaya, xxvi–xxviii.

episode. If we accept it—and I think we should [1]—we have to face the further question: Why was the episode inserted in the Dîgha? It is given there in the middle of the account of the cremation of the Buddha at Kusinârâ. It has very little to do either with what precedes, or with what follows it; and is said to have taken place away from Kusinârâ. The outburst itself was of little importance in the long story of the Buddha's last days; and (in the older order as preserved in the Dîgha) is immediately overwhelmed by Mahâ Kassapa's apt quotation from the Master's words. Have we not here a very similar motive, acting on either the same or very similar minds? Is it not precisely the part played by this anecdote in the traditional account of the First Council that led the compilers of the Dîgha to find a place for it in the Book of the Great Decease? They might so easily have left it out. As it stands it only breaks in upon the narrative. And, apart from the tradition about the First Council, it had no importance.

There has been much discussion both for and against the authenticity of this First Council. Is this really necessary? Oldenberg's analysis of the comparative date of the different parts of the Vinaya has shown conclusively that the record, as we have it, is later than the Council of Vesâlî, that is at least a hundred years later than the meeting whose proceedings it purports to record. What can be the value of so late a record? It may be objected to this that though the extant record is late the tradition may be older. No one can prove that it was not. But this would not help matters at all. We must then point out that the details as given are, as one might expect, quite inaccurate [2].

Space will only allow of one example being taken.

It is well known that all the ancient sacred literatures of the world have grown up gradually, and are a mosaic of earlier

---

[1] It does not quite follow that the Vinaya is borrowing direct from the Dîgha. That may be so. But the Subhadda story may have been in existence before either Dîgha or Vinaya was put into its present shape. If so, it was doubtless current in the form now preserved by the Dîgha; and was changed by the compilers of the Vinaya. Both Oldenberg (*loc. cit.*) and Franke (J. P. T. S., 1908, 8–12) suppose the Vinaya to be borrowing from the Dîgha. It is quite possible that the two books—Dîgha and Vinaya—may have been put together, as we now have them, at the same time.

[2] It is admitted there were no reporters present. There were at the time of the Buddha's death no mechanical means available for writing anything beyond the most meagre notes.

and later material. The Buddhist Pi/akas form no exception. As regards the Nikâyas I have shown this elsewhere in considerable detail[1]. Now the record, as we have it, presupposes the existence, already at the time of the Buddha's death, of the Five Nikâyas in their present arrangement!

It follows that both on general principles of comparative criticism, and on consideration of a particular instance in this special case, the details given us in the Vinaya about the First Council cannot be trusted. But it does not follow, as a matter of certainty, that there was no Council at all. It is quite possible, and even probable, that the Order held a 'General Chapter,' as we should call it, soon after the Buddha's death. They kept no proper minutes of the meeting. We may conjecture what happened at it, but it would be only conjecture. And we must continue patiently, from the incidental references in the books themselves, to formulate a probable theory as to the method in which the literature gradually sprang up. The record handed down to us in the Vinaya is authentic enough ; but only *in the only way in which any such record can be considered authentic*, that is, as evidence of beliefs held at the date at which it was composed.

---

[1] 'Dialogues,' I, x–xx; 'Buddhist India,' 161–208.

THE BOOK OF THE GREAT DECEASE.

CHAPTER I.]

1. [**72**] Thus have I heard. The Exalted One was once dwelling in Râjagaha, on the hill called the Vulture's Peak. Now at that time Ajâtasattu, the son of the queen-consort of the Videha clan[1], the king of Magadha, had made up his mind to attack the Vajjians; and he said to himself, 'I will strike at these Vajjians, mighty and powerful[2] though they be, I will root out these Vajjians, I will destroy these Vajjians, I will bring these Vajjians to utter ruin!'

2. So he spake to the brahmin Vassakâra (the Rain-maker), prime-minister of Magadha, and said:—

---

[1] Ajâtasattu Vedehiputto. The first word is not a personal name but an official epithet, 'he against whom there has arisen no (worthy or equal) foe' (so already in the Rig Veda but Sum. 131 different). The second gives us the maiden family, or tribal (not personal) name of his mother. Her name, according to a Tibetan authority quoted by Rockhill, 'Life of the Buddha,' p. 63, was Vâsavî.

Persons of distinction are scarcely ever mentioned by name in Indian Buddhist books, a rule applying more especially to kings, but extended not unfrequently to private persons. Thus Upatissa, the disciple whom the Buddha himself declared to be 'the second founder of the kingdom of righteousness,' is referred to either as Dhamma-senâpati or as Sâriputta; epithets of corresponding origin to those in the text. See above, Vol. I, pp. 193–5.

By the Jains Ajâtasattu is called Kûnika or Konika, which again is probably not the name given to him at the rice-eating (the ceremony corresponding to infant baptism), but a nickname acquired in after-life.

[2] Evammahiddhike evammahânubhâve. There is nothing magical or supernatural about the iddhi here referred to. Etena tesam samagga-bhâvam kathesi says the commentator simply: thus referring the former adjective to the power of union, as he does the second to the power derived from practice in military tactics (hatthisippâdîhi). See above, Vol. I, p. 273.

'Come now, brahmin, do you go to the Exalted One, and bow down in adoration at his feet on my behalf, and inquire in my name whether he is free from illness and suffering, and in the enjoyment of ease and comfort and vigorous health.   Then tell him that Ajâtasattu, son of the Vedehî, the king of Magadha, in his eagerness to attack the Vajjians, has resolved, "I will strike at these Vajjians, mighty and powerful though they be, I will root out these Vajjians, I will destroy these Vajjians, I will bring these Vajjians to utter ruin!"   And bear carefully in mind whatever the Exalted One may predict, and repeat it to me. For the Buddhas speak nothing untrue!'

3. [**73**] Then the brahmin Vassakâra, the Rain-maker, hearkened to the words of the king, saying, 'Be it as you say.'   And ordering a number of state carriages to be made ready, he mounted one of them, left Râjagaha with his train, and went to the Vulture's Peak, riding as far as the ground was passable for carriages and then alighting and proceeding on foot to the place where the Exalted One was.   On arriving there he exchanged with the Exalted One the greetings and compliments of politeness and courtesy, sat down respectfully by his side (and then delivered to him the message even as the king had commanded [1]).

4. Now at that time the venerable Ânanda was standing behind the Exalted One, and fanning him. And the Blessed One said to him :—' Have you heard, Ânanda, that the Vajjians foregather often and frequent the public meetings of their clan?'

'Lord, so I have heard,' replied he.

'So long, Ânanda,' rejoined the Blessed One, 'as the Vajjians foregather thus often, and frequent the public meetings of their clan; so long may they be expected not to decline, but to prosper.'

(And in like manner questioning Ânanda, and receiving a similar reply, the Exalted One declared

---

[1] The wording of § 2 is here repeated.

as follows the other conditions which would ensure the welfare of the Vajjian confederacy[1].)

[74] 'So long, Ânanda, as the Vajjians meet together in concord, and rise in concord, and carry out their undertakings in concord—so long as they enact nothing not already established, abrogate nothing that has been already enacted, and act in accordance with the ancient institutions of the Vajjians, as established in former days—so long as they honour and esteem and revere and support the Vajjian elders, and hold it a point of duty to hearken to their words—so long as no women or girls belonging to their clans are detained among them by force or abduction—[75] so long as they honour and esteem and revere and support the Vajjian shrines[2] in town or country, and allow not the proper offerings and rites, as formerly given and performed, to fall into desuetude—so long as the rightful protection, defence, and support shall be fully provided for the Arahants among them, so that Arahants from a distance may enter the realm, and the Arahants therein may live at ease—so long may the Vajjians be expected not to decline, but to prosper.'

5. Then the Exalted One addressed Vassakâra the brahmin and said :—

'When I was once staying, O brahmin, at Vesâlî at the Sârandada Shrine[3], I taught the Vajjians these conditions of welfare ; and so long as these conditions shall continue to exist among the Vajjians, so long as the Vajjians shall be well instructed in those conditions, so long may we expect them not to decline, but to prosper.'

'We may expect then,' answered the brahmin, 'the welfare and not the decline of the Vajjians when they are possessed of any one of these conditions of welfare, how much more so when they are possessed of all

---

[1] In the text there is a question, answer, and reply with each clause.

[2] Cetiyâni, which Sum. Vil. explains as Yakkha-cetiyâni.

[3] The commentator adds that this was a vihara erected on the site of a former shrine of the Yakkha Sârandada. The teaching referred to is set out in full at A. IV, 16, but the persons taught are there called Licchavis.

the seven. [76] So, Gotama, the Vajjians cannot be overcome by the king of Magadha; that is not in battle, without diplomacy or breaking up their alliance[1]. And now, Gotama, we must go; we are busy and have much to do.'

'Whatever you think most fitting, O brahmin,' was the reply. And the brahmin Vassakâra, the Rainmaker, delighted and pleased with the words of the Exalted One, rose from his seat, and went his way.

6. Now soon after he had gone the Exalted One addressed the venerable Ânanda, and said :—' Go now, Ânanda, and assemble in the Service Hall such of the brethren[2] as live in the neighbourhood of Râjagaha.'

And he did so; and returned to the Exalted One, and informed him, saying :—

'The company of the brethren, lord, is assembled, let the Exalted One do as seemeth to him fit.'

And the Exalted One arose, and went to the Service

---

[1] 'Overcome' is literally 'done' (karanîya), but the word evidently has a similar sense to that which ' done ' occasionally has in colloquial English. Upalâpana, which I have only met with here, must mean 'humbug, cajolery, diplomacy;' see the use of the verb upa-lâpeti, at S. I, 102; Vin. II, 119; IV, 139; Jât. II, 266, 267; IV, 56. Sum. Vil. explains it, at some length, as making an alliance, by gifts, with hostile intent, which comes to much the same thing. The root, I think, is lî.

[2] The word translated 'brethren' throughout is in the original bhikkhu, a word most difficult to render adequately by any word which would not, to Christians and in Europe, connote something different from the Buddhist idea. A bhikkhu, literally ' beggar,' was a disciple who had joined Gotama's order; but the word refers to their renunciation of worldly things, rather than to their consequent mendicancy; and they did not really beg in our modern sense of the word. Hardy has ' priests;' I have elsewhere used ' monks' and sometimes ' beggars' and ' members of the order.' This last is, I think, the best rendering; but it is too long for constant repetition, as in this passage, and too complex to be a really good version of bhikkhu. The members of the order were not priests, for they had no priestly powers. They were not monks, for they took no vow of obedience, and could leave the order (and constantly did so and do so still) whenever they chose. They were not beggars, for they had none of the mental and moral qualities associated with that word. ' Brethren ' connotes very much the position in which they stood to one another; but I wish there were a better word to use in rendering bhikkhu.

Hall; and when he was seated, he addressed the brethren, and said :—

'I will teach you, O mendicants, seven conditions of the welfare of a community. Listen well and attend, and I will speak.'

'Even so, lord,' said the brethren, in assent, to the Exalted One ; and he spake as follows :—

'So long, O mendicants, as the brethren foregather oft, and frequent the formal meetings of their Order— so long as they meet together in concord, and rise in concord, and carry out in concord the duties of the Order—[77] so long as the brethren shall establish nothing that has not been already prescribed, and abrogate nothing that has been already established, and act in accordance with the rules of the Order as now laid down—so long as the brethren honour and esteem and revere and support the elders of experience and long standing, the fathers and leaders of the Order, and hold it a point of duty to hearken to their words— so long as the brethren fall not under the influence of that craving which, springing up within them, would give rise to renewed existence—so long as the brethren delight in a life of solitude—so long as the brethren so train their minds in self-possession that good men among their fellow-disciples shall come to them, and those who have come shall dwell at ease—so long may the brethren be expected, not to decline, but to prosper. So long as these seven conditions shall continue to exist among the brethren, so long as they are well-instructed in these conditions, so long may the brethren be expected not to decline, but to prosper.

7. 'Other seven conditions of welfare will I teach you, O brethren. Listen well, and attend, and I will speak.'

And on their expressing their assent, he spake as follows :—

[78] 'So long as the brethren shall not engage in, or be fond of, or be connected with business—so long as the brethren shall not be in the habit of, or be fond of, or be partakers in idle talk—so long as the brethren

shall not be addicted to, or be fond of, or indulge in
slothfulness—so long as the brethren shall not frequent,
or be fond of, or indulge in society—so long as the
brethren shall neither have, nor fall under the influence
of, wrong desires [1]—so long as the brethren shall not
become the friends, companions, or intimates of evil-
doers—so long as the brethren shall not come to a stop
on their way (to Nirvana in Arahantship [2]) because they
have attained to any lesser thing—so long may the
brethren be expected not to decline, but to prosper.

'So long as these conditions shall continue to exist
among the brethren—so long as they are instructed in
these conditions—so long may the brethren be expected
not to decline, but to prosper.

8. 'Other seven conditions of welfare will I teach
you, O brethren.   Listen well, and attend, and I will
speak.'

And on their expressing their assent, he spake as
follows :—

'So long as the brethren shall be full of faith,
modest in heart, afraid of wrong doing [3], full of learning,
[79] strong in energy, active in mind, and full of
wisdom—so long may the brethren be expected not to
decline, but to prosper.

'So long as these conditions shall continue to exist
among the brethren—so long as they are instructed in

---

[1] The blundering misstatement that Buddhism teaches the suppres-
sion of desire (not of wrong desire) is still occasionally met with.   The
question is fully discussed in Mrs. Rhys Davids's article on ' The Will
in Buddhism' (J.R.A.S., 1898).

[2] This is an interesting analogue to Philippians iii. 13 :—'I count not
myself to have apprehended : but this one thing I do, forgetting those
things which are behind, and reaching forth unto those things which
are before, I press toward the mark,' &c.   See also below, Chap. V,
§ 68.

[3] The exact distinction between hiri and ottappa is here explained
by Buddhaghosa as loathing sin as contrasted with fear of sin.   But
this is rather a gloss than an exact and exclusive definition.   Ahirikâ
is shamelessness, anotappam frowardness.   At Jât. I, 207 we find
hiri described as subjective, and ottappa as objective, modesty of
heart as contrasted with decency in outward behaviour.   See further
Mrs. Rhys Davids in ' Buddhist Psychology,' p. 20.

these conditions—so long may the brethren be expected
not to decline, but to prosper.

9. 'Other seven conditions of welfare will I teach
you, O brethren. Listen well, and attend, and I will
speak.'

And on their expressing their assent, he spake as
follows :—

'So long as the brethren shall exercise themselves
in the sevenfold higher wisdom, that is to say, in
mental activity, search after truth, energy, joy, peace,
earnest contemplation, and equanimity of mind—so
long may the brethren be expected not to decline, but
to prosper.

'So long as these conditions shall continue to exist
among the brethren—so long as they are instructed in
these conditions—so long may the brethren be expected
not to decline, but to prosper.

10. 'Other seven conditions of welfare will I teach
you, O brethren. Listen well, and attend, and I will
speak.'

And on their expressing their assent, he spake as
follows :—

'So long as the brethren shall exercise themselves
in the realization of the ideas of the impermanency
of all phenomena, bodily or mental, the absence [in
them of any abiding principle] of any "soul," of
corruption, of the danger of wrong thoughts, of the
necessity of getting rid of them, of purity of heart,
of Nirvana—so long may the brethren be expected not
to decline, but to prosper.

[80] 'So long as these conditions shall continue to
exist among the brethren—so long as they are instructed in these conditions—so long may the brethren
be expected not to decline but to prosper.

11. 'Six conditions of welfare will I teach you,
O brethren. Listen well, and attend, and I will
speak.'

And on their expressing their assent, he spake
as follows :—

'So long as the brethren shall persevere in kindness

of action, speech, and thought towards their fellow-disciples, both in public and in private—so long as they shall divide without partiality, and share in common with their upright companions, all such things as they receive in accordance with the just provisions of the Order, down even to the mere contents of a begging-bowl—so long as the brethren shall live among the saints in the practice, both in public and in private, of those virtues which [unbroken, intact, unspotted, unblemished] are productive of freedom [1], and praised by the wise; which are untarnished [by the desire of future life, or by the belief in the efficacy of outward acts] [2]; and which are conducive to concentration of heart—so long as the brethren shall live among the saints, cherishing, both in public and in private, that noble and saving insight which leads to the complete destruction of the sorrow of him who acts according to it—so long may the brethren be expected not to decline, but to prosper.

[81] 'So long as these six conditions shall continue to exist among the brethren—so long as they are instructed in these six conditions—so long may the brethren be expected not to decline, but to prosper.'

12. Now it was while the Exalted One was staying there at Râjagaha on the Vulture's Peak that he held that comprehensive religious talk with the brethren, saying:—'Such and such is upright conduct; such and such is earnest contemplation; such and such is intelli-

---

[1] Buddhaghosa takes this in a spiritual sense. He says:—'These virtues are bhujissâni because they bring one to the state of a free man by delivering him from the slavery of craving.'

[2] The commentator explains:—'These virtues are called aparâmatthâni because they are untarnished by craving or delusion, and because no one can say of him who practises them, "you have been already guilty of such and such a fault." Craving is here the hope of a future life in heaven, and delusion the belief in the efficacy of rites and ceremonies (the two nissayas), which are condemned as unworthy inducements to virtue. At A. III, 132 these five qualities are called phâsu-vihârâ, states of bliss.

gence. Great becomes the fruit, great the advantage of earnest contemplation, when it is set round with upright conduct. Great becomes the fruit, great the advantage of intellect when it is set round with earnest contemplation. The mind set round with intelligence is set quite free from the Intoxications, that is to say, from the Intoxication of Sensuality, from the Intoxication of Becoming, from the Intoxication of Delusion, from the Intoxication of Ignorance[1].'

13. Now when the Exalted One had sojourned at Râjagaha as long as he thought fit, he addressed the venerable Ânanda, and said :—' Come, Ânanda, let us go to Ambala*tth*ikâ.'

' So be it, lord!' said Ânanda in assent, and the Exalted One, with a large company of the brethren, proceeded to Ambala*tth*ikâ.

14. There the Exalted One stayed in the king's house and held that comprehensive religious talk with the brethren, saying :—' Such and such is upright conduct; such and such is earnest contemplation; such and such is intelligence. Great becomes the fruit, great the advantage of earnest contemplation, when it is set round with upright conduct. Great

---

[1] This paragraph is spoken of as if it were a well-known summary, and it is constantly repeated below. The word I have here rendered ' earnest contemplation' is samâdhi, which occupies in the Five Nikâyas very much the same position as faith does in the New Testament; and this section shows that the relative importance of samâdhi, paññâ, and sîla played a part in early Buddhism just as the distinction between faith, reason, and works did afterwards in Western theology. It would be difficult to find a passage in which the Buddhist view of the relation of these conflicting ideas is stated with greater beauty of thought, or equal succinctness of form. See further Rhys Davids's ' The Yogâvacara's Manual of Indian Mysticism,' pp. xxv foll., and above; Vol. I, p. 156. Also E. W. West, ' Pahlavi Texts,' III, 37 ; Anguttara I, 233 ; Itivuttaka, No. 59.

The expression ' set round with' is in Pâli paribhâvita. In a constantly recurring simile (M. I, 104; S. III, 153) eggs are said to be paribhâvitâni by a brooding hen. In medicine the word means ' charged with, impregnated with.' See Jât. I, 380; IV, 407; and compare Mil. 361, 382, 394. Comp. Bhag. Gîtâ III, 38 for this simile.

becomes the fruit, great the advantage of intellect when it is set round with earnest contemplation. The mind set round with intelligence is set quite free from the Intoxications, that is to say, from the Intoxication of Sensuality, from the Intoxication of Becoming, from the Intoxication of Delusion, from the Intoxication of Ignorance.'

15. Now when the Exalted One had sojourned at Ambala*tth*ikâ as long as he thought fit, he addressed the venerable Ânanda, and said :—' Come, Ânanda, let us go on to Nâlandâ [1].'

'So be it, lord!' said Ânanda, in assent, to the Exalted One.

Then the Exalted One proceeded, with a great company of the brethren, to Nâlandâ; and there, at Nâlandâ, the Exalted One stayed in the Pâvârika mango grove.

16. [2] Now the venerable Sâriputta came to the place where the Exalted One was, and having saluted him, took his seat respectfully at his side, [82] and said :— 'Lord! such faith have I in the Exalted One, that methinks there never has been, nor will there be, nor is there now any other, whether wanderer or brahmin, who is greater and wiser than the Exalted One, that is to say, as regards the higher wisdom.'

'Grand and bold are the words of thy mouth, Sâriputta: verily, thou hast burst forth into a song of ecstasy! of course then thou hast known all the Exalted Ones who in the long ages of the past have been Able, Awakened Ones [3], comprehending their

---

[1] Afterwards the seat of the famous Buddhist University for so many centuries the centre of learning in India.

[2] The following conversation is also given at length in the Sampasadâniya Suttanta of the Dîgha Nikâya, and a third time in the Satipa*tth*âna Sa*m*yutta of the Sa*m*yutta Nikâya (S. V, 159). It was evidently a very popular passage, and is quite possibly the one referred to in Asoka's Bhabra Edict as the 'Question of Upatissa,' that is, of Sâriputta.

[3] Arahant Buddhas. The meaning of these words must have been very present to the minds of those who used them at the time of the rise of what we call Buddhism; and there was little or no difference

minds with yours, and aware what their conduct was, what their wisdom, what their mode of life, and what the emancipation they attained to?'

'Not so, O lord!'

'Of course then thou hast perceived all the Exalted Ones who in the long ages of the future shall be Able Awakened Ones comprehending [in the same manner their whole minds with yours]?'

'Not so, O lord!'

'But at least then, O Sâriputta, thou knowest me as the Able Awakened One now alive, and hast penetrated my mind [in the manner I have mentioned]?'

'Not even that, O lord!'

'You see then, Sâriputta, that you know not the hearts of the Able Awakened Ones of the past and of the future. [83] Why therefore are your words so grand and bold? Why do you burst forth into such a song of ecstasy?'

17. 'O lord! I have not the knowledge of the hearts of the Able Awakened Ones that have been, and are to come, and now are. I only know the lineage of the faith.

'Just, lord, as a king might have a border city, strong in its foundations, strong in its ramparts and towers, and with only one gate; and the king might have a watchman there, clever, expert, and wise, to stop all strangers and admit only men well known. And he, on patrolling in his sentry walks over the approaches all round the city, might not so observe all the joints and crevices in the ramparts of that city as to know where even a cat could get out. He might well be satisfied to know that all living things of larger size that entered or left the city, would have to do so

---

between the connotation of the two terms. As time went on the two were more and more differentiated, and hardened into technical terms. See Samyutta III, 65 on the difference between the two: and see Samyutta I, 233; III, 160; IV, 175 for very old explanations of Arahâ, and Paṅsambhidâ I, 172 for an ancient commentary on the meaning of Buddha.

by that gate.   Thus only is it, lord, that I know the
lineage of the faith.

'I know that the Able Awakened Ones of the past,
putting away all hankering after the world, ill-will,
sloth, worry and perplexity—those five Hindrances,
mental faults which make the understanding weak;—
training their minds in the four kinds of mental
activity; thoroughly exercising themselves in the
sevenfold higher wisdom, received the full fruition of
Enlightenment.   And I know that the Able Awakened
Ones of the times to come will [do the same].   And
I know that the Exalted One, the Able Awakened
One of to-day, has [done so] now [1].'

18. [84] There too at Nâlandâ in the Pâvârika
mango grove the Exalted One held that comprehensive religious talk with the brethren, saying :—' Such
and such is upright conduct; such and such is earnest
contemplation ; such and such is intelligence.   Great
becomes the fruit, great the advantage of earnest contemplation, when it is set round with upright conduct.
Great becomes the fruit, great the advantage of intellect when it is set round with earnest contemplation.
The mind set round with intelligence is set quite free
from the Intoxications, that is to say, from the Intoxication of Sensuality, from the Intoxication of Becom-

---

[1] The tertium quid of the comparison is the completeness of the
knowledge.   Sâriputta acknowledges that he was wrong in jumping
to the wide conclusion that his own lord and master was the wisest of
all the teachers of the different religious systems that were known to
him.   So far—after the cross-examination by the Buddha—he admits
that his knowledge does not reach.   But he maintains that he does
know that which is, to him, after all the main thing, namely, that all
the Buddhas must have passed through the process here laid down as
leading up to the Enlightenment of Arahantship.

All the details he gives are details, not of Buddhahood, but of
Arahantship.   He makes no distinction between the two states of
attainment.   This is most important for the history of that Buddhology,
which, in after centuries, was the main factor in the downfall of
Buddhism.

ing, from the Intoxication of Delusion, from the Intoxication of Ignorance.'

19. Now when the Exalted One had sojourned as
long as he thought fit at Nâlandâ, he addressed the
venerable Ânanda, and said :—' Come, Ânanda, let us
go on to Pâṭaligâma.'

'So be it, lord!' said Ânanda, in assent, to the
Exalted One.

Then the Exalted One proceeded, with a great company of the brethren, to Pâṭaligâma.

20. Now the disciples at Pâṭaligâma heard of his
arrival there, and they went on to the place where he
was, took their seats respectfully beside him, and invited him to their village rest-house.   And the Exalted
One signified, by silence, his consent.

21. Then the Pâṭaligâma disciples seeing that he
had accepted the invitation, rose from their seats, and
went away to the rest-house, bowing to the Exalted
One and keeping him on their right as they passed
him.   On arriving there they strewed all the rest-house
with fresh sand, placed seats in it, set up a water-pot,
and fixed an oil lamp.   Then they returned to the
Exalted One, and saluting him they stood beside him,
and told him what they had done and said :—' It is
time for you to do what you deem most fit.'

22. [85] And the Exalted One robed himself, took
his bowl and other things, went with the brethren to
the rest-house, washed his feet, entered the hall, and
took his seat against the centre pillar, with his face
towards the east.   And the brethren also, after washing their feet, entered the hall, and took their seats
round the Exalted One, against the western wall, and
facing the east.   And the Pâṭaligâma disciples too,
after washing their feet, entered the hall, and took
their seats opposite the Exalted One, against the
eastern wall, and facing towards the west.

23. Then the Exalted One addressed the Pâṭaligâma
disciples, and said :—' Fivefold, O householders, is the
loss of the wrong-doer through his want of rectitude.
In the first place the wrong-doer, devoid of rectitude,

falls into great poverty through sloth; in the next place his evil repute gets noised abroad; thirdly, whatever society he enters—whether of nobles, brahmins, heads of houses, or men of a religious order—he enters shyly and confused; fourthly, he is full of anxiety when he dies; and lastly, on the dissolution of the body, after death, he is reborn into some unhappy state of suffering or woe [1]. This, O householders, is the fivefold loss of the evil-doer!

24. [86] 'Fivefold, O householders, is the gain of the well-doer through his practice of rectitude. In the first place the well-doer, strong in rectitude, acquires great wealth through his industry; in the next place, good reports of him are spread abroad; thirdly, whatever society he enters—whether of nobles, brahmins, heads of houses, or members of a religious order—he enters confident and self-possessed; fourthly, he dies without anxiety; and lastly, on the dissolution of the body, after death, he is reborn into some happy state in heaven. This, O householders, is the fivefold gain of the well-doer.'

25. When the Exalted One had thus taught the lay disciples at Pâ*aligâma, and incited them, and roused them, and gladdened them, far into the night with religious discourse, he dismissed them, saying :— 'The night is far spent, O householders. It is time for you to do what you deem most fit.' 'Even so, lord!' answered the disciples of Pâ*aligâma, and they rose from their seats, and bowing to the Exalted One, and keeping him on their right hand as they passed him, they departed thence.

And the Exalted One, not long after the disciples

---

[1] Four such states are mentioned, apâya, duggati, vinipâto, and nirayo, all of which are temporary states. The first three seem to be synonyms. The last is one of the four divisions into which the first is usually divided, and is often translated hell; but not being an eternal state, and not being dependent or consequent upon any judgement, it cannot be accurately so rendered. See p. 51.

of Pâ*t*aligâma had departed thence, entered into his
private chamber [1].

26. At that time Sunîdha and Vassakâra, the chief
ministers of Magadha, were building a fortress at
Pâ*t*aligâma to repel the Vajjians, [87] and there were
a number of fairies who haunted in thousands the plots
of ground there. Now, wherever ground is so occupied
by powerful fairies, they bend the hearts of the most
powerful kings and ministers to build dwelling-places
there, [and fairies of middling and inferior power bend
in a similar way the hearts of middling or inferior kings
and ministers [2].]

27. And the Blessed One, with great and clear
vision, surpassing that of ordinary men, saw thousands
of those fairies haunting Pâ*t*aligâma. And he rose up
very early in the morning, and said to Ânanda:—'Who
is it then, Ânanda, who is building a fortress at
Pâ*t*aligâma?'

'Sunîdha and Vassakâra, lord, the chief ministers of
Magadha, are building a fortress there to keep back
the Vajjians.'

28. 'They act, Ânanda, as if they had consulted with
the Tâvati*m*sa angels.' [And telling him of what he
had seen, and of the influence such fairies had, he
added]:—'And as far, Ânanda, as Aryan people resort,
as far as merchants travel, this will become the chief
city, Pâ*t*ali-putta, a centre for the interchange of all
kinds of wares. [88] But three dangers will hang over
Pâ*t*ali-putta, that of fire, that of water, and that of
dissension among friends [3].'

---

[1] Compare Vinaya III, 93.
[2] The curious popular belief as to good and bad fairies haunting
the sites of houses gave rise to a quack science, akin to astrology,
called vatthu-vijjâ, which Buddhaghosa explains here at some
length, and which is frequently condemned elsewhere in the Five
Nikâyas. See, for instance, I of the Mahâ-silam, translated above,
Vol. I, p. 18. The belief is turned to ridicule in the edifying legend,
No. 40, in my 'Buddhist Birth Stories,' pp. 326-34.
[3] This paragraph is of importance to the orthodox Buddhist as
proving the Buddha's power of prophecy and the authority of the

29. Now Sunîdha and Vassakâra, the chief ministers of Magadha, proceeded to the place where the Exalted One was. And when they had come there they exchanged with the Exalted One the greetings and compliments of politeness and courtesy, and stood there respectfully on one side. And, so standing, Sunîdha and Vassakâra, the chief ministers of Magadha, spake thus to the Exalted One :—

'May the venerable Gotama do us the honour of taking his meal, together with the company of the brethren, at our house to-day.' And the Exalted One signified, by silence, his consent.

30. Then when Sunîdha and Vassakâra, the chief ministers of Magadha, perceived that he had given his consent, they returned to the place where they dwelt. And on arriving there, they prepared sweet dishes of boiled rice, and cakes ; and informed the Exalted One, saying :—

'The hour of food has come, O Gotama, and all is ready.'

And the Exalted One robed himself early, took his bowl with him, and repaired, with the brethren, to the dwelling-place of Sunîdha and Vassakâra, and sat down on the seat prepared for him. And with their own hands they set the sweet rice and the cakes before the brethren with the Buddha at their head, and waited on them till they had had enough. And when the Exalted One had finished eating his meal, the ministers brought a low seat, and sat down respectfully at his side.

31. And when they were thus seated the Exalted One gave thanks in these verses :—

'Wheresoe'er the prudent man shall take up his abode

Buddhist scriptures. To those who conclude that such a passage must have been written after the event that is prophesied (if any), it may be valuable evidence of the age both of the Vinaya and of this Mahâ Parinibbâna Suttanta. See the note at 'Vinaya Texts,' II, 102.

Let him support the brethren there, good men of
    self-control,
And give the merit of his gifts to the deities who
    haunt the spot [1].
Revered, they will revere him: honoured, they
    honour him again ;
Are gracious to him as a mother to her own, her
    only son.
And the man who has the grace of the gods, good
    fortune he beholds.'

32. [89] And when he had thanked the ministers in
these verses he rose from his seat and departed thence.
And they followed him as he went, saying, ' The gate
the Samana Gotama goes out by to-day shall be called
Gotama's gate, and the ferry at which he crosses the
river shall be called Gotama's ferry.' And the gate
he went out at was called Gotama's gate.

33. But the Exalted One went on to the river. And
at that time the river Ganges was brimful and over-
flowing ; and wishing to cross to the opposite bank,
some began to seek for boats, some for rafts of wood,
whilst some made rafts of basket-work. Then the
Exalted One as instantaneously as a strong man would
stretch forth his arm, or draw it back again when he
had stretched it forth, vanished from this side of the
river, and stood on the further bank with the company
of the brethren.

34. And the Exalted One beheld the people who
wished to cross to the opposite bank looking some of
them for boats and some of them for rafts of wood,
and some of them for rafts of basket-work ; and as he
beheld them he brake forth at that time into this
song :—

---

[1] Tâsam dakkhinam âdise. See Therî Gâthâ 307, 311;
Mil. 294.

' They who have crossed the ocean drear
Making a solid path across the pools—
Whilst the vain world ties its basket rafts—
These are the wise, these are the saved indeed![1] '

End of the First Portion for Recitation.

---

[1] That is, those who cross the ' ocean drear ' of taṇhâ, or craving ; avoiding by means of the ' dyke' or causeway of the Aryan Path, the ' pools ' or shallows of lust, and ignorance, and delusion (comp. Dhp. 91), whilst the vain world looks for salvation from rites, and ceremonies, and gods,—' these are the wise, these are the saved indeed ! '

CHAPTER II.

1. [90] Now the Exalted One addressed the venerable Ânanda, and said :—' Come, Ânanda, let us go on to Koṭigâma.'

'So be it, lord!' said Ânanda, in assent, to the Exalted One.

The Exalted One proceeded with a great company of the brethren to Koṭigâma ; and there he stayed in the village itself [1].

2. And at that place the Exalted One addressed the brethren, and said :—' It is through not understanding and grasping four Aryan Truths, O brethren, that we have had to run so long, to wander so long in this weary path of transmigration, both you and I !

'And what are these four ?'

'The Aryan truth about sorrow ; the Aryan truth about the cause of sorrow ; the Aryan truth about the cessation of sorrow ; and the Aryan truth about the path that leads to that cessation. But when these Aryan truths are grasped and known the craving for future life is rooted out, that which leads to renewed becoming is destroyed, and then there is no more birth ![2]'

3. Thus spake the Exalted One ; and when the Happy One had thus spoken, then again the Teacher said :—[91]

'By not seeing the Aryan Truths as they really are,
Long is the path that is traversed through many
  a birth ;

---

[1] As will be observed from the similar passages that follow, there is a regular sequence of clauses in the set descriptions of the Buddha's movements. The last clause should specify the particular grove or house where the Exalted One stayed ; but it is also (in this and one or two other cases) inserted with due regularity even when it adds nothing positive to the sense.

[2] Compare below, Chapter IV, §§ 2, 3 ; p. 131.

> When these are grasped, the cause of rebirth is removed,
> The root of sorrow uprooted, and then there is no more birth.'

4. There too, while staying at Ko*t*igâma, the Exalted One held that comprehensive religious talk with the brethren, saying :—' Such and such is upright conduct ; such and such is earnest contemplation ; such and such is intelligence. Great becomes the fruit, great the advantage of earnest contemplation, when it is set round with upright conduct. Great becomes the fruit, great the advantage of intellect when it is set round with earnest contemplation. The mind set round with intelligence is set quite free from the Intoxications, that is to say, from the Intoxication of Sensuality, from the Intoxication of Becoming, from the Intoxication of Delusion, from the Intoxication of Ignorance.'

5. Now when the Exalted One had remained as long as he thought fit at Ko*t*igâma, he addressed the venerable Ânanda, and said:—'Come, Ânanda, let us go on to the Nâdikas.'

' So be it, lord!' said Ânanda, in assent, to the Exalted One.

And the Exalted One proceeded to the Nâdikas with a great company of the brethren ; and there, at Nâdika, the Exalted One stayed in the Brick Hall[1].

---

[1] At first Nâdika is (twice) spoken of in the plural number (a clan-name); but then, thirdly, in the last clause, in the singular (a local name derived from the clan-name). Buddhaghosa explains this by saying that there were two villages of the same name on the shore of the same piece of water. The ' Brick Hall ' was the public resting-place for travellers, and the name is noteworthy as almost all buildings were then of wood.

The expression used here is an idiomatic phrase descriptive of the arrival of travellers at a place :—' and there, at X. so and so stayed in Y.' where X. is the name of the town or village, and Y. is the lodging-place the traveller occupies. (See just above in § 1 for a good instance.) The first name, the name X., is always the name of the

6. And the venerable Ânanda went to the Exalted One and paid him reverence and took his seat beside him. And when he was seated, he addressed the Exalted One, and said :—' The brother named Sâ*l*ha has died at Nâdika, lord. Where has he been reborn, and what is his destiny? The sister named Nandâ has died, lord, at Nâdika. Where is she reborn, and what is her destiny?' [92] [And in the same terms he inquired concerning the lay disciple Sudatta, and the devout lady Sugata, the lay disciples Kakudha, and Kâlinga, and Nika*t*a, and Ka*t*issabha, and Tu*tth*a, and Santu*tth*a, and Bhadda, and Subhadda.]

7. 'The brother named Sâ*l*ha, Ânanda, by the destruction of the Intoxications has by himself, and in this world, known and realized and attained to Arahantship, to emancipation of heart and to emancipation of mind. The sister named Nandâ, Ânanda, has, by the complete destruction of the five bonds that bind people to these lower worlds of lust, become an inheritor of the highest heavens, there to pass entirely away, thence never to return. The devout Sudatta, Ânanda, by the complete destruction of the three bonds, and by the reduction to a minimum of lust, ill-will, and stupidity, has become a Sakadâgâmin, who on his first return to this world will make an end of sorrow. The devout Sugata, Ânanda, by the complete destruction of the three bonds, has become converted, is no longer liable to be reborn in a state of suffering, and is assured of hereafter attaining to the enlightenment [of Arahantship][1]. The devout Kakudha, Ânanda, by the complete destruction of the five bonds that bind people to these lower worlds of lust, has become an inheritor of the highest heavens, there to pass entirely away, thence never to return. [The same of Kâlinga, Nika*t*a,

___

town, and never an adjective in agreement with the second name. It seems simple enough; but even the best Sanskritists appear sometimes to be unfamiliar with the force of this Pâli idiom.

[1] See Rhys Davids's 'Buddhism,' pp. 108–10; above, Vol. I, pp. 190–2; below, at VI, 6, and in the translation of D. II, 201; also Divyâvadâna, pp. 533–4.

Ka*t*issabha, Tu*tth*a, Santu*tth*a, Bhadda, and Subhadda, [**93**] and with more than fifty devout men in Nâdika.] More than ninety devout men in Nâdika, who have died, Ânanda, have by the complete destruction of the three bonds, and by the reduction of lust, ill-will and stupidity, become Sakadâgâmins, who on their first return to this world will make an end of sorrow. More than five hundred devout men of Nâdika who have died, Ânanda, have by the complete destruction of the three bonds become converted, are no longer liable to be reborn in a state of suffering, and are assured of hereafter attaining the enlightenment [of Arahantship].

8. 'Now there is nothing strange in this, Ânanda, that a human being should die ; but that as each one does so you should come to me, and inquire about them in this manner, that is wearisome to me. I will, therefore, teach you a way of truth, called the Mirror of Truth, which if a disciple of the noble ones possess he may, if he should so desire, himself predict of himself :—"Purgatory is destroyed for me, and rebirth as an animal, or a ghost, or in any place of woe. I am converted, I am no longer liable to be reborn in a state of suffering, and am assured of hereafter attaining to the enlightenment [of Arahantship]."

9. 'What then, Ânanda, is this Mirror of Truth ? [It is the consciousness that] the disciple of the Arahants is in this world possessed of faith in the Buddha— believing the Exalted One to be the Arahant, the Fully-enlightened One, Wise, Upright, Happy, World-knowing, Supreme, the Bridler of men's wayward hearts, the Teacher of gods and men, the Exalted and Awakened One. And that he [the disciple] is possessed of faith in the Truth—believing the Truth to have been proclaimed by the Exalted One, of advantage in this world, passing not away, welcoming all, leading to salvation, and to be attained to by the wise, each one for himself. And that he [the disciple] is possessed of faith in the Order—believing the multitude of the disciples of the Exalted One who are walking in the

four stages of the noble eightfold path, the righteous,
the upright, the just, the law-abiding—[94] believing
this church of the Exalted One to be worthy of honour,
of hospitality, of gifts, and of reverence; to be the
supreme sowing ground of merit for the world; to be
possessed of the virtues beloved by the good, virtues
unbroken, intact, unspotted, unblemished, virtues which
make men truly free, virtues which are praised by the
wise, are untarnished by the desire of future life or by
the belief in the efficacy of outward acts, and are conducive to concentration of heart [1].

'This, Ânanda, is the way, the Mirror of Truth,
which if a disciple of the noble ones possess he may, if
he should so desire, himself predict of himself :—" Purgatory is destroyed for me; and rebirth as an animal,
or a ghost, or in any place of woe. I am converted;
I am no longer liable to be reborn in a state of suffering, and am assured of finally attaining to the enlightenment [of Arahantship]."'

10. There, too, at the Brick Hall at Nâdika the
Exalted One held that comprehensive religious talk
with the brethren, saying :—'Such and such is upright
conduct; such and such is earnest contemplation; such
and such is intelligence. Great becomes the fruit,
great the advantage of earnest contemplation, when it
is set round with upright conduct. Great becomes the
fruit, great the advantage of intellect when it is set
round with earnest contemplation. The mind set
round with intelligence is set quite free from the
Intoxications, that is to say, from the Intoxication of
Sensuality, from the Intoxication of Becoming, from
the Intoxication of Delusion, from the Intoxication of
Ignorance.'

11. Now when the Exalted One had remained as
long as he wished at Nâdika, he addressed Ânanda,
and said :—'Come, Ânanda, let us go on to Vesâli.'

---

[1] See above, I, 11.

'So be it, lord!' said Ânanda, in assent, to the Exalted One.

Then the Exalted One proceeded, with a great company of the brethren, to Vesâli; and there at Vesâli the Exalted One stayed at Ambapâli's grove.

12. Now there the Exalted One addressed the brethren, and said :—'Let a brother, O mendicants, be mindful and self-possessed; this is our instruction to you[1].

'And how does a brother become mindful?

'Herein, O mendicants, a brother continues as to the body, so to look upon the body that he remains strenuous, [95] self-possessed, and mindful, having overcome both the hankering and the dejection common in the world. [And in the same way as to feelings, moods, or ideas, he continues so to look upon each] that he remains strenuous, self-possessed, and mindful, having overcome both the hankering and the dejection common in the world.

13. 'And how does a brother become self-possessed?

'He acts, O mendicants, in full presence of mind whatever he may do, in going out or coming in, in looking forward or in looking round, in bending in his arm or in stretching it forth, in wearing his robes or in carrying his bowl, in eating or drinking, in masticating or swallowing, in obeying the calls of nature, in walking or standing or sitting, in sleeping or waking, in talking and in being silent.

'Thus let a brother, O mendicants, be mindful and self-possessed; this is our instruction to you[2].'

---

[1] Quoted Mil. 378.

[2] This doctrine of being 'mindful and self-possessed' is one of the lessons most frequently inculcated in the Pâli Piṭakas, and is one of the 'Seven Jewels of the Law.' It is fully treated of in each of the Nikâyas, forming the subject of the Maha Satippaṭṭhâna Suttanta in the Dîgha Nikâya, and the Satippaṭṭhâna Suttanta of the Majjhima Nikâya, and the Satippaṭṭhâna Saṃyutta of the Saṃyutta Nikâya, as well as of various passages in the Anguttara Nikâya, and of the Vibhaṅga. See above, Vol. I, pp. 80, 81; and the translation, below, of pp. 290 foll. of the text. The point is there discussed in detail.

Buddhaghosa has no comment here on the subject itself, reserving

14. [1] Now the courtezan Ambapâli heard that the Exalted One had arrived at Vesâli, and was staying there at her mango grove. And ordering a number of state vehicles to be made ready, she mounted one of them, and went forth with her train from Vesâli towards her garden. She went in the carriage as far as the ground was passable for carriages; there she alighted; and she proceeded on foot to the place where the Exalted One was, and took her seat respectfully on one side. And when she was thus seated the Exalted One instructed, aroused, incited, and gladdened her with religious discourse.

Then she—instructed, aroused, incited, and gladdened with his words—addressed the Exalted One, and said:—

'May the Exalted One do me the honour of taking his meal, together with the brethren, at my house to-morrow?'

And the Exalted One gave, by silence, his consent. Then when Ambapâli the courtezan saw that the Exalted One had consented, she rose from her seat and bowed down before him, and keeping him on her right hand as she passed him, she departed thence.

---

what he has to say for the comment on the Suttantas devoted entirely to it; but he observes in passing that the reason why the Exalted One laid stress, at this particular time and place, on the necessity of being 'mindful and thoughtful,' was because of the imminent approach of the beautiful courtezan in whose grove they were staying. The use of the phrase sati upa*tth*âpetabbâ below, Chap. V, 9 (text, p. 141), in reference to the way in which women should be treated, is quite in accordance with this explanation. But see the next note.

[1] From this point down to the words 'he rose from his seat,' in II, 24 is, with a few unimportant variations, word for word the same as Vinaya, Vol. I, pp. 231–3. But the passage there follows immediately after the verses translated above, I, 34, so that the events here (in §§ 14–18) localized at Vesâli, are there localized at Ko*s*igâma. Our section II, 5 is then inserted between our sections II, 18 and II, 19; and our section II, 11 does not occur at all, the Exalted One only reaching Ambapâli's grove when he goes there (as in our section II, 19) to partake of the meal to which he had been invited. Buddhaghosa passes over this apparent discrepancy in silence.

15. [96] Now the Licchavis of Vesâli heard that the Exalted One had arrived at Vesâli, and was staying at Ambapâli's grove. And ordering a number of state carriages to be made ready, they each mounted one of them and went forth with their train from Vesâli. Some of them were dark, dark in colour, and wearing dark clothes and ornaments : some of them were fair, fair in colour, and wearing light clothes and ornaments : some of them were red, ruddy in colour, and wearing red clothes and ornaments : some of them were white, pale in colour, and wearing white clothes and ornaments.

16. And Ambapâli drove up against the young Licchavis, axle to axle, wheel to wheel, and yoke to yoke, and the Licchavis said to Ambapâli the courtezan : —'How is it, Ambapâli, that thou drivest up against us thus ?'

'My lords, I have just invited the Exalted One and his brethren for their morrow's meal,' said she.

'Ambapâli! give up this meal to us for a hundred thousand,' said they.

'My lords, were you to offer all Vesâli with its subject territory, I would not give up so honourable a feast!'

Then the Licchavis cast up their hands, exclaiming : —'We are outdone by this mango girl! we are out-reached by this mango girl[1]!' and they went on to Ambapâli's grove.

17. When the Exalted One saw the Licchavis approaching in the distance, he addressed the brethren, and said :—

'O brethren, let those of the brethren who have never seen the Tâvatimsa gods, gaze upon this company of the Licchavis, behold this company of the Licchavis, compare this company of the Licchavis— for they are even as a company of Tâvatimsa gods[2].'

---

[1] Literally 'by this woman.' But I have tried to reproduce the evident word-play. Ambapâli means mango grower, one who looks after mangoes.

[2] The Tâvatimsa-devâ are the gods in the heaven of the Great

18. [97] And when they had ridden as far as the ground was passable for carriages, the Licchavis alighted there, and then went on foot to the place where the Exalted One was, and took their seats respectfully by his side. And when they were thus seated the Exalted One instructed and roused and incited and gladdened them with religious discourse [1].

Then they—instructed and roused and incited and gladdened with his words—addressed the Exalted One, and said :—'May the Exalted One do us the honour of taking his meal, together with the brethren, at our house to-morrow?'

'O Licchavis, I have promised to dine to-morrow with Ambapâli the courtezan,' was the reply.

Then the Licchavis cast up their hands, exclaiming : —'We are outdone by this mango girl! we are out-reached by this mango girl'! And expressing their thanks and approval of the words of the Exalted One, they rose from their seats and bowed down before the Exalted One, and keeping him on their right hand as they passed him, they departed thence.

19. And at the end of the night Ambapâli the courtezan made ready in her mansion sweet rice and cakes, and announced the time to the Exalted One, saying:—'The hour, lord, has come, and the meal is ready!'

And the Exalted One who had dressed himself early in the morning, took his bowl, and his robe, and went with the brethren to the place where Ambapâli's mansion was : and when he had come there he seated himself on the seat prepared for him. And Ambapâli

---

Thirty-Three, the principal deities of the Vedic Pantheon. See A. III, 239; Sum. I, 310; Mahâvastu I, 262.

[1] The Malâlankâra-vatthu gives the substance of the discourse on this occasion. 'The princes had come in their finest and richest dress; in their appearance they vied in beauty with the nats (or angels). But foreseeing the ruin and misery that was soon to come upon them all, the Buddha exhorted his disciples to entertain a thorough contempt for things that are dazzling to the eyes, but essentially perishable and unreal in their nature.'—Bigandet, 2nd ed., p. 260.

the courtezan set the sweet rice and cakes before the
Order, with the Buddha at their head, and waited upon
them till they refused any more.

And when the Blessed One had quite finished his
meal, and had cleansed the bowl and his hands, the
courtezan had a low stool brought, and [98] sat down
at his side, and addressed the Exalted One, and said :
—' Lord, I present this pleasaunce to the order of
mendicants, of which the Buddha is the chief.' And
the Exalted One accepted the gift; and after instructing, and rousing, and inciting, and gladdening her with
religious discourse, he rose from his seat and departed
thence.[1]

20. While at Ambapâli's mango grove the Exalted
One held that comprehensive religious talk with the
brethren, saying :—' Such and such is upright conduct ;
such and such is earnest contemplation ; such and such
is intelligence. Great becomes the fruit, great the
advantage of earnest contemplation, when it is set
round with upright conduct. Great becomes the fruit,
great the advantage of intellect when it is set round
with earnest contemplation. The mind set round with
intelligence is set quite free from the Intoxications,
that is to say, from the Intoxication of Sensuality, from
the Intoxication of Becoming, from the Intoxication of
Delusion, from the Intoxication of Ignorance.'

21. Now when the Exalted One had remained so
long as he wished at Ambapâli's grove, he addressed
Ânanda, and said :—' Come, Ânanda, let us go on to
Beluva [2].'

---

[1] Bishop Bigandet says:—' In recording the conversion of
a courtezan named Apapalika, her liberality and gifts to Budha and
his disciples, and the preference designedly given to her over princes
and nobles, who, humanly speaking, seemed in every respect better
entitled to attentions—one is almost reminded of the conversion of
' a woman that was a sinner,' mentioned in the Gospels ('Legend of
the Burmese Budha,' 2nd ed., p. 258).

[2] The Vinaya (I, 233) says they went to the Great Wood near

'So be it, lord,' said Ânanda, in assent, to the Exalted One.

Then the Exalted One proceeded, with a great company of the brethren, to Beluva, and there the Exalted One stayed in the village itself.

22. Now the Exalted One there addressed the brethren, and said :—'O mendicants, do you take up your abode round about Vesâlî, each according to the place where his friends, acquaintances, and intimates may live, for the retreat in the rainy season [for vassa]. I shall enter upon the rainy season here at Beluva.'

'So be it, lord!' said those brethren, in assent, to the Exalted One.   And they entered upon the rainy season round about Vesâlî, each according to the place where his friends, acquaintances, and intimates lived : [**99**] whilst the Exalted One stayed even there at Beluva.

23. Now when the Exalted One had thus entered upon the rainy season, there fell upon him a dire sickness, and sharp pains came upon him, even unto death. But the Exalted One, mindful and self-possessed, bore them without complaint.

Then this thought occurred to the Exalted One :—'It would not be right for me to pass away without addressing the disciples, without taking leave of the Order. Let me now, by a strong effort of the will, bend this sickness down again, and keep my hold on life till the allotted time be come [1].'

And the Exalted One, by a strong effort of the will, bent that sickness down again, and kept his hold on life till the time he fixed upon should come. And the sickness abated upon him.

24. Now very soon after the Blessed One began to recover. And when he had quite got rid of the sickness, he came out from his lodging, and sat down in the shadow thereof on a seat spread out there. And

Vesâlî, that is, it skips the context here as far as III, 64. Our sections 27–35 are in the Samyutta V, 152–4.

[1] Compare Divyâvadâna 203.

the venerable Ânanda went to the place where the
Exalted One was, and saluted him, and took a seat respectfully on one side, and addressed the Exalted One,
and said :—' I have beheld, lord, how the Exalted
One was in health, and I have beheld how the Exalted
One had to suffer.   And though at the sight of the
sickness of the Exalted One my body became weak
as a creeper, and the horizon became dim to me, and
my faculties were no longer clear [1], yet notwithstanding
I took some little comfort from the thought that the
Exalted One would not pass away until at least he had
left instructions as touching the Order.'

25. [100] 'What, then, Ânanda ? Does the Order
expect that of me ? I have preached the truth without
making any distinction between exoteric and esoteric
doctrine ; for in respect of the truths, Ânanda, the
Tathâgata has no such thing as the closed fist of
a teacher, who keeps some things back [2].   Surely,
Ânanda, should there be any one who harbours the
thought, "It is I who will lead the brotherhood," or,
'The Order is dependent upon me," it is he who should
lay down instructions in any matter concerning the
Order.   Now the Tathâgata, Ânanda, thinks not that
it is he who should lead the brotherhood, or that the
Order is dependent upon him.   Why then should he
leave instructions in any matter concerning the Order ?
I too, O Ânanda, am now grown old, and full of years,
my journey is drawing to its close, I have reached my
sum of days, I am turning eighty years of age ; and
just as a worn-out cart, Ânanda, can be kept going
only with the help of thongs, so, methinks, the body of
the Tathâgata can only be kept going by bandaging it
up [3].   It is only, Ânanda, when the Tathâgata, by

[1] Compare A. III, 69.
[2] Compare Jâtaka II, 221, 250; Mil. 144.
[3] Vegha-missakena, the meaning of which is not clear. The
Malâlankâra-vatthu, as rendered by Bigandet, has 'repairs.' The
Sumangala Vilâsinî agrees, but in such a way as to throw no light on
the derivation of the word. In the Samyutta Nikâya (V, 153) the

ceasing to attend to any outward thing, becomes
plunged by the cessation of any separate sensation in
that concentration of heart which is concerned with no
material object—it is only then that the body of the
Tathâgata is at ease[1].

26. [2] 'Therefore, O Ânanda, be ye lamps unto yourselves. Be ye a refuge to yourselves. Betake yourselves to no external refuge. Hold fast to the Truth
as a lamp. Hold fast as a refuge to the Truth. Look
not for refuge to any one besides yourselves. And
how, Ânanda, is a brother to be a lamp unto himself,
a refuge to himself, betaking himself to no external
refuge, holding fast to the Truth as a lamp, holding fast
as a refuge to the Truth, looking not for refuge to any
one besides himself?

'Herein, O mendicants, a brother continues, as to
the body, so to look upon the body that he remains
strenuous, self-possessed, and mindful, having overcome both the hankering and the dejection common in
the world. [And in the same way] as to feelings . . .
moods . . . ideas, he continues so to look upon each
that he remains strenuous, self-possessed, and mindful,
having overcome both the hankering and the dejection
common in the world.

[101] 'And whosoever, Ânanda, either now or after
I am dead, shall be a lamp unto themselves, and
a refuge unto themselves, shall betake themselves to
no external refuge, but holding fast to the Truth as

Burmese Phayre MS. reads vekhamissakena and another Burmese
MS. vedha—but SS. all read vegha. The Siamese edition has ve/u.
My Dîgha Nikâya confirms Childers's reading, which no doubt
correctly represents the uniform tradition of the Ceylon MSS. On
the use of the word missaka at the end of a compound see Jâtaka
II, 8, 420, 433; and compare M. I, 82; Thera-gâthâ 143; Mil. 159;
and the discussion in 'J.P.T.S.,' 1884, pp. 97-101.

[1] This is very interesting as giving what is, no doubt, the original
meaning of animitta as applied to ceto-samâdhi. See my
'Yogâvacara's Manual of Indian Mysticism,' p. xxvii.

[2] This section recurs at S. V, 163, compare III, 42, and the
example given at V, 221.

their lamp, and holding fast as their refuge to the Truth, shall look not for refuge to any one besides themselves—it is they, Ânanda, among my bhikkhus, who shall reach the very topmost Height!—but they must be anxious to learn[1].'

End of the Second Portion for Recitation.

[1] Buddhaghosa says:—'Tamatagge is for tamagge. The "t" in the middle is used for euphony. This word means, "These are the most pre-eminent, the very chief." Having, as above stated, broken every bond of darkness (tama), those bhikkhus of mine, Ânanda, will be at the very top, in the highest condition. They will be at the very top of whom? Those bhikkhus who are willing to learn, and those who exercise themselves in the four ways of being mindful and thoughtful, they shall be at the top of all (the rest). Thus does he make Arahantship the three-peaked height of his discourse' (compare on this last phrase Nibbânena desanâkutam ganhâti, Jâtaka I, 275, 393, 401; and see also I, 114). Uttama, the highest (scil. bhava, condition), is used absolutely of Arahantship or Nirvana at Jâtaka I, 96; Aggaphala occurs in the same sense at Jâtaka I, 114; and even Phalagga at Mahâvamsa XV, 209. The last words, 'but they must be anxious to learn,' seem to me to be an afterthought. It is only those who are thoroughly determined to work out their own salvation, without looking for safety to any one else, even to the Buddha himself, who will, whilst in the world, enter into and experience Nirvana. But, of course, let there be no mistake, merely to reject the vain baubles of the current superstitious beliefs is not enough. There is plenty to learn and to acquire, of which enough discourse is elsewhere.

CHAPTER III.

1.[1] [102] Now the Exalted One robed himself early in the morning, and taking his bowl in the robe, went into Vesâlî for alms. When, after he had returned from the round for alms, he had finished eating the rice, he addressed the venerable Ânanda, and said :— 'Take up the mat, Ânanda; I will go and spend the day at the Châpâla Shrine.'

'So be it, lord!' said the venerable Ânanda, in assent, to the Exalted One. And taking up the mat he followed step for step behind the Exalted One.

2. So the Exalted One proceeded to the Châpâla Shrine, and when he had come there he sat down on the mat spread out for him, and the venerable Ânanda took his seat respectfully beside him. Then the Exalted One addressed the venerable Ânanda, and said :— 'How delightful a spot, Ânanda, is Vesâlî, and how charming the Udena Shrine, and the Gotamaka Shrine, and the Shrine of the Seven Mangoes, and the Shrine of Many Sons, and the Sârandada Shrine, and the Châpâla Shrine [2]!

3. [103] 'Ânanda, whosoever has developed, prac- tised, dwelt on, expanded and ascended to the very heights of the four paths to Iddhi [3], and so mastered them as to be able to use them as a vehicle, and as a

---

[1] 1–20 recur in A. IV, 308 foll.; 1–10 in Udâna VI, 1, and S. V, 259 foll. Compare Divy., pp. 200–8.

[2] Shrines of pre-Buddhistic worship. They were probably trees and barrows; but as no excavations have yet been made at Vesâlî the point is uncertain. The Anglo-Indian use of the word Chetiya, as equivalent to our Temple, is quite wrong.

[3] Iddhi. The four paths are :—(1) will, (2) effort, (3) thought, and (4) investigation, each united to earnest thought and the struggle against evil. On the Iddhi to be reached by them see above, Vol. I, pp. 272, 273; and the translator's 'Buddhism,' pp. 174–7. The whole set of participles is used elsewhere of other conditions of mind. So, for instance, of universal love (mettâ) at A. V, 342, quoted Jâtaka II, 61, Mil. 198. An ancient commentary on them is preserved at Pa/is. I, 172.

basis, he, should he desire it, could remain in the same birth for an aeon or for that portion of the aeon which had yet to run. Now the Tathâgata has thoroughly practised and developed them [in all respects as just more fully described], and he could, therefore, should he desire it, live on yet for an aeon, or for that portion of the aeon which has yet to run.'

4. But even though a suggestion so evident and a hint so clear were thus given by the Exalted One, the venerable Ânanda was incapable of comprehending them; [104] and he besought not the Exalted One, saying :—' Vouchsafe, lord, to remain during the aeon ! Live on through the aeon, O Happy One ! for the good and the happiness of the great multitudes, out of pity for the world, for the good and the gain and the weal of gods and men !' So far was his heart possessed by the Evil One [1].

5. A second and a third time did the Exalted One [say the same thing, and a second and a third time was Ânanda's heart thus hardened].

6. Then the Exalted One addressed the vener-

---

[1] Yathâ tam Mârena pariyu*tth*itacitto. Here ta*m* is the indeclinable particle, yathâ ta*m* introducing an explanation. My MS. of the Digha Nikâya and the Turnour MS. of the Sumangala Vilâsinî read parivu*tth*ita, and either spelling is correct. The fact is that the 'y' or 'v' in such cases is even less than euphonic; it is an assistance not to the speaker, but merely to the writer. Thus in the Sinhalese duwanawâ, 'to run,' the spoken word is duanawâ, and the 'w' is written only to avoid the awkward use in the middle of a written word of the initial sign for the sound 'a'. That the speakers of Pâli found no difficulty in pronouncing two vowels together is abundantly proved by numerous instances. The writers of Pâli, in those cases in which the second vowel begins a word, use without hesitation the initial sign; but in the middle of the word this would be so ungainly that they naturally prefer to insert a consonantal sign *to carry the vowel sign*. The varying readings I have pointed out are a strong confirmation of the correctness of the pronunciation of modern native scholars (in this case pari-u*tth*ita); and we may the more readily adopt it as the question is not really one concerning the pronunciation of Pâli, but concerning the use which modern native copyists make of their own alphabet. I would pronounce therefore pari-utthita-citto. See Windisch, 'Mara und Buddha,' p. 40; M. I, 433-4; Vin. II, 289; IV, 94, 229.

able Ânanda, and said :—' You may leave me, Ânanda, awhile, and do whatsoever now seemeth to thee fit.'

' So be it, lord ! ' said the venerable Ânanda, in assent, to the Exalted One, and passing him on the right sat down at the foot of a certain tree not far off thence.

7. Now not long after the venerable Ânanda had been gone, Mâra, the Evil One, approached the Exalted One and stood beside him. And so standing there, he addressed the Exalted One in these words :—

' Pass away now, lord ; let the Exalted One now die. Now is the time for the Exalted One to pass away —even according to the word which the Exalted One spoke when he said [1] :—" I shall not die, O Evil One ! until the brethren and sisters of the Order, and until the lay-disciples of either sex [2] shall have become true hearers, wise and well trained, ready and learned, carrying the doctrinal books in their memory, masters of the lesser corollaries that follow from the larger doctrine, correct in life, walking according to the precepts—until they, having thus themselves learned the doctrine, shall be able to tell others of it, preach it, make it known, establish it, open it, minutely explain it and make it clear—until they, when others start vain doctrine easy to be refuted by the truth, shall be able in refuting it, to spread the wonder-working [3] truth abroad ! "

8. ' And now, lord, the brethren and sisters of the order and the lay-disciples of either sex have become [all this], are able to do [all this]. [105] Pass away now therefore, lord ; let the Exalted One now die ! The time has come for the Exalted One to pass away—

---

[1] The words here quoted were spoken by the Buddha, after he had been enjoying the first bliss of Nirvana, under the goatherd's Nigrodha tree (see below, ch. III, § 34).

[2] The whole paragraph is repeated, here and below, § 35, for each of these classes of persons.

[3] Sappaṭihâriyaṃ dhammaṃ. (Comp. the opposite idea appaṭihîra-kataṃ bhâsitaṃ, D. I, 193, 239.) The two ideas are contrasted at KV. 561.

even according to the word which he spake when he
said, "I shall not die, O Evil One! until this pure
religion of mine shall have become successful, prosperous, wide-spread, and popular in all its full extent—
until, in a word, it shall have been well proclaimed
among men." And now, lord, this pure religion of
thine has become [all this]. Pass away now therefore,
lord; let the Exalted One now die! The time has
come for the Exalted One to pass away!'

9. [106] And when he had thus spoken, the Exalted
One addressed Mâra, the Evil One, and said :—'O
Evil One! make thyself happy, the death of the Tathâgata shall take place before long. At the end of three
months from this time the Tathâgata will pass away.'

10. Thus the Exalted One while at the Shrine of
Châpâla deliberately and consciously rejected the rest
of his natural term of life [1]. And on his so rejecting it
there arose a mighty earthquake, awful and terrible,
and the thunders of heaven burst forth. [107] And
when the Exalted One beheld this, he broke out at that
time into this hymn of exultation :—

'His sum of life the sage renounced,
  The cause of life immeasurable or small;
With inward joy and calm, he broke,
  Like coat of mail, his life's own cause! [2]'

11.[3] Now the following thought occurred to the

[1] Âyu-saṃkhâram ossaji. The difficult term Âyu-saṃkhâra
must here have the meaning in which it is used at Majjhima I,
pp. 295, 296; Saṃyutta II, 266; Jâtaka IV, 215. He renounced those
tendencies, potentialities, which in the ordinary course of things, would
otherwise have led to the putting together of, the building up of, more
life (that is, of course, in this birth. Any more life in a future birth
he had already renounced when, under the Wisdom Tree, he attained
Nirvana).

[2] This verse is obscure and possibly corrupt. See Windisch,
'Mara und Buddha,' pp. 37, 72; Ud. VI, 1; S. V, 263; Div. 203.

[3] The narrative is now interrupted by the insertion of paragraphs
which at first sight seem to be quite out of place. But the connexion,
or want of connexion, between them and the main story is very

venerable Ânanda:—'Wonderful indeed and marvellous is it that this mighty earthquake should arise, awful and terrible, and that the thunders of heaven should burst forth! What may be the proximate, what the remote cause of the appearance of this earthquake?'

12. Then the venerable Ânanda went up to the place where the Blessed One was, and did obeisance to the Exalted One, and seated himself respectfully at one side, and said:—'Wonderful indeed and marvellous is it that this mighty earthquake should arise, awful and terrible, and that the thunders of heaven should burst forth! What may be the proximate, what the remote cause of the appearance of this earthquake?'

13. 'Eight are the proximate, eight the remote causes, Ânanda, for the appearance of a mighty earthquake. What are the eight? This great earth, Ânanda, is established on water, the water on wind, and the wind rests upon space. And at such a time, Ânanda, as the mighty winds blow, the waters are shaken by the mighty winds as they blow, and by the moving water the earth is shaken. These are the first causes, proximate and remote, of the appearance of a mighty earthquake [1].

14. [108] 'Again, Ânanda, a recluse or a brahmin of great [intellectual] power, and who has the feelings

---

suggestive as to the way in which the Suttanta was put together. The whole chapter is an answer to a possible objection, either from outsiders or from weaker members of the fold, that if the Buddha were really so great why did he die at all. The suggested answer is that he could have lived on if he had so wished; but he did not wish because he had certain kinds of power and insight and self-mastery which prevented him from doing so. For the purpose of this answer these paragraphs, already in existence among the Suttas current in the community, and dealing with these powers, are here repeated without any such connecting argument as we should find under similar circumstances, in a modern (written) book of apologetics. The argument suggested by them follows exactly the same lines as that in the Mahâli Suttanta, translated in the former volume (Number VI of the 'Dialogues').

[1] Windisch, 'Mara und Buddha,' 61, adduces a number of interesting parallels, from European writers, to this curious old theory of earthquakes.

of his heart well under his control ; or a god or fairy (devatâ [1]) of great might and power,—when such a one by intense meditation on the idea of the minutest portion of earth and on the idea of the widest expanse of water [has succeeded in realizing the comparative value of things] he can make this earth move and tremble and be shaken violently [2]. These are the second causes, proximate and remote, of the appearance of a mighty earthquake.

---

[1] Devatâ is a fairy, god, genius, or angel. I am at a loss how to render this word without conveying an erroneous impression to those not familiar with ancient ideas, and specially with ancient Indian ideas, of the spirit world. It includes gods of all sorts; tree and river nymphs; the kindly fairies or ghosts who haunt houses (see my 'Buddhist Birth Stories,' Tale 40); spirits in the ground (see above, I, 26); the angels who minister at the great renunciation, the temptation, and the death of the Buddha ; the guardian angels who watch over men, and towns, and countries; and many other similar beings. 'Celestial beings' would be wholly inapplicable, for instance, to the creatures referred to in the curious passage above (I, 26). 'Superhuman being' would be an inaccurate rendering ; for all these light and airy shapes come below, and after, man in the Buddhist order of precedence. 'Spirit' being used of the soul inside the human body, and of the human soul after it has left the body, and figuratively of mental faculties—none of which are included under devatâ—would suggest ideas inconsistent with that of the Pâli wcrd. As there is therefore no appropriate general word I have chosen, for each passage where the expression occurs, the word used in English of the special class more particularly referred to in the passage of the text. Here all kinds of devatâs being referred to, and there being no word in English for them all, I have ventured to put the word devatâ into my version, and to trouble the reader with this note.

[2] Buddhaghosa here tells a long story how Sangharakkhita Sâmaṇera, the nephew of Nâga Thera, attained Arahantship on the day of his admission to the order ; and at once proceeded to heaven, and standing on the pinnacle of the palace of the king of the gods, shook the whole place with his big toe ; to the great consternation and annoyance of the exalted dwellers therein ! There is no doubt a real truth in the idea that deep thought can shake the universe, and make the palaces of the gods to tremble, just as faith is said in Matthew xxi. 21 to be able to remove mountains, and cause them to be cast into the sea. But these figurative expressions have, in Buddhism, become a fruitful soil for the outgrowth of superstitions and misunderstandings. The train of early Buddhist speculation in this field has yet to be elucidated.

15. 'Again, Ânanda, when a Bodhisatta consciously and deliberately leaves his [temporary] form in the heaven of delight and descends into his mother's womb, then is this earth made to quake and tremble and is shaken violently. These are the third causes, proximate and remote, of the appearance of a mighty earthquake [1].

16. 'Again, Ânanda, when a Bodhisatta deliberately and consciously quits his mother's womb, then the earth quakes and trembles and is shaken violently. This is the fourth cause, proximate and remote, of the appearance of a mighty earthquake.

17. 'Again, Ânanda, when a Tathâgata arrives at the supreme and perfect enlightenment, then this earth quakes and trembles and is shaken violently. This is the fifth cause, proximate and remote, of the appearance of a mighty earthquake.

18. 'Again, Ânanda, when a Tathâgata founds the sublime kingdom of righteousness, then this earth quakes and trembles and is shaken violently. This is the sixth cause, proximate and remote, of the appearance of a mighty earthquake.

19. 'Again, Ânanda, when a Tathâgata consciously and deliberately rejects the remainder of his life, then this earth quakes and trembles and is shaken violently.

---

[1] The Bodhisatta's voluntary incarnation is looked upon by the Buddhists as a great act of renunciation, and curious legends have gathered about it. One is that on the night when she conceived his mother dreamt that a white elephant entered her side. The account will be found at length in my 'Buddhist Birth Stories' (pp. 62-4), and the earthquake is there mentioned in terms identical with those in the text. As I have pointed out in 'Buddhism' (p. 184), the white elephant legend is one of those hallowed sun stories by which half-converted Indians strove to embellish the life-story of the Teacher whose followers they had become. In the Lalita Vistara (Calc. ed., p. 63) the entrance of the elephant into Mâyâ precedes the dream; but though the ignorant may have therefore accepted it as a fact, it is of course only a figure of speech—and I venture to think from the Indian standpoint, a beautiful figure of speech—to express the incarnation of divine mildness and majesty in a human form. The use of such a figure is not confined to India. In one of the Apocryphal Gospels, the Gospel according to the Hebrews, the incarnation of the divine gentleness and love is expressed by saying that a dove from heaven 'entered into' the human form.

This is the seventh cause, proximate and remote, of the appearance of a mighty earthquake.

20. 'Again, Ânanda, when a Tathâgata passes entirely [109] away in that utter passing away in which nothing whatever is left behind, then this earth quakes and trembles and is shaken violently. This is the eighth cause, proximate and remote, of the appearance of a mighty earthquake.'

21. 'Now of eight kinds, Ânanda, are these assemblies. Which are the eight? Assemblies of nobles, brahmins, householders and wanderers, and of the angel hosts of the Guardian Kings, of the Great Thirty-Three, of the Mâras, and of the Brahmâs.

22. 'Now I call to mind, Ânanda, how when I used to enter into an assembly of many hundred [1] nobles, before I had seated myself there or talked to them or started a conversation with them, I used to become in colour like unto their colour, and in voice like unto their voice. Then with religious discourse I used to instruct and incite, and quicken them, and fill them with gladness. But they knew me not when I spoke, and would say :—"Who may this be who thus speaks? a man or a god?" Then having instructed, incited, quickened, and gladdened them with religious discourse, I would vanish away. But they knew me not even when I vanished away : and would say:—"Who may this be who has thus vanished away? a man or a god?"

23. [And in the same words the Exalted One spake of how he had been used to enter into assemblies of each of the other of the eight kinds, and of how he had not been made known to them either in speaking or in vanishing away.] 'Now these, Ânanda, are the eight assemblies.'

---

[1] Windisch, 'Mara und Buddha,' p. 75, makes this number refer to the number of entrances, and quotes Itivuttaka, p. 15, in support. The Singhalese version (p. 758) is as above.

24. [110] 'Now these, Ânanda, are the eight positions of Mastery [over the delusion arising from the
apparent permanence of external things [1]]. What are
the eight ?

25. 'When a man having subjectively the idea of
form sees forms external to himself which are finite,
and pleasant or unpleasant to the sight, and having
mastered them, is conscious that he knows and sees—
this is the first position of mastery.

26. 'When a man having subjectively the idea of
form sees èxternally forms which are boundless, and
pleasant or unpleasant to the sight, and having mastered them, is conscious that he knows and sees—this
is the second position of mastery.

27. 'When a man without the subjective idea of form
sees forms external to himself which are finite, and
pleasant or unpleasant to the sight, and having mastered them, is conscious that he knows and sees—this
is the third position of mastery.

28. 'When a man without the subjective idea of
form sees externally forms external to himself which
are boundless, and pleasant or unpleasant to the sight,
and having mastered them, is conscious that he knows
and sees—this is the fourth position of mastery.

29. 'When a man without the subjective idea of
form sees externally forms external to himself that are
blue, blue in colour, blue in appearance, and reflecting
blue,—just, for instance, as the flax blossom is blue in
colour, blue in appearance, and reflecting blue ; or, again,

---

[1] This and the next paragraph are based upon the Buddhist belief
as to the long-vexed question between the Indian schools who represented more or less closely the European Idealists and Realists.
When cleared of the many repetitions inserted for the benefit of the
repeaters or reciters, the fundamental idea seems to be that the great
necessity is to get rid of the delusion that what one sees and feels is
real and permanent. Nothing is real and permanent but character.

The so-called eight Positions of Mastery are merely an expansion of
the first two of the following eight Stages of Deliverance, and the whole
argument is also expressed in another form in the passage on the nine
successive 'Cessations,' of which an abstract will be found in Childers,
sub voce nirodha.

as that fine muslin of Benares, of delicate finish on both
sides, is blue in colour, blue in appearance, and reflecting blue,—when a man without the subjective idea of
form sees externally forms which, just in that way, are
blue, blue in colour, blue in appearance, and reflecting
blue, and having mastered them, is conscious that he
knows and sees—that is the fifth position of mastery.'

30–2. [111] [The sixth, seventh, and eighth positions of mastery are explained in words identical with
those used to explain the fifth ; save that yellow, red,
and white are respectively substituted throughout for
blue ; and the Kanikara flower, the Bandhu-givaka
flower, and the morning star are respectively substituted for the flax blossom, as the first of the two
objects given as examples.]

33.[1] [112] ' Now these stages of Deliverance, Ânanda
[from the hindrance to thought arising from the sensations and ideas due to external forms], are eight in
number.   Which are the eight ?

' A man possessed of form sees forms—this is the
first stage of deliverance.

' Unaware of his own form, he sees forms external to
himself—this is the second stage of deliverance.

' With the thought " it is well," he becomes intent—
this is the third stage of deliverance.

' By passing quite beyond all idea of form, by
putting an end to all idea of sensory impact [2], by paying
no attention to the idea of multiformity, he, thinking
" it is all infinite space," reaches [mentally] and remains in the state of mind in which the idea of the
infinity of space is the only idea that is present—this
is the fourth stage of deliverance.

' By passing quite beyond all idea of space being the
infinite basis, he, thinking " it is all infinite reason,"

---

[1] These have already occurred in the Mahâ Nidâna (p. 70 of the
text).   The English version here is made somewhat fuller.
[2] On these technical terms see Mrs. Rhys Davids's ' Buddhist Psychology,' pp. 72, 182, 204.

reaches [mentally] and remains in the state of mind to which the infinity of reason is alone present—this is the fifth stage of deliverance.

'By passing quite beyond the consciousness of the infinity of reason, he, thinking "nothing at all exists," reaches [mentally] and remains in the state of mind to which nothing at all is specially present—this is the sixth stage of deliverance.

'By passing quite beyond all idea of nothingness he reaches [mentally] and remains in the state of mind to which neither ideas nor the absence of ideas are specially present—this is the seventh stage of deliverance.

'By passing quite beyond the state of "neither ideas nor the absence of ideas" he reaches [mentally] and remains in the state of mind in which both sensations and ideas have ceased to be—this is the eighth stage of deliverance.

'Now these, Ânanda, are the eight stages of Deliverance.'

34. 'On one occasion, Ânanda, I was resting under the goatherd's Nigrodha tree on the bank of the river Nerañjarâ immediately after having reached the great enlightenment. Then Mâra, the Evil One, came, Ânanda, to the place where I was, and standing beside me he addressed me in the words :—" Pass away now, lord, from existence! Let the Exalted One now die! Now is the time for the Exalted One to pass away!"

35. [113] 'And when he had thus spoken, Ânanda, I addressed Mâra, the Evil One, and said :—" I shall not pass away, O Evil One ! until not only the brethren and sisters of the Order, but also the lay-disciples of either sex shall have become true hearers, wise and well trained, ready and learned, carrying the doctrinal books in their memory, masters of the lesser corollaries that follow from the larger doctrine, correct in life, walking according to the precepts—until they, having thus themselves learned the doctrine, shall be able to tell others of it, preach it, make it known, establish it, open it, minutely explain it and make it clear—until

they, when others start vain doctrine easy to be refuted by the truth, shall be able in refuting it to spread the wonder-working truth abroad! I shall not die until this pure religion of mine shall have become successful, prosperous, wide-spread, and popular in all its full extent—until, in a word, it shall have been well proclaimed among men!"

36. 'And now again to-day, Ânanda, at Châpâla's Shrine Mâra, the Evil One, came to the place where I was, and standing beside me addressed me [in the same words].

37. [114] 'And when he had thus spoken, Ânanda, I answered him and said:—" Make thyself happy, the passing away of the Tathâgata shall take place before long. At the end of three months from this time the Tathâgata will pass away!"

'And now again, Ânanda, the Tathâgata has to-day at Châpâla's Shrine consciously and deliberately rejected the rest of his allotted term of life.'

38. [115] And when he had thus spoken the venerable Ânanda addressed the Exalted One, and said:—'Vouchsafe, lord, to remain during the aeon: live on through the kalpa, O Exalted One! for the good and the happiness of the great multitudes, out of pity for the world, for the good and the gain and the weal of gods and men!'

'Enough now, Ânanda, beseech not the Tathâgata!' was the reply. 'The time for making such request is past.'

39. And again, the second time, the venerable Ânanda besought the Exalted One [in the same words. And he received from the Exalted One the same reply].

And again, the third time, the venerable Ânanda besought the Exalted One [in the same words].

'Hast thou faith, Ânanda, in the wisdom of the Tathâgata?'

'Even so, lord!'

'Now why, then, Ânanda, dost thou trouble the Tathâgata even until the third time?'

40. 'From his own mouth have I heard from the Exalted One, from his own mouth have I received

this saying :—" Whosoever has developed, practised, dwelt on, expanded, and ascended to the very heights of the four paths to Iddhi, and so mastered them as to be able to use them as a vehicle, and as a basis, he, should he desire it, could remain in the same birth for an aeon, or for that portion of the aeon which had yet to run."   Now the Tathâgata has thoroughly practised and developed them [in all respects as just now fully described], and he could, therefore, should he desire it, live on yet for an aeon, or for that portion of the aeon which has yet to run.'

'Hast thou faith, Ânanda ? '

' Even so, lord ! '

' Then, O Ânanda, thine is the fault, thine is the offence—in that when a suggestion so evident and a hint so clear were thus given thee by the Tathâgata, thou wast yet incapable of comprehending them, and thou besoughtest not the Tathâgata, saying :—" Vouchsafe, lord, to remain during the aeon for the good and the happiness of the great multitudes, out of pity for the world, for the good and the gain and the weal of gods and men." If thou shouldst then have so besought the Tathâgata, the Tathâgata might have rejected the appeal even to the second time, but the third time he would have granted it. Thine, therefore, O Ânanda, is the fault, thine is the offence!

41. ' On one occasion,. Ânanda, I was dwelling at Râjagaha, on the hill called the Vulture's Peak.   Now there, Ânanda, I spoke to thee, and said :—[116] " How pleasant a spot, Ânanda, is Râjagaha; how pleasant is this Vulture's Peak.   Whosoever, Ânanda, has developed, practised, dwelt on, expanded, and ascended to the very heights of the four paths to Iddhi, and so mastered them as to be able to use them as a vehicle, and as a basis, he, should he desire it, could remain in the same birth for an aeon, or for that portion of the aeon which had yet to run.   Now the Tathâgata has thoroughly practised and developed them [in all respects as just now fully described], and he could, therefore, should he desire it, live on yet for an aeon, or for

that portion of the aeon which has yet to run." But even when a suggestion so evident and a hint so clear were thus given thee by the Tathâgata, thou wast yet incapable of comprehending them, and thou besought-est not the Tathâgata, saying :—"Vouchsafe, lord, to remain during the aeon. Live on, O Exalted One! through the aeon for the good and the happiness of the great multitudes, out of pity for the world, for the good and the gain and the weal of gods and men." If thou shouldst then have so besought the Tathâgata, the Tathâgata might have rejected the appeal even to the second time, but the third time he would have granted it. Thine, therefore, O Ânanda, is the fault, thine is the offence!

42. 'On one occasion, Ânanda, I was dwelling at that same Râjagaha in the Banyan Grove—on one occasion at that same Râjagaha at the Robbers' Cliff—on one occasion at that same Râjagaha in the Satta-pañni cave on the slope of Mount Vebhâra—on one occasion at that same Râjagaha at the Black Rock on the slope of Mount Isigili—on one occasion at that same Râjagaha in the Sîtavana Grove in the mountain cave Sappasondika—on one occasion at that same Râjagaha in the Tapoda Grove—on one occasion at that same Râjagaha in the Bambu Grove in the Squirrels' Feed-ing Ground—on one occasion at that same Râjagaha in Jîvaka's Mango Grove—on one occasion at that same Râjagaha in the Deer Forest at Maddakucchi.

43. 'Now there too, Ânanda, I spoke to thee, and said :—"How pleasant, Ânanda, is Râjagaha; how pleasant the Vulture's Peak ; how pleasant the Banyan tree of Gotama; how pleasant the Robbers' Cliff; how pleasant the Sattapañni cave on the slope of Mount Vebhâra; how pleasant the Black Rock on the slope of Mount Isigili ; how pleasant the mountain cave of the Serpent's Pool in the Sîtavana Grove; how pleasant the Tapoda Grove ; how pleasant the Squirrels' Feeding Ground in the Bambu Grove ; how pleasant Jîvaka's Mango Grove ; how pleasant the Deer Forest at Maddakucchi!"

44. [117] ' " Whosoever, Ânanda, has developed, practised, dwelt on, expanded, and ascended to the very heights of the four paths to Iddhi, and so mastered them as to be able to use them as a vehicle, and as a basis, he, should he desire it, could remain in the same birth for an aeon, or for that portion of the aeon which had yet to run. Now the Tathâgata has thought out and thoroughly practised them [in all respects as just now fully described], and might, should he desire it, remain alive for an aeon, or for that portion of an aeon which has yet to run." But even when a suggestion so evident and a hint so clear were thus given thee by the Tathâgata, thou wast yet incapable of comprehending them, and thou besought-est not the Tathâgata, saying :— " Vouchsafe, lord, to remain during the aeon. Live on, O Exalted One! through the aeon for the good and the happiness of the great multitudes, out of pity for the world, for the good and the gain and the weal of gods and men." If thou shouldst then have so besought the Tathâgata, the Tathâgata might have rejected the appeal even to the second time, but the third time he would have granted it. Thine, therefore, O Ânanda, is the fault, thine is the offence !

45. 'On one occasion, Ânanda, I was residing here at Vesâlî at the Udena Shrine. And there too, Ânanda, I spoke to thee, and said :— " How pleasant, Ânanda, is Vesâlî: how pleasant the Udena Ketiya. Whosoever, Ânanda, has thought out, developed, prac-tised, dwelt on, expanded, and ascended to the very heights of the four paths to Iddhi, and so mastered them as to be able to use them as a vehicle, and as a basis, he, should he desire it, could remain in the same birth for an aeon, or for that portion of the aeon which had yet to run. Now the Tathâgata has thought out and thoroughly practised them [in all respects as just now fully described], and might, should he desire it, remain alive for an aeon, or for that portion of an aeon which has yet to run." But when a suggestion so evident and a hint so clear were thus

given thee by the Tathâgata, thou wast yet incapable
of comprehending them, and thou besoughtest not
the Tathâgata, saying :—" Vouchsafe, Lord, to remain
during the aeon.   Live on, O Exalted One ! through
the aeon for the good and the happiness of the great
multitudes, out of pity for the world, for the good and
the gain and the weal of gods and men."   If thou
shouldst then have so besought the Tathâgata, the
Tathâgata might have rejected the appeal even to
the second time, but the third time he would have
granted it.   Thine, therefore, O Ânanda, is the fault,
thine is the offence !

46. [118] 'On one occasion, Ânanda, I was dwelling
here at Vesâlî at the Gotamaka Shrine—on one
occasion here at Vesâlî at the Shrine of the Seven
Mangoes—on one occasion here at Vesâlî at the
Bahuputta Shrine,—on one occasion here at Vesâlî
at the Sârandada Shrine [and on each occasion I spoke
to thee, Ânanda, in the same words].

47. 'And now to-day, Ânanda, at the Châpâla
Shrine, I spoke to thee, and said :—" How delightful
a spot, Ânanda, is Vesâlî, how charming the Udena
Shrine, and the Gotamaka Shrine and the Shrine of
the Seven Mangoes, and the Shrine of Many Sons,
and the Sârandada Shrine, and the Châpâla Shrine.
Whosoever, Ânanda, has developed, practised, dwelt
on, expanded, and ascended to the very heights of the
four paths to Iddhi, and so mastered them as to be
able to use them as a vehicle and as a basis, he, should
he desire it, could remain in the same birth for an
aeon or for that portion of the aeon which had yet
to run.   Now the Tathâgata has thoroughly practised
and developed them [in all respects as just more fully
described], and he could, therefore, should he desire it,
live on yet for an aeon, or for that portion of the aeon
which has yet to run."   But even when a suggestion
so evident and a hint so clear were thus given thee,
Ânanda, by the Tathâgata, thou wast yet incapable
of comprehending them, and thou besoughtest not the
Tathâgata, saying :—" Vouchsafe, lord, to remain during

the aeon. Live on, O Exalted One! through the aeon for the good and the happiness of the great multitudes, out of pity for the world, for the good and the gain and the weal of gods and men." If thou shouldst then have so besought the Tathâgata, the Tathâgata might have rejected the appeal even to the second time, but the third time he would have granted it. Thine, therefore, O Ânanda, is the fault, thine is the offence!'

48. ' But now, Ânanda, have I not formerly declared to you that it is in the very nature of all things, near and dear unto us, that we must divide ourselves from them, leave them, sever ourselves from them ? How, then, Ânanda, can this be possible—whereas anything whatever born, brought into being, and organized, contains within itself the inherent necessity of dissolution—how then can this be possible that such a being should not be dissolved ? No such condition can exist! And that which, Ânanda, has been relinquished, cast away, renounced, rejected, and abandoned by the Tathâgata—the remaining sum of life surrendered by him—verily with regard to that the word has gone forth from the Tathâgata, saying :—" The passing away of the Tathâgata shall take place before long. [119] At the end of three months from this time the Tathâgata will die!" That the Tathâgata for the sake of living should repent him again of that saying—this can no wise be![1]

'Come, Ânanda, let us go to the Kûṭâgâra Hall, to the Mahâvana.'

---

[1] I do not understand the connexion of ideas between this paragraph and the idea repeated with such tedious iteration in the preceding paragraphs. The two seem to be in marked contrast, if not in absolute contradiction. Perhaps we have here the older tradition ; and certainly this paragraph is more in accordance with the general impression of the character, and with the other sayings, of Gotama as handed down in the Pâli Piṭakas.

'Even so, lord!' said the venerable Ânanda, in assent, to the Exalted One.

49. Then the Exalted One proceeded, and Ânanda with him, to the Mahâvana, to the Kû*t*âgâra Hall: and when he had arrived there he addressed the venerable Ânanda, and said :—

'Go now, Ânanda, and assemble in the Service Hall such of the brethren as reside in the neighbourhood of Vesâlî.'

'Even so, lord!' said the venerable Ânanda, in assent, to the Exalted One.   And when he had assembled in the Service Hall such of the brethren as resided in the neighbourhood of Vesâlî, he went to the Exalted One and saluted him and stood beside him.   And standing beside him, he addressed the Exalted One, and said :—

'Lord! the assembly of the brethren has met together.   Let the Exalted One do even as seemeth to him fit.'

50. Then the Exalted One proceeded to the Service Hall, and sat down there on the mat spread out for him.   And when he was seated the Exalted One addressed the brethren, and said :—

'Therefore, O brethren—ye to whom the truths I have perceived have been made known by me—having thoroughly made yourselves masters of them, practise them, meditate upon them, and spread them abroad; in order that pure religion may last long and be perpetuated, in order that it may continue to be for the good and happiness of the great multitudes, out of pity for the world, to the good and the gain and the weal of gods and men!

'Which then, O brethren, are the truths which, when I had perceived, I made known to you, which when you have mastered it behoves you to practise, meditate upon, and spread abroad, in order that pure religion may last long and be perpetuated, in order that it may continue to be for the good and the happiness of the great multitudes, out of pity for the world, to the good and the gain and the weal of gods and men?

[120] ' They are these :—

The four earnest meditations,
The fourfold great struggle against evil,
The four roads to saintship,
The five moral powers,
The five organs of spiritual sense,
The seven kinds of wisdom, and
The Aryan eightfold path.

These, O brethren, are the truths which, when I had perceived, I made known to you, which when you have mastered it behoves you to practise, meditate upon, and spread abroad, in order that pure religion may last long and be perpetuated, in order that it may continue to be for the good and the happiness of the great multitudes, out of pity for the world, to the good and the gain and the weal of gods and men ! '

51. And the Exalted One exhorted the brethren, and said :—

' Behold now, O brethren, I exhort you, saying :— "All component things must grow old. Work out your salvation with diligence. The final extinction of the Tathâgata will take place before long. At the end of three months from this time the Tathâgata will die !"

' My age is now full ripe, my life draws to its close :
I leave you, I depart, relying on myself alone !
Be earnest then, O brethren, holy, full of thought !
Be steadfast in resolve ! Keep watch o'er your own
    hearts !
Who wearies not, but holds fast to this truth and
    law [1],
Shall cross this sea of life, shall make an end of
    grief.'

End of the Third Portion for Recitation [2].

---

[1] Dhamma and vinaya. The Buddhist religion, as just summarized, and the regulations of the Order.

[2] It is of great interest to notice what are the points upon which Gotama, in this last address to his disciples, and at the solemn time,

when death was so near at hand, is reported to have lain such emphatic 'stress. Unfortunately we have only a fragment of the address, and, as it would seem from its commencement, only the closing fragment. This, however, is in the form of a summary, consisting of an enumeration of certain aggregates, the details of which must have been as familiar to the early Buddhists as the details of similar numerical terms—such as the ten commandments, the twelve tribes, the seven deadly sins, the four gospels, and so on—afterwards were to the Christians. This summary of the Buddha's last address may fairly be taken as a summary of Buddhism, which thus appears to be simply a system of earnest self-culture and self-control.

The following are the details of the aggregate technical terms·used in the above summary, but it will be understood that the English equivalents used give rather a general than an exact representation of the ideas expressed by the Pâli ones. To attempt more would demand a treatise rather than a note.

The four Earnest Meditations are:—

1. Meditation on the body.
2. Meditation on the sensations.
3. Meditation on the ideas.
4. Meditation on reason and character.

The fourfold Great Struggle against evil is divided into:—

1. The struggle to prevent evil arising.
2. The struggle to put away evil states which have arisen.
3. The struggle to produce goodness not previously existing.
4. The struggle to increase goodness when it does exist.

The four Roads to Saintship are four means by which Iddhi (see above, § 3, note) is to be acquired. They are:—

1. The will to acquire it united to earnest meditation and the struggle against evil.
2. The necessary exertion united to earnest meditation and the struggle against evil.
3. The necessary preparation of the heart united to earnest meditation and the struggle against evil.
4. Investigation united to earnest meditation and the struggle against evil.

The five moral powers (balâni) are said to be the same as the next class, called organs (indriyâni). It is no doubt most remarkable that, in a summary like this, two classes out of seven should be absolutely identical except in name. The difference of name is altogether too unimportant to account, by itself, for the distinction made. Either the currently accepted explanation of one of the two aggregate terms must be incorrect, or we must look for some explanation of the repetition other than the mere desire to record the double title. Is it impossible that the one class was split into two to bring the number of the classes up to the sacred number seven, corresponding to the seven Ratanas of a Cakkavatti?

The details of both classes are :—

1. Faith. 2. Energy. 3. Thought. 4. Contemplation. 5. Wisdom.

The seven kinds of Wisdom are :—

1. Energy. 2. Thought. 3. Contemplation. 4. Investigation (of Scripture). 5. Joy. 6. Repose. 7. Serenity.

The Aryan Eightfold Path consists of :—

1. Right views. 2. High aims. 3. Right speech. 4. Upright conduct. 5. A harmless livelihood. 6. Perseverance in well-doing. 7. Intellectual activity. 8. Right rapture.

CHAPTER IV.

1. [122] Now the Exalted One early in the morning robed himself, and taking his bowl, entered Vesâlî for alms; and when he had passed through Vesâlî, and had eaten his meal and was returning from his alms-seeking he gazed at Vesâlî with an elephant look [1] and addressed the venerable Ânanda, and said :—'This will be the last time, Ânanda, that the Tathâgata will behold Vesâlî. Come, Ânanda, let us go on to Bhanda-gâma.'

'Even so, lord!' said the venerable Ânanda, in assent, to the Exalted One.

And the Exalted One proceeded with a great company of the brethren to Bhanda-gâma; and there the Exalted One stayed in the village itself.

2. There the Exalted One addressed the brethren, and said :—'It is through not understanding and grasping four truths [2], O brethren, that we have had to run so long, to wander so long in this weary path of transmigration—both you and I.

'And what are these four? The noble conduct of life, the noble earnestness in meditation, the noble kind of wisdom, and the noble salvation of freedom. [123] But when noble conduct is realized and known, when noble meditation is realized and known, when noble wisdom is realized and known, when noble freedom is realized and known—then is the craving for future life rooted out, that which leads to renewed existence is destroyed, and there is no more birth.'

---

[1] Nâgâpalokitam Vesâliyam apaloketvâ. The Buddhas were accustomed, says Buddhaghosa, on looking backwards to turn the whole body round as an elephant does; because the bones in their neck were firmly fixed, more so than those of ordinary men!

[2] Or Conditions (Dhammâ). They must, of course, be carefully distinguished from the better known Four Noble Truths above, p. 96.

3. Thus spake the Exalted One; and when the Happy One had thus spoken, then again the Teacher said [1] :—

'Righteousness, earnest thought, wisdom, and freedom sublime—
These are the truths realized by Gotama, far-renowned.
Knowing them, he, the knower, proclaimed the truth to the brethren.
The master with eye divine, the quencher of griefs, is at peace [2].'

4. There too, while staying at Bhanda-gâma, the Exalted One held that comprehensive religious talk with the brethren, saying :—'Such and such is upright conduct; such and such is earnest contemplation; such and such is intelligence. Great becomes the fruit, great the advantage of earnest contemplation, when it is set round with upright conduct. Great becomes the fruit, great the advantage of intellect when it is set round with earnest contemplation. The

---

[1] This is merely a stock phrase for introducing verses which repeat the idea of the preceding phrase (see above, paragraph 32). It is an instructive sign of the state of mind in which such records are put together, that these verses could be ascribed to Gotama himself without any feeling of the incongruity involved.

[2] The last word, Parinibbuto, was misunderstood by Childers. It is used in the Nikâyas of living persons in the sense of set free (from evil), at peace. In one passage (M. I, 446) it is even used of a living horse. In all of these passages Childers's rendering 'extinguished, extinct, dead' would be quite inexplicable. Such passages are Majjhima I, 45, 235, 251 ; II, 102; Thera-gâthâ 5, 7, 8, 9, &c. ; Sutta Nipâta 359, 758 ; Samyutta III, 26, 54 ; Itivuttaka 52, 56 ; Dhammapada 89. The same usage is still found in later books (Milinda 50 ; Jâtaka IV, 303, 453). But, just as in the somewhat analogous Christian expression *entered into rest*, the word (still in its ordinary meaning as above) is once or twice used, figuratively, of Arahants who have died. They are at peace, set free. There is no word in the Buddhist phrase corresponding to the Christian 'entered.' The Buddhists never say *entered into Nirvana* of a deceased person. So far as I know the phrase occurs only once (Sutta Nipâta 514), and then it is used of a living person.

mind set round with intelligence is set quite free from
the Intoxications, that is to say, from the Intoxication
of Sensuality, from the Intoxication of Becoming, from
the Intoxication of Delusion, from the Intoxication of
Ignorance.'

5, 6. Now when the Exalted One had remained at
Bha*nd*a-gâma as long as he desired, he addressed
the venerable Ânanda, and said:—'Come, Ânanda,
let us go to Hatthi-gâma.'

[Then in similar words, end of § 1 and §§ 2, 3, and 4
repeated, it is related how the Buddha went there, and
then on to Amba-gâma, and then on to Jambugâma,
at each place holding similar discourses; and then
went on to Bhoga-nagara.]

7. Now there at Bhoga-nagara the Exalted One
stayed at the Ânanda Shrine.

There the Exalted One addressed the brethren
and said:—'I will teach you, O brethren, these four
Great Authorities[1].　Listen thereto, and give good
heed, and I will speak.'

[124] 'Even so, lord!' said the brethren, in assent[2],
to the Exalted One, and the Exalted One spoke as
follows:—

8. 'In the first place, brethren, a brother may say
thus:—" From the mouth of the Exalted One himself

---

[1] The meaning of mahâpadesa is not quite clear.　Perhaps it
should be rendered 'true authorities.'　I have followed Buddhaghosa in
taking apadesa as the last part of the compound.　He says:—mahâ-
padesâ ti mahâ-okâse mahâ-apadese vâ.　Buddhâdayo
mahante mahante apadisitva vuttâni mahâkara*n*âni ti attho,
'the causes (authorities) alleged when referring to Buddha and other
great men.'　Mr. Samarasekara takes it as mahâ-padesa.

[2] I ought perhaps to have explained why I have ventured to differ
from Childers in the rendering of the common word patisu*n*âti.
The root śru seems to have meant 'to sound' before it meant 'to
hear'; and, whether this be so or not, pati-su*n*âti means not
simply 'to consent,' but 'to answer (assentingly).'　It has been pointed
out to me that answer was formerly *andswerian* where *swerian* is
probably not unrelated to the root svar, 'to sound.'

XVI. MAHÂ PARINIBBÂNA SUTTANTA.

have I heard, from his own mouth have I received it. This is the truth, this the law, this the teaching of the Master." The word spoken, brethren, by that brother should neither be received with praise nor treated with scorn. Without praise and without scorn every word and syllable should be carefully understood and then put beside the Suttas [the stock paragraphs learnt by heart in the community] and compared with the Vinaya [the rules of the Order][1]. If when so compared they do not harmonize with the Suttas, and do not fit in with the rules of the Order, then you may come to the con- clusion :—" Verily, this is not the word of the Exalted One, and has been wrongly grasped by that brother." Therefore, brethren, you should reject it. But if they harmonize with the Suttas and fit in with the rules of the Order, then you may come to the conclusion :— "Verily, this is the word of the Exalted One, and has been well grasped by that brother." This, brethren, you should receive as the first Great Authority.

9. 'Again, brethren, a brother may say thus :—" In such and such a dwelling-place there is a company of the brethren with their elders and leaders. From the mouth of that company have I heard, face to face have I received it. This is the truth, this the law, this the teaching of the Master." The word spoken, brethren, by that brother should neither be received with praise nor treated with scorn. Without praise and without scorn every word and syllable should be carefully understood, and then put beside the Suttas and compared with the rules of the Order. If when so compared they do not harmonize with the Suttas, and do not fit in with the rules of the Order, then you may come to the conclusion :—" Verily, this is not the word of the Exalted One, and has been wrongly grasped by that company of the brethren." Therefore, brethren, you should reject it. But if they harmonize

---

[1] Sutte otâretabbâni vinaye sandassetabbâni, where one would expect to find the word Pi*t*aka if it had been in use when this passage was first written or composed.

with the Suttas and fit in with the rules of the Order, then you may come to the conclusion :—[125] "Verily, this is the word of the Exalted One, and has been well grasped by that company of the brethren." This, brethren, you should receive as the second Great Authority.

10. 'Again, brethren, a brother may say thus :—" In such and such a dwelling-place there are dwelling many elders of the Order, deeply read, holding the faith as handed down by tradition, versed in the truths, versed in the regulations of the Order, versed in the summaries of the doctrines and the law. From the mouth of those elders have I heard, from their mouth have I received it. This is the truth, this the law, this the teaching of the Master." The word spoken, brethren, by that brother should neither be received with praise nor treated with scorn. Without praise and without scorn every word and syllable should be carefully understood, and then put beside the Suttas and compared with the rules of the Order. If when so compared they do not harmonize with the Suttas and do not fit in with the rules of the Order, then you may come to the conclusion :—" Verily, this is not the word of the Exalted One, and has been wrongly grasped by those elders." Therefore, brethren, you should reject it. But if they harmonize with the Suttas and fit in with the rules of the Order, then you may come to the conclusion :—" Verily, this is the word of the Exalted One, and has been well grasped by those elders." This, brethren, you should receive as the third Great Authority.

11. 'Again, brethren, a brother may say :—" In such and such a dwelling-place there is there living a brother, deeply read, holding the faith as handed down by tradition, versed in the truths, versed in the regulations of the Order, versed in the summaries of the doctrines and the law. From the mouth of that elder have I heard, from his mouth have I received it. This is the truth, this the law, this the teaching of the Master." The word spoken, brethren, by that

brother should neither be received with praise nor treated with scorn. Without praise and without scorn every word and syllable should be carefully understood, and then put beside the Suttas and compared with the rules of the Order. If when so compared they do not harmonize with the Suttas, and do not fit in with the rules of the Order, then you may come to the conclusion :—" Verily, this is not the word of the Exalted One, and has been wrongly grasped by that brother." Therefore, brethren, you should reject it. But if they harmonize with the Suttas and fit in with the rules of the Order, then you may come to the conclusion :— [126] "Verily, this is the word of the Exalted One, and has been well grasped by that brother." This, brethren, you should receive as the fourth Great Authority.

' These, brethren, are the Four Great Authorities.'

12. There too, the Exalted One held that comprehensive religious talk with the brethren, saying :—' Such and such is upright conduct; such and such is earnest contemplation; such and such is intelligence. Great becomes the fruit, great the advantage of earnest contemplation, when it is set round with upright conduct. Great becomes the fruit, great the advantage of intellect when it is set round with earnest contemplation. The mind set round with intelligence is set quite free from the Intoxications, that is to say, from the Intoxication of Sensuality, from the Intoxication of Becoming, from the Intoxication of Delusion, from the Intoxication of Ignorance.'

13. Now when the Exalted One had remained as long as he desired at Bhoga-gâma, he addressed the venerable Ânanda, and said :—' Come, Ânanda, let us go on to Pâvâ.'

' Even so, lord!' said the venerable Ânanda, in assent to the Exalted One. And the Exalted One proceeded with a great company of the brethren to Pâvâ.

And there at Pâvâ the Exalted One stayed at the Mango Grove of Chunda, who was by family a smith.

14. Now Chunda, the worker in metals, heard that the Exalted One had come to Pâvâ, and was staying there in his Mango Grove.

And Chunda, the worker in metals, went to the place where the Exalted One was, and saluting him took his seat respectfully on one side. And when he was thus seated, the Exalted One instructed, aroused, incited, and gladdened him with religious discourse.

15. Then he, instructed, aroused, incited, and gladdened by the religious discourse, addressed the Exalted One, and said:—'May the Exalted One do me the honour of taking his meal together with the brethren, at my house to-morrow?'

And the Exalted One signified, by silence, his consent.

16. Then seeing that the Exalted One had consented, [127] Chunda, the worker in metals, rose from his seat and bowed down before the Exalted One, and keeping him on his right hand as he passed him, departed thence.

17. Now at the end of the night, Chunda, the worker in metals, made ready in his dwelling-place sweet rice and cakes, and a quantity of truffles [1]. And he

---

[1] Sûkara-maddava. See the note in my translation of the Milinda (1890), Vol. I, p. 244. Dr. Hoey informs me that the peasantry in these districts are still very fond of a bulbous root, a sort of truffle, found in the jungle, and called sûkara-kanda. Mr. K. E. Neumann, in his translation of the Majjhima (1896), p. xx, has collected several similar instances of truffle-like roots, or edible plants, having such names. The Sinhalese translation of the Dîgha (London and Colombo, 1905), p. 796, simply repeats the Pâli word. Buddhists do not attach much importance to the point. They have been mostly vegetarians, and are increasingly so. But their scheme of ethics works from within; and the Buddha expressly refused, in the case of Devadatta's schism, to lay down any hard and fast rule as to abstinence from flesh as food. It is perhaps of importance that the food prepared by Chunda and eaten by the Buddha is called Bhatta (below, § 21): this is not used elsewhere of meat.

announced the hour to the Exalted One, saying :—'The hour, lord, has come, and the meal is ready.'

18. And the Exalted One robed himself early in the morning, and taking his bowl, went with the brethren to the dwelling-place of Chunda, the worker in metals. When he had come thither he seated himself on the seat prepared for him. And when he was seated he addressed Chunda, the worker in metals, and said :—'As to the truffles you have made ready, serve me with them, Chunda : and as to the other food, the sweet rice and cakes, serve the brethren with it.'

'Even so, lord!' said Chunda, the worker in metals, in assent, to the Blessed One. And the truffles he had made ready he served to the Exalted One ; whilst the other food, the sweet rice and cakes, he served to the members of the Order.

19. Now the Exalted One addressed Chunda, the worker in metals, and said :—'Whatever truffles, Chunda, are left over to thee, those bury in a hole. I see no one, Chunda, on earth nor in Mâra's heaven, nor in Brahma's heaven, no one among Samanas and Brâhmanas, among gods, and men, by whom, when he has eaten it, that food can be properly assimilated, save by a Tathâgata.'

'Even so, lord!' said Chunda, the worker in metals, in assent, to the Exalted One. And whatever truffles remained over those he· buried in a hole. And he went to the place where the Exalted One was ; and when he had come there, took his seat respectfully on one side. And when he was seated, the Exalted One instructed and aroused and incited and gladdened Chunda, the worker in metals, with religious discourse. And the Exalted One then rose from his seat and departed thence.

20. Now when the Exalted One had eaten the rice prepared by Chunda, the worker in metals, there fell upon him a dire sickness, the disease of dysentery, and sharp pain came upon him, even unto death. [128] But the Exalted One, mindful and self-possessed, bore it without complaint.

And the Exalted One addressed the venerable Ânanda, and said :—' Come, Ânanda, let us go on to Kusinârâ.'

' Even so, lord!' said the venerable Ânanda, in assent, to the Exalted One.

' When he had eaten Chunda's food,
The copper-smith's—thus have I heard—
He bore with fortitude the pain,
The sharp pain even unto death!

When he had eaten, from the truffles in the food
There fell upon the teacher sickness dire,
Then after nature was relieved the Exalted One
        announced and said :
' I now am going on to Kusinârâ[1].'

---

21. Now the Exalted One went aside from the path to the foot of a certain tree; and when he had come there he addressed the venerable Ânanda, and said :—' Fold, I pray you, Ânanda, the robe in four; and spread it out for me. I am weary, Ânanda, and must rest awhile!'

' Even so, lord!' said the venerable Ananda, in assent, to the Exalted One, and spread out the robe folded fourfold.

22. And the Exalted One seated himself on the seat prepared for him; and when he was seated, he addressed the venerable Ânanda, and said :—' Fetch me, I pray you, Ânanda, some water. I am thirsty, Ânanda, and would drink.'

When he had thus spoken, the venerable Ananda said to the Exalted One :—' But just now, lord, about five hundred carts have gone over. That water stirred up by the wheels has become shallow and flows fouled and turbid. [129] This river Kakuttha, lord, not far off, is clear and pleasant, cool and transparent, easy to

---

[1] 'It should be understood,' says Buddhaghosa, 'that these are verses by the Theras who held the council.' And he repeats this at §§ 38, 41. These here seem to be two different versifications of the same legend.

get down into, and delightful. There the Exalted
One may both drink the water, and cool his limbs.'

23. Again the second time the Exalted One
addressed the venerable Ânanda, and said :—'Fetch
me, I pray you, Ânanda, some water. I am thirsty,
Ânanda, and would drink.'

And again the second time the venerable Ananda
said to the Exalted One :—'But just now, lord, about
five hundred carts have gone over. That water stirred
up by the wheels has become shallow and flows fouled
and turbid. This river Kaku*tth*a, lord, not far off, is
clear and pleasant, cool and transparent, easy to get
down into, and delightful. There the Exalted One
may both drink the water, and cool his limbs.'

24. Again the third time the Exalted One addressed
the venerable Ânanda, and said :—'Fetch me, I pray
you, Ânanda, some water. I am thirsty, Ânanda, and
would drink.'

'Even so, lord!' said the venerable Ananda, in
assent, to the Exalted One : and taking a bowl he
went down to the streamlet. And lo! the streamlet
which, stirred up by the wheels, was but just now
become shallow, and was flowing fouled and turbid,
had begun, when the venerable Ânanda came up to it,
to flow clear and bright and free from all turbidity.

25. Then Ânanda thought :—' How wonderful, how
marvellous is the great might and power of the Tathâgata![1] For this streamlet which, stirred up by the
wheels, was but just now become shallow and was
flowing foul and turbid, now, as I come up to it, is
flowing clear and bright and free from all turbidity.'

And taking water in the bowl he returned towards
the Exalted One ; and when he had come where the
Exalted One was he said to him :—' How wonderful,

---

[1] This is a most unusual way of speaking of the Buddha. In the
Suttantas believers are represented as addressing him as bhante, lord
or sir (the same form as that used by junior members of the Order in
addressing their seniors); and as speaking of him by the epithet
Bhagavâ the Exalted One. Unbelievers address him as bho
Gotama, and speak of him as the Sama*n*a Gotama.

how marvellous is the great might and power of the
Tathâgata ! For this streamlet which, stirred up by
the wheels, was but just now become shallow and was
flowing foul and turbid, now, as I come up to it, is
flowing clear and bright and free from all turbidity.
Let the Exalted One drink the water ! Let the Happy
One drink the water ! '

Then the Exalted One drank of the water.

---

26. [130] Now at that time a man named Pukkusa [1],
a young Mallian, a disciple of Âlâra Kâlâma's, was
passing along the high road from Kusinârâ to Pâvâ.

And Pukkusa, the young Mallian, saw the Exalted
One seated at the foot of a tree. On seeing him, he
went up to the place where the Exalted One was, and
when he had come there he saluted the Exalted One,
and took his rest respectfully on one side. And when
he was seated Pukkusa, the young Mallian, said to the
Exalted One :—' How wonderful a thing it is, lord!
and how marvellous, that those who have gone forth
out of the world should pass their time in a state of
mind so calm !

27. ' Formerly, lord, Âlâra Kâlâma was once walking along the high road ; and leaving the road he sat
himself down under a certain tree to rest during the
heat of the day. Now, lord, five hundred carts passed
by one after the other, each close to Âlâra Kâlâma.
And a certain man, who was following close behind
that caravan of carts, went up to the place where Âlâra
Kâlâma was, and when he was come there he spake as
follows to Âlâra Kâlâma :—

' " But, lord, did you see those five hundred carts
go by ? "

' " No, indeed, I saw them not."

---

[1] The Pukkusas were one of the despised tribes. Compare M. II,
152 ; A. II, 85 ; PP. IV, 19 ; Jât. IV, 205, 306 ; Lalita Vistara
XXI, 17. But Buddhaghosa says Pukkusa must here be simply
a name, as the Mallas were Khattiyas. He adds that this Pukkusa
was the owner of the five hundred carts that had just passed by ; and
that Âlâra Kâlâma was called Âlâra because he was Dîgha-pingalo,
Kâlâma being his family name.

' " But, lord, did you hear the sound of them ? "
' " No, indeed, sir, I heard not their sound."
' " But, lord, were you then asleep ? "
' " No, sir, I was not asleep."
' " But, lord, were you then conscious ? " '
' " Even so, sir."

' " So that you, lord, though you were both conscious and awake, neither saw, nor heard the sound of five hundred carts passing by, one after the other, and each close to you. Why, lord, even your robe was sprinkled over with the dust of them ! " '

' " It is even so, sir." '

' Then thought that man :—" How wonderful a thing is it, and how marvellous, that those who have gone forth out of the world should pass their time in a state of mind so calm ! [131] So much so that a man though being both conscious and awake, neither sees, nor hears the sound of five hundred carts passing by, one after the other, and each close to him."

' And after giving utterance to his deep faith in A/âra Kâlâma, he departed thence.'

28. ' Now what think you, Pukkusa, which is the more difficult thing either to do or to meet with—that a man, being conscious and awake, should neither see, nor hear the sound of five hundred carts passing by, one after the other, close to him,—or that a man, being conscious and awake, should neither see, nor hear the sound thereof when the falling rain goes on beating and splashing, and the lightnings are flashing forth, and the thunderbolts are crashing ? '

29. ' What in comparison, lord, can these five hundred carts do, or six or seven or eight or nine or ten hundred, yea, even hundreds and thousands of carts ? That certainly is more difficult, both to do and to meet with, that a man, being conscious and awake, should neither see, nor hear the sound thereof when the falling rain goes on beating and splashing, and the lightnings are flashing forth, and the thunderbolts are crashing.'

30. ' Now on one occasion, Pukkusa, I was dwelling

at Âtumâ, and was at the Threshing-floor. And at that time the falling rain began to beat and to splash, and the lightnings to flash forth, and the thunderbolts to crash; and two peasants, brothers, and four oxen were killed. Then, Pukkusa, a great multitude of people went forth from Âtumâ, and went up to the place where the two peasants, brothers, and the four oxen, lay killed.'

31. 'Now at that time, Pukkusa, I had gone forth from the Threshing-floor, and was walking up and down thinking at the entrance to the Threshing-floor. And a certain man came, Pukkusa, out of that great multitude of people, up to the place where I was; and when he came up he saluted me, and took his place respectfully on one side. And as he stood there, Pukkusa, I said to the man:—

32. '"Why then, sir, is this great multitude of people assembled together?"'

[132] '" But just now, the falling rain began to beat and to splash, and the lightnings to flash forth, and the thunderbolts to crash; and two peasants, brothers, were killed, and four oxen. Therefore is this great multitude of people gathered together. But where, lord, were you?"'

'" I, sir, have been here all the while."

'" But, lord, did you see it?"

'" I, sir, saw nothing."

'" But, lord, did you hear it?"

'" I, sir, heard nothing."

'" Were you then, lord, asleep?"

'" I, sir, was not asleep."

'" Were you then conscious, lord?"

'" Even so, sir."

'" So that you, lord, being conscious and awake, neither saw, nor heard the sound thereof when the falling rain went on beating and splashing, and the lightnings were flashing forth, and the thunderbolts were crashing."'

'"That is so, sir."

33. 'Then, Pukkusa, the thought occurred to that man:—

'" How wonderful a thing is it, and marvellous, that those who have gone forth out of the world should pass their time in a state of mind so calm!—so that a man, being conscious and awake, neither sees, nor hears the sound thereof when the falling rain is beating and splashing, and the lightnings are flashing forth, and the thunderbolts are crashing." And after giving utterance to his deep faith in me, he departed from me [with the customary demonstrations of respect].'

34. And when he had thus spoken, Pukkusa, the young Mallian, addressed the Blessed One in these words :—' Now I, lord, as to the faith that I had in Âlâra Kâlâma, that I winnow away as in a mighty wind, and wash it away as in a swiftly running stream. Most excellent, lord, are the words of thy mouth, most excellent! Just as if a man were to set up that which is thrown down, or were to reveal that which is hidden away, or were to point out the right road to him who has gone astray, or were to bring a lamp into the darkness, so that those who have eyes can see external forms—just even so, lord, has the truth been made known to me, in many a figure, by the Exalted One. [133] And I, even I, betake myself, lord, to the Exalted One as my refuge, to the Truth, and to the Brotherhood. May the Exalted One accept me as a disciple, as a true believer, from this day forth, as long as life endures! [1] '

35. Now Pukkusa, the young Mallian, addressed a certain man and said :—' Fetch me, I pray you, my good man, a pair of robes of cloth of gold, burnished and ready for wear.'

' So be it, sir!' said that man, in assent, to Pukkusa, the young Mallian; and he brought a pair of robes of cloth of gold, burnished and ready for wear.

---

[1] This is a stock phrase constituting the final answer of a hitherto unconverted man at the end of one of those argumentative dialogues by which Gotama overcame opposition or expounded the truth. After a discussion of exalted themes it fits in very appropriately; here and elsewhere it is incongruous and strained. See below, V, 50.

And the Mallian Pukkusa presented the pair of robes of cloth of gold, burnished and ready for wear, to the Exalted One, saying :—' Lord, this pair of robes of burnished cloth of gold is ready for wear.   May the Exalted One show me favour and accept it at my hands !'

' In that case, Pukkusa, robe me in one, and Ânanda in one.'

' Even so, lord !' said Pukkusa, in assent, to the Exalted One ; and in one he robed the Exalted One, and in one, Ânanda.

36. Then the Exalted One instructed and aroused and incited and gladdened Pukkusa, the young Mallian, with religious discourse.   And Pukkusa, the young Mallian, when he had been instructed and aroused and incited and gladdened by the Exalted One with religious discourse, arose from his seat, and bowed down before the Exalted One; and keeping him on his right hand as he passed him, departed thence.

37. Now not long after the Mallian Pukkusa had gone, the venerable Ânanda placed that pair of robes of cloth of gold, burnished and ready for wear, on the body of the Exalted One ; and when it was so placed on the body of the Exalted One it appeared to have lost its splendour [1] !

And the venerable Ânanda said to the Exalted One:— ' How wonderful a thing is it, lord, and how marvellous, that the colour of the skin of the Exalted One should

[1] To understand what is here represented to have happened one must understand the mode in which the Buddhist Wanderers wore their robes.   There was no tailoring at all.   The set of three robes was simply three lengths of cotton cloth about a yard wide.   One piece, folded in half, was wrapped round the body.   Another piece covered the limbs from the waist to the ankles.   It was supported by a girdle and went three or four times round.   The third piece was put on over this last, went twice round the legs, and then the rest of it was thrown over the left shoulder, and passed under the right arm across the body.   See below, ch. V, § 19.

Pukkusa had placed the two lengths of cloth, shawl-wise, over the shoulders of the recipients.   When he left them Ânanda assisted the Buddha to put them on as Nos. 1 and 3 of a set of robes.

be so clear, so exceeding bright! For when I placed even this pair of robes of burnished cloth of gold and ready for wear on the body [134] of the Exalted One, lo! it seemed as if it had lost its splendour!'

'It is even so, Ânanda. There are two occasions, Ânanda, on which the colour of the skin of a Tathâgata becomes clear and exceeding bright. What are the two?

'On the night, Ânanda, on which a Tathâgata attains to the supreme and perfect insight, and on the night in which he passes finally away in that utter passing away which leaves nothing whatever to remain—on these two occasions the colour of the skin of the Tathâgata becomes clear and exceeding bright.

38. 'And now this day, Ânanda, at the third watch of the night, in the Upavattana of Kusinârâ, in the Sâla Grove of the Mallians, between the twin Sâla trees, the utter passing away of the Tathâgata will take place. Come, Ânanda! Let us go on to the river Kakutthâ.'

'Even so, lord!' said the venerable Ânanda, in assent, to the Exalted One.

> The pair of robes of cloth of gold,
> All burnished, Pukkusa had brought,
> Clad on with them the Master then
> Shone forth in colour like to gold [1]!

39. Now the Exalted One with a great company of the brethren went on to the river Kakutthâ; and when he had come there, he went down into the water, and bathed, and drank. And coming up out again on the other side he went on to the Mango Grove.

---

[1] We have here the commencement of the legend which afterwards grew into an account of an actual 'transfiguration' of the Buddha. It is very curious that it should have taken place soon after the Buddha had announced to Ânanda his approaching death, and that in the Buddhist Sutta it should be connected so closely with that event; for a similar remark applies also to the Transfiguration mentioned in the Gospels.

And when he was come there he addressed the
venerable Chundaka, and said :—' Fold, I pray you,
Chundaka, a robe in four and spread it out. I am
weary, Chundaka, and would lie down.'

' Even so, lord !' said the venerable Chundaka, in
assent, to the Exalted One. And he folded a robe
in four, and spread it out.

40. And the Exalted One laid himself down on his
right side, with one foot resting on the other ; and
calm and self-possessed he meditated, intending to
rise up again in due time.   [135] And the venerable
Chundaka seated himself there in front of the Exalted
One.

41. The Buddha to Kakutthâ's river came,
Whose clear and pleasant waters limpid flow.
He plunged beneath the stream wearied and worn,
The Buddha without equal in the world !
When he had bathed and drunk, the teacher then
Crossed o'er, the brethren thronging round his steps ;
The Blessed Master, preaching the while the truth,
The Mighty Sage came to the Mango Grove.
There spake he to the brother Chundaka :—
' Spread me the fourfold robe out as a couch.'
Urged by the Holy One, he quickly spread
The fourfold robe in order on the ground.
The Master laid him down, wearied and worn ;
And there, before him, Chunda took his seat.

42. And the Exalted One addressed the venerable
Ânanda, and said :—' Now it may happen, Ânanda,
that some one should stir up remorse in Chunda the
smith, by saying :—" This is evil to thee, Chunda, and
loss to thee in that when the Tathâgata had eaten his
last meal from thy provision, then he died." Any such
remorse, Ânanda, in Chunda the smith should be
checked by saying:—" This is good to thee, Chunda, and
gain to thee, in that when the Tathâgata had eaten his
last meal from thy provision, then he died. From the
very mouth of the Exalted One, Chunda, have I heard,

from his own mouth have I received this saying :—
' These two offerings of food are of equal fruit, and of
equal profit, and of much greater fruit and much greater
profit than any other—and which are the two ? [136]
The offering of food which, when a Tathâgata has
eaten, he attains to supreme and perfect insight; and
the offering of food which, when a Tathâgata has
eaten, he passes away by that utter passing away in
which nothing whatever remains behind—these two
offerings of food are of equal fruit and of equal profit,
and of much greater fruit and of much greater profit than
any others. There has been laid up by Chunda the
smith a karma redounding to length of life, redounding
to good birth, redounding to good fortune, redounding to
good fame, redounding to the inheritance of heaven, and
of sovereign power.' " In this way, Ânanda, should be
checked any remorse in Chunda the smith [1].'

43. Then the Exalted One, perceiving how the
matter stood, uttered on that occasion this hymn of
exultation :—

' To him who gives shall virtue be increased ;
In him who curbs himself, no anger can arise ;
The righteous man casts off all evil ways,
And by the rooting out of lust, and bitterness,
And all infatuation, is at peace !'

End of the Fourth Portion for Recitation, containing
The Episode of Â*l*âra.

---

[1] Here, and above pp. 137–9, we have spelt the name of the smith,
in English, as it is pronounced in Pâli, and should be pronounced in
English.

CHAPTER V.

1. [137] Now the Exalted One addressed the venerable Ânanda, and said :—'Come, Ânanda, let us go on to the Sâla Grove of the Mallas, the Upavattana of Kusinârâ, on the further side of the river Hiranyavatî.'

'Even so, lord!' said the venerable Ânanda, in assent, to the Exalted One.

And the Exalted One proceeded with a great company of the brethren to the Sâla Grove of the Mallas, the Upavattana of Kusinârâ, on the further side of the river Hiranyavatî : and when he had come there he addressed the venerable Ânanda, and said :—

'Spread over for me, I pray you, Ânanda, the couch with its head to the north, between the twin Sâla trees[1]. I am weary, Ânanda, and would lie down.'

'Even so, lord!' said the venerable Ânanda, in assent, to the Exalted One. And he spread a covering over the couch with its head to the north, between the twin Sâla trees. And the Exalted One laid himself down on his right side, with one leg resting on the other ; and he was mindful and self-possessed.

---

2. Now at that time the twin Sâla trees were all one mass of bloom with flowers out of season ; and

---

[1] According to the commentator 'tradition says that there was a row of Sâla trees at the head (sîs'a) of that couch, and another at its foot, one young Sâla tree being close to its head, and another close to its foot. The twin Sâla trees were so called because the two trees were equally grown in respect of the roots, trunks, branches, and leaves. There was a couch there in the park for the special use of the (periodically elected) chieftain of the Mallas, and it was this couch which the Exalted One asked Ânanda to make ready.'

There is no further explanation of the term uttara-sîsaka*m*, which may have been the name for a slab of wood or stone reserved on great occasions for the use of the leaders of the neighbouring republic, but available at other times for passers-by.

all over the body of the Tathâgata [1] these dropped
and sprinkled and scattered themselves, out of reverence for the successor of the Buddhas of old.   And
heavenly Mandârava flowers, too, and heavenly sandalwood powder came falling from the sky, and all over
the body of the Tathâgata they descended and sprinkled
[138] and scattered themselves, out of reverence for
the successor of the Buddhas of old.   And heavenly
music was sounded in the sky, out of reverence for
the successor of the Buddhas of old.   And heavenly
songs came wafted from the skies, out of reverence
for the successor of the Buddhas of old!

3. Then the Exalted One addressed the venerable
Ânanda and said:—'The twin Sâla trees are all one
mass of bloom with flowers out of season; all over the
body of the Tathâgata these drop and sprinkle and
scatter themselves, out of reverence for the successor
of the Buddhas of old.   And heavenly Mandârava
flowers, too, and heavenly sandal-wood powder come
falling from the sky, and all over the body of the
Tathâgata they descend and sprinkle and scatter themselves, out of reverence for the successor of the
Buddhas of old.   And heavenly music sounds in the
sky, out of reverence for the successor of the Buddhas
of old.   And heavenly songs come wafted from the
skies, out of reverence for the successor of the Buddhas
of old!

'Now it is not thus, Ânanda, that the Tathâgata is
rightly honoured, reverenced, venerated, held sacred
or revered.   But the brother or the sister, the devout
man or the devout woman, who continually fulfils all
the greater and the lesser duties, who is correct in life,
walking according to the precepts—it is he who rightly
honours, reverences, venerates, holds sacred, and
reveres the Tathâgata with the worthiest homage.

---

[1] We have here the unusual case of the Buddha being called Tathâgata, not by himself, but by à third person, the compiler of the
Suttanta. The paragraph is perhaps moulded by inadvertence on the
next one. But see § 10. Compare the note above on IV, 25.

Therefore, O Ânanda, be ye constant in the fulfilment of the greater and of the lesser duties, and be ye correct in life, walking according to the precepts ; and thus Ânanda, should it be taught.'

4. Now at that time the venerable Upavâna was standing in front of the Exalted One, fanning him. And the Exalted One was not pleased with Upavâna, and he said to him :—' Stand aside, O brother, stand not in front of me !'

Then this thought sprang up in the mind of the venerable Ânanda :—[139] 'This venerable Upavâna had long been in close personal attendance and service on the Exalted One. And now, at the last moment, the Exalted One is not pleased with Upavâna, and has said to him :—" Stand aside, O brother, stand not in front of me!" What may be the cause and what the reason that the Exalted One is not pleased with Upavâna, and speaks thus with him ?'

5. And the venerable Ânanda said to the Exalted One :—' This venerable Upavâna has long been in close personal attendance and service on the Exalted One. And now, at the last moment, the Exalted One is not pleased with Upavâna, and has said to him :—" Stand aside, O brother, stand not in front of me !" What may be the cause and what the reason that the Exalted One is not pleased with Upavâna, and speaks thus with him ?'

' In great numbers, Ânanda, are the gods of the ten world-systems assembled together to behold the Tathâgata. For twelve leagues, Ânanda, around the Sâla Grove of the Mallas, the Upavattana of Kusinârâ, there is no spot in size even as the pricking of the point of the tip of a hair which is not pervaded by powerful spirits [1]. And the spirits, Ânanda, are mur-

---

[1] Buddhaghosa explains that even twenty to sixty angels or gods (devatâyo) could stand âragga-koti-nittûdana- (MS. nittaddana-) matte pi, ' on a point pricked by the extreme point of a gimlet,' without inconveniencing one another (aññam aññam avyâbâdhenti). It is most curious to find this exact analogy to the notorious discussion as to how many angels could stand on the point

muring, and say :—" From afar have we come to behold
the Tathâgata. Few and far between are the Tathâgatas, the Arahant Buddhas who appear in the world :
and now to-day, in the last watch of the night, the
death of a Tathâgata will take place; and this eminent
brother stands in front of the Tathâgata, concealing
him, and in his last hour we are prevented from
beholding the Tathâgata"; thus, Ânanda, do the
spirits murmur.'

6. ' But of what kind of spirits is the Exalted One
thinking ? '

' There are spirits, Ânanda, in the sky, but of
worldly mind, who dishevel their hair and weep, who
stretch forth their arms and weep, [140] who fall
prostrate on the ground, and roll to and fro in anguish
at the thought :—" Too soon will the Exalted One die!
Too soon will the Exalted One pass away! Full
soon will the Light of the world vanish away [1]!"

' There are spirits, too, Ânanda, on the earth,
and of worldly mind, who tear their hair and weep,
who stretch forth their arms and weep, who fall pros-

---

of a needle in a commentary written at just that period of Buddhist
history which corresponds to the Middle Ages of Christendom. The
passage in the text does not really imply or suggest any such doctrine,
though the whole episode is so absurd that the author of the text
could not have hesitated to say so, had such an idea been the common
belief of the early Buddhists. With these sections should be compared the similar sections in Chapter VI, of which these are perhaps
merely an echo.

There is no comment on nittûdana, but there can be little doubt
that Childers's conjectural reading is correct.

[1] It is literally, ' the Eye in the world will vanish away,' where Eye
is of course used figuratively of that by the aid of which spiritual truths
can be perceived, corresponding exactly to the similar use in Europe
of the word Light. The Master is often called ' He with the Eye,'
' He of the Spiritual Eye' (see, for instance, the last verses in this
Book), and here by a bold figure of speech he is called the Eye itself,
which was shortly about to vanish away from the world, the means
of spiritual insight which was no longer to be available for the common
use of all men. But this is, it will be noticed, only the lament of the
foolish and ignorant.

trate on the ground, and roll to and fro in anguish at the thought :—"Too soon will the Exalted One die! Too soon will the Happy One pass away! Full soon will the Eye of the world disappear from sight."

'But the spirits who are free from passion bear it, calm and self-possessed, mindful of the saying which begins:—"Impermanent indeed are all component things. How then is it possible [whereas anything whatever, when born, brought into being, and organized, contains within itself the inherent necessity of dissolution— how then is it possible that such a being should not be dissolved? No such condition can exist[1]!"]

7. 'In times past, lord, the brethren, when they had spent the rainy season in different districts, used to come to see the Tathâgata, and we used to receive those very reverend brethren to audience, and to wait upon the Exalted One. But, lord, after the end of the Exalted One, we shall not be able to receive those very reverend brethren to audience, and to wait upon the Exalted One.'

8. 'There are these four places, Ânanda, which the believing clansman should visit with feelings of reverence. Which are the four?

'The place, Ânanda, at which the believing man can say :—"Here the Tathâgata was born!" is a spot to be visited with feelings of reverence.

'The place, Ânanda, at which the believing man can say :—"Here the Tathâgata attained to the supreme and perfect insight!" is a spot to be visited with feelings of reverence.

'The place, Ânanda, at which the believing man can say:—"Here was the kingdom of righteousness set on foot by the Tathâgata!" is a spot to be visited with feelings of reverence.

'The place, Ânanda, at which the believing man can say :—"Here the Tathâgata passed finally away in that utter passing away which leaves nothing whatever to

---

[1] The words in brackets have been inserted from par. III, 48 above. See par. VI, 19 below.

remain behind!" is a spot to be visited with feelings of reverence. [141] These are the four places, Ânanda, which the believing clansman should visit with feelings of reverence.

'And there will come, Ânanda, to such spots, believers, brethren and sisters of the Order, or devout men and devout women, and will say :—" Here was the Tathâgata born!" or, " Here did the Tathâgata attain to the supreme and perfect insight!" or, "Here was the kingdom of righteousness set on foot by the Tathâgata!" or, "Here the Tathâgata passed away in that utter passing away which leaves nothing whatever to remain behind!"

'And they, Ânanda, who shall die while they, with believing heart, are journeying on such pilgrimage, shall be reborn after death, when the body shall dissolve, in the happy realms of heaven.'

---

9. 'How are we to conduct ourselves, lord, with regard to womankind?'

'As not seeing them, Ânanda.'

'But if we should see them, what are we to do?'

'No talking, Ânanda.'

'But if they should speak to us, lord, what are we to do?'

'Keep wide awake, Ânanda.'

---

10. 'What are we to do, lord, with the remains of the Tathâgata?'

'Hinder not yourselves, Ânanda, by honouring the remains of the Tathâgata. Be zealous, I beseech you, Ânanda, in your own behalf! Devote yourselves to your own good! Be earnest, be zealous, be intent on your own good! There are wise men, Ânanda, among the nobles, among the brahmins, among the heads of houses, who are firm believers in the Tathâgata; and they will do due honour to the remains of the Tathâgata.

11. ¹ 'But what should be done, lord, with the remains of the Tathâgata?'

'As men treat the remains of a king of kings, so, Ananda, should they treat the remains of a Tathâgata.'

'And how, lord, do they treat the remains of a king of kings²?'

'They wrap the body of a king of kings, Ananda, in a new cloth. When that is done they wrap it in carded cotton wool³. When that is done they wrap it in a new cloth, [142] and so on till they have wrapped the body in five hundred successive layers of both kinds. Then they place the body in an oil vessel of iron, and cover that close up with another oil vessel of iron⁴. They then build a funeral pyre of all kinds

---

¹ This conversation occurs also below (VI, 17), and the older tradition probably had it only in that connexion.

² King of kings is an adequate rendering of the 'King of the Rolling Wheel,' the wheels of whose chariot roll unhindered through the land; that is to say, a king whose power no other king can dispute, who is an acknowledged overlord. The idea, which is explained very fully in the next Suttanta, may have arisen with the rise of the Kosala power; but it may also be later. If we could trace its history it would afford us a guide to the date at which the Mahâ Parinibbâna Suttanta assumed its present form.

³ Buddhaghosa explains this passage thus:—'As Benares cloth, by reason of its fineness of texture, does not take the oil, he therefore says:—"with vihata cotton wool," that is, with cotton wool that has been well forced asunder.' The technical use of the word, as applied to cotton wool, has only been found in this passage. It usually means 'torn' with grief.

⁴ Ayasâya tela-doniyâ, where one would expect âyasâya, but my MS. of the Dîgha Nikâya confirms twice over here, and twice again below (VI, 33, 35) the reading given by Childers. Buddhaghosa says the word here means gold. Ayas was originally used for bronze, and only later for iron also, and at last exclusively of iron. As kamsa is already a common word for bronze in very early Buddhist Pâli texts, I think âyasa (not ayasa) would here mean 'of iron.' When Buddhaghosa says it is here a name for gold, we can only conclude that iron had become, in his time, a metal which he might fairly consider too base for the purpose proposed. The whole process as described is not very intelligible; and one might suppose that ayasa after all had nothing to do with any metal, and was a technical term descriptive of some particular size or shape or colour of oil vessel. But it is frequently found in the MSS. when iron is clearly meant. Thus in the

of perfume, and burn the body of the king of kings.
And then at the four cross roads they erect a cairn [1]
to the king of kings. This, Ânanda, is the way in
which they treat the remains of a king of kings.

'And as they treat the remains of a king of kings,
so, Ânanda, should they treat the remains of the
Tathâgata. At the four cross roads a cairn should
be erected to the Tathâgata. And whosoever shall
there place garlands or perfumes or paint, or make
salutation there, or become in its presence calm in
heart—that shall long be to them for a profit and
a joy.'

12. 'The men, Ânanda, worthy of a cairn, are four
in number. Which are the four?

'A Tathâgata, an Able Awakened One, is worthy
of a cairn. One awakened for himself alone is
worthy of a cairn [2]. A true hearer of the Tathâgata
is worthy of a cairn. A king of kings is worthy of a
cairn.

'And on account of what circumstance, Ananda, is
a Tathâgata, an Able Awakened One, worthy of a
cairn?

'At the thought, Ananda:—" This is the cairn of that
Exalted One, of that Able Awakened One," the hearts
of many shall be made calm and happy; and since
they there had calmed and satisfied their hearts they
will be reborn after death, when the body has dissolved, in the happy realms of heaven. It is on
account of this circumstance, Ânanda, that a Tathâgata, an Able Awakened One, is worthy of a cairn.

popular verse at Sa*m*yutta I, 77 on which a Jâtaka is based (II, 140),
which is inserted in the ' Anthologies' (Dhammapada 345, Khar. MS.
No. 102), and twice quoted in the Netti (35, 153), the MSS. have both
forms in spite of the metre favouring the long vowel. In this passage
both Paññânanda's Colombo edition of 1877, and Samarasekara's
version (Col. and Lond. 1905) have the short vowel only.

[1] Thûpa. A solid mound or tumulus or barrow, in the midst of
which the bones and ashes are to be placed. The dome of St. Paul's
as seen from the Thames Embankment gives a very good idea of one
of the later of these Buddhist monumental mounds.

'And on account of what circumstance, Ânanda, is one awakened for himself alone [1] worthy of a cairn?

'At the thought, Ânanda:—"This is the cairn of that Exalted One awakened for himself alone" [143] the hearts of many shall be made calm and happy; and since they there had calmed and satisfied their hearts they will be reborn after death, when the body has dissolved, in the happy realms of heaven. It is on account of this circumstance, Ânanda, that one awakened for himself alone is worthy of a cairn.

'And on account of what circumstance, Ânanda, is a true hearer of the Exalted One, the Able Awakened One, worthy of a cairn?

'At the thought, Ânanda:—"This is the cairn of that true hearer of the Exalted Able Awakened One," the hearts of many shall be made calm and happy; and since they there had calmed and satisfied their hearts they will be reborn after death, when the body has dissolved, in the happy realms of heaven. It is on account of this circumstance, Ânanda, that a true hearer of the Exalted One, the Able Awakened One, is worthy of a cairn.

'And on account of what circumstance, Ânanda, is a king of kings worthy of a cairn?

'At the thought, Ânanda:—"This is the cairn of that righteous king who ruled in righteousness," the hearts of many shall be made calm and happy; and since they there had calmed and satisfied their hearts they will be reborn after death, when the body has dissolved, in the happy realms of heaven. It is on account of this circumstance, Ânanda, that a king of kings is worthy of a cairn.

'These four, Ânanda, are the persons worthy of a cairn.'

13. 'Now the venerable Ânanda went into the Vihâra [2], and stood leaning against the lintel of the

---

[1] Pacceka-buddho. One who has attained to the supreme and perfect insight; but dies without proclaiming the truth to the world.

[2] The expression that Ânanda went 'into the Vihâra' at the end of a conversation represented as having taken place in the Sâla Grove,

door, and weeping at the thought :—'Alas! I remain
still but a learner, one who has yet to work out· his
own perfection [1]. And the Master is about to pass
away from me—he who is so kind!'

Now the Exalted One called the brethren, and
said :—'Where then, brethren, is Ânanda?'

'The venerable Ânanda, lord, has gone into the
Vihâra, and stands leaning against the lintel of the
door, and weeping at the thought :—"Alas! I remain
still but a learner, one who has yet to work out his
own perfection. And the Master is about to pass
away from me—he who is so kind!"'

And the Exalted One called a certain brother, and
said :—'Go now, brother, and call Ânanda in my name,
and say:—"Brother Ânanda, the Master calls for thee"'
[144].

'Even so, lord!' said that brother, in assent, to
the Exalted One. And he went up to the place where
the Exalted One was : and when he had come there,
he said to the venerable Ânanda :—'Brother Ânanda,
the Master calls for thee.'

'Very well, brother,' said the venerable Ananda,
in assent, to that brother. And he went up to the
place where the Exalted One was, and when he had
come there, he bowed down before the Exalted One,
and took his seat respectfully on one side.

14. Then the Exalted One said to the venerable
Ânanda, as he sat there by his side :—'Enough,
Ânanda! Do not let yourself be troubled; do not
weep! Have I not already, on former occasions,
told you that it is in the very nature of all things

---

would seem to point to the fact that this episode originally stood in
some other connexion. Buddhaghosa attempts to explain away the
discrepancy by saying that Vihâra here means Maṇḍala. As the
spot was the place for the performance of the communal ceremonies
of the clan there was most likely a Maṇḍala there, and there must,
from the context below, § 25, have been also some small closed-in
building, a hut or cottage. It is only this latter that could have been
called a Vihâra.

[1] Ânanda had entered the Noble Path, but had not yet reached the
end of it. He had not attained to Nirvana.

most near and dear unto us that we must divide ourselves from them, leave them, sever ourselves from
them? How, then, Ânanda, can this be possible—
whereas anything whatever born, brought into being,
and organized, contains within itself the inherent
necessity of dissolution—how, then, can this be possible, that such a being should not be dissolved? No
such condition can exist! For a long time, Ânanda,
have you been very near to me by acts of love, kind
and good, that never varies[1], and is beyond all
measure. For a long time, Ânanda, have you been
very near to me by words of love, kind and good, that
never varies, and is beyond all measure. For a long
time, Ânanda, have you been very near to me by
thoughts of love, kind and good, that never varies,
and is beyond all measure. You have done well,
Ânanda! Be earnest in effort, and you too shall soon
be free from the Intoxications—[of sensuality, and
individuality, and delusion, and ignorance.][2]!'

15. Then the Exalted One addressed the brethren,
and said:—'Whosoever, brethren, have been Able
Awakened Ones through the long ages of the past,
they also had servitors just as devoted to those Exalted
Ones as Ânanda has been to me.

'He is a clever man, brethren, is Ananda, and
wise[3]. He knows when it is the right time for the
brethren or for the sisters of the Order, for devout
men [145] and devout women, for a king, or for a king's
ministers, or for other teachers or for their disciples,
to come and visit the Tathâgata.

16. 'Brethren, there are these four wonderful and
marvellous qualities in Ânanda. Which are the four?

---

[1] A dvayena, which Buddhaghosa explains as not being that kind
of love which is now one thing and now another, or which varies in
the presence or the absence of the object loved.

[2] That is, you too shall become an Arahant, shall attain Nirvana in
this life.

[3] A word has here slipped out of the text, medhâvî should stand
before jânâti.

'If, brethren, a number of the brethren of the Order should come to visit Ânanda, they are filled with joy on beholding him ; and if Ânanda should then preach the truth to them, they are filled with joy at the discourse; while the company of brethren is ill at ease, brethren, when Ânanda is silent.

'If, brethren, a number of the sisters of the Order, . . . or of devout men, . . . or of devout women, should come to visit Ânanda, they are filled with joy on beholding him ; and if Ânanda should then preach the truth to them, they are filled with joy at the discourse; while the company of sisters is ill at ease, brethren, when Ânanda is silent.

'Brethren, there are these four wonderful and marvellous qualities in a king of kings. What are the four?

'If, brethren, a number of nobles, or brahmins, or heads of houses, or members of a religious order should come to visit a king of kings, they are filled with joy on beholding him; and if the king of kings should then speak, they are filled with joy at what is said; while they are ill at ease, brethren, when the king of kings is silent [146].

'Just so, brethren, are the four wonderful and marvellous qualities in Ânanda.

'If, brethren, a number of the brethren of the Order, or of the sisters of the Order, or of devout men, or of devout women, should come to visit Ânanda, they are filled with joy on beholding him ; and if Ânanda should then preach the truth to them, they are filled with joy at the discourse; while the company of brethren is ill at ease, brethren, when Ânanda is silent.

'Now these, brethren, are the four wonderful and marvellous qualities that are in Ânanda.'

---

17. When he had thus spoken,[1] the venerable Ânanda said to the Exalted One:—

---

[1] From here down to the end of section 18 is found also, nearly word for word, in the beginning of the Mahâ-Sudassana Suttanta, translated below.

'Let not the Exalted One die in this little wattle-and-daub town, in this town in the midst of the jungle, in this branch township[1]. For, lord, there are other great cities, such as Champâ, Râjagaha, Sâvatthi, Sâketa, Kosambi, and Benares. Let the Exalted One die in one of them. There there are many wealthy nobles and brahmins and heads of houses, believers in the Tathâgata, who will pay due honour to the remains of the Tathâgata[2].'

'Say not so, Ânanda! Say not so, Ânanda, that this is but a small wattle-and-daub town, a town in the midst of the jungle, a branch township.

18. 'Long ago, Ânanda, there was a king, by name Mahâ-Sudassana, a king of kings, a righteous man who ruled in righteousness, Lord of the four quarters of the earth, conqueror, the protector of his people, possessor of the seven royal treasures. This Kusinârâ, Ânanda, was the royal city of King Mahâ-Sudassana, under the name of Kusâvati, and on the east and on the west it was twelve leagues in length, and on the north and on the south it was seven leagues in breadth.

'That royal city Kusâvati, Ânanda, was mighty and prosperous [147] and full of people, crowded with men, and provided with all things for food. Just, Ânanda, as the royal city of the gods, Âlakamandâ by name, is mighty, prosperous, and full of people, crowded with the gods, and provided with all kinds of food, so.

---

[1] Kudda-nagarake ti patirûpake sambâdhe khuddakanagare. Uggangala-nagarake ti visama-nagarake (S. V, fol. thau) Kudda, if this explanation be right, seems to be merely an old and unusual form for kshudra, and the Burmese correction into khudda to be unnecessary: but I venture to think it is more likely to be = kudya, and to mean a wall built of mud and sticks, or what is called in India, of wattle and daub. When Buddhaghosa explains uggangala as 'lawless,' he is expressing his view that a town in the jungle is likely to be a heathen, pagan sort of place.

[2] With reference to Childers's note in his Dictionary on mahâsâlâ, with which every one must entirely agree, Buddhaghosa's explanation of the word will be interesting as a proof (if proof be needed) that the Ceylon scholars are not always trustworthy. He says:—Khattiyamahâsâlâ ti khattiya-mahâsârâ, sârapattâ mahakhattiyâ. Eso nayo sabbatha.

Ânanda, was the royal city Kusâvatî mighty and prosperous, full of people, crowded with men, and provided with all kinds of food.

'Both by day and by night, Ânanda, the royal city Kusâvatî resounded with the ten cries ; that is to say, the noise of elephants, and the noise of horses, and the noise of chariots ; the sounds of the drum, of the tabor, and of the lute ; the sound of singing, and the sounds of the cymbal and of the gong ; and lastly, with the cry :—" Eat, drink, and be merry !"'

19. Go now, Ânanda, and enter into Kusinârâ, and inform the Mallas of Kusinârâ, saying :—" This day, O Vâseṭṭhas, in the last watch of the night, the final passing away of the Tathâgata will take place. Be favourable herein, O Vâseṭṭhas, be favourable. Give no occasion to reproach yourselves hereafter, saying :— 'In our own village did the death of our Tathâgata take place, and we took not the opportunity of visiting the Tathâgata in his last hours.'"'

'Even so, lord,' said the venerable Ânanda, in assent, to the Exalted One; and he robed himself and taking his bowl, entered into Kusinârâ attended by another member of the order[1].

20. Now at that time the Mallas of Kusinârâ were assembled in the council hall on some [public] affair [2].

---

[1] Literally 'Put on his under-garment, and taking his uppergarment and his bowl, &c.' This sounds complicated; and why should he take his bowl ? The Wanderers when at their lodging places on their travels lived (naturally in that beautiful climate) in undress—with only one robe on, the one from the waist to the feet. When they set out for the village on a visit, or on any ceremonious occasion, they put on the second robe, and (just as a European often carries his great-coat on his arm) carried the third with them. At some convenient spot near the village they would put this also on, and enter—so to speak—in full canonicals. And the bowl belonged to, formed part of, their official costume. See J. I, 55 ; III, 379 ; Sum. I, 45, 186; and the note above on Ch. IV, § 37, p. 145.

[2] Kenaḱid eva karaṇîyena. Professor Pischel, in his edition of the Assalâyana Sutta (p. 1), prints this expression kenaḱi devakaraṇîyena, and translates it (p. 28), 'for some religious purpose.' It

And the venerable Ânanda went to the council hall of the Mallas of Kusinârâ; and when he had arrived there, he informed them, saying :—' This day, O Vâse-*tth*as, in the last watch of the night, the final passing away of the Tathâgata will take place. Be favourable herein, O Vâse*tth*as, be favourable. Give no occasion to reproach yourselves hereafter, saying :—" In our own village [148] did the death of our Tathâgata take place, and we took not the opportunity of visiting the Tathâgata in his last hours." '

21. And when they had heard this saying of the venerable Ânanda, the Mallas with their young men and maidens and their wives were grieved, and sad, and afflicted at heart. And some of them wept, dishevelling their hair, and stretched forth their arms and wept, fell prostrate on the ground, and rolled to and fro in anguish at the thought :—' Too soon will the Exalted One die! Too soon will the Happy One pass away! Full soon will the Light of the world vanish away!'

Then the Mallas, with their young men and maidens and their wives, being grieved, and sad, and afflicted at heart, went to the Sâla Grove of the Mallas, to the Upavattana, and to the place where the venerable Ânanda was.

22. Then the venerable Ânanda thought :—' If I allow the Mallas of Kusinârâ, one by one, to pay their respects to the Exalted One, the whole of the Mallas of Kusinârâ will not have been presented to the Exalted One until this night brightens up into the dawn. Let me, now, cause the Mallas of Kusinârâ to stand in groups, each family in a group, and so present them to the Exalted One, saying :—" Lord! a Malla of such and such a name, with his children, his wives, his retinue, and his friends, humbly bows down at the feet of the Exalted One." '

And the venerable Ânanda caused the Mallas of

___

seems to me that he has been misled by the commentary, which really presupposes the more correct division.

Kusinârâ to stand in groups, each family in a group, and so presented them to the Exalted One, and said :—
'Lord! a Malla of such and such a name, with his children, his wives, his retinue, and his friends, humbly bows down at the feet of the Exalted One.'

And after this manner the venerable Ânanda presented all the Mallas of Kusinârâ to the Exalted One in the first watch of the night.

23. Now at that time a Wanderer named Subhadda, who was not a believer, was dwelling at Kusinârâ. And the Wanderer Subhadda heard the news :—' This very day, they say, in the third watch of the night, will take place the final passing away of the Samana Gotama.'

[149] Then thought the Wanderer Subhadda :—'This have I heard from fellow Wanderers old and well stricken in years, teachers and disciples, when they said :—" Sometimes and full seldom do Tathâgatas appear in the world, the Able Awakened Ones." Yet this day, in the last watch of the night, the final passing away of the Samana Gotama will take place. Now a certain feeling of uncertainty has sprung up in my mind; and this faith have I in the Samana Gotama, that he, methinks, is able so to present the truth that I may get rid of this feeling of uncertainty.'

24. Then the Wanderer Subhadda went to the Sâla Grove of the Mallas, to the Upavattana of Kusinârâ, to the place where the venerable Ânanda was.

And when he had come there he said to the venerable Ânanda :—' Thus have I heard from fellow Wanderers, old and well stricken in years, teachers and disciples, when they said :—" Sometimes and full seldom do Tathâgatas appear in the world, the Able Awakened Ones." Yet this day, in the last watch of the night, the final passing away of the Samana Gotama will take place. Now a certain feeling of uncertainty has sprung up in my mind ; and this faith have I in the Samana Gotama, that he, methinks, is able so to present the truth that I may get rid of this feeling of uncertainty. O that I, even I, Ânanda, might be allowed to see the Samana Gotama!'

And when he had thus spoken the venerable Ânanda said to the Wanderer Subhadda :—'Enough! friend Subhadda. Trouble not the Tathâgata. The Exalted One is weary.'

And again the Wanderer Subhadda [made the same request in the same words, and received the same reply]: and the third time the Wanderer Subhadda [made the same request in the same words, and received the same reply]. [150]

25. Now the Exalted One overheard this conversation of the venerable Ânanda with the Wanderer Subhadda. And the Exalted One called the venerable Ânanda, and said :—' It is enough, Ânanda! Do not keep out Subhadda. Subhadda, Ânanda, may be allowed to see the Tathâgata. Whatever Subhadda may ask of me, he will ask from a desire for knowledge, and not to annoy me. And whatever I may say in answer to his questions, that he will quickly understand.'

Then the venerable Ânanda said to Subhadda, the Wanderer :—'Enter in, friend Subhadda; for the Exalted One gives you leave.'

26. Then Subhadda, the Wanderer, went in to the place where the Exalted One was, and saluted him courteously, and after exchanging with him the compliments of esteem and of civility, he took his seat on one side. And when he was thus seated, Subhadda, the Wanderer, said to the Exalted One :—' The leaders in religious life [1] who are heads of companies of

---

[1] Samana-brâhmanâ, which compound may possibly mean Samanas and Brâhmanas as it has usually been rendered, but I think not necessarily. Not one of those here specified were brahmins by birth, as is apparent from the Sumangala Vilâsinî on the Sâmañña-Phala Suttanta, §§ 3–7. Compare the use of Kshatriya-brahmano, ' a soldier priest,' a Kshatriya who offered sacrifice ; and of Brâhmano, absolutely, as an epithet of an Arahant. In the use of the word samana there seems to me to be a hopeless confusion between, a complete mingling of the meanings of, the two roots śram and śam (which, in Pâli, would both become sam). It connotes both asceticism

disciples and students, teachers of students, well
known, renowned, founders of schools of doctrine,
esteemed as good men by the multitude—to wit,
Pûra*n*a Kassapa, Makkhali of the cattle-pen, A*g*ita of
the garment of hair, Ka*kk*âyana of the Pakudha tree,
Sañ*g*aya the son of the Bela*tth*i slave-girl, and
Niga*nth*a of the Nâtha clan [151]—have they all,
according to their own assertion, thoroughly understood things? or have they not? or are there some
of them who have understood, and some who have
not?'

'Enough, Subhadda! Let this matter rest whether
they, according to their own assertion, have thoroughly
understood things, or whether they have not, or
whether some of them have understood and some
have not! The truth, Subhadda, will I teach you.
Listen well to that, and give ear attentively, and
I will speak!'

'Even so, lord!' said the Wanderer Subhadda, in
assent, to the Exalted One.

27. And the Exalted One spake:—'In whatsoever
doctrine and discipline, Subhadda, the Aryan eightfold
path is not found, neither in it is there found a man of
true saintliness of the first, or of the second, or of the
third, or of the fourth degree. And in whatsoever
doctrine and discipline, Subhadda, the Aryan eightfold
path is found, in it is found the man of true saintliness
of the first, and the second, and the third, and the
fourth degree[1]. Now in this doctrine and discipline,
Subhadda, is found the Aryan eightfold path, and in it

---

and inward peace, and might best be rendered 'devotee,' were it not
for the intellectual inferiority implied by that word in our language.
A Sama*n*a-brahmin should therefore mean a man of any birth, who by
his saintliness of life, by his renunciation of the world, and by his
reputation as a religious thinker, had acquired the position of a quasi-
brahmin and was looked up to by the people with as much respect as
they looked up to a brahmin by birth. Compare further my 'Buddhist
Birth Stories,' vol. I, p. 260; and see J. I, 57, 187; M. I, 285-6,
400; II, 54; A. I, 180; III, 228.

[1] On these degrees in the religious life, see M. I, 63; A. II, 238.
They are described in my 'Buddhism' (21st ed., pp. 108 foll.).

too, are found, Subhadda, the men of true saintliness
of all the four degrees.   Void are the systems of
other teachers—void of true saints.   And in this
one, Subhadda, may the brethren live the Life that's
Right, so that the world be not bereft of Arahants [1].

> ' But twenty-nine was I when I renounced
> The world, Subhadda, seeking after Good.
> For fifty years and one year more, Subhadda,
> Since I went out, a pilgrim have I been
> Through the wide realm of System and of Law—
> Outside of that no victory can be won! [2]

' Yea, not of the first, [152] nor of the third, nor of the
fourth degree.   Void are the systems of other teachers
—void of true saints.   But in this one, Subhadda, may
the brethren live the perfect life, that the world be not
bereft of Arahants.'

---

[1] Arahants are those who have reached Nirvana, the 'supreme
goal, the highest fruit' of the Aryan Eightfold Path.   To live 'the
Life that's Right' (sammâ) is to live in the Noble Path, each of the
eight divisions of which is to be sammâ, round, right and perfect,
normal and complete.   To live right (sammâ) is therefore to have :—
(1) Right views, free from superstition ; (2) right aims, high and worthy
of the intelligent and earnest man ; (3) right speech, kindly, open,
truthful ; (4) right conduct, in all concerns of life ; (5) right livelihood,
bringing hurt or danger to no living thing ; (6) right perseverance, in
all the other seven ; (7) right mindfulness, the watchful, active mind ;
(8) right contemplation, earnest thought on the deep mysteries of life.
In each of these the word right is sammâ, and the whole paragraph
being on the Aryan Path, the allusion is certainly to this central
doctrine of the Buddhist Dhamma.
Buddhaghosa says that bhikkhu sammâ viharati, who, having
himself entered the Aryan Path, leads his brother into it, and this is,
no doubt, good Buddhism.   But it is a practical application of the
text, a theological exegesis, and not a philological explanation.   Even
so it seems to lay the stress too much on 'bereft,' and too little on
' Arahants.'
[2] Literally ' There is no samana.'   See note on § 26.   I have
followed, though with some doubt, Childers's punctuation.   Buddhaghosa refers padesa-vatti to samano ; and ito, not to padesa, but
to magga, understood ; and it is quite possible that this is the correct
explanation.   On samâdhikâni see the comment at Jâtaka II, 383 :
Watters, 'On Yüan Chwâng,' II, 33, and Ed. Hardy, ' Buddhismus,'
p. 44.   Both Paññânanda and Samarasekhara render it as above.

28. And when he had thus spoken, Subhadda, the Wanderer, said to the Exalted One :—'Most excellent, lord, are the words of thy mouth, most excellent! Just as if a man were to set up that which is thrown down, or were to reveal that which is hidden away, or were to point out the right road to him who has gone astray, or were to bring a lamp into the darkness, so that those who have eyes can see external forms;—just even so, lord, has the truth been made known to me, in many a figure, by the Exalted One. And I, even I, betake myself, lord, to the Exalted One as my refuge, to the truth, and to the Order. I would fain be accepted as a probationer under the Exalted One, as a full member in his Order.'

29. 'Whosoever, Subhadda, has formerly been a follower of another doctrine, and thereafter desires to be received into the higher or the lower grade in this doctrine and discipline, he remains on probation for the space of four months; and at the end of the four months, the brethren, exalted in spirit, receive him into the lower or into the higher grade of the order. Nevertheless in this case I acknowledge the difference in persons.'

'If, lord, whosoever has formerly been a follower of another doctrine, and then desires to be received into the higher or the lower grade in this doctrine and discipline,—if, in that case, such a person remains on probation for the space of four months; and at the end of the four months, the brethren, exalted in spirit, receive him into the lower or into the higher grade of the Order—I too, then, will remain on probation for the space of four months; and at the end of the four months let the brethren, exalted in spirit, receive me into the lower or into the higher grade of the Order!'

But the Exalted One called the venerable Ânanda, and said :—'As it is, Ânanda, receive Subhadda into the Order!'

'Even so, lord!' said the venerable Ânanda, in assent, to the Exalted One.

30. And Subhadda, the Wanderer, said to the venerable Ânanda :—'Great is your gain, friend Ânanda, great is your good fortune, friend Ânanda, in that you all have been sprinkled with the sprinkling of discipleship in this brotherhood at the hands of the Master himself!'

[153] So Subhadda, the Wanderer, was received into the higher grade of the Order under the Exalted One; and from immediately after his ordination the venerable Subhadda remained alone and separate, earnest, zealous, and resolved. And ere long he attained to that supreme goal of the higher life[1], for the sake of which the clansmen go out from all and every household gain and comfort to become houseless wanderers—yea, that supreme goal did he, by himself, and while yet in this visible world, bring himself to the knowledge of, and continue to realize, and to see face to face! And he became conscious that birth was at an end, that the higher life had been fulfilled, that all that should be done had been accomplished, and that after this present life there would be no beyond!

So the venerable Subhadda became yet another among the Arahants; and he was the last disciple whom the Exalted One himself converted[2].

End of the Hiraññavatiya portion, being the
Fifth Portion for Recitation.

---

[1] That is, Nirvana. Compare Mangala Sutta 10, 11, and the Dhammapada, verses 180, 354, and above, Chap. I, § 7.

[2] Buddhaghosa says that the last five words in the text (the last twelve words in my translation) were added by the Theras who held the Council. On Subhadda's ordination he has the following interesting note :—'The Thera (that is, Ânanda), they say, took him on one side, poured water over his head from a water vessel, made him repeat the formula of meditation on the impermanency of the body (see my "Buddhist Birth Stories," p. 161), shaved off his hair and beard, clad him in the yellow robes, made him repeat the "Three Refuges," and led him back to the Exalted One. The Exalted One himself admitted him then into the higher rank of the brotherhood, and pointed out to

him a subject for meditation (kamma*tthâ*na). He accepted this, and walking up and down in a quiet part of the grove, he thought and meditated upon it, till overcoming the Evil Spirit, he had acquired Arahantship, and with it the discriminating knowledge of all the Scriptures (Pa*t*isambhidâ). Then, returning, he came and took his seat beside the Exalted One.'

According to this, no set ceremony for ordination (Saṅgha-kamma*m*), as laid down in the Vinaya, took place; and it is other-wise probable that no such ceremony was usual in the earliest days of Buddhism.

CHAPTER VI.

1. [**154**] Now the Exalted One addressed the venerable Ânanda, and said :—' It may be, Ânanda, that in some of you the thought may arise, " The word of the master is ended, we have no teacher more! " But it is not thus, Ananda, that you should regard it. The Truths, and the Rules of the Order, which I have set forth and laid down for you all, let them, after I am gone, be the Teacher to you.'

---

2. 'Ânanda! when I am gone address not one another in the way in which the brethren have heretofore addressed each other—with the epithet that is, of " Âvuso " (Friend). A younger brother may be addressed by an elder with his name, or his family name, or the title " Friend." But an elder should be addressed by a younger brother as "Sir" or as " Venerable Sir[1]."'

---

3. 'When I am gone, Ânanda, let the Order, if it should so wish, abolish all the lesser and minor precepts[2].'

4. 'When I am gone, Ânanda, let the higher penalty be imposed on brother Channa.'

'But what, lord, is the higher penalty?'

'Let Channa say whatever he may like, Ânanda, the

---

[1] **Bhante** or **âyasmâ**. This question has been fully discussed by Prof. Franke in the ' Journal of the Pâli Text Society,' 1908.

[2] According to tradition (trans. by Rhys Davids and Oldenberg, ' Vinaya Texts,' III, 377 foll.) the Order considered this matter shortly after the Buddha's death, and declined to avail themselves of this permission. As to what these lesser precepts were see Rhys Davids, ' Questions of King Milinda,' I, 202 foll.

brethren should neither speak to him, nor exhort him,
nor admonish him [1].'

---

5. Then the Exalted One addressed the brethren,
and said :—' It may be, brethren, that there may be
doubt or misgiving in the mind of some brother as to
the Buddha, or the doctrine, or the path, or the method[2].
Inquire, brethren, freely. Do not have to reproach
yourselves [155] afterwards with the thought :—" Our
teacher was face to face with us, and we could not
bring ourselves to inquire of the Exalted One when
we were face to face with him."'

And when he had thus spoken the brethren were
silent.

And again the second and the third time the Exalted
One addressed the brethren, and said :—' It may be,
brethren, that there may be doubt or misgiving in the
mind of some brother as to the Buddha, or the doctrine,
or the path, or the method. Inquire, brethren, freely.
Do not have to reproach yourselves afterwards with
the thought :—" Our teacher was face to face with us,
and we could not bring ourselves to inquire of the
Exalted One when we were face to face with him."'

And even the third time the brethren were silent.

Then the Exalted One addressed the brethren, and
said :—' It may be, brethren, that you put no questions
out of reverence for the teacher. Let one friend com-
municate to another.'

And when he had thus spoken the brethren were
silent.

6. And the venerable Ânanda said to the Exalted

---

[1] This brother is represented as an obstinate, perverse man ; so
destitute of the proper *esprit de corps* that he dared to take part with
the sisterhood, and against the brotherhood, in a dispute which had
arisen between them. But after the social penalty here referred to
had been duly imposed upon him, even his proud and independent
spirit was tamed ; he became humble ; his eyes were opened ; and he,
also, attained to the ' supreme goal ' of the Buddhist faith. (The
passages are shown in the index to ' Vinaya Texts.')

[2] Comp. D. II, 287.

One :—' How wonderful a thing is it, lord, and how
marvellous ! Verily, I believe that in this whole
assembly of the brethren there is not one brother who
has any doubt or misgiving as to the Buddha, or the
doctrine, or the path, or the method ! '

' It is out of the fullness of faith that thou hast
spoken, Ânanda ! But, Ânanda, the Tathâgata knows
for certain that in this whole assembly of the brethren
there is not one brother who has any doubt or misgiving as to the Buddha, or the doctrine, or the path,
or the method ! For even the most backward, Ânanda,
of all these five hundred brethren has become converted, is no longer liable to be born in a state of
suffering, and is assured of hereafter attaining to the
Enlightenment [of Arahantship] [1].

7. Then the Exalted One addressed the brethren,
and said :—[156] ' Behold now, brethren, I exhort you,
saying :—" Decay is inherent in all component things !
Work out your salvation with diligence ! " '
This was the last word of the Tathâgata !

8. Then the Exalted One entered into the first stage
of Rapture [2]. And rising out of the first stage he
passed into the second. And rising out of the second
he passed into the third. And rising out of the third
stage he passed into the fourth. And rising out of
the fourth stage of Rapture, he entered into the state
of mind to which the infinity of space is alone present [3].
And passing out of the mere consciousness of the
infinity of space he entered into the state of mind
to which the infinity of thought is alone present.
And passing out of the mere consciousness of the

---

[1] Compare above, Chap. II, § 7. By ' the most backward ' according to Buddhaghosa, the Exalted One referred to Ânanda, and he said
this to encourage him.
[2] The full text and an explanation of this Rapture will be found in
the translator's ' Buddhism,' pp. 174–6.
[3] Compare above, Chap. III, § 33, p. 119.

infinity of thought he entered into a state of mind to
which nothing at all was specially present. And
passing out of the consciousness of no special object
he fell into a state between consciousness and unconsciousness. And passing out of the state between
consciousness and unconsciousness he fell into a state
in which the consciousness both of sensations and of
ideas had wholly passed away[1].

Then the venerable Ânanda said to the venerable
Anuruddha :—' O my lord, O Anuruddha, the Exalted
One is dead!'

'Nay! brother Ânanda, the Exalted One is not
dead. He has entered into that state in which both
sensations and ideas have ceased to be!'

9. Then the Exalted One passing out of the state
in which both sensations and ideas have ceased to be,
entered into the state between consciousness and unconsciousness. And passing out of the state between
consciousness and unconsciousness he entered into
the state of mind to which nothing at all is specially
present. And passing out of the consciousness of no
special object he entered into the state of mind to
which the infinity of thought is alone present. And
passing out of the mere consciousness of the infinity
of thought he entered into the state of mind to which
the infinity of space is alone present. And passing
out of the mere consciousness of the infinity of space
he entered into the fourth stage of Rapture. And
passing out of the fourth stage he entered into the
third. And passing out of the third stage he entered
into the second. And passing out of the second he
entered into the first. And passing out of the first
stage of Rapture he entered into the second. And
passing out of the second stage he entered into the

---

[1] These nine states are called in the Milinda, p. 176, the nine
Anupubba-Vihâras. We have therefore, in this list, a technical,
scholastic, attempt to describe the series of ideas involved in what was
considered the highest thought. No one, of course, can have known
what actually did occur ; and the eight boundary lines between the
nine states are purely conjectural.

third. And passing out of the third stage he entered into the fourth stage of Rapture. And passing out of the last stage of Rapture he immediately expired.

---

10. When the Exalted One died there arose, at the moment of his passing out of existence, a mighty earthquake, terrible and awe-inspiring : and the thunders of heaven burst forth [157].

When the Exalted One died, Brahmâ Sahampati, at the moment of his passing away from existence, uttered this stanza :—

> They all, all beings that have life, shall lay
> Aside their complex form—that aggregation
> Of mental and material qualities,
> That gives them, or in heaven or on earth,
> Their fleeting individuality!
> E'en as the teacher—being such a one,
> Unequalled among all the men that are,
> Successor of the prophets of old time,
> Mighty by wisdom, and in insight clear—
>   Hath died! [1]'

When the Exalted One died, Sakka, the king of the gods, at the moment of his passing away from existence, uttered this stanza :—

> ' They're transient all, each being's parts and powers,
> Growth is their very nature, and decay.

---

[1] Brahmâ, the first cause, the highest result of Indian theological speculation, the one God of the Indian Pantheists, is represented as using expressions full of deep allusions to the most characteristic Buddhist doctrines. The Samussaya is the result of the temporary collocation of the 'aggregations' (khandha) of mental and material qualities which give to each being (bhûto, that is, man, animal, god, ghost, fairy, or what not) its outward and visible shape, its individuality. Loka is here not the world in our sense, but the 'locality' in the Buddhist universe which such an individual occupies until it is dissolved. (Comp. Chap. II, §§ 12, 26.) Brahmâ appears therefore as a veritable Doctor in theology, and I have been obliged to expand the translation to bring out all the meaning in the text.

They are produced, they are dissolved again :
To bring them all into subjection—that is bliss [1].

When the Exalted One died, the venerable Anuruddha, at the moment of his passing away from
existence, uttered these stanzas :—

'When he who from all craving want was free,
Who to Nirvana's tranquil state had reached,
When the great sage finished his span of life,
No gasping struggle vexed that steadfast heart !

All resolute, and with unshaken mind,
He calmly triumphed o'er the pain of death.
E'en as a bright flame dies away, so was
The last emancipation of his heart.'

---

[1] On this celebrated verse see below the Introduction to Mahâ-
Sudassana-Suttanta. It must be the original of the first verse in the
Chinese work, Fa Kheu Pi Hu (Beal, Dhammapada, p. 32), though it
is there so changed that every clause has lost its point.

'Whatever exists is without endurance,
And hence the terms 'flourishing' and 'decaying.'
A man is born, and then he dies.
Oh, the happiness of escaping from this condition!'

The very meaning which is here the most essential connotation of
sankhâra is lost in the phrase 'whatever exists.' By a misappre-
hension of the, no doubt, difficult word Dhamma, which, however,
never means 'term,' the second clause has lost its point. And by
a grammatical blunder the third clause in the Chinese confines the
doctrine, erroneously, to man. In a Chinese tale, called Ngan shih
niu, translated by Mr. Beal, in the 'Indian Antiquary' for May, 1880,
the following verses occur ; and they are possibly another reflection of
this stanza :—

'All things that exist are transitory,
They must of necessity perish and disappear ;
Though joined together, there must be separation ;
Where there is life there must be death.'

Compare the constantly repeated phrase :—'Whatsoever hath an
origin in that is inherent the necessity of dissolution.' The perception of this is emphatically called the Eye for the Truth ; and the
doctrine is referred to in the next section.

When the Exalted One died, the venerable Ânanda, at the moment of his passing away from existence, uttered this stanza :—

> 'Then was there terror!
> Then stood the hair on end!
> When he endowed with every grace—
> The supreme Buddha—died![1]'

[2]When the Exalted One died, of those of the brethren who were not yet free from the passions, some stretched out their arms and wept, and some fell headlong on the ground, rolling to and fro in anguish at the thought :—[158] 'Too soon has the Exalted One died! Too soon has the Happy One passed away! Too soon has the Light gone out in the world!'

But those of the brethren who were free from the passions [the Arahants] bore their grief collected and composed at the thought :—' Impermanent are all component things! How is it possible that [they should not be dissolved]?'

11. Then the venerable Anuruddha exhorted the brethren, and said :—' Enough, my brethren! Weep not, neither lament! Has not the Exalted One formerly declared this to us, that it is in the very nature of all things near and dear unto us, that we must divide ourselves from them, leave them, sever ourselves from them? How then, brethren, can this be possible—that whereas anything whatever born, brought into being, and organized, contains within itself the inherent necessity of dissolution—how then can this be possible that such a being should not be dissolved? No such

---

[1] In these four stanzas we seem to have the way in which the death of the Buddha would be regarded, as the early Buddhist thought, by four representative persons—the exalted God of the theologians ; the Jupiter of the multitude (allowing in the case of each of these for the change in character resulting from their conversion to Buddhism) ; the holy, thoughtful Arahant; and the loving, childlike disciple.

[2] Nearly = V, § 6; and below, VI, 19.

condition can exist! Even the spirits, brethren, will reproach us [1].'

'But of what kind of spirits, Sir, is the venerable Anuruddha thinking?'

'There are spirits, brother Ânanda, in the sky, but of worldly mind, who dishevel their hair and weep, and stretch forth their arms and weep, fall prostrate on the ground, and roll to and fro in anguish at the thought:—"Too soon has the Exalted One died! Too soon has the Light gone out in the world!"

'There are spirits, too, Ânanda, on the earth, and of worldly mind, who tear their hair and weep, and stretch forth their arms and weep, fall prostrate on the

---

[1] Ugghâyanti. I have followed the reading of my own MS., which is confirmed by the Sumangala Vilâsinî and the Mâlâlankara-vatthu. Vigghâyanti, which Childers reads, would be questionable Buddhism. The spirits do not become extinct; that is, not as a general rule, as would be implied by the absolute statement:—'Even the spirits, brethren, become extinct.' It is no doubt true that all spirits, from the lowest to the highest, from the most insignificant fairy to the God of theological speculation, are regarded as temporary. But when they cease to exist as gods or spirits (devatâ), they do not go out, they are not extinguished (vigghâyanti); they continue to exist in some other form. And though that other form would, from the European point of view, be a different being, as there would be no continuity of consciousness, no passage of a 'soul' from the one to the other; it would, from the Buddhist point of view, be the same being, as it would be the resultant effect of the same Karma. There would follow on the death of a devatâ, not extinction, but a trans-mutation of force, a transmigration of character, a passing on, an inheritance of Karma. Only in the exceedingly rare case of an anâgâmin, of which an instance will be found above Chap. II, § 7, could it be said that a spirit becomes extinct.

The expression 'of worldly mind,' here and above in V, 6, is in Pâli pathavi-saññiniyo, an ambiguous phrase which has only as yet been found in this connexion. The word is here opposed to vîtarâga, 'free from passion,' and I have therefore taken it in a spiritual sense. There is another possibility, viz. that it is used in an intellectual sense, 'making the idea of earth present to their mind'; and this would be in accordance with the use of saññi in the Kasina meditations, in which spirits, like men, were supposed to indulge; see Dîgha II, 108. But how easily, especially in Buddhism, the intellectual merges into the religious may be seen from such a Kasina phrase as marana-saññino, used at Mahâvamsa V, 159, of good men.

ground, and roll to and fro in anguish at the thought :—
" Too soon has the Blessed One died !   Too soon has
the Happy One passed away !   Too soon has the
Light gone out in the world !"

' But the spirits who are free from passion bear it,
calm and self-possessed, mindful of the saying which
begins :—" Impermanent indeed are all component
things.   How then is it possible [. . . that such a being
should not be dissolved] ? [1] " '

12. Now the venerable Anuruddha and the venerable
Ânanda spent the rest of that night in religious discourse.   Then the venerable Anuruddha said to the
venerable Ânanda :—' Go now, brother Ânanda, into
Kusinârâ and inform the Mallas of Kusinârâ, saying:—
" The Exalted One, O Vâse*tth*as, is dead ; do, then,
whatever seemeth to you fit ! " '

' Even so, lord !' said the venerable Ânanda, in
assent, to the venerable Anuruddha.   And having
robed himself early in the morning, he took his bowl,
and went into Kusinârâ with one of the brethren as
an attendant [159].

Now at that time the Mallas of Kusinârâ were
assembled in the council hall concerning that very
matter.

And the venerable Ânanda went to the council hall
of the Mallas of Kusinârâ ; and when he had arrived
there, he informed them, saying :—' The Blessed One,
O Vâse*tth*as, is dead ; do, then, whatever seemeth to
you fit !'

And when they had heard this saying of the venerable Ânanda, the Mallas, with their young men and
their maidens and their wives, were grieved, and sad,
and afflicted at heart.   And some of them wept,
dishevelling their hair, and some stretched forth their
arms and wept, and some fell prostrate on the ground,
and some reeled to and fro in anguish at the thought :—
' Too soon has the Exalted One died !   Too soon has

---

[1] See the end of the first paragraph of this section.

the Happy One passed away! Too soon has the
Light gone out in the world!'

13. Then the Mallas of Kusinârâ gave orders to
their attendants, saying :—'Gather together perfumes
and garlands, and all the music in Kusinârâ!'

And the Mallas of Kusinârâ took the perfumes and
garlands, and all the musical instruments, and five
hundred suits of apparel, and went to the Upavattana,
to the Sâla Grove of the Mallas, where the body of
the Exalted One lay. There they passed the day in
paying honour, reverence, respect, and homage to the
remains of the Exalted One with dancing, and hymns,
and music, and with garlands and perfumes ; and in
making canopies of their garments, and preparing
decoration wreaths to hang thereon [1].

Then the Mallas of Kusinârâ thought :—

'It is much too late to burn the body of the Exalted
One to-day. Let us now perform the cremation
to-morrow.' And in paying honour, reverence, respect,
and homage to the remains of the Exalted One with
dancing, and hymns, and music, and with garlands and
perfumes ; and in making canopies of their garments,
and preparing decoration wreaths to hang thereon,
they passed the second day too, and then the third day,
and the fourth, and the fifth, and the sixth day also.

14. Then on the seventh day the Mallas of Kusinârâ [160] thought :—

---

[1] The dress of the Mallas consisted probably of mere lengths of
muslin or cotton cloth ; and a suit of apparel consisted of two or, at
the outside, of three of these—one to wrap around the loins, one to
throw over the shoulders, and one to use as a turban. To make
a canopy on occasions of state they would join such pieces together ;
to make the canopy into a tent they would simply add walls of the
same material ; and the only decoration, as simple as it is beautiful,
would be wreaths of flowers, or single lotuses, hanging from the roof,
or stretched along the sides. Every civil servant travelling on duty
in remote districts in Ceylon has such a tent or canopy put up for him
by the peasantry.

'Let us carry the body of the Exalted One, by the south and outside, to a spot on the south, and outside of the city,—paying it honour, and reverence, and respect, and homage, with dance, and song, and music, with garlands and perfumes,—and there, to the south of the city, let us perform the cremation ceremony!'

And thereupon eight chieftains among the Mallas bathed their heads, and clad themselves in new garments with the intention of bearing the body of the Exalted One. But, behold, they could not lift it up!

Then the Mallas of Kusinârâ said to the venerable Anuruddha :—'What, lord, can be the reason, what can be the cause, that eight chieftains of the Mallas who have bathed their heads, and clad themselves in new garments with the intention of bearing the body of the Exalted One, are unable to lift it up?'

'It is because you, O Vâse*tth*as, have one purpose, and the spirits have another purpose.'

15. 'But what, lord, is the purpose of the spirits?'

'Your purpose, O Vâse*tth*as, is this :—Let us carry the body of the Exalted One, by the south and outside, to a spot on the south, and outside of the city,—paying it honour, and reverence, and respect, and homage, with dance, and song, and music, with garlands and perfumes,—and there, to the south of the city, let us perform the cremation ceremony. But the purpose of the spirits, Vâse*tth*as, is this :—Let us carry the body of the Exalted One by the north to the north of the city, and entering the city by the north gate, let us bring it through the midst of the city into the midst thereof. And going out again by the eastern gate,—paying honour, and reverence, and respect, and homage to the body of the Exalted One, with heavenly dance, and song, and music, and garlands, and perfumes,—let us carry it to the shrine of the Mallas called Maku*t*a-bandhana, to the east of the city, and there let us perform the cremation ceremony.'

'Even according to the purpose of the spirits, so, lord, let it be.'

16. Then immediately all Kusinârâ down even to
the dust bins and rubbish heaps became strewn knee-
deep with Mandârava flowers from heaven! and while
both the spirits from the skies, and the Mallas of
Kusinârâ upon earth, paid honour, and reverence, and
respect, and homage to the body of the Exalted One.
with dance, and song, and music, [161] with garlands,
and with perfumes, they carried the body by the north
to the north of the city; and entering the city by the
north gate they carried it through the midst of the
city into the midst thereof; and going out again by
the eastern gate they carried it to the shrine of the
Mallas, called Makuta-bandhana; and there, to the
east of the city, they laid down the body of the Exalted
One[1].

17[2]. Then the Mallas of Kusinârâ said to the venerable Ânanda :—'What should be done, lord, with the
remains of the Tathâgata?'

'As men treat the remains of a king of kings,
so, Vâsetthas, should they treat the remains of a
Tathâgata.'

'And how, lord, do they treat the remains of a king
of kings?'

'They wrap the body of a king of kings, Vâsetthas,
in a new cloth. When that is done they wrap it in
carded cotton wool. When that is done they wrap it
in a new cloth,—and so on till they have wrapped the
body in five hundred successive layers of both kinds.
Then they place the body in an oil vessel of iron,
and cover that close up with another oil vessel of iron.
They then build a funeral pyre of all kinds of perfumes,

---

[1] The point of this interesting legend is that the inhabitants of an
Indian village of that time would have considered it a desecration or
pollution to bring a dead body into or through their village.
Authorities differ as to the direction in which it should be taken to
avoid this. The old custom, according to Caland (p. 23) was to take
it to the East or the West. Later priestly books (Manu, for instance,
V, 92) say to the North. The Mallas wanted to go to the South.
The remedy proposed by the spirits who are shocked at this im-
propriety, is more shocking still.

[2] Compare Chap. V, §§ 11, 12.

and burn the body of the king of kings. And then at the four cross roads they erect a cairn to the king of kings. This, Vâse*tth*as, is the way in which they treat the remains of a king of kings.

'And as they treat the remains of a king of kings, so, Vâse*tth*as, should they treat the remains of the Tathâgata. At the four cross roads a cairn should be erected to the Tathâgata. And whosoever shall there place garlands or perfumes or paint, or make salutation there, or become in its presence calm in heart—that shall long be to them for a profit and a joy.'

18. Therefore the Mallas gave orders to their attendants, saying :—' Gather together all the carded cotton wool of the Mallas!'

Then the Mallas of Kusinârâ wrapped the body of the Exalted One in a new cloth. And when that was done, they wrapped it in carded cotton wool. And when that was done, they wrapped it in a new cloth, [162]—and so on till they had wrapped the body of the Exalted One in five hundred layers of both kinds. And then they placed the body in an oil vessel of iron, and covered that close up with another oil vessel of iron. And then they built a funeral pyre of all kinds of perfumes, and upon it they placed the body of the Exalted One.

19. Now at that time the venerable Mahâ Kassapa was journeying along the high road from Pâvâ to Kusinârâ with a great company of the brethren, with about five hundred of the brethren. And the venerable Mahâ Kassapa left the high road, and sat himself down at the foot of a certain tree.

Just at that time a certain naked ascetic [1] who had picked up a Mandârava flower in Kusinârâ was coming along the high road to Pâvâ.

Now the venerable Mahâ Kassapa saw the naked ascetic coming in the distance ; and when he had seen him he said to that naked ascetic :—

[1] An Âjîvaka. See the note above at Vol. I, p. 71.

'O friend! surely thou knowest our Master?'

'Yea, friend! I know him. This day the Samana Gotama has been dead a week! That is how I obtained this Mandârava flower.'

On that of those of the brethren who were not yet free from the passions, some stretched out their arms and wept, and some fell headlong on the ground, and some reeled to and fro in anguish at the thought:—'Too soon has the Exalted One died! Too soon has the Happy One passed away! Too soon has the Light gone out in the world!'

But those of the brethren who were free from the passions [the Arahants] bore their grief self-possessed and composed at the thought :—'Impermanent are all component things! How is it possible that [they should not be dissolved]?'

----

20. Now at that time a brother named Subhadda, who had been received into the Order in his old age, was seated in that company [1].

And Subhadda the recruit in his old age said to those brethren :—'Enough, sirs! Weep not, neither lament! We are well rid of the great Samana. We used to be annoyed by being told:—"This beseems you, this beseems you not." But now we shall be able to do whatever we like; and what we do not like, that we shall not have to do!'

But the venerable Mahâ Kassapa exhorted the brethren :—'Enough, my brethren! Weep not, neither lament! [163] Has not the Exalted One formerly declared this, that it is in the very nature of all things near and dear unto us that we must divide ourselves

----

[1] At p. xxvi of the Introduction to his edition of the Vinaya, Prof. Oldenberg identifies this Subhadda with Subhadda the last convert, mentioned above at the end of Chap. V. They are different persons; the last convert being represented as a man of high character, incapable of the conduct here ascribed to this Subhadda. The last convert was a brahmin, traditionally supposed to be younger brother to Aññâ Kondañña, the first convert; this Subhadda had been a barber in the village Âtumâ.

from them, leave them, sever ourselves from them ?
How then, brethren, can this be possible—whereas
anything whatever born, brought into being, and
organized contains within itself the inherent necessity
of dissolution—how then can this be possible that such
a being should not be dissolved ? No such condition
can exist ! '

___

21. Now just at that time four chieftains of the
Mallas had bathed their heads and clad themselves in
new garments with the intention of setting on fire the
funeral pyre of the Exalted One. But, behold, they
were unable to set it alight!

Then the Mallas of Kusinârâ said to the venerable
Anuruddha :—' What, lord, can be the reason, and
what the cause [of this] ? '

' The purpose of the spirits, O Vâse*tth*as, is
different.'

' But what, sir, is the purpose of the spirits ? '

' The purpose of the spirits, O Vâse*tth*as, is this :—
That venerable brother Mahâ Kassapa is now journeying along the way from Pâvâ to Kusinârâ with a great
company of the brethren, with five hundred brethren.
The funeral pyre of the Exalted One shall not catch
fire until the venerable Mahâ Kassapa shall have been
able reverently to salute the feet of the Exalted One.'

' Even according to the purpose of the spirits so, sir,
let it be !'

22. Then the venerable Mahâ Kassapa went on to
Maku*t*a-bandhana of Kusinârâ, to the shrine of the
Mallas, to the place where the funeral pyre of the
Exalted One was. And when he had come up to it
he arranged his robe on one shoulder ; and after bowing down with clasped hands, he thrice walked
reverently round the pyre, and then, uncovering the
feet, he bowed down in reverence at the feet of the
Exalted One.

And those five hundred brethren arranged their
robes on one shoulder ; and bowing down with clasped

hands, they thrice walked reverently round the pyre, and then bowed down in reverence at the feet of the Exalted One [**164**].

And when the homage of the venerable Mahâ Kassapa and of those five hundred brethren was ended, the funeral pyre of the Exalted One caught fire of itself [1].

23. Now as the body of the Exalted One burned itself away, from the skin and the integument, and the flesh, and the nerves, and the fluid of the joints, neither soot nor ash was seen. Only the bones remained behind. Just as one sees no soot or ash when ghee or oil is burned; so, as the body of the Exalted One burned itself away, from the skin and the integument, and the flesh, and the nerves, and the fluid of the joints, neither soot nor ash was seen. Only the bones remained behind. And of those five hundred pieces of raiment the very innermost and outermost were both consumed.

And when the body of the Exalted One had been burnt up, there came down streams of water from the sky and extinguished the funeral pyre of the Exalted One; and there burst forth streams of water from the storehouse of the waters [beneath the earth], and extinguished the funeral pyre of the Exalted One. The Mallas of Kusinârâ also brought water scented

---

[1] It is possible that we have here the survival of some ancient custom. Spence Hardy appropriately refers to a ceremony among Jews (of what place or time is not mentioned) in the following terms:— 'Just before a Jew is taken out of the house to be buried, the relatives and acquaintances of the departed stand round the coffin; when the feet are uncovered; and each in rotation lays hold of the great toes, and begs pardon for any offence given to the deceased, and requests a favourable mention of them in the next world' ('Manual of Buddhism,' p. 348).

The Buddhist bhikkhus in Siam and the great majority of those in Ceylon (the adherents of the Siyam-samâgama) always keep one shoulder uncovered. It is evident that the bhikkhus in Burma and those in Ceylon, who belong to the Amara-pura-samâgama, are more in accordance with ancient custom in wearing the robe ordinarily over both shoulders.

with all kinds of perfumes, and extinguished the funeral pyre of the Exalted One [1].

Then the Mallas of Kusinârâ surrounded the bones of the Exalted One in their council hall with a lattice work of spears, and with a rampart of bows; and there for seven days they paid honour, and reverence, and respect, and homage to them with dance, and song, and music, and with garlands and perfumes.

24. Now the king of Magadha, Ajâtasattu, the son of the queen of the Videha clan, heard the news that the Exalted One had died at Kusinârâ.

Then the king of Magadha, Ajâtasattu, the son of the queen of the Videha clan, sent a messenger to the Mallas, saying,—' The Exalted One was a Kshatriya and so am I.   I am worthy to receive a portion of the relics of the Exalted One.   Over the remains of the Exalted One will I put up a sacred cairn, and in their honour will I celebrate a feast!'

And the Licchavis of Vesâlî heard the news that the Exalted One had died at Kusinârâ.   And the Licchavis of Vesâlî sent a messenger to the Mallas, saying:—'The Exalted One was a Kshatriya and so are we [165]. We are worthy to receive a portion of the relics of the Exalted One.   Over the remains of the Exalted One will we put up a sacred cairn, and in their honour will we celebrate a feast!'

And the Sâkiyas of Kapila-vatthu heard the news that the Exalted One had died at Kusinârâ.   And the

[1] There is something very quaint in the way in which the faithful Mallas are here represented as bringing coals to Newcastle.   The 'storehouse of the waters' is in Pâli udaka-sâlâ, on which Buddhaghosa has two theories: first, that the Sâla trees around shed down a miraculous rain from their trunks and branches and leaves; and next, that the waters burst up from the earth and became as it were a diadem of crystal round the pyre.   On the belief that water thus burst up miraculously through the earth, see 'Buddhist Birth Stories,' pp. 64, 67.   If the reading be correct it is scarcely possible that sâlâ can here have anything to do with Sâla trees; but the other interpretation is open to the objections that sâlâ means an open hall rather than a storehouse, and that the belief in a 'storehouse of water' has not, as yet, been found elsewhere.

Sâkiyas of Kapila-vatthu sent a messenger to the Mallas, saying :—'The Exalted One was the pride of our race. We are worthy to receive a portion of the relics of the Exalted One. Over the remains of the Exalted One will we put up a sacred cairn, and in their honour will we celebrate a feast!'

And the Bulis of Allakappa heard the news that the Exalted One had died at Kusinârâ. And the Bulis of Allakappa sent a messenger to the Mallas, saying:—'The Exalted One was a Kshatriya and so are we. We are worthy to receive a portion of the relics of the Exalted One. Over the remains of the Exalted One will we put up a sacred cairn, and in their honour will we celebrate a feast!'

And the Koliyas of Râmagâma heard the news that the Exalted One had died at Kusinârâ. And the Koliyas of Râmagâma sent a messenger to the Mallas, saying:—'The Exalted One was a Kshatriya and so are we. We are worthy to receive a portion of the relics of the Exalted One. Over the remains of the Exalted One will we put up a sacred cairn, and in their honour will we celebrate a feast!'

And the brahmin of Vethadîpa heard the news that the Exalted One had died at Kusinârâ. And the brahmin of Vethadîpa sent a messenger to the Mallas, saying:—'The Exalted One was a Kshatriya, and I am a brahmin. I am worthy to receive a portion of the relics of the Exalted One. Over the remains of the Exalted One will I put up a sacred cairn, and in their honour will I celebrate a feast!'

And the Mallas of Pâvâ heard the news that the Exalted One had died at Kusinârâ.

Then the Mallas of Pâvâ sent a messenger to the Mallas, saying :—'The Exalted One was a Kshatriya and so are we. We are worthy to receive a portion of the relics of the Exalted One. Over the remains of the Exalted One will we put up a sacred cairn, and in their honour will we celebrate a feast!'

25. When they heard these things the Mallas of Kusinârâ spoke to the assembled crowds, saying :— [166] 'The Exalted One died in our village domain. We will not give away any part of the remains of the Exalted One!'

When they had thus spoken, Dona the brahmin addressed the assembled crowds, and said :—

'Hear, gracious sirs, one single word from me.
Forbearance was our Buddha wont to teach.
Unseemly is it that over the division
Of the remains of him who was the best of beings
Strife should arise, and wounds, and war!
Let us all, sirs, with one accord unite
In friendly harmony to make eight portions.
Wide spread let cairns spring up in every land
That in the Light of the world mankind may trust!'

'Do thou then, O brahmin, thyself divide the remains of the Exalted One equally into eight parts, with fair division[1].'

'Be it so, sirs!' said Dona the brahmin, in assent, to the assembled brethren. And he divided the remains of the Exalted One equally into eight parts, with fair division. And he said to them :—'Give me, sirs, this vessel, and I will set up over it a sacred cairn, and in its honour will I establish a feast.'

And they gave the vessel to Dona the brahmin.

26. And the Moriyas of Pipphalivana heard the news that the Exalted One had died at Kusinârâ.

Then the Moriyas of Pipphalivana sent a messenger to the Mallas, saying :—'The Exalted One was a Kshatriya and so are we. We are worthy to receive a portion of the relics of the Exalted One. Over the remains of the Exalted One will we put up a sacred cairn, and in their honour will we celebrate a feast!'

And when they heard the answer, saying :—'There is

---

[1] Here again the commentator expands and adds to the comparatively simple version of the text.

no portion of the remains of the Exalted One left over. The remains of the Exalted One are all distributed,' then they took away the embers.

---

27. So the king of Magadha, Ajâtasattu, the son of the queen of the Videha clan, made a cairn in Râjagaha over the remains of the Exalted One, and celebrated a feast [167].

And the Licchavis of Vesâli made a cairn in Vesâli over the remains of the Exalted One, and celebrated a feast.

And the Sâkiyas of Kapila-vatthu made a cairn in Kapila-vatthu over the remains of the Exalted One, and celebrated a feast.

And the Bulis of Allakappa made a cairn in Allakappa over the remains of the Exalted One, and celebrated a feast.

And the Koliyas of Râmagâma made a cairn in Râmagâma over the remains of the Exalted One, and celebrated a feast.

And Vethadîpaka the brahmin made a cairn in Vethadîpa over the remains of the Exalted One, and celebrated a feast.

And the Mallas of Pâvâ made a cairn in Pâvâ over the remains of the Exalted One, and celebrated a feast.

And the Mallas of Kusinârâ made a cairn in Kusinârâ over the remains of the Exalted One, and celebrated a feast.

And Dona the brahmin made a cairn over the vessel [in which the remains had been collected] and celebrated a feast.

And the Moriyas of Pipphalivana made a cairn over the embers, and celebrated a feast.

Thus were there eight cairns (Thupas) for the remains, and one for the vessel, and one for the embers. This was how it used to be [1].

---

[1] Here closes Buddhaghosa's long and edifying commentary. He has no note on the following verses, which he says were added by

[28. Eight measures of relics there were of him of
the far-seeing eye,
Of the best of the best of men.   In India seven are
worshipped,
And one measure in Râmagâma, by the kings of the
serpent race.
One tooth, too, is honoured in heaven, and one in
Gandhâra's city,
One in the Kâlinga realm, and one more by the
Nâga race.
Through their glory the bountiful earth is made
bright with offerings painless—
For with such are the Great Teacher's relics best
honoured by those who are honoured,
By gods and by Nâgas and kings, yea, thus by the
noblest of humans—
Bow down with clasped hands!
Hard, hard is a Buddha to meet with through
hundreds of ages!]

End of the Book of the Great Decease.

Theras in Ceylon. The additional verse found in the Phayre MS.
was in the same way probably added in Burma.

INTRODUCTION

TO THE

MAHÂ-SUDASSANA-SUTTANTA.

THIS Suttanta is an expansion of the conversation recorded in the Book of the Great Decease (above, Ch. V, § 17).

The same legend recurs as the Mahâ-Sudassana Jâtaka, No. 95 in Mr. Fausböll's edition. As the latter differs in several important particulars from our Suttanta, it is probably not taken directly from it, but is merely derived from the same source. To facilitate comparison between the two I add here a translation of the Jâtaka.

The part enclosed in square brackets [ ] is the so-called Story of the Present: and the whole was probably written in Ceylon in the fifth century of our era. There is every reason to believe, for the reasons given in my 'Buddhist India' (pp. 201–7), that the stories themselves belong to a very early period in the history of Buddhism and are, many of them, older even than Buddhism. We may be sure that if this particular story had been abstracted by the author of the commentary from our Suttanta, he would not have ventured to introduce such serious changes into what he regarded as sacred writ.

MAHÂ-SUDASSANA JÂTAKA.

['How transient are all component things.' This the Master told when lying on his death-couch, concerning that word of Ânanda the Thera, when he said:—'Do not, O Exalted One, die in this little town,' and so on.

When the Tathâgata was at the Jetavana [1] he thought:—

---

[1] It is not easy with our present materials to reconcile the apparently conflicting statements with regard to the Buddha's last journey. According to the Mâlâlankâra-vatthu this refers here to a residence at the Jetavana, which took place between the end of § 23 in Chap. II in the Book of the Great Decease, and the beginning of § 24.

Mr. Fausböll, by his punctuation, includes these words in the following thought ascribed to the Exalted One, but I think they only describe the time at which the thought is supposed to have arisen.

'The Thera Sâriputta, who was born at Nâlagâma, has died, on the day of the full moon in the month of Kattika, in the chamber in which he had been born [1]; and Mahâ-Moggallâna in the latter, the dark half of that same month. As my two chief disciples are thus dead, I too will pass away at Kusinârâ.' Thereupon he proceeded straight on to that place, and lay down on the Uttarasîsaka couch, between the twin Sâla trees, never to rise again.

Then the venerable Ânanda besought him, saying:—'Let not the Exalted One die in this little township, in this little town in the jungle, in this branch township. Let the Exalted One die in one of the other great cities, such as Râjagaha, and the rest!'

But the Master answered:—' Say not, Ânanda, that this is a little township, a little town in the jungle, a branch township. I was dwelling formerly in this town at the time when I was Sudassana, the king of kings; and then it was a great city, surrounded by a jewelled rampart, twelve leagues in length!'

And at the request of the Thera, he, telling the tale, uttered the Mahâ-Sudassana-Sutta [2].]

Now on that occasion when Queen Subhaddâ saw Mahâ-Sudassana when he had come down out of the Palace of Righteousness, and was lying down, not far off, on the appropriate couch, spread out in the grove of the seven kinds of gems, and when she said:—' Thine, O king, are these four and eighty thousand cities, of which the chief is the royal city of Kusâvatî. Set thy heart on these';—

Then replied Mahâ-Sudassana: 'Speak not thus, O queen! but exhort me rather, saying:—" Cast away desire for these, long not after them [3]."'

---

[1] The text reads ' at Varaka.' But this is a mistake. The word which has puzzled Mr. Fausböll is ovaraka. The modern name of the village, afterwards the site of the famous Buddhist university of Nâlandâ, is Baragaon. The full-moon day in Kattika is the first of December. An account of the death of Sâriputta will be found in the Mâlâlankâra-vatthu (Bigandet, 'Legend,' &c., 3rd ed., II, 1–25), and of the murder of Moggallâna by the Niganthas in the Dhammapada commentary (Fausböll, p. 298 seq.), of which Spence Hardy's account ('Manual of Buddhism,' p. 338) is nearly a translation; and Bigandet's account (loc. cit., pp. 25–7) is an abridgement.

[2] In the earliest description of this conversation (above, 'Book of the Great Decease,' V, 17) there is no mention of this. But it is inserted most incongruously in the present Suttanta.

[3] Both these speeches are different from those given on the same occasion in the Suttanta below.

And when she asked:—'.Why so, O king?' 'To-day my time is come, and I shall die!' was his reply[1].

Then the weeping queen, wiping her eyes, brought herself with difficulty and distress to address him accordingly. And having spoken, she wept, and lamented; and the other four and eighty thousand women wept too, and lamented; and of the attendant courtiers not one could restrain himself, but all also wept.

But the Bodisat stopped them all, saying:—'Enough, my friends! Be still!' And he exhorted the queen, saying:— 'Neither do thou, O queen, weep: neither do thou lament. For down even unto a grain of sesamum fruit there is no such thing as a compound which is permanent! All are transient, all have the inherent quality of dissolution!'

And when he had so said, he further uttered this stanza:—

> 'How transient are all component things!
> Growth is their nature and decay:
> They are produced, they are dissolved again:
> To bring them into full subjection, that is bliss[2].'

[In these verses the words 'How transient are all component things!' mean 'Dear lady Subhaddâ, wheresoever and by whatsoever causes made or come together, compounds[3],—that is, all those things which possess the essential constituents [whether material or mental] of existing things[4],—all these compounds are impermanence itself. For of these form[5] is impermanent, reason[6] is impermanent, the [mental] eye[7] is impermanent, and qualities[8] are impermanent. And whatever treasure there be, whether conscious or unconscious, that is transitory. Understand therefore "How transient are all component things!"

'And why? "Growth is their nature and decay." These, all, have the inherent quality of coming into [individual] existence, and have also the inherent quality of growing old; or [in other words] their very nature is to come into existence and to be broken up. Therefore should it be understood that they are impermanent.

'And since they are impermanent, when "they are produced, they are dissolved again." Having come into existence,

---

[1] This question and answer are not in the Suttanta.

[2] All this is omitted in the Suttanta. It is true the verse occurs there, but it is placed in the mouth of the Teacher, after the account of Mahâ-Sudassana's death.

[3] Sankhârâ.   [4] Khandâyatanâdayo.   [5] Rûpam.
[6] Viññânam.   [7] Cakkhum.   [8] Dhammâ.

having reached a state [1], they are surely dissolved. For all these things come into existence, taking an individual form; and are dissolved, being broken up. To them as soon as there is birth, there is what is called a state; as soon as there is a state, there is what is called disintegration [2]. For to the unborn there is no such thing as state, and there is no such thing as a state which is without disintegration. Thus are all compounds, having attained to the three characteristic marks [of impermanency, pain, and want of any abiding principle], subject, in this way and in that way, to dissolution. All these component things therefore, without exception, are impermanent, momentary, despicable, unstable, disintegrating, trembling, quaking, unlasting, sure to depart [3], only for a time [4], and without substance; as temporary as a phantom, as the mirage, or as foam!

' How then in these, dear lady Subhaddâ, can you feel any sign of satisfaction? Understand rather than "to bring them into subjection, that is bliss." For to bring them into subjection, since it involves mastery over the whole circle of transmigration, is the same as Nirvana. That and this are one [5]. And there is no other bliss than that.']

And when Mahâ-Sudassana had thus brought his discourse to a point with the ambrosial great Nirvana, and had made exhortation also to the rest of the great multitude, saying:— ' Give gifts! Observe the precepts! Keep the sacred days [6]!' he became an inheritor of the world of the gods.

[When the Master had concluded this lesson in the truth, he summed up the Jâtaka, saying:— ' She who was then Subhaddâ the queen was the mother of Râhula, the great adviser was Râhula, the rest of the retinue the Buddha's retinue, and Mahâ-Sudassana I myself.']

The word translated ' component things ' or ' compounds ' is sankhârâ, literally confections, from kar, ' to make,' and sam, ' together.' It is a word very frequently used in Buddhist writings, and a word consequently of many different connotations; and there is, of course, no exactly corresponding word

---

[1] Thiti.   [2] Bhango.
[3] Pâyâtâ, literally ' departed.' The forms payâti and payâto, given by Childers, should be corrected into pâyâti and pâyâto.
[4] Tâvakâlika. See Jâtaka I, 121, where the word is used of a cart let out on hire for a time only.
[5] Tad ev ekam ekam, which is not altogether without ambiguity.
[6] This paragraph, too, is omitted in the Suttanta.

in English. 'Production' would often be very nearly correct, although it fails entirely to give the force of the preposition sam; but a greater objection to that word is the fact that it is generally used, not of things that have come into being of themselves, but of things that have been produced by some one else. It suggests, if it does not imply, a producer; which is contrary to the whole spirit of the Buddhist passages in which the word saṅkhârâ occurs. In this important respect the word 'compound' is a much more accurate translation, though it lays somewhat too much stress on the sam.

The term Confections (to coin a rendering) is sometimes used to denote all things which have been brought together, made up, by pre-existing causes; phenomena in general. In this sense it includes, as the commentator here points out, all those material or mental qualities which unite to form an individual, a separate thing or being, whether conscious or unconscious.

It is more usually used, (with special reference to their origin from pre-existing causes, and with allusion to the wider meanings just above explained), of the mental confections only, the mental constituents, of all sentient beings generally, or of man alone. In this sense it forms by itself one of the five classes or aggregates (khandha) into which the material and mental qualities of each separate individual are divided in Buddhist writings—the class of dispositions, capabilities, and all that goes together to make what we call character. This class has naturally enough been again divided and subdivided; and a full list of the Confections in this sense, as now acknowledged by orthodox Buddhists, will be found in my manual 'Buddhism' (pp. 91, 92). At the time when the Five Nikâyas reached their present form, no such elaborate list of Confections in detail seems to have been made; but the general sense of the word was, as is quite clear from the passages in which it occurs, the idea which these details together convey. It is this second and more usual meaning of the term which is more especially emphasized in the concluding verse of the above stanza.

Turning now to the Suttanta itself, we find that the portion of the legend omitted in the Jâtaka throws an unexpected light upon the tale; for it commences with a long description of the riches and glory of Mahâ-Sudassana, and reveals in its details the instructive fact that the legend is nothing more nor less than a spiritualized sun-myth.

It cannot be disputed that the sun-myth theory has become greatly discredited, and with reason, by having been used too

carelessly and freely as an explanation of religious legends
of different times and countries which have really no historical
connexion with the earlier awe and reverence inspired by the
sun. The very mention of the word sun-myth is apt to call
forth a smile of incredulity, and the indubitable truth which
s the basis of the theory has not sufficed to protect it from
the shafts of ridicule. The 'Book of the Great King of Glory'
seems to afford a useful example both of the extent to which
the theory may be accepted, and of the limitations under
which it should always be applied.

It must at once be admitted that whether the whole story
is based on a sun-story, or whether certain parts or details
of it are derived from things first spoken about the sun, or not,
it is still essentially Buddhistic. A large proportion of its
contents has nothing at all to do with the worship of the sun;
and even that which has, had not, in the mind of the author,
when the book was put together. Whether indebted to a
sun-myth or not, it is therefore perfectly true and valid evidence
of the religious belief of the people among whom it was
current; and no more shows that the Buddhists were unconscious sun-worshippers than the story of Samson, under
any theory of its possible origin, would prove the same of
the Jews.

What we really have is a kind of wonderful fairy tale,
a gorgeous poem, in which an attempt is made to describe in
set terms the greatest possible glory and majesty of the
greatest possible king, in order to show that all is vanity, save
only righteousness—just such a poem as a Jewish prophet
might have written of Solomon in all his glory. It would
have been most strange, perhaps impossible, for the author
to refrain from using the language of the only poets he knew,
who had used their boldly figurative language in an attempt
to describe the appearance of the sun.

To trace back all the rhetorical phrases of our Sutta to their
earliest appearance in the Vedic hymns would be an interesting task of historical philology, though it would throw more
light upon Buddhist forms of speech than upon Buddhist forms
of belief. In M. Senart's valuable work, 'La Légende du
Bouddha,' he has already done this with regard to the seven
treasures (mentioned in the early part of the Suttanta) on the
basis of the corresponding passage in the later Buddhist
Sanskrit poem called the Lalita Vistara. The description
of the royal city and of its wondrous Palace of Righteousness
has been probably originated by the author, though on the
same lines; and it reminds one irresistibly, in many of its
expressions, of the similar, but simpler and more beautiful

poem in which a Jewish author, some three or four centuries afterwards, described the heavenly Jerusalem.

When the Northern Buddhists, long afterwards, had smothered the simple teaching of the founder of their religion under the subtleties of theological and metaphysical speculation, and had forgotten all about the Aryan Path, their goal was no longer a change of heart in the Arahantship to be reached on earth, but a life of happiness, under a change of outward condition, in a heaven of bliss beyond the skies. One of the most popular books among the Buddhists of China and Japan is a description of this heavenly paradise of theirs, called the Sukhavâtî-vyûha, the 'Book of the Happy Country.' It is instructive to find that several of the expressions used are word for word the same as the corresponding phrases in our much older 'Book of the Great King of Glory.'

Incidentally the details given in this Suttanta enable us to judge as to what was considered, at the time when it was put together, to be the greatest possible luxury and glory of the mightiest and most righteous king. In spite of the exuberance of some of the language used, the luxury is after all curiously simple, and mostly of an out-of-door kind. A summary of the conclusions which can be drawn from the sacred books of the Buddhists as to the social and economic condition of the Ganges valley, at the time when those books were composed, will be found in my 'Buddhist India,' ch. IV–VI. The very simple character of the luxury here depicted is in accordance with the evidence there given.

[XVII. MAHÂ-SUDASSANA-SUTTANTA.

THE GREAT KING OF GLORY[1].

CHAPTER I.|

1. [169] Thus have I heard. The Exalted One was once staying at Kusinârâ in the Upavattana, the Sâla grove of the Mallas, between the twin Sâla trees, at the time of his death.

2. Now the venerable Ânanda went up to the place where the Exalted One was, and bowed down before him, and took his seat respectfully on one side. And when he was so seated, the venerable Ânanda said to the Exalted One :—

'Let not the Exalted One die in this little wattle-and-daub town, in this town in the midst of the jungle, in this branch township. For, lord, there are other great cities, such as Champâ, Râjagaha, Sâvatthi, Sâketa, Kosambi, and Benares. Let the Exalted One die in one of them. There there are many wealthy nobles and brahmins and heads of houses, believers in the Tathâgata, who will pay due honour to the remains of the Tathâgata.'

3. 'Say not so, Ânanda! Say not so, Ânanda, that this is but a small wattle-and-daub town, a town in the midst of the jungle, a branch township. Long ago, Ânanda, there was a king, by name Mahâ-Sudassana, a king of kings, a righteous man who ruled in righteousness, an anointed Kshatriya[2], Lord of the four quarters

---

[1] Sudassana means 'beautiful to see, having a glorious appearance,' and is the name of many kings and heroes in Indian legend.

[2] Khattiyo muddhâvasitto, which does not occur in the Mahâparinibbâna, the Mahâpadâna, and the Lakkhana Suttantas, and other places where this stock description of a king of kings is found. It is omitted also in the Lalita Vistara. The Burmese Phayre MS. of the

of the earth, conqueror, the protector of his people, possessor of the seven royal treasures. [170] This Kusinârâ, Ânanda, was the royal city of king Mahâ-Sudassana, under the name of Kusâvatî, and on the east and on the west it was twelve leagues in length, and on the north and on the south it was seven leagues in breadth. That royal city Kusâvatî, Ânanda, was mighty, and prosperous, and full of people, crowded with men, and provided with all things for food. Just, Ânanda, as the royal city of the gods, A*l*akamandâ by name, is mighty, prosperous, and full of people, crowded with the gods, and provided with all kinds of food, so, Ânanda, was the royal city Kusâvatî mighty and prosperous, full of people, crowded with men, and provided with all kinds of food. Both by day and by night, Ânanda, the royal city Kusâvatî resounded with the ten cries ; that is to say, the noise of elephants, and the noise of horses, and the noise of chariots ; the sounds of the drum, of the tabor, and of the lute ; the sound of singing, and the sounds of the cymbal and of the gong·; and lastly, with the cry:—" Eat, drink, and be merry[1]!" '

4. 'The royal city Kusâvatî, Ânanda, was surrounded by Seven Ramparts. Of these, one rampart was of gold, and one of silver, and one of beryl, and one of crystal, and one of agate, and one of coral, and one of all kinds of gems !

5. 'To the royal city Kusâvatî, Ânanda, there were Gates of four colours. One gate was of gold, and one of silver, and one of jade, and one of crystal. [171] At each gate seven pillars were fixed ; in height as three times or as four times the height of a man. And one pillar was of gold, and one of silver, and one of beryl, and one of crystal, and one of agate, and one of coral, and one of all kinds of gems.

India Office reads here muddâbhisitto, but this is an unnecessary correction. The epithet is probably inserted here from § 7 below.
[1] This enumeration is found also at Jâtaka I, 3, only that the chank is added there—wrongly, for that makes the number of cries eleven.

6. 'The royal city Kusâvatî, Ânanda, was surrounded by Seven Rows of Palm Trees. One row was of palms of gold, and one of silver, and one of beryl, and one of crystal, and one of agate, and one of coral, and one of all kinds of gems.

'And the Golden Palms had trunks of gold, and leaves and fruits of silver. And the Silver Palms had trunks of silver, and leaves and fruits of gold. And the Palms of Beryl had trunks of beryl, and leaves and fruits of crystal. And the Crystal Palms had trunks of crystal, and leaves and fruits of beryl. And the Agate Palms had trunks of agate, and leaves and fruits of coral. And the Coral Palms had trunks of coral, and leaves and fruits of agate. And the Palms of every kind of Gem had trunks and leaves and fruits of every kind of gem.

[1] 'And when those rows of palm trees, Ânanda, were shaken by the wind, there arose a sound sweet, and pleasant, and charming, and intoxicating.

'Just, Ânanda, as the five kinds of instruments yield, when well played upon, to the skilful man, a sound sweet, and pleasant, and charming, and intoxicating—[172] just even so, Ânanda, when those rows of palm trees were shaken by the wind, there arose a sound sweet, and pleasant, and charming, and intoxicating.

'And whoever, Ânanda, in the royal city Kusâvatî were at that time gamblers, drunkards, and given to

---

[1] This section should be compared with one in the Sukhâvatî-vyûha, translated by Professor Max Müller as follows (' Journal of the Royal Asiatic Society,' 1880, p. 170):—

'And again, O Sâriputra, when those rows of palm trees and strings of bells in that Buddha country are moved by the wind, a sweet and enrapturing sound proceeds from them. Yes, O Sâriputra, as from a heavenly musical instrument consisting of a hundred thousand kotis of sounds, when played by Aryas, a sweet and enrapturing sound proceeds; a sweet and enrapturing sound proceeds from those rows of palm trees and strings of bells moved by the wind.

'And when the men there hear that sound, reflection on Buddha arises in their body, reflection on the Law, reflection on the Assembly.'

Compare also below, § 32, and Jâtaka I, 32.

drink, they used to dance round together to the sound
of those palms when shaken by the wind.'

---

7. 'The Great King of Glory, Ânanda, was the
possessor of Seven Precious Things, and was gifted
with Four Marvellous Powers.

'What are those seven?

[1] 'In the first place, Ânanda, when the Great King
of Glory, on the Sabbath day[2], on the day of the full
moon, had purified himself, and had gone up into the
upper story of his palace to keep the sacred day, there
then appeared to him the heavenly Treasure of the
Wheel,[3] with its nave, its tire, and all its thousand
spokes complete.

'When he beheld it the Great King of Glory
thought:—

'"This saying have I heard, 'When a king of the
warrior race, an anointed king, has purified himself on
the Sabbath day, on the day of the full moon, and has
gone up into the upper story of his palace to keep the
sacred day; if there appear to him the heavenly Treasure of the Wheel, with its nave, its tire, and all its
thousand spokes complete—that king becomes a king
of kings invincible.' May I, then, become a king of
kings invincible[4]."

8. 'Then, Ânanda, the Great King of Glory rose
from his seat, and reverently uncovering from one
shoulder his robe, he held in his left hand a pitcher,
and with his right hand he sprinkled water up over the
Wheel, as he said:—

'"Roll onward, O my lord, the Wheel! O my lord,
go forth and overcome!"

'Then the wondrous Wheel, Ânanda, rolled onwards

---

[1] The following enumeration is found word for word in several
other Pâli Suttas, and occurs also, in almost identical terms, in the
Lalita Vistara (Calcutta edition, pp. 14–19).

[2] Uposatha, a weekly sacred day; being full-moon day, new-moon
day, and the two equidistant intermediate days.   Comp. § 12.

[3] This is the disk of the sun.

[4] A king of the rolling wheel.

towards the region of the East, and after it went the Great King of Glory, and with him his army, horses, and chariots, and elephants, and men. [173] And in whatever place, Ânanda, the Wheel stopped, there the Great King of Glory took up his abode, and with him his army, horses, and chariots, and elephants, and men.

9. 'Then, Ânanda, all the rival kings in the region of the East came to the Great King of Glory and said :—

'"Come, O mighty king! Welcome, O mighty king! All is thine, O mighty king! Do thou, O mighty king, be a Teacher to us!"

'Thus spake the Great King of Glory :—" Ye shall slay no living thing. Ye shall not take that which has not been given. Ye shall not act wrongly touching the bodily desires. Ye shall speak no lie. Ye shall drink no maddening drink. Ye shall eat as ye have eaten [1]."

'Then, Ânanda, all the rival kings in the region of the East became subject unto the Great King of Glory.

10. 'But the wondrous Wheel, Ânanda, having plunged down into the great waters in the East, rose up out again, and rolled onward to the region of the South [and there all happened as had happened in the region of the East. And in like manner the wondrous Wheel rolled onward to the extremest boundary of the West and of the North ; and there, too, all happened as had happened in the region of the East].

11. [174] ' Now when the wondrous Wheel, Ânanda, had gone forth conquering and to conquer over the whole earth to its very ocean boundary, it returned back again to the royal city of Kusâvatî and remained fixed on the open terrace in front of the entrance to the inner apartments of the Great King of Glory, as

---

[1] Yathâbhuttam bhuñjatha. Buddhaghosa has no comment on this. I suppose it means, 'Observe the rules current among you regarding clean and unclean meats.' If so, the Great King of Glory disregards the teaching of the Âmagandha Sutta (translated in my 'Buddhism,' p. 131).

a glorious adornment to the inner apartments of the Great King of Glory.

'Such, Ânanda, was the wondrous Wheel which appeared to the Great King of Glory.'

12. 'Now further, Ânanda, there appeared to the Great King of Glory the Elephant Treasure [1], all white, seven-fold firm [2], wonderful in power, flying through the sky—the Elephant-King, whose name was " The Changes of the Moon [3]."

'When he beheld it the Great King of Glory was pleased at heart at the thought :—

'" Auspicious were it to ride upon the Elephant, if only it would submit to be controlled !"

'Then, Ânanda, the wondrous Elephant—like a fine elephant of noble blood long since well trained—submitted to control.

'And long ago, Ânanda, when the Great King of Glory, to test that wondrous Elephant, had mounted on to it early in the morning, it passed over along the broad earth to its very ocean boundary, and then returned again, in time for the morning meal, to the royal city of Kusâvati [4].

'Such, Ânanda, was the wondrous Elephant that appeared to the Great King of Glory.

13. 'Now further, Ânanda, there appeared to the Great King of Glory the Horse Treasure [5], all white

---

[1] Hatthi-ratana.

[2] Satta-ppatittho, that is, perhaps, in regard to its four legs, two tusks, and trunk. The expression is curious, and Buddhaghosa has no note upon it. It is quite possible that it merely signifies ' exceeding firm,' the number seven being used without any hard and fast interpretation.

[3] Uposatho. In the Lalita Vistara its name is ' Wisdom' (Bodhi). Uposatha is the name for the sacred day of the moon's changes—first, and more especially the full-moon day; next, the new-moon day; and lastly, the days equidistant between these two. It was, therefore, a weekly sacred day, and, as Childers says, may often be well rendered ' Sabbath.'

[4] Compare on this and § 29 my ' Buddhist Birth Stories,' p. 85, where a similar phrase is used of Kanthaka.

[5] Assa-ratanam.

with a crow-black head, and a dark mane, wonderful
in power, flying through the sky—the Charger-King,
whose name was "Thunder-cloud[1]."

'When he beheld it, the Great King of Glory was
pleased at heart at the thought :—

'" Auspicious were it to ride upon that Horse if only
it would submit to be controlled !"

[175] ' Then, Ânanda, the wondrous Horse—like a
fine horse of the best blood long since well trained—
submitted to control.

' When long ago, Ânanda, the Great King of Glory,
to test that wondrous Horse, mounted on to it early in
the morning, it passed over along the broad earth to its
very ocean boundary and then returned again, in time
for the morning meal, to the royal city of Kusâvatî.

' Such, Ânanda, was the wondrous Horse that appeared to the Great King of Glory.

14. ' Now further, Ânanda, there appeared to the
Great King of Glory the Gem-Treasure[2]. That Gem
was the Ve*luriya, bright, of the finest species, with
eight facets, excellently wrought, clear, transparent, perfect in every way.

' The splendour, Ânanda, of that wondrous Gem
spread round about a league on every side.

' When, long ago, Ânanda, the Great King of Glory,
to test that wondrous Gem, set all his fourfold army in
array and raised aloft the Gem upon his standard top,
he was able to march out in the gloom and darkness of
the night.

' And then too, Ânanda, all the dwellers in the
villages round about, set about their daily work,
thinking :—" The daylight hath appeared."

---

[1] Valâhako. Compare the Valâhassa-Jâtaka (Fausböll, No. 196),
of which the Chinese story translated by Mr. Beal at pp. 332–40 of his
' Romantic History,' &c., is an expanded and altered version. In the
Valâhakâ Sa*myutta of the Sa*myutta Nikâya the spirits of the skies are
divided into U*nha-valâhakâ Devâ, Sîta-valâhakâ Devâ, Abbha-
valâhakâ Devâ, Vâta-valâhakâ Devâ, and Vassa-valâhakâ
Devâ, that is, the cloud-spirits of cold, heat, air, wind, and rain
respectively.

[2] Ma*ni-ratana*m.

'Such, Ânanda, was the wondrous Gem that appeared to the Great King of Glory.'

---

15. 'Now further, Ânanda, there appeared to the
Great King of Glory the Woman-Treasure [1], graceful in
figure, beautiful in appearance, charming in manner,
and of the most fine complexion ; neither very tall, nor
very short ; neither very stout, nor very slim ; neither
very dark, nor very fair ; surpassing human beauty, she
had attained unto the beauty of the gods [2].

'The touch too, Ânanda, of the skin of that wondrous
Woman was as the touch of cotton or of cotton wool ;
in the cold her limbs were warm, in the heat her limbs
were cool ; while from her body was wafted the perfume
of sandal wood and from her mouth the perfume of the
lotus.

'That Pearl among Women too, Ânanda, used to
rise up before the Great King of Glory, [176] and after
him retire to rest ; pleasant was she in speech, and ever
on the watch to hear what she might do in order so to
act as to give him pleasure.

'That Pearl among Women too, Ânanda, was never,
even in thought, unfaithful to the Great King of Glory—
how much less then could she be so with the body !

'Such, Ânanda, was the Pearl among Women who
appeared to the Great King of Glory.'

---

16. 'Now further, Ânanda, there appeared unto the
Great King of Glory a Wonderful Treasurer [3], possessed,

---

[1] Itthi-ratanam.

[2] The above description of an ideally beautiful woman is of frequent
occurrence.

[3] Gahapati-ratanam.   The word gahapati has been hitherto
usually rendered 'householder,' but this may often, and would certainly
here, convey a wrong impression.   There is no single word in English
which is an adequate rendering of the term, for it connotes a social
condition now no longer known among us.   The gahapati was the
head of a family, the representative in a village community of a family,
the *pater familias*.   So the god of fire, with allusion to the sacred
fire maintained in each household, is called in the Rig-veda the
grihapati, the *pater familias*, of the human race.   It is often

through good deeds done in a former birth, of a marvellous power of vision by which he could discover
treasure, whether it had an owner or whether it had
not.

'He went up to the Great King of Glory, and said :—

'"Do thou, O King, take thine ease! I will deal
with thy wealth even as wealth should be dealt
with."

'Long ago, Ânanda, the Great King of Glory, to test
that wonderful Treasurer, went on board a boat, and
had it pushed out into the current in the midst of the
river Ganges. Then he said to the wonderful steward :—

'"I have need, O Treasurer, of yellow gold!"

'"Let the ship then, O Great King, go alongside
either of the banks."

'"It is here, O Treasurer, that I have need of yellow
gold."

'Then the wonderful Treasurer reached down to the
water with both his hands, and drew up a jar full of
yellow gold, and said to the Great King of Glory :—

'"Is that enough, O Great King? Have I done
enough, O Great King?"

'And the Great King of Glory replied :—

'"It is enough, O Treasurer. You have done
enough, O Treasurer. You have offered me enough,
O Treasurer!" [177]

'Such was the wonderful Treasurer, Ânanda, who
appeared to the Great King of Glory.'

---

used in opposition to brâhma*n*a very much as we used 'yeoman'
in opposition to 'clerk' (Jâtaka I, 83); and the two combined are
used in opposition to people of other ranks and callings held to be
less honourable than that of clerk or yeoman (Jâtaka I, 218). The
compound brâhma*n*a-gahapatika as a collective term comes to
be about equivalent to 'priests and laymen' (see, for instance, below,
§ 21, and Vinaya I, 35, 36). Then again the gahapati is distinct from
the subordinate members of the family, who had not the control and
management of the common property (Sâmañña Phala Suttanta 133,
= Tevijja Suttanta I, 47); and it is this implication of the term that
is emphasized in the text. Buddhaghosa uses, as an explanatory
phrase, the words se*tth*i-gahapati.

17. 'Now further, Ânanda, there appeared to the Great King of Glory a Wonderful Adviser [1], learned, clever, and wise; and qualified to lead the Great King of Glory to undertake what he ought to undertake, and to leave undone what he ought to leave undone.

'He went up to the Great King of Glory, and said :—

'" Do thou, O King, take thine ease! I will be thy guide."

'Such, Ânanda, was the wonderful Adviser who appeared to the Great King of Glory.

'The Great King of Glory was possessed of these Seven Precious Things.

18. 'Now, further, Ânanda, the Great King of Glory was gifted with Four Marvellous Gifts [2].

'What are the Four Marvellous Gifts?

'In the first place, Ânanda, the Great King of Glory was graceful in figure, handsome in appearance, pleasing in manner, and of most beautiful complexion, beyond what other men are.

'The Great King of Glory, Ânanda, was endowed with this First Marvellous Gift.

19. 'And besides that, Ânanda, the Great King of Glory was of long life, and of many years, beyond those of other men.

'The Great King of Glory, Ânanda, was endowed with this Second Marvellous Gift.

20. 'And besides that, Ânanda, the Great King of Glory was free from disease, and free from bodily suffering; and his internal fire was neither too hot nor too cold, but such as to promote good digestion, beyond that of other men [3].

---

[1] Parinâyaka-ratanam. Buddhaghosa says that he was the eldest son of the king. The Lalita Vistara makes him a general.

[2] The Four Iddhis. Here again, as elsewhere, it will be noticed that there is nothing supernatural about these four Iddhis. See the passages quoted above, Vol. I, pp. 272 foll. They are merely attributes accompanying or forming part of the majesty (iddhi) of the King of kings.

[3] The same thing is said of Ratthapâla in the Ratthapâla Sutta, where Gogerly renders the whole passage:—' Ratthapâla is healthy, free from pain, having a good digestion and appetite, being troubled with

'The Great King of Glory, Ânanda, was endowed with this Third Marvellous Gift.

21. [178] 'And besides that, Ânanda, the Great King of Glory was beloved and popular with priests and with laymen alike. Just, Ânanda, as a father is near and dear to his own sons, just so, Ânanda, was the Great King of Glory beloved and popular with priests and with laymen alike. And just, Ânanda, as his sons are near and dear to a father, just so, Ânanda, were priests and laymen alike near and dear to the Great King of Glory.

'Once, Ânanda, the Great King of Glory marched out with all his fourfold army to the pleasure ground. There, Ânanda, the priests and laymen went up to the Great King of Glory, and said :—

'"O King, pass slowly by, that we may look upon thee for a longer time!"

'But the Great King of Glory, Ânanda, addressed his charioteer, and said :—

'"Drive on the chariot slowly, charioteer, that I may look upon my people [priests and laymen] for a longer time!"

'This was the Fourth Marvellous Gift, Ânanda, with which the Great King of Glory was endowed.

'These are the Four Marvellous Gifts, Ânanda, with which the Great King of Glory was endowed.'

22. 'Now to the Great King of Glory, Ânanda, there occurred the thought :—

---

no excess of either heat or cold' ('Journal of the Ceylon Asiatic Society,' 1847–8, p. 98). The gahani is a supposed particular organ or function situate at the junction of the stomach and intestines. Moggallâna explains it, udare tu tathâ pâcanalasmim gahani (Abhidhâna-ppadîpikâ 972), where Subhûti's Sinhalese version is 'kukshi, pâkâgni,' and his English version, 'the belly, the internal fire which promotes digestion.' Buddhaghosa explains samavipâkiyâ kammaga-tejo-dhâtuyâ, and adds :—'If a man's food is dissolved the moment he has eaten it, or if it remains like a lump, he has not the samavepâkini gahani, but he who has appetite (bhattacchando) when the time for food comes round again, he has the samavepâkini gahani,'—which is delightfully naïve.

'"Suppose, now, I were to make Lotus-ponds in the spaces between these palms, at every hundred bow-lengths."

'Then, Ânanda, the Great King of Glory, in the spaces between those palms, at distances of a hundred bow-lengths, made Lotus-ponds.

'And those Lotus-ponds, Ânanda, were faced with tiles of four kinds. One kind of tile was of gold, and one of silver, and one of beryl, and one of crystal.

'And to each of those Lotus-ponds, Ânanda, there were four flights of steps, of four different kinds. One flight of steps was of gold, and one of silver, and one of beryl, and one of crystal. [179] The flight of golden steps had balustrades of gold, with the cross bars and the figure-head of silver. The flight of silver steps had balustrades of silver, with the cross bars and the figure-head of gold. The flight of beryl steps had balustrades of beryl, with the cross bars and the figure-head of crystal. The flight of crystal steps had balustrades of crystal, with cross bars and figure-head of beryl.

'And round those Lotus-ponds there ran, Ânanda, a double railing. One railing was of gold, and one was of silver. The golden railing had its posts of gold, and its cross bars and its capitals of silver. The silver railing had its posts of silver, and its cross bars and its capitals of gold[1].

---

[1] Pokkharani, the word translated Lotus-pond, is an artificial pool or small lake for water-plants. There are some which are probably nearly as old as this passage still in good preservation in Anurâdhapura in Ceylon. Each is oblong, and has its tiles and its four flights of steps, and some had railings. The balustrades, cross bars, figure-head, and railings are in Pâli thambha, sûciyo, unhîsa, and vedikâ, of the exact meaning of which I am not quite confident. They do not occur in the description of the Lotus-lakes in Sukhâvatî. General Cunningham says that the cross bars of the Buddhist railings are called sûciyo in the inscriptions at Bharahat ('The Stupa of Bharhut,' p. 127). Buddhaghosa, who is good enough to tell us the exact number of the ponds—to wit, 84,000, has no explanation of these words, merely saying that of the two vedikâs one was at the limit of the tiles and one at the limit of the parivena. See below § 31 ; and Rhys Davids, 'Buddhist India,' Figures 6, 7 ; pp. 74–6.

23. 'Now, to the Great King of Glory, Ânanda, there occurred the thought :—

'"Suppose, now, I were to have flowers of every season planted in those Lotus-ponds for all the people to have garlands to put on[1]—to wit, blue water-lilies and blue lotuses, white lotuses and white water-lilies."

[And the king had such flowers planted there accordingly.]

'Now, to the Great King of Glory, Ânanda, occurred the thought :—

'"Suppose, now, I were to place bathing-men on the banks of those Lotus-ponds, to bathe such of the people as come there from time to time."

[And the king had such bathing-men placed there accordingly.]

'Now, to the Great King of Glory, Ânanda, occurred the thought :—

'"Suppose, now, I were to establish a perpetual grant by the banks of those Lotus-ponds—to wit, food for the hungry, drink for the thirsty, raiment for the naked, means of conveyance for those who have need of it, couches for the tired, wives for those who want wives, gold for the poor, and money for those who are in want."

[180] 'Then, Ânanda, the Great King of Glory established a perpetual grant by the banks of those Lotus ponds—to wit, food for the hungry, drink for the thirsty, raiment for the naked, means of conveyance for those who needed it, couches for the tired, wives for those who wanted wives, gold for the poor, and money for those who were in want.'

24. 'Now, Ânanda, the people [priests and laymen] went to the Great King of Glory, taking with them much wealth.   And they said :—

'"This abundant wealth, O King, have we brought

---

[1] Literally 'have garlands planted for all the people to put on'—an elliptical expression revealing the ideas of that early time as to the only possible use of flowers.   I think the reading should be anavaram.

here for the use of the King of kings.   Let the King accept it of us!'"

'"I have enough wealth, my friends, laid up for myself, the produce of righteous taxation. Do you keep this, and take away more with you!"

'When those men were thus refused by the King they went aside and considered together, saying :—

'"It would not beseem us now, were we to take back this wealth to our own houses. Suppose, now, we were to build a mansion for the Great King of Glory."

'Then they went to the Great King of Glory, and said :—

'"A mansion would we build for thee, O King!"

'Then, Ânanda, the Great King of Glory signified, by silence, his consent.'

---

25. 'Now, Ânanda, when Sakka, the king of the gods, became aware in his mind of the thoughts that were in the heart of the Great King of Glory, he addressed Vissakamma the god, and said :—

'"Come now, Vissakamma, create me a mansion for the Great King of Glory—a palace which shall be called 'Righteousness'."

'"Even so, lord!" said Vissakamma, in assent, Ânanda, to Sakka, the king of the gods. [181] And as instantaneously as a strong man might stretch forth his folded arm, or draw in his arm again when it was stretched forth, so quickly did he vanish from the heaven of the Great Thirty-Three, and appeared before the Great King of Glory.

'Then, Ânanda, Vissakamma the god said to the Great King of Glory :—

'"I would create for thee, O King, a mansion—a palace which shall be called 'Righteousness'!"

'Then, Ânanda, the Great King of Glory signified, by silence, his consent.

'So Vissakamma the god, Ânanda, created for the Great King of Glory a mansion—a palace to be called "Righteousness".'

26. 'The Palace of Righteousness, Ânanda, was
on the east and on the west a league in length,
and on the north and on the south half a league in
breadth.

'The ground-floor, Ânanda, of the Palace of Righteousness, in height as three times the height to which a
man can reach, was built of bricks, of four kinds. One
kind of brick was of gold, and one of silver, and one
of beryl, and one of crystal.

'To the Palace of Righteousness, Ânanda, there
were eighty-four thousand pillars of four kinds. One
kind of pillar was of gold, and one of silver, and one of
beryl, and one of crystal.

'The Palace of Righteousness, Ânanda, was fitted
up with seats of four kinds. One kind of seat was of
gold, and one of silver, and one of beryl, and one of
crystal.

'In the Palace of Righteousness, Ânanda, there were
twenty-four staircases of four kinds. One staircase was
of gold, and one of silver, and one of beryl, and one of
crystal. The staircase of gold had balustrades of gold,
with the cross bars and the figure-head of silver. The
staircase of silver had balustrades of silver, with the
cross bars and the figure-head of gold. [182] The
staircase of beryl had balustrades of beryl, with the
cross bars and the figure-head of crystal. The staircase of crystal had balustrades of crystal, with cross
bars and figure-head of beryl.

'In the Palace of Righteousness, Ânanda, there were
eighty-four thousand chambers of four kinds. One
kind of chamber was of gold, and one of silver, and one
of beryl, and one of crystal.

'In the golden chamber a silver couch was spread;
in the silver chamber a golden couch; in the beryl
chamber a couch of ivory; and in the crystal chamber
a couch of coral.

'At the door of the golden chamber there stood a
palm tree of silver; and its trunk was of silver, and its
leaves and fruits of silver.

'At the door of the beryl chamber there stood a palm

tree of crystal ; and its trunk was of crystal, and its leaves and fruits of beryl.

'At the door of the crystal chamber there stood a palm tree of beryl ; and its trunk was of beryl, and its leaves and fruits of crystal.'·

27. 'Now there occurred, Ânanda, to the Great King of Glory this thought :—

' " Suppose, now, I were to make a grove of palm trees, all of gold, at the entrance to the chamber of the Great Complex ¹, under the shade of which I may pass the heat of the day."

'Then, Ânanda, the Great King of Glory made a grove of palm trees, all of gold, at the entrance to the chamber of the Great Complex, under the shade of which he might pass the heat of the day.

28. 'The Palace of Righteousness, Ânanda, was surrounded by a double railing. [183] One railing was of gold, and one was of silver. The golden railing had its posts of gold, and its cross bars and its figure head of silver. The silver railing had its posts of silver, and its cross bars and its figure-head of gold.

29. 'The Palace of Righteousness, Ânanda, was hung round with two networks of bells. One network of bells was of gold, and one was of silver. The golden network had bells of silver, and the silver network had bells of gold.

'And when those networks of bells, Ânanda, were shaken by the wind there arose a sound sweet, and pleasant, and charming, and intoxicating.

'Just, Ânanda, as the seven kinds of instruments yield, when well played upon, to the skilful man, a sound sweet, and pleasant, and charming, and intoxicating—just even so, Ânanda, when those networks of

---

¹ Mahâvyûhassa kû/âgârassa dvâre. The 'Great Complex' contains a double allusion, in the same spirit in which the whole legend has been worked out : (1) To the Great Complex as a name of the Sun God regarded as a unity of the deities ; and (2) To the Great Complex as a name of a particular kind of deep religious meditation or speculation.

bells were shaken by the wind, there arose a sound sweet, and pleasant, and charming, and intoxicating.

' And whoever, Ânanda, in the royal city Kusâvatî were at that time gamblers, drunkards, and given to drink, they used to dance round together to the sound of those networks of bells when shaken by the wind.'

---

30. ' When the Palace of Righteousness, Ânanda, was finished it was hard to look at, destructive to the eyes.   Just, Ânanda, as in the last month of the rains in the autumn time, when the sky has become clear and the clouds have vanished away, the sun, springing up along the heavens, is hard to look at, and destructive to the eyes—[184] just so, Ânanda, when the Palace of Righteousness was finished was it hard to look at, and destructive to the eyes.'

---

31. ' Now there occurred, Ânanda, to the Great King of Glory this thought :—

' " Suppose, now, in front of the Palace of Righteousness, I were to make a Lotus-lake to bear the name of ' Righteousness '."

' Then, Ânanda, the Great King of Glory made a Lotus-lake to bear the name of " Righteousness ".

' The Lake of Righteousness, Ânanda, was on the east and on the west a league in length, and on the north and on the south half a league in breadth.

' The Lake of Righteousness, Ânanda, was faced with tiles of four kinds.   One kind of tile was of gold, and one of silver, and one of beryl, and one of crystal.

' The Lake of Righteousness, Ânanda, had four and twenty flights of steps, of four different kinds.   One flight of steps was of gold, and one of silver, and one of beryl, and one of crystal.   The flight of golden steps had balustrades of gold, with the cross bars and the figure-head of silver.   The flight of silver steps had balustrades of silver, with the cross bars and the figure-head of gold.   The flight of beryl steps had balustrades of beryl, with the cross bars and the figure-head of crystal. The flight of crystal steps had balustrades of crystal, with cross bars and figure-head of beryl.

'Round the Lake of Righteousness, Ânanda, there ran a double railing. One railing was of gold, and one was of silver. The golden railing had its posts of gold, and its cross bars and its capitals of silver. The silver railing had its posts of silver, and its cross bars and its capitals of gold.

32. 'The Lake of Righteousness, Ânanda, was surrounded by seven rows of palm trees. One row was of palms of gold, and one of silver, and one of beryl, and one of crystal, and one of agate, and one of coral, and one of all kinds of gems.

'And the golden palms had trunks of gold, and leaves and fruits of silver. [185] And the silver palms had trunks of silver, and leaves and fruits of gold. And the palms of beryl had trunks of beryl, and leaves and fruits of crystal. And the crystal palms had trunks of crystal, and leaves and fruits of beryl. And the agate palms had trunks of agate, and leaves and fruits of coral. And the coral palms had trunks of coral, and leaves and fruits of agate. And the palms of every kind of gem had trunks and leaves and fruits of every kind of gem.

'And when those rows of palm trees, Ânanda, were shaken by the wind, there arose a sound sweet, and pleasant, and charming, and intoxicating.

'Just, Ânanda, as the seven kinds of instruments yield, when well played upon, to the skilful man, a sound sweet, and pleasant, and charming, and intoxicating,—just even so, Ânanda, when those rows of palm trees were shaken by the wind, there arose a sound sweet, and pleasant, and charming, and intoxicating.

'And whosoever, Ânanda, in the royal city Kusâvatî were at that time gamblers, drunkards, and given to drink, they used to dance round together to the sound of those palms when shaken by the wind.'

33. 'When the Palace of Righteousness, Ânanda, was

finished, and the Lotus-lake of Righteousness was
finished, the Great King of Glory entertained with all
good things those of the Wanderers who, at that time,
were held in high esteem, and those of the brahmins
who, at that time, were held in high esteem.   Then he
ascended up into the Palace of Righteousness.'

End of the First Portion for Recitation.

CHAPTER II.

1. ' Now there occurred, Ânanda, this thought to the Great King of Glory :—

' " Of what previous character, now, may this be the fruit, of what previous character the result, that I am now so mighty and so great ? "

[186] 'And then occurred, Ânanda, to the Great King of Glory this thought :—

' " Of three qualities is this the fruit, of three qualities the result, that I am now so mighty and so great,— that is to say, of giving, of self-conquest, and of self-control [1]." '

---

2. ' Now the Great King of Glory, Ânanda, ascended up into the chamber of the Great Complex ; and there he broke out into a cry of intense emotion :—

' " Stay here, O thoughts of lust!
Stay here, O thoughts of ill-will!
Stay here, O thoughts of hatred!
Thus far only, O thoughts of lust!
Thus far only, O thoughts of ill-will!
Thus far only, O thoughts of hatred! "

3. ' And when, Ânanda, the Great King of Glory had entered the chamber of the Great Complex, and had seated himself upon the couch of gold, having put away all passion and all unrighteousness, he entered into, and remained in, the First Rapture,—a state of joy and ease, born of seclusion, full of reflection, full of investigation.

' By suppressing reflection and investigation, he entered into, and remained in, the Second Rapture,—

---

[1] I have here translated kamma by ' previous character' and by ' quality.' The easiest plan would, no doubt, have been to preserve in the translation the technical term karma, which is explained at some length in ' Buddhism,' pp. 99–106.

a state of joy and ease, born of serenity, without reflection, without investigation, a state of elevation of mind, of internal calm.

'By absence of the longing after joy, he remained indifferent, conscious, self-possessed, experiencing in his body that ease which the noble ones announce, saying:— "The man indifferent and self-possessed is well at ease," and thus he entered into, and remained in, the Third Rapture.

'By putting away ease, by putting away pain, by the previous dying away both of gladness and of sorrow, he entered into, and remained in, the Fourth Rapture,— a state of purified self-possession and equanimity, without ease, and without pain [1].

4. 'Then, Ânanda, the Great King of Glory went out from the chamber of the Great Complex, and entered the golden chamber and sat himself down on the silver couch. And he let his mind pervade one quarter of the world with thoughts of Love; and so the second quarter, and so the third, and so the fourth. And thus the whole wide world, above, below, around, and everywhere, did he continue to pervade with heart of Love, far-reaching, grown great, and beyond measure, free from the least trace of anger or ill-will.

'And he let his mind pervade one quarter of the world with thoughts of Pity; and so the second quarter, and so the third, and so the fourth. And thus the whole wide world, above, below, around, and everywhere, did he continue to pervade with heart of Pity, far-reaching, grown great, and beyond measure, free from the least trace of anger or ill-will.

'And he let his mind pervade one quarter of the

---

[1] The above paragraphs are an endeavour to express the inmost feelings when they are first strung to the uttermost by the intense effects of deep religious emotion, and then feel the effects of what may be called, for want of a better word, the reaction. Most deeply religious natures have passed through such a crisis; and though the feelings are perhaps really indescribable, this passage is dealing, not with a vain mockery, but with a very real event in spiritual experience. It implies neither hypnotism nor trance.

world with thoughts of Sympathy; and so the second quarter, and so the third, and so the fourth. And thus the whole wide world above, below, around, and everywhere, did he continue to pervade with heart of Sympathy, far reaching, grown great, and beyond measure, free from the least trace of anger or ill-will.

'And he let his mind pervade one quarter of the world with thoughts of Equanimity[1]; [187] and so the second quarter, and so the third, and so the fourth. And thus the whole wide world, above, below, around, and everywhere, did he continue to pervade with heart of Equanimity, far-reaching, grown great, and beyond measure, free from the least trace of anger or ill-will.

5. 'The Great King of Glory, Ânanda, had four and eighty thousand cities, the chief of which was the royal city of Kusâvatî:

'Four and eighty thousand palaces, the chief of which was the Palace of Righteousness:

'Four and eighty thousand chambers, the chief of which was the chamber of the Great Complex:

'Four and eighty thousand divans, of gold, and silver, and ivory, and sandal wood, spread with long-haired rugs, and cloths embroidered with flowers, and magnificent antelope skins; covered with lofty canopies; and provided at both ends with purple cushions:

'Four and eighty thousand state elephants, with trappings of gold, and gilded flags, and golden coverings of network,—of which the king of elephants, called "the Changes of the Moon," was chief:

'Four and eighty thousand state horses, with trappings of gold, and gilded flags, and golden coverings of network,—of which "Thunder-cloud," the king of horses, was the chief:

'Four and eighty thousand chariots, with coverings of the skins of lions, and of tigers, and of panthers,—

---

[1] These are the four Appamaññas or infinite feelings, also called (e.g. below, § 13) the four Brahma-vihâras or Sublime Conditions. They are here very appropriately represented to follow immediately after the state of feeling described in the Raptures; but they ought to be the constant companions of a good Buddhist.

of which the chariot called "the Flag of Victory" was the chief:

'Four and eighty thousand gems, of which the Wondrous Gem was the chief:

'Four and eighty thousand wives, of whom Subhaddâ, the Queen of Glory[1], was the chief: [188]

'Four and eighty thousand yeomen, of whom the Wonderful Steward was the chief:

'Four and eighty thousand nobles, of whom the Wonderful Adviser was the chief:

'Four and eighty thousand cows, with jute trappings, and horns tipped with bronze:

'Four and eighty thousand myriads of garments, of delicate textures, of flax, and cotton, and silk, and wool:

'Four and eighty thousand dishes, in which, in the evening and in the morning rice was served[2].'

---

6. 'Now at that time, Ânanda, the four and eighty thousand state elephants used to come every evening and every morning to be of service to the Great King of Glory.

'And this thought occurred to the Great King of Glory :—

'"These eighty-four thousand elephants come every evening and every morning to be of service to me. Suppose, now, I were to let the elephants come in alternate forty-two thousands, once each, every alternate hundred years!"

'Then, Ânanda, the Great King of Glory said to the Great Adviser :—

'"O, my friend, the Great Adviser! these eighty-four thousand elephants come every evening and every morning to be of service to me. Now, let the elephants

---

[1] Subhaddâ Devî. Subhaddâ, 'glorious, magnificent,' is a not uncommon name both for men and women in Buddhist and post-Buddhistic Hindu literature.

[2] Most of the trappings and cloths here mentioned are the same as those referred to in the Moralities translated above, Vol. I, pp. 11, 12. The whole paragraph is four times repeated below.

come, O my friend, the Great Adviser, in alternate forty-two thousands, [189] once each, every alternate hundred years!"

' " Even so, lord!" said the Wonderful Adviser, in assent, to the Great King of Glory.

'From that time forth, Ânanda, the elephants came in alternate forty-two thousands, once each, every alternate hundred years.'

---

7. 'Now, Ânanda, after the lapse of many years, of many hundred years, of many thousand years, there occurred to the Queen of Glory this thought :—

' " 'Tis long since I have beheld the Great King of Glory. Suppose, now, I were to go and visit the Great King of Glory."

'Then, Ânanda, the Queen of Glory said to the women of the harem :—

' " Arise now, dress your hair, and clothe yourselves in fresh raiment. 'Tis long since we have beheld the Great King of Glory. Let us go and visit the Great King of Glory!"

' " Even so, lady!" said the women of the harem, Ânanda, in assent, to the Queen of Glory. And they dressed their hair, and clad themselves in fresh raiment, and came near to the Queen of Glory.

'Then, Ânanda, the Queen of Glory said to the Great Adviser :—

' " Arrange, O Great Adviser, the fourfold army in array. 'Tis long since I have beheld the Great King of Glory. I am about to go to visit the Great King of Glory."

' " Even so, O Queen!" said the Great Adviser, Ânanda, in assent, to the Queen of Glory. And he set the fourfold army in array, and had the fact announced to the Queen of Glory in the words :—

' " The fourfold army, O Queen, is set for thee in array. Do now whatever seemeth to thee fit."

8. [190] 'Then, Ânanda, the Queen of Glory, with the fourfold army, repaired, with the women of the harem, to the Palace of Righteousness. And when she

had arrived there she mounted up into the Palace of Righteousness, and went on to the chamber of the Great Complex. And when she had reached it, she stopped and leant against the side of the door.

'When, Ânanda, the Great King of Glory heard the noise he thought:—

'"What, now, may this noise, as of a great multitude of people, mean?"

'And going out from the chamber of the Great Complex, he beheld the Queen of Glory standing leaning up against the side of the door. And when he beheld her, he said to the Queen of Glory:—

'"Stop there, O Queen! Enter not!"'

9. 'Then the Great King of Glory, Ânanda, said to one of his attendants:—

'"Arise, good man! take the golden couch out of the chamber of the Great Complex, and make it ready under that grove of palm trees which is all of gold."

'"Even so, lord!" said the man, in assent, to the Great King of Glory. And he took the golden couch out of the chamber of the Great Complex, and made it ready under that grove of palm trees which was all of gold.

'Then, Ânanda, the Great King of Glory laid himself down in the dignified way a lion does; and lay with one leg resting on the other, calm and self-possessed.'

10. 'Then, Ânanda, there occurred to the Queen of Glory this thought:—

'"How calm are all the limbs of the Great King of Glory! How clear and bright is his appearance! O may it not be that the Great King of Glory is dead[1]!'

'And she said to the Great King of Glory:—

'"Thine, O King, are those four and eighty thousand

---

[1] On the approach of death, explains the commentator, people are transfigured, shine forth. This idea may be the source of the legend of the Transfiguration translated above, p. 146, 'Book of the Great Decease,' IV, 37.

cities, the chief of which is the royal city of Kusâvatî. Arise, O King, re-awaken thy desire for these! quicken thy longing after life! [191]

' " Thine, O King, are those four and eighty thousand palaces, the chief of which is the Palace of Righteousness. Arise, O King, re-awaken thy desire for these, quicken thy longing after life.

' " Thine, O King, are those four and eighty thousand chambers, the chief of which is the chamber of the Great Complex. Arise, O King, re-awaken thy desire for these, quicken thy longing after life.

' " Thine, O King, are those four and eighty thousand divans, of gold, and silver, and ivory, and sandal wood, spread with long-haired rugs, and cloths embroidered with flowers, and magnificent antelope skins, covered with lofty canopies, and provided at both ends with purple cushions. Arise, O King, re-awaken thy desire for these, quicken thy longing after life.

' " Thine, O King, are those four and eighty thousand state elephants, with trappings of gold, and gilded flags, and golden coverings of network,—of which the king of elephants, called 'the Changes of the Moon,' is chief. Arise, O King, re-awaken thy desire for these, quicken thy longing after life.

' " Thine, O King, are those four and eighty thousand state horses, with trappings of gold, and gilded flags, and golden coverings of network,—of which ' Thunder-cloud,' the king of horses, is the chief. Arise, O King, re-awaken thy desire for these, quicken thy longing after life.

' " Thine, O King, are those four and eighty thousand chariots, with coverings of the skins of lions, and of tigers, and of panthers,—of which the chariot called ' the Flag of Victory' is the chief. Arise, O King, re-awaken thy desire for these, quicken thy longing after life.

' " Thine, O King, are those four and eighty thousand gems, of which the Wondrous Gem is the chief. Arise, O King, re-awaken thy desire for these, quicken thy longing after life.

' " Thine, O King, are those four and eighty thousand wives, of whom the Queen of Glory is the chief. Arise, O King, re-awaken thy desire for these, quicken thy longing after life.

' " Thine, O King, are those four and eighty thousand yeomen, of whom the Wonderful Steward is the chief. Arise, O King, re-awaken thy desire for these, quicken thy longing after life.

' " Thine, O King, are those four and eighty thousand nobles, of whom the Wonderful Adviser is the chief. Arise, O King, re-awaken thy desire for these, quicken thy longing after life.

' " Thine, O King, are those four and eighty thousand cows, with jute trappings, and horns tipped with bronze. Arise, O King, re-awaken thy desire for these, quicken thy longing after life [192].

' " Thine, O King, are those four and eighty thousand myriads of garments, of delicate textures, of flax, and cotton, and silk, and wool. Arise, O King, re-awaken thy desire for these, quicken thy longing after life.

' " Thine, O King, are those four and eighty thousand dishes, in which, in the evening and in the morning, rice is served. Arise, O King, re-awaken thy desire for these, quicken thy longing after life." '

---

11. 'When she had thus spoken, Ânanda, the Great King of Glory said to the Queen of Glory :—

' " Long hast thou addressed me, O Queen, in pleasant words, much to be desired, and sweet. Yet now in this last time you speak in words unpleasant, disagreeable, not to be desired."

' " How then, O King, shall I address thee ? "

' " Thus, O Queen, shouldst thou address me—The nature of all things near and dear to us, O King, is such that we must leave them, divide ourselves from them, separate ourselves from them [1]. Pass not away,

---

[1] The Pâli words are the same as those at the beginning of the constantly repeated longer phrase to the same effect in the 'Book of the Great Decease.'

O King, with longing in thy heart. Sad is the death of him who longs, unworthy is the death of him who longs[1]. Thine, O King, are these four and eighty thousand cities, the chief of which is the royal city of Kusâvatî. Cast away desire for these, long not after life.

'"Thine, O King, are these four and eighty thousand palaces, the chief of which is the Palace of Righteousness. Cast away desire for these, long not after life.

[193] '"Thine, O King, are these four and eighty thousand chambers, the chief of which is the chamber of the Great Complex. Cast away desire for these, long not after life.

'"Thine, O King, are these four and eighty thousand divans, of gold, and silver, and ivory, and sandalwood, spread with long-haired rugs, and cloths embroidered with flowers, and magnificent antelope skins, covered with lofty canopies, and provided at both ends with purple cushions. Cast away desire for these, long not after life.

'"Thine, O King, are these four and eighty thousand state elephants, with trappings of gold, and gilded flags, and golden coverings of network,—of which the king of elephants, called 'the Changes of the Moon,' is the chief. Cast away desire for these, long not after life.

'"Thine, O King, are these four and eighty thousand state horses, with trappings of gold, and gilded flags, and golden coverings of network,—of which 'Thundercloud,' the king of horses, is the chief. Cast away desire for these, long not after life.

'"Thine, O King, are these four and eighty thousand chariots, with coverings of the skins of lions, and of tigers, and of panthers,—of which the chariot called 'the Flag of Victory' is the chief. Cast away desire for these, long not after life.

'"Thine, O King, are these four and eighty thousand gems, of which the Wondrous Gem is the chief. Cast away desire for these, long not after life.

[1] Compare Jâtaka, No. 34.

' " Thine, O King, are these four and eighty thousand wives, of which the Queen of Glory is the chief.　Cast away desire for these, long not after life.

' " Thine, O King, are these four and eighty thousand yeomen, of whom Wonderful Steward is the chief. Cast away desire for these, long not after life.

' " Thine, O King, are these four and eighty thousand nobles, of whom the Wonderful Adviser is the chief. Cast away desire for these, long not after life.

' " Thine, O King, are these four and eighty thousand cows, with jute trappings, and horns tipped with bronze. Cast away desire for these, long not after life.

[194] ' " Thine, O King, are these four and eighty thousand myriads of garments, of delicate textures, of flax, and cotton, and silk, and wool.　Cast away desire for these, long not after life.

' " Thine, O King, are these four and eighty thousand dishes, in which, in the evening and in the morning, rice is served.　Cast away desire for these, long not after life." '

12. 'When he thus spake, Ânanda, the Queen of Glory wept and poured forth tears.

'Then, Ânanda, the Queen of Glory wiped away her tears, and addressed the Great King of Glory, and said :

' " The nature of all things near and dear to us, O King, is such that we must leave them, divide ourselves from them, separate ourselves from them. Pass not away, O King, with longing in thy heart. Sad is the death of him who longs, unworthy is the death of him who longs.　Thine, O King, are these four and eighty thousand cities, the chief of which is the royal city of Kusâvatî.　Cast away desire for these, long not after life.

' " Thine, O King, are these four and eighty thousand palaces, the chief of which is the Palace of Righteousness.　Cast away desire for these, long not after life.

' " Thine, O King, are these four and eighty thousand chambers, the chief of which is the chamber of the

Great Complex. Cast away desire for these, long not after life.

'"Thine, O King, are these four and eighty thousand divans, of gold, and silver, and ivory, and sandalwood, spread with long-haired rugs, and cloths embroidered with flowers, and magnificent antelope skins, covered with lofty canopies, and provided at both ends with purple cushions. Cast away desire for these, long not after life.

'"Thine, O King, are these four and eighty thousand state elephants, with trappings of gold, and gilded flags, and golden coverings of network,—of which the king of elephants, called 'the Changes of the Moon,' is the chief. Cast away desire for these, long not after life.

'"Thine, O King, are these four and eighty thousand state horses, with trappings of gold, and gilded flags, and golden coverings of network,—[195] of which 'Thunder-cloud,' the king of horses, is the chief. Cast away desire for these, long not after life.

'"Thine, O King, are these four and eighty thousand chariots, with coverings of the skins of lions, and of tigers, and of panthers,—of which the chariot called 'the Flag of Victory' is the chief. Cast away desire for these, long not after life.

'"Thine, O King, are these four and eighty thousand gems, of which the Wondrous Gem is the chief. Cast away desire for these, long not after life.

'"Thine, O King, are these four and eighty thousand wives, of whom the Queen of Glory is the chief. Cast away desire for these, long not after life.

'"Thine, O King, are these four and eighty thousand yeomen, of whom the Wonderful Steward is the chief. Cast away desire for these, long not after life.

'"Thine, O King, are these four and eighty thousand nobles, of whom the Wonderful Adviser is the chief. Cast away desire for these, long not after life.

'"Thine, O King, are these four and eighty thousand cows, with jute trappings, and horns tipped with bronze. Cast away desire for these, long not after life.

'"Thine, O King, are these four and eighty thousand

myriads of garments, of delicate textures, of flax, and cotton, and silk, and wool. Cast away desire for these, long not after life.

' " Thine, O King, are these four and eighty thousand dishes, in which, in the evening and in the morning, rice is served. Cast away desire for these, long not after life." '

13. ' Then immediately, Ânanda, the Great King of Glory died. Just, Ânanda, as when a yeoman has eaten a hearty meal he becomes all drowsy, just so were the feelings he experienced, Ânanda, as death came upon the Great King of Glory.

[196] 'When the Great King of Glory, Ânanda, had died, he came to life again in the happy world of Brahmâ.

'For eight and forty thousand years, Ânanda, the Great King of Glory lived the happy life of a prince, for eight and forty thousand years he was viceroy and heir-apparent, for eight and forty thousand years he ruled the kingdom, and for eight and forty thousand years he lived, as a layman, the noble life in the Palace of Righteousness. And then, when full of noble thoughts he died, he entered, after the dissolution of the body, the world of Brahmâ[1].'

14. ' Now it may be, Ânanda, that you may think " The Great King of Glory of that time was another person." But, Ânanda, you should not view the matter thus. I at that time was the Great King of Glory.

'Mine at that time were the four and eighty thousand cities, of which the chief was the royal city of Kusâvatî.

'Mine were the four and eighty thousand palaces, of which the chief was the Palace of Righteousness.

---

[1] The 'noble thoughts' are the Brahma-vihâras, the sublime conditions described above, Chap. II, § 4. The 'noble life' is the Brahmacariya*m*, which does not mean the same as it does in Sanskrit. The adjective Brahma may have reference here also to the subsequent (and consequent?) rebirth in the Brahmaloka.

'Mine were the four and eighty thousand chambers, of which the chief was the chamber of the Great Complex.

'Mine were the four and eighty thousand divans, of gold, and silver, and ivory, and sandalwood, spread with long-haired rugs, and cloths embroidered with flowers, and magnificent antelope skins, covered with lofty canopies, and provided at both ends with purple cushions.

'Mine were the four and eighty thousand state elephants, with trappings of gold, and gilded flags, and golden coverings of network,—of which the king of elephants, called " the Changes of the Moon," was the chief.

'Mine were the four and eighty thousand state horses, with trappings of gold, and gilded flags, and golden coverings of network,—of which " Thunder-cloud," the king of horses, was the chief.

'Mine were the four and eighty thousand chariots [197] with coverings of the skins of lions, and of tigers, and of panthers,—of which the chariot called " the Flag of Victory " was the chief.

'Mine were the four and eighty thousand gems, of which the Wondrous Ge 1 was the chief.

'Mine were the four and eighty thousand wives, of whom the Queen of Glory was the chief.

'Mine were the four and eighty thousand yeomen, of whom the Wonderful Steward was the chief.

'Mine were the four and eighty thousand nobles, of whom the Wonderful Adviser was the chief.

'Mine were the four and eighty thousand cows, with jute trappings, and horns tipped with bronze.

'Mine were the four and eighty thousand myriads of garments, of delicate textures, of flax, and cotton, and silk, and wool.

'Mine were the four and eighty thousand dishes, in which, in the evening and in the morning, rice was served.'

15. 'Of those four and eighty thousand cities, Ânanda, one was that city in which, at that time, I used to dwell—to wit, the royal city of Kusâvatî.

'Of those four and eighty thousand palaces, too, Ânanda, one was that palace in which, at that time, I used to dwell—to wit, the Palace of Righteousness.

'Of those four and eighty thousand chambers, too, Ânanda, one was that chamber in which, at that time, I used to dwell—to wit, the chamber of the Great Complex.

'Of those four and eighty thousand divans, too, Ânanda, one was that divan which, at that time, I used to occupy—to wit, one of gold, or one of silver, or one of ivory, or one of sandalwood.

'Of those four and eighty thousand state elephants, too, Ânanda, one was that elephant which, at that time, I used to ride—to wit, the king of elephants, "the Changes of the Moon."

[198] 'Of those four and eighty thousand horses, too, Ânanda, one was that horse which, at that time, I used to ride—to wit, the king of horses, "the Thunder-cloud."

'Of those four and eighty thousand chariots, too, Ânanda, one was that chariot in which, at that time, I used to ride—to wit, the chariot called "the Flag of Victory."

'Of those four and eighty thousand wives, too, Ânanda, one was that wife who, at that time, used to wait upon me—to wit, either a lady of noble birth, or a Velâmikâni.

'Of those four and eighty thousand myriads of suits of apparel, too, Ânanda, one was the suit of apparel which, at that time, I wore—to wit, one of delicate texture, of linen, or cotton, or silk, or wool.

'Of those four and eighty thousand dishes, too, Ânanda, one was that dish from which, at that time, I ate a measure of rice and the curry suitable thereto.'

---

16. 'See, Ânanda, how all these things are now past, are ended, have vanished away. Thus impermanent, Ânanda, are component things; thus transitory, Ânanda, are component things; thus untrustworthy,

Ânanda, are component things. Insomuch, Ânanda, is it meet to be weary of, is it meet to be estranged from, is it meet to be set quite free from the bondage of all component things!'

17. 'Now I call to mind, Ânanda, how in this spot my body had been six times buried.   And when I was dwelling here as the righteous king who ruled in righteousness, the lord of the four regions of the earth, the conqueror, the protector of his people, the possessor of the seven royal treasures—that was the seventh time.

'But I behold not any spot, Ânanda, in the world of men and gods, nor in the world of Mâra, nor in the world of Brâhma—no, not among the race of Samanas or Brahmins, of gods or men,—where the Tathâgata for the eighth time will lay aside his body [1].'

Thus spake the Exalted One; and when the Happy One had thus spoken, once again the Teacher said :—

'How transient are all component things!
Growth is their nature and decay;
They are produced, they are dissolved again;
To bring them all into subjection—that is bliss [2].'

End of the Mahâ-Sudassana-Suttanta.

---

[1] The whole of this conversation between the Great King of Glory and the Queen is very much shorter in the Jâtaka. This may be perhaps partly explained by the narrative style in which the stories are composed—a style incompatible with the repetitions of the Suttas, and confined to the facts of the story.

But I think that no one can read this Suttanta in comparison with the short passage found in the 'Book of the Great Decease' (above, Chap. V, § 18) without feeling that the latter is the more original of the two, and that the legend had not, when that passage or episode was first composed, attained to its present extended form.

[2] On this celebrated verse, see the note at Mahâparinibbâna Suttanta VI, 16, where it is put into the mouth of Sakka, the king of the gods. The principal word, samkhâra (states, or things, or phenomena), is discussed in the Introduction to this Suttanta. See the 'Journal of the Pâli Text Society' for 1909, and below, p. 248.

INTRODUCTION

TO THE

JANA-VASABHA SUTTANTA.

JUST as the Mahâ-Sudassana is based on one paragraph now incorporated in the Book of the Great Decease, and the Sampasâdaniya is based on another, so our present Suttanta is based on a third.

In the other two cases it is probable, but not certain, that the expansion is later than the paragraph. In this case the available evidence, small as it is, points to a more decisive conclusion. It is easy to point out that probably no one can read the opening paragraphs of the Jana-vasabha, with the episode about the Nâdika adherents in the Book of the Great Decease [1] in his mind, without seeing at once that the latter is older. It is not so easy to point out why—so much depends, in the comparison of two passages of literature, on the personal equation, so evasive are the slight *nuances* of meaning when it is attempted to set them forth at length.

But this can be said. In the Book of the Great Decease the rebirths of certain followers at Nâdika are explained. In the Jana-vasabha, for the sake of the story that follows about Bimbisâra, the well-known king of Magadha, it was necessary to include Magadha; and it was desirable to emphasize Magadha. Magadha is accordingly left out in the first list of localities, and special reasons are then given why it should be included. The story begins by stating that the Buddha used to tell how adherents of the new teaching, who belonged to one or other of ten tribes, had fared in their rebirths. As an example of how he did so the paragraph about the adherents in Nâdika—which is not one of the ten tribes just mentioned—is given word for word. Now, unless that paragraph had been before the story-teller he would surely have given, as an example, one or other, or all, of the ten tribes. As it stands the Nâdika paragraph, and indeed the mention of Nâdika at all, is out of place. On the supposition that the

---

[1] Dîgha II, 91–93.

prologue to the story was composed on the basis of the
Nâdika paragraph, additions necessary or desirable for the sake
of the subsequent story being added to it, everything explains
itself, and is in good order.

It is perhaps as well to repeat the caution that it would
not follow that the Jana-vasabha, as we have it, is younger
than the Mahâ-parinibbâna, as we have it. The Nâdika
paragraph may have been in existence, as a separate episode,
before both of them. The collection (Nikâya) containing
both may have been put together, from older material of
varying dates, at the same time [1]. And this is, in point of
fact, what seems, in the present state of our knowledge to have
been, most probably, the case.

After the prologue, here discussed, the story turns into a
fairy tale, quite well told, and very edifying, and full of subtle
humour [2]. The manner in which the gods, even the highest,
give themselves away, must have been quite satisfactory to the
adherents of the new doctrine, and is quite on a par with
the famous passage in the Kevaddha [3]. Just as the supreme
being of the priestly speculation is there raised to the highest
pinnacle of power and glory that words are able to express,
only to be then described as confessing ignorance; so here,
after his imposing entry into the Council Hall of the gods, he
materializes himself into the form of a Gandharva only to
propagate among them the new gospel. Just previously the
gods have been rejoiced to find that adherents of the new
Teacher, who have died and been reborn among them, outshine them all in radiance and glory; and Sakka, the king of
the gods, has voiced their satisfaction in a hymn of praise to
the Teacher, and his doctrine of the reign (not of the gods
but) of Law.

The irony of it all falls rather flat now. Brahmâ and Sakka
are mere names to us, void of vitality or power. So confident
are we that there are no beings in the universe, worth considering, except human beings, that the whole story seems
simply absurd; and so strange to us is a narrative composed,
not to be read, but to be recited, that however clearly the
necessity for them is explained, the repetitions continue to jar
upon our sense of literary fitness.

It was far different then. Having no books (in our sense of
the word) they liked and looked for the repetitions. The
mixture of irony and earnestness appealed to their literary

---

[1] See above, p. 73.
[2] Compare above, Vol. I, pp. 160–63.
[3] Translated above, Vol. I, pp. 280 ff.

taste. And they all accepted as a matter of course the
existence of gods and fairies, and ethereal beings of varied
character and radiance. We cannot therefore be surprised to
find that this group of Suttantas all directed to the one purpose of persuading the people that the gods were on the side
of the reforming party, attained a lasting success. Even when
the Buddhists, some centuries after the death of the Buddha,
began to write in Sanskrit, they still quoted from these Pâli
mythological legends, and from those passages of them which
seem to our taste the most bizarre [1].

There are two expressions in our Suttanta which merit a
longer discussion than is possible in a note. These are
  kenacid eva karanîyena and
  yâvad eva manussehi suppakâsitam
In each case the question arises whether the *d* is to be taken
as added for euphony, or whether it should be taken with the
following eva to form the word deva, god.

Buddhaghosa comments on the former phrase when it
occurs in the Assalâyana (M. II, 147). There certain
brahmins are said to be staying at Sâvatthi kenacid eva
karanîyena (as Sir Robert Chalmers prints it), that is, 'on
some business or other.' Prof. Pischel, however, in the separate
edition he published at Chemnitz in 1880, prints it kena ci
devakaranîyena, that is 'on some matter connected with
worship of the gods.' The Papañca Sûdanî has kenacidevâti
yaññûpâsanâdinâ aniyamita-kiccena, 'on some undeter-
mined matter such as sacrifice, worship, or so on.' This is an
explanation of the *meaning* of the phrase as found in that
connexion, and not a direction as to whether the phrase contains the word deva or the word eva. The gloss would be
equally correct in either case. In our Suttanta the phrase
occurs in § 11 where Jana-vasabha is sent by one god to
another kenacid eva karanîyena. Here it seems quite
unnecessary to mention that he was sent ' on business referring
to the god,' and the phrase may well be taken in its ordinary
sense as, for instance, in the Mahâ-parinibbâna (D. II, 147).
There Ânanda goes to the Mallas to announce the impending
death of the Buddha and finds them assembled in their Mote
Hall kenacid eva karanîyena—clearly, in this connexion
' on some business or other.' (Cp. D. II, 159.) It may, indeed,
be objected that the clansmen may have been consulting about
some business ' connected with the gods.' That seems, how-

---

[1] See further the remarks in ' Buddhist India,' pp. 219 ff.

ever, unlikely. If really meant it would have been expressed otherwise. And frankly it is most doubtful whether the suggested phrase deva-karanîya 'god-business' is really a good Pâli idiom at all. The best conclusion therefore, in the present state of our knowledge of that idiom, is that the right reading is eva, not deva, and that the phrase always means 'on some business or other.'

The other case is more difficult. The phrase occurs at the end of the epilogue to our Suttanta. It recurs in the Sampasâdaniya (D. III, 122). In both places it is evidently an excerpt from the stock episode found in the Anguttara IV, 308 ff., the Samyutta V, 258 ff., and the Udâna VI, 1, and incorporated in the Mahâ-parinibbâna (D. II, 102 ff., see especially pp. 106, 114). There the Buddha refuses to die till certain things have been accomplished. These are (1) until the Bhikkhus shall have become true hearers, wise and well trained, &c.—(2) until they, having themselves learned the doctrine, shall be able to tell others of it, preach it, expound it, &c.—(3) until they shall be able, by the truth, to refute vain doctrine—(4) until the way of good life shall have become wide spread and popular—(5) yavad eva manussehi pakâsitam, apparently meaning 'until it shall have been well proclaimed among men' (or perhaps 'by men' as Prof. Windisch renders, Mara and Buddha, p. 72). The same set of conditions is then repeated, reading for 'Bhikkhus,' 'Bhikkhunis,' 'laymen' and 'lay women' respectively. The conditions, it will be observed, are all of them conditions to obtain among humans. Nevertheless the Divyâvadâna (p. 202), in Sanskritising (or re-writing) the passage, doubles the d (yavad devamanushyebhyah), and so introduces the gods— 'until it shall have been well proclaimed among (or by) gods and men.' Later tradition does the same. Buddhaghosa brings in the gods in his comments on the Dîgha passages. But the question is, did the version of the episode, as originally composed, have this meaning? The context is against it. Another constantly repeated phrase about the reform being 'for the good and the weal and the gain of gods and men,' is, as Dr. Estlin Carpenter suggests to me, in its favour. But it may be precisely the haunting memory of that phrase that influenced the author of the version included in the Divyâvadâna, and also Buddhaghosa. When once the gods got in, it would be most difficult to dislodge them. There the matter must, for the present, be left.

THUS have I heard.

1. [200][1] The Exalted One was once staying in
Nâdika, at the Brick House. Now at that time the
Exalted One was wont to make declarations as to the
rebirths of such followers (of the doctrine) as had
passed away in death among the tribes round about
on every side—among the Kâsis and Kosalans, the
Vajjians and Mallas, the Chetis and Vamsas, the Kurus
and Panchâlas, the Macchas and Sûrasenas—saying:
' Such an one has been reborn there, and such an
one there[2]. From Nâdika upwards of fifty adherents,
who passed away in death after having completely
destroyed the Five Bonds that bind people to this
world[3], have become inheritors of the highest heavens,
there to pass utterly away, thence never to return.
Full ninety adherents in Nâdika, who have passed
away in death after having completely destroyed the
Three Bonds, and reduced to a minimum lust ill-will
and delusion, have become Once-returners, and on
their first return to this world shall make an end of
pain. Over five hundred adherents of Nâdika, who
have passed away in death after having completely
destroyed the Three Bonds, and become converted,
cannot be reborn in any state of woe, but are assured
of attaining to the Insight (of the higher stages of
the Path).'

2. [201] Now the adherents at Nâdika, when they
heard these revelations, were pleased, gladdened and
filled with joy and happiness at these solutions by the

---

[1] See above pp. 97 ff., and the notes there.
[2] For the details see above, p. 98, § 7.
[3] See ' Dialogues,' I, pp. 200, 201.

Exalted One of the problems that had been put to him.

3. Now the venerable Ânanda heard [of these declarations made by the Exalted One, and of the satisfaction felt by the adherents at Nâdika].

4. And this idea occurred to him :—' But there were also [202] adherents in Magadha, many of them, and of long religious experience, who have passed away in death. One might think that Anga and Magadha were void of adherents who have passed away in death. For they too had entire faith in the Buddha the Law and the Order, they had fulfilled the moral precepts. And yet concerning them, since they passed away in death, nothing has been declared by the Exalted One. It were surely a good thing to evoke a response as to them ; for much folk would believe, and would hereafter enter into bliss. Then too there was Seniya Bimbisâra, king of Magadha, righteous and ruling righteously, benign to priests and laymen, to town-folk and country-folk. His fame are men verily spreading abroad saying :—" Dead is our so righteous king of righteous rule who made us so happy ! How well have we lived in the kingdom of that righteous king !" Now he too had entire faith in the Buddha the Law and the Order, and fulfilled the moral precepts. And people verily have also said, " Seniya Bimbisâra, king of Magadha, who up to the day of his death was given to praises of the Exalted One, is dead." Concerning him who has passed away in death nothing has been declared by the Exalted One. It were surely a good thing to evoke a response as to him ; for much folk would believe, and would here-after enter into bliss. Moreover the Exalted One attained supreme Insight in Magadha. Now where that took place, how should there be no declaration from the Exalted One concerning adherents in Magadha who have passed away in death ? [203] If the Exalted One declare nothing concerning them they will be hurt. And since they would be hurt, how can the Exalted One keep silence ? '

5, 6. Having thus pondered, alone and privately, concerning the Magadhese adherents, the venerable Ânanda rose up the next morning and came into the presence of the Exalted One, and being come, saluted him and sat down on one side.   And so sitting, he told the Exalted One [all that he had heard and thought [1]]. [204] And when he had made an end of thus speaking before the Exalted One, he rose from his seat, saluted the Exalted One rightwise, and went away.

7. Then the Exalted One, not long after the venerable Ânanda had gone away, robed himself in the morning and, taking a bowl and cloak, went forth for alms to Nâdika.   And when he had walked through Nâdika for alms, after his meal, when he had come back again from his round for alms and bathed his feet, he entered the Brick House and sat down on a seat made ready, thinking over and cogitating upon and concentrating his whole mind on the Magadhese adherents, saying to himself : ' I will find out their future, their fate after this life, whither these good men are bound, what their destiny is.'   And he, the Exalted One, saw the Magadhese adherents, whither they were bound, [205] and what their destiny was.   Then at eventide the Exalted One, arising from his meditation, went out of the Brick House, and sat down on a mat spread in the shade behind the lodging place.

8. Then the venerable Ânanda came into the presence of the Exalted One, saluted him and sat down on one side.   Thus seated he said to the Exalted One :—' My lord the Exalted One looks serene, his complexion shines forth, as it were, owing to the tranquillity of his faculties.   Has the lord the Exalted One spent a pleasant day ?'

9. 'When you had made that speech to me, Ânanda, concerning the Magadhese adherents and had gone away, I, when I had gone to Nâdika for alms, had dined, returned, bathed my feet and entered the Brick House, sat me down on a mat spread there and thought

---

[1] Repeated from §§ 1, 2, 4, nearly word for word.

over, cogitated upon, and concentrated my whole mind
on those Magadhese adherents, resolving to know
their future, their fate after this life, whither these good
men were bound, what their destiny would be.   And
I saw, Ânanda, those Magadhese adherents, whither
the good men were bound, what their destiny would
be.   Thereupon an invisible spirit made himself heard,
saying :—" I am Jana-vasabha, O Exalted One ; I am
Jana-vasabha, O Welcome One ! "   Now do you allow,
Ânanda, that you have ever heard of any one bearing
such a name as Jana-vasabha ? '

'I confess, lord, that I have never heard of one
bearing such a name as Jana-vasabha.   Moreover,
lord, on hearing such a name as Jana-vasabha, I am
thrilled with excitement [1], and I fancy [206] it can be
no ordinary spirit who bears such a name as Jana-
vasabha [2].'

10. 'After those words had been spoken, Ânanda,
the spirit himself appeared before me, a splendid
presence.   And he made a second utterance :—" I am
Bimbisâra, O Exalted One!   I am Bimbisâra, O
Welcome One!   'Tis now the seventh time, lord, that
I am reborn into the communion of the great King
Vessavana.   Deceased as a human king, I am in
heaven become a non-human king.

Hence seven, thence seven, in all fourteen rebirths—
So much I know of lives I've lived in the long past.

Long, lord, have I, who am destined not to be reborn in states of woe, been conscious of that destiny,
and now is there desire in me to become a Once-
returner."

'Wonderful is this, marvellous is this that you, the
venerable spirit Jana-vasabha, tell me :—" Long have
I who am destined not to be reborn in states of woe,

---

[1] Literally, the down of my skin bristles.
[2] Literally, the ' Bull of the Folk,' that is glorious among the people.
The name seems scarcely to justify the good Ânanda's excitement,
as such epithets were then, as now, common enough in India.   But it
is part of the art of the story-teller to make a mystery of it.

been conscious of that destiny;" and again:—" Now is
there desire in me to become a Once-returner." How
has it come about that Jana-vasabha the venerable
spirit recognizes his attainment to a distinction so
splendid?'

11. "Nowise save through thy word, O Exalted One,
nowise save through thy word, O Blessed One! From
the moment when I had gone over, in absolute and
entire faith to the Exalted One, from that moment,
lord, [207] did I who am destined not to be reborn in
states of woe, been conscious of that destiny; and I now
desire to become a Once-returner. Now, lord, I have
been sent on a message concerning some business by
King Vessava*n*a to King Virû*l*haka; and on my way
I saw the Exalted One entering the Brick House,
and sitting down to think over, to cogitate upon, to
concentrate his whole mind upon the deceased Magadhese adherents, in the resolve to know their future,
their fate after this life; whither the good men are
bound, what their destiny is. Now it was only the
moment before, lord, that I had heard face to face
and had understood from his own mouth from King
Vessava*n*a, how he had said to his assembly whither
those good men were bound, and what their destiny
was, so it occurred to me that I would visit the Exalted
One, and I would announce it to him. These, lord,
are the two reasons why I came forth to visit the
Exalted One[1].

12[2]. In days gone by, lord, in days long long gone by,
it came to pass that on the night of the feast of the
fifteenth day at the full moon in the month for entering
upon Retreat[3], the month Âsâ*l*hi, the whole of the
gods in the retinue of the Thirty-Three were assembled

---

[1] These two reasons are: firstly, that he had heard a statement
by Vessava*n*a; secondly, that (having noticed, on his way, how the
Exalted One had been thinking on that very matter) he wished to
report it to him.

[2] Recurs slightly altered below, Mahâ-Govinda Suttanta, § 2.

[3] Vassûpanâyika. Vassa is here used in its technical sense of
the yearly Retreat during the rains. See A. I, 51; Vin. I, 137.

together, seated in the hall of Good Counsel. And
around them on every side a vast celestial company
was seated; and at the four quarters of the firmament
sat the Four Great Kings. There was Dhatara*tth*a,
king of the East, seated facing the west, presiding
over his host; Virû*l*haka, king of the South, seated
facing the north, presiding over his host; Virûpakkha,
king of the West, seated facing the east, presiding
over his host; and Vessava*n*a, king of the North,
seated facing the south, presiding over his host. [208]
Whenever, lord, all the gods in the heaven of the
Thirty-Three are assembled and seated in their hall of
Good Counsel, with a vast celestial company seated
around them on every side, and with the Four Great
Kings at the four quarters of the firmament, this is the
order of the seats of the Four. After that come our
seats. And those gods, lord, who had been recently
reborn in the hosts of the Thirty-Three because they
had lived the higher life under the Exalted One, they
outshone the other gods in appearance and in glory.
And thereat, lord, the Thirty-Three were glad and
of good cheer, were filled with joy and happiness,
saying:—"Verily, sirs, the celestial hosts are waxing,
the titanic hosts are waning."

13. Now, lord, Sakka, ruler of the gods, when he
saw the satisfaction felt by the retinue of the Three-
and-Thirty, expressed his approval in these verses:—

The Three-and-Thirty, verily, both gods and lord,
    rejoice,
Tathâgata they honour and the cosmic law sublime [1],
Whereas they see the gods new-risen, beautiful and
    bright,
Who erst the holy life had lived, under the Happy
    One,
The Mighty Sage's hearers, who had won to higher
    truths [2],

---

[1] Literally, 'and the fair Normness of the Norm,' that is, the rule,
not of gods, but of Law.

[2] Visesûpagatâ. See above, Vol. I, p. 296: 'attains to distinc-

Come hither; and in glory all the other gods out-
    shine.
This they behold right gladly, both lord and Thirty-
    Three,
Tathâgata they honour and the cosmic law sublime.

Hereat [**209**], lord, the Three-and-Thirty Gods were
even more abundantly glad and of good cheer and
filled with joy and happiness, saying :—" Verily the
celestial hosts are waxing, the titanic hosts are
waning ! "

14. Then, lord, concerning the object for which the
Three-and-Thirty gods were assembled in their seats
in the Hall of Good Counsel, they took counsel and
deliberated about it ; and with respect to that object
the Four Great Kings were addressed, and with respect
to that object the Four Great Kings were admonished,
standing by their seats :—

The uttered word th' admonished Kings accepted there,
Serene in mind and calm they stood each at his place.

15. Then, lord, a splendid light came forth out of
the North, and a radiance shone around surpassing the
divine glory of the gods. And, lord, then did Sakka,
king of the gods, say to the retinue of the Thirty-
Three :—" According, friends, to the signs now seen,—
the light that ariseth, the radiance that appeareth—
Brahmâ will be manifested. For this is the herald
sign of the manifestation of Brahmâ to wit, when the
light ariseth and the glory shineth [1] " :—

The portents now are seen, so Brahmâ draweth nigh,
For this is Brahmâ's sign, this glorious splendour vast.

16. Then, lord, the gods of the Thirty-Three sat
down in their own places, saying :—" We will ascertain
what shall be the result of this radiance, when we have

---

tion so excellent.' Perhaps this technical phrase is to be taken here
(as in § 28) in its ordinary sense. It would then mean : ' who have
attained to the distinction of rebirth among the gods.'

[1] So also in the Kevaddha (p. 200, translated above, Vol. I, p. 281).

realized it, we will go to meet him. The Four Great Kings also sat down in their own places, saying the same. [210] And when they had heard this, the gods of the Three-and-Thirty were all together agreed :—" We will ascertain what shall be the result of this radiance ; when we have realized it, we will go to meet him."

17. When, lord, Brahmâ Sanamkumâra[1] appears before the Thirty-Three gods, he appears as a (relatively) gross personality which he has specially created. For Brahmâ's usual appearance is not sufficiently materialized to impress the vision of the Thirty-Three Gods. And, lord, when Brahmâ Sanamkumâra appears before the Thirty-Three Gods, he outshines the other gods in colour and in glory. Just, lord, as a figure made of gold outshines the human frame, so, when Brahmâ Sanamkumâra appears before the Thirty-Three Gods, does he outshine the other gods in colour and in glory. And when, lord, Brahmâ Sanamkumâra appears before the Thirty-Three Gods, there is no god in all that assembly that salutes him, or rises up, or invites him to be seated. They all sit in silence, with clasped hands and cross-legged, thinking :—" Of whichever god Brahmâ Sanamkumâra now desires anything, he will sit down on that god's divan." And by whichever god he does sit down, that god is filled with a sublime satisfaction, a sublime happiness, even as a Kshatriya king newly anointed and crowned is filled with a sublime satisfaction, a sublime happiness.

18. [211] So, lord, Brahmâ Sanamkumâra having created a grosser personality and become in appearance as the youth Five-crest[2], manifested himself thus to the gods of the company of the Thirty-Three. Rising up into the air he sat down cross-legged in the sky. Just, lord, as easily as a strong man might sit down cross-legged on a well-spread divan or a smooth piece of

---

[1] See Vol. I, p. 121.
[2] Pañcasikha, which became a famous name in Indian legends, and was adopted by Saivite and Sânkhya writers. It is nowhere explained what, or how disposed, his five crests were.

ground, even so did Brahmâ Sana*m*kumâra, rising up
into the air, sit down cross-legged in the sky.   And
seeing the tranquillity of the gods of the company of
the Thirty-Three he expressed his pleasure in these
verses :—

The Three-and-Thirty, verily, both gods and lord,
    rejoice,
Tathâgata they honour and the cosmic law sublime,
Whereas they see these gods new-risen, beautiful and
    bright,
Who erst the holy life had lived, under the Happy
    One,
The Mighty Sage's hearers, who had won to higher
    truths,
Come hither; and in glory all the other gods out-
    shine.
This they behold right gladly, both lord and Thirty-
    Three,
Tathâgata they honour and the cosmic law sublime.

19. This was the matter of Brahmâ Sana*m*kumâra's
speech.   And he spoke it with a voice of eightfold
characteristics—in a voice that was fluent, intelligible,
sweet, audible, continuous, distinct, deep, and resonant.
And whereas, lord, Brahmâ Sana*m*kumâra communi-
cated with that assembly by his voice, the sound thereof
did not penetrate beyond the assembly.   He whose
voice has these eight characteristics is said to be
Brahmâ-voiced.

20. Then, lord, Brahmâ Sana*m*kumâra, having
created thirty-three shapes of himself [212], sitting each
on the couch of each of the Thirty-Three Gods, thus
addressed the Gods :—

"Now what think ye, my lord gods Thirty-and-
Three?   Inasmuch as the Exalted One hath acted for
the welfare of the peoples, for the happiness of the
peoples, out of pity for the world, for the advantage,
for the welfare, for the happiness of gods and men,
they, whoever they be, Sirs, who have taken the
Buddha for their refuge, the Truth for their refuge,

the Order for their refuge, they, on the dissolution of
the body after death, have been reborn, some of them
into the communion of the Paranimmita-Vasavattî
gods, some of them into the communion of the Tusita
gods, or of the gods in the retinue of Yâma, or of the
Thirty-Three Gods, or of the Four Great Kings.
Those who fill the number of the lowest group, they
go to fill the number of the Gandharva host."

21. This was the matter of Brahmâ Sana*m*kumâra's
speech.   And he spoke it with such a voice, that each
god fancied [1] :—" He who is on my divan, he alone
hath spoken."

Speaks but one Brahmâ-shape, the Thirty-Three all
        speak ;
Silently sits one shape, they all in silence sit.
Then all the Three-and-Thirty with their king too
        think,
He who is on my couch, 'tis he alone that spake [2].

22. Then, lord, Brahmâ Sana*m*kumâra betook himself to one end [of the Hall] and then [213] sitting down
on the divan of Sakka, lord of the gods, addressed the
Thirty-Three Gods :—

" Now what think ye, my lord gods Thirty-and-Three,
of the completeness wherewith the Exalted One, who
knows, who sees, the Arahant, Buddha Supreme, hath
revealed the Four Ways to Iddhi for the development, thereof, for proficiency therein, for the elaboration thereof ?   Which are the Four Ways ?   In the
first place a brother practises that way which is compounded of concentration and effort with desire.   In
the second place a brother practises that way which is
compounded of concentration and effort with energy.
In the third place a brother practises that way which

---

[1] In the text read so so devo.

[2] The first couplet of this verse, oddly enough it seems to us, was
a great favourite.   It survived among the Buddhists for many centuries, and is extant in its Sanskritised form in the Divyâvadâna,
p. 166; and also in the Madhyamaka V*ri*tti, p. 118 of the edition
published by the Buddhist Text Society.

is compounded of concentration and effort with a
[dominant] idea. In the fourth place a brother practises that way which is compounded of concentration
and effort with investigation. These, sir, are the Four
Ways to Iddhi revealed by the Exalted One who
knows, who sees, the Arahant, Buddha Supreme, for the
development thereof, for proficiency therein, for the
elaboration thereof[1]. Now those recluses or brahmins
who, in past times, have enjoyed Iddhi in one or more
of its forms, they have all done so through practice
and improvement in just these Four Ways. And
those recluses or brahmins who, in future times, will
enjoy Iddhi in one or more of its forms, they
will all do so through practice and improvement in
just these Four Ways. And those recluses or brahmins
who, at the present time, enjoy Iddhi in one or more
of its forms, they all do so through practice and improvement in just these Four Ways.

Do ye see, my lord gods Thirty-and-Three, in me
a potency of Iddhi like that?"

"Yea, Brahmâ."

"I too, Sirs, through practice and improvement in
just these Four Ways to Iddhi [214], have acquired
such power and potency therein."

23. Such was the matter of Brahmâ Sanaṃkumâra's
speech. And having thus spoken he addressed the
Thirty-Three Gods :—

"Now what think ye, my lord gods Thirty-and-
Three, of the Three Avenues for arriving at Bliss
manifested by the Exalted One who knows, who sees,
by the Arahant, Buddha Supreme? Which are the
Three?

In the first place, Sirs, take a brother who is living
in indulgence in the pleasures of sense, in association
with bad conditions. He on a certain occasion hears
the Aryan Truth, studies it and acquires both the main

---

[1] There are two sorts of Iddhi, the worldly and the spiritual. On
the former see above, Vol. I, pp. 272, 3; and on the latter Dîgha III,
112, 113.

and the subsidiary doctrines. Having come to this hearing, studying and acquisition, he takes to a life detached from the pleasures of sense, not associated with bad conditions. Under these circumstances he experiences ease and more than ease, happiness. Just as a feeling of complacency may develop into gladness, so does for him, under those circumstances, first ease arise, and, then more than ease, happiness. This, Sirs, is the First Avenue for arriving at Bliss manifested by the Exalted One . . . Buddha Supreme.

24. In the next place, Sirs, take a brother in whom the grosser conditions precedent [1] to action, speech and thought are not entirely calmed down. He on a certain occasion hears the Aryan Truth preached, studies it and acquires both the main and subsidiary doctrines. Having arrived at this hearing, studying and acquisition, the grosser conditions precedent to action, speech and thought in him become entirely calmed down. And from this ease is experienced, and then more than ease, happiness. Just as a feeling of complacency may develop into gladness, so does for him, under those circumstances, first ease arise and then more than ease, happiness. [215] This, Sirs, is the Second Avenue for arriving at Bliss manifested by the Exalted One . . . Buddha Supreme.

25. In the third place, Sirs, take the case of a brother who does not really know that ' This is good,' ' This is bad,' ' This is wrong,' ' This is not wrong,' ' This is to be followed,' ' This is to be avoided,' ' This is base,' ' This is excellent,' ' This is of mixed dark and bright quality.' He on a certain occasion hears the Aryan Truth, studies it and acquires the main and subsidiary doctrines. Having arrived at this hearing, study and acquisition, he now really knows that ' This is good,' he really knows that ' This is bad,' ' This is wrong,' ' This is not wrong,' ' This is to be followed,' ' This is to be avoided,' ' This is base,' ' This is

---

[1] Saṅkhârâ. This paragraph throws light on the celebrated verse given above, p. 232.

excellent,' ' This is of mixed dark and bright quality.'
For him thus knowing, thus seeing, ignorance is put
away, wisdom has arisen. From this extinction of
ignorance, from the arising of wisdom, a sense of ease
arises and, then more than ease, happiness. Just as
a feeling of complacency may develop into gladness, so
does for him, under these circumstances, first ease
arise, and then more than ease, happiness. This, Sirs,
is now the Third Avenue for arriving at Bliss manifested
by the Exalted One who knows, who sees, Arahant,
Buddha Supreme.

These, Sirs, are [216] the Three Avenues for
arriving at Bliss manifested by the Exalted One, who
knows and sees, the Arahant, Buddha Supreme."

26. On this matter, lord, did Brahmâ Sana*m*kumâra
speak. And having so spoken he addressed the
Thirty-Three Gods :—

"Now what think ye, my lord gods Thirty-and-
Three, of the completeness wherewith the Exalted
One, who knows, who sees, the Arahant, Buddha
Supreme, hath revealed the Four Inceptions of Mindfulness [1] for attaining to the Good. And which are the
Four ? Take, Sirs, a brother who abides subjectively
watchful over the body, ardent self-possessed mindful,
that he may discern the unhappiness arising from
coveting the things of the world. So, subjectively
watchful, he attains to right concentration and right
calm. He, having right concentration and right calm
in his physical being, evokes knowledge of and insight
into all other physical forms external to himself. So,
again, he abides subjectively watchful over his feelings
. . . over his heart, . . . over his ideas, ardent self-
possessed mindful, that he may discern the unhappiness
arising from coveting the things of the world. So,
subjectively watchful, he attains to right concentration
and right calm. He, having right concentration and
right calm in his feelings . . . his heart . . . his ideas,

---

[1] The four Satipa*tth*ânas.

evokes knowledge of and insight into the ideas of others external to himself.

These, Sirs, are the Four Inceptions of Deliberation for attaining to the Good completely revealed by the Exalted One, who knows, who sees, the Arahant, Buddha Supreme."

27. On this matter did Brahmâ Sana*m*kumâra speak. And having spoken he addressed the Thirty-Three Gods :—

"Now what think ye, my lord gods Thirty-and-Three, of the completeness wherewith the Exalted One, who knows, who sees, the Arahant, Buddha Supreme, hath revealed the Seven Requisites of Intellectual Concentration [1], for practice of right Rapture, for the perfecting of Rapture? Which are the Seven? Right views, right intention, right speech, right action, right livelihood, [217] right effort, right mindfulness. That concentration of thought, Sirs, which is prepared by these seven factors, is called the Noble Right Rapture together with its bases, together with its requisites. Right intention suffices to maintain right views, right speech suffices to maintain right intention, right action suffices to maintain right speech, right livelihood suffices to maintain right action, right effort suffices to maintain right livelihood, right mindfulness suffices to maintain right effort, right rapture suffices to maintain right mindfulness, right knowledge suffices to maintain right rapture, right freedom suffices to maintain right knowledge.

If any one uttering right speech, Sirs, were to say :— 'Well hath the Exalted One proclaimed the Truth,— the Norm that in this life beareth fruit, that avails not for a time only [2], that welcometh every one, that leadeth away and onward, that each one who hath intelligence may of and by himself understand!' Then in saying :

"Wide opened are the portals to Nirvana!"

---

[1] Samâdhi-parikkhârâ.
[2] akâlika. The opposite tâvakâlika occurs above, p. 195.

He would be rightly saying that. For, Sirs, the doctrine well proclaimed by the Exalted One is all that; and

"Wide opened are the portals to Nirvana!"

For, Sirs, whosoever has unwavering[1] faith in the Buddha, unwavering faith in the Truth, unwavering faith in the Order, and is endowed with the virtues pleasing to the Noble Ones; and whatsoever new gods have appeared in our midst, led hither by the Law, to wit more than twenty-four lacs of Magadha disciples now dead and gone[2]; these all through complete destruction of the Three Bonds, have become converted, and cannot be reborn in any state of woe, but are assured of attaining to the Insight (of the highest stages of the Path). [218] Moreover there are here Once-returners;

"But of that other Breed to tell,
Of higher merit[3], lo! the tale
I cannot reckon, lest perchance
I should offend against the truth."

28. This, lord, was the matter of Brahmâ Sana*m*-kumâra's speech. And concerning what he had spoken, the reflection arose in the mind of the Great King Vessava*n*a:—"Wonderful truly is it, Sirs, marvellous is it, that there should be so glorious a Teacher, so glorious a proclaiming of the Truth, and that such glorious avenues to distinction[4] should be made known!"

---

[1] Avecca, not as Childers thought from ava + eti but from a + vi + eti. Buddhaghosa says acala. Veti (not in Childers) is to wane (see S. I, 135; A. II, 51; KV. 66; Asl. 329), but one can scarcely say 'unwaning faith.'

[2] The reading is uncertain. As it stands the deceased disciples belong only to the second group—the new gods. It is quite possible that it is intended to include them also among the men of faith and virtue in the first group.

[3] These must be Anâgâmins, Non-returners, those who, reborn in one of the heavens, will attain Arahantship there, without returning at all to this world.

[4] Visesâdhigamâ. See note above on § 13.

Then, lord, Brahmâ Sana*m*kumâra discerning this reflection in the mind of the Great King Vessava*n*a, spake thus to him :—

"Now what thinks my lord, the Great King Vessava*n*a? There both has been in past times, a Teacher so glorious, a proclaiming of the Truth so glorious, a making known such glorious avenues to distinction, and there will be also in future times a Teacher so glorious, [214] a proclaiming of the Truth so glorious, a making known such glorious avenues to distinction."

---

29. This was the matter whereof Brahmâ Sana*m*kumâra spoke to the Thirty-Three Gods. And this matter the Great King Vessava*n*a, when he had, in his own person, heard it and assented to it, reported to his own following. And this matter the spirit Jana-vasabha, when he had in his own person heard it so reported by Vessava*n*a, reported to the Exalted One. And this matter the Exalted One, when he had in his own person heard it and assented to it, and had also intuitively discerned it, reported to Ânanda. And this matter the venerable Ânanda, when he had in his own person heard it from the Exalted One and assented to it, reported to the brethren and the sisterhood, to believing laymen and laywomen. And the System waxed influential and prosperous and expanded and broadened with the numbers that joined, so well was it spread abroad among men.[1]

Here endeth Jana-vasabha's Story.

---

[1] Afterwards interpreted to mean ' gods and men' (see pp. 235, 236). But the last two sentences refer here to men and women only. To put in the gods spoils the climax.

INTRODUCTION

TO THE

MAHÂ-GOVINDA SUTTANTA.

THIS Suttanta is certainly, in some respects, among the most interesting in the collection; and for the history of the literature is of great importance.

The subject is twofold, both necessary points at the time, and both scarcely intelligible, without a little attention, to modern Western minds. Even in the East, and to Buddhists, the story now seems somewhat strange and antiquated. The success of the method of argument here adopted has been so far complete that the need of the argument has ceased, the point of view has changed, and the Suttanta, among the most popular in early times, is now, compared to others dealing with the positive side of the doctrine, considered of minor value.

The two points are those of the brahmins and the gods. The method of the argument is not to argue about anything; to accept the opponents' position throughout, and simply to out-flank it by making the gods and the brahmins *themselves* act and speak as quite good Buddhists, and take for granted the Buddhist position on ethical matters. This is of course, from one point of view, logically absurd. No militant brahmin, in favour of the pecuniary or social advantages allowed to brahmins by birth, would speak or act thus. No god, as he was supposed by his worshippers to be (and he existed only as such), would speak or act thus. But the composer (or composers) of the Govinda knew this quite well. And he is (or they are) scrupulously polite. The actions imputed to the brahmin and the gods, the words put into their mouths, are quite admirable. No one can blame the story-teller that they happen also to be Buddhist. The question as to what the good brahmin ought to be, what a good god ought to do or say, is quietly begged in the most delicate way. On this point —the ethical doctrine—the narrator is thoroughly in earnest; and he no less thoroughly enjoys the irony of the incongruities involved. It is the fashion to label all Buddhist writings, without discrimination, as insufferably dull; and the fashion will be kept up, no doubt, among those who do not see the point of the really very able way in which, sometimes, it is all done. But we may be permitted to appreciate a clever story (even with a moral) in spite of the fact that the story part is a story—all make-believe, none of it historically true.

It has been pointed out above (Vol. I, 208), how a brahmin law book, at a time when the increasing respect paid to Wanderers and Bhikkhus threatened loss of prestige and profit to the sacrificing priests, puts into the mouth of Prajâpati the ferocious remark that he who praises such people (the wandering teachers, &c.) 'becomes dust and perishes.' The writer hoped (quite in vain as it turned out) to gain acceptance for his view by attributing it to a deity. This polemical device was quite in accord with the literary ethics of the day. The choice of the god has an artistic touch, and the anecdote *se non è vero è ben trovato*. Quite a number of other instances might be quoted from Indian books of all ages, though not from Pâli works later than the Nikâyas, nor from works written in Ceylon or Burma. And they are found also in other lands and other literatures. The device is peculiar, not to India, but to a certain stage in religious beliefs and literary taste. It is not in reality so good a device as, at first sight, it seems to be. There are many instances, like the one just quoted, where it has altogether failed. As applied here, in the Govinda, the device has failed as regards the brahmins[1]. Where it has had a measure of success (that is, where the opinion thus fathered on a deity has become more or less an accepted opinion), it probably owes more to its validity, or to its appeal to the feeling of the times, than to the help of the deity invoked. The reader may be reminded that the habit of assuming that the deity is on one's own side, of taking it for granted that He shares one's own opinions, comes out quite clearly in modes of expression in constant use, even by very exalted personages, in the Europe of to-day.

Our Suttanta introduces us, in the first scene of the play, to heaven. There the gods rejoice at the increase in their numbers through the appearance, in their midst, of new gods produced by the good Karma of the followers of the new view of life put forward by Gotama. The king of the gods voices their satisfaction in a hymn; and then utters, in eight paragraphs, a eulogy on the Buddha. In scene two the still higher god, Mahâ-brahmâ, appears. He desires to hear the eulogy, which is accordingly repeated for his benefit. He approves of it, and

---

[1] This question has been fully discussed, and the reasons for the failure given, above, Vol. I, pp. 105, 138 ff., and especially 141.

adds that the Exalted One had long been as wise as that. In support of this he then tells the story which forms the second act, as it were, in many scenes. Here we have Brahmâ's view (that is, the view of the author or authors of the Govinda) concerning the ideal brahmin. It is really very funny ; whether we compare it with the actual brahmin of to-day, or with the brahmin as described in the epics and the law books, or with the brahmin as he probably really was in the Buddha's time. The last must have been in the authors' mind all the time ; and the incongruity, though quite courteous, is sufficiently startling.

The episode told in Act I, Scenes 1 and 2, has already occurred, nearly word for word, in the Jana-vasabha :—

Jana-vasabha 12, 13 = Govinda 2, 3.

       „   14–19 =   „   14–18.

The intervening passage (Govinda 4–13) contains Sakka's eulogy. A eulogy is also part of the Jana-vasabha (§§ 22 ff.). But it is there put, at a later stage in the episode, into the mouth of Brahmâ, and deals accordingly with much deeper matters [1].

What is the conclusion to be drawn from these facts ? They would be explained if the episode had existed in the community before either of these Suttantas had been put into its present shape ; and had been so popular that it had been worked up, by different authors, in slightly differing ways. Or the author or authors of either Suttanta might have altered an episode, already incorporated in the other, to harmonize better with the particular lines of his own story. In that case it must be the Govinda version that is the later. In it the eulogy is put into the mouth of Sakka, and altered to suit that divinity, because Brahmâ's speech was wanted for the story to follow. In either case it is evident that, at the time when these Suttantas were put together as we have them, the legendary material current among the community was still in a fluid, unstable, condition, so that it was not only possible, it was considered quite the proper thing, to add to or alter it.[2]

---

[1] This difference in the mental endowments of the two gods,—the one the mere king of the gods, an Indian Zeus ; and the other the Great First Cause, the outcome of the hightest speculation—is always carefully observed in the various speeches ascribed, in the early Buddhist texts, to these divinities. See above, p. 175, for another instance.

[2] The doctrinal material stands on a different footing. Already in 1877 I ventured to point out the difference (in ' Buddhism,' pp. 86–7), and the point has since increasingly forced itself upon my notice.

The whole story is retold, in a Sanskrit dialect and in different phraseology and order, in the Mahâvastu. The following table will make the degree of the resemblance and difference plain.

Mahâ-govinda Suttanta.	Govindîya Sutta in Mahâvastu.
§ 1	Vol. III, p. 197
2	198
4	199
5, 6	200
8	201
9	200
10	201
12	201
13	198
17	203
19–27	202
29	204
30	205
31, 32	206
34	207
35, 36	208
37, 38	209
43, 44	210, 11
45	212
46	213, 14
47	215
48	217
49	218
50	216
51	219
56	220
57, 58	222
60	223
61	215

Now we do not know exactly when and where Buddhists began to write in Sanskrit, though it was probably in Kashmir some time before the beginning of our era. They did not then *translate* into Sanskrit any Pâli book. They wrote new books. And the reason for this was twofold. In the first place they had already come to believe things very different from those contained in the canon; they were no longer in full sympathy with it. In the second place, though Pâli was never the vernacular of Kashmir, it was widely known there, and even very probably still used for literary work; translations were therefore not required.

This gives a possible explanation of the most astounding

Professor Windisch (in 'Die Composition des Mahâvastu,' Leipzig, 1909, p. 494) supports this view.

fact we know about the Mahâvastu. It purports to be the Vinaya (that is, the Rules regulating the outward conduct of the members of the Order), as held by the school of the Lokottara-vâdins. In M. Senart's admirable edition it fills three bulky volumes. There is not, from beginning to end of them, even one single Rule of the Order! No explanation has been given of this extraordinary state of things, though it was pointed out at once on the publication of the edition[1]. Prof. Windisch in his able discussion (just above referred to) of the actual contents of the book does not refer to this remarkable omission.

The old Vinaya begins with the Sutta Vibhanga, that is, the Rules themselves elucidated by discussion of their origin and meaning. This occupies 615 pages in Oldenberg's editions. Then follow in 660 pages the Khandhakas, twenty-two in number, dealing with various points of Canon Law. At the beginning of these is an Introduction, explaining how the Order arose; and at the end an Appendix, on the Councils[2]. This old Vinaya has never been translated into Sanskrit. The Mahâvastu is based on the Introduction to the Khandhakas, rewritten, added to, enormously expanded, and arranged according to the order of the Pâli Nidâna Kathâ. Now why did the Lokottara-vâdins, in their Vinaya, omit practically the whole of the Vinaya, and confine themselves to rewriting the Introduction to what is only a part of the Vinaya? Why did not they also rewrite the rest? May it be because, when they wrote, the old rules and explanations, with which they did not quarrel in the least, were still well known and used in the original Pâli, or in some closely cognate shape?[3]

It must have been from some such cognate recension, and not from our Pâli text, that the Govinda story was Sanskritised. The differences between the Dîgha and the Mahâvastu are too great to have arisen at one stage. The whole point of the story in the Dîgha is the way in which Brahmâ describes his

---

[1] Rhys Davids, J. R. A. S., 1898, 424.

[2] There is a supplementary work, the Parivâra, much shorter, and consisting mainly of what we should now call examination papers. This volume, though most interesting from the point of view of the history of Indian education, presupposes the old Vinaya, and is later.

As is well known the Khandhakas come first in Oldenberg's edition, but the order in the MSS. is as above. See for instance Oldenberg's 'Catalogue of the Pâli MSS. in the India Office Library,' J. P. T. S., 1882, p. 59.

[3] Compare Oldenberg's remarks on the Chinese translations of Vinaya at the end of his introduction to the Pâli Text.

ideal brahmin as quite emancipated from animistic superstitions
and practices. He gains access to Brahmâ by practising (with
reference, no doubt, to the closing scene of the Mahâ-Sudassana,
and also to the Tevijjâ and other passages) the Rapture of
Mercy, one of the Brahma-vihâras, or Sublime Conditions.
The Mahâvastu is not satisfied with that. It makes him add
to it the kindling of the mystic Fire, Agni (D. II, 239 and
Mhvst. III, 210). The paean of delight at the arrival of the
new gods (D. II, 227 and Mhvst. III, 203) is introduced in the
Mahâvastu by the words: 'He (Brahmâ) addressed them in
verses.' But it gives only one verse. The others are found
in the Dîgha. Perhaps their ethical standpoint did not appeal
any more to the Lokottara-vâdins. In the eulogy on the
Buddha (D. II, 222 and Mhvst. III, 199) the Mahâvastu mentions
that there are eight points concerning which the Buddha was
worthy of praise. It gives, however, only seven, differing in
order and meaning from the eight given in the Dîgha. Verbal
differences throughout the whole story are found in almost every
paragraph.

In column 136 of Bunyiu Nanjio's catalogue of Chinese
Buddhist books we find mentioned a translation of the Mahâ-
Govinda evidently from some recension different from the Pâli.
It would be interesting to know whether there has, in this
version, been preserved an intermediate stage between the
Dîgha and the Mahâvastu.

[220] THUS have I heard.

1. The Exalted One was once staying at Râjagaha on Vulture-peak Hill. Now when the night was far spent, Five-crest of the Gandharva fairies,[1] beautiful to see, irradiating the whole of Vulture-peak, came into the presence of the Exalted One, and saluted him, and stood on one side. So standing Five-crest the Gandharva addressed the Exalted One, and said :—

' The things, lord, that I have seen, the things I have noted when in the presence of the gods in the heaven of the Three-and-Thirty, I would tell to the Exalted One.'

' Tell thou me, Five-crest,' said the Exalted One.

2. ' In days gone by, lord, in days long long gone by, on the Fifteenth, the holy-day, at the Feast of the Invitations[2] on the night of full moon, all the gods in the heaven of the Thirty-Three were assembled, sitting in their Hall of Good Counsel. And a vast celestial company was seated round about, and at the four quarters of the firmament sat the Four Great Kings. There was Dhataraṭṭha, king of the East, seated facing the west, presiding over his host; Virûḍhaka, king of the South, seated facing the north, presiding over his host; [221] Virûpakkha, king of the West, seated facing the east, presiding over his host; and Vessavaṇa, king of the North, seated facing the south, presiding over his host. Whenever, lord, all the gods in the heaven of the Thirty-Three are assembled, and seated in their Hall of Good Counsel, with the vast celestial company seated around them, and with the Four Great Kings at the four quarters of the firma-

---

[1] Pañcasikho Gandhabbo. See above, p. 244.
[2] Pavâraṇâ.

ment, this is the order of the seats of the four. After that come our seats. And those gods, lord, who had been recently reborn in the hosts of the Three-and-Thirty because they had lived the higher life under the Exalted One, they outshone the other gods in appearance and in glory. Thereat, verily, lord, the Three-and-Thirty gods were glad and of good cheer, were filled with joy and happiness, saying, " Verily, sirs, the celestial hosts are waxing; the hosts of the titans are waning!"

3. 'Then Sakka, lord, ruler of the gods, when he saw the satisfaction felt by the Three-and-Thirty gods, expressed his approval in these verses :—

The Three-and-Thirty, verily, both gods and lord, rejoice,
Tathâgata they honour and the cosmic law sublime,
Whereas they see these gods new-risen, beautiful and bright,
Who erst the holy life had lived, under the Happy One,
The Mighty Sage's hearers, who had won to higher truths,
Come hither ; and in glory all the other gods outshine.
This they behold right gladly, both lord and Thirty-Three,
Tathâgata they honour and the cosmic law sublime.

' Hereat, lord, [222] the Three-and-Thirty gods were even more abundantly glad and of good cheer, and filled with joy and happiness, saying : " Verily, sirs, the celestial hosts are waxing ; the hosts of the titans are waning!"

4. 'Then Sakka, lord, perceiving the satisfaction of the Three-and-Thirty gods, addressed them thus :—

" Is it your wish, gentlemen, to hear eight truthful items in praise of that Exalted One ? "

" It is our wish, sir, to hear them."

' Then Sakka, lord, ruler of the gods, uttered before

the Three-and-Thirty gods these eight truthful items in praise of the Exalted One :—

5. "Now what think ye, my lords gods Three-and-Thirty? Inasmuch as the Exalted One has so wrought for the good of the many, for the happiness of the many, for the advantage, the good, happiness of gods and men, out of compassion for the world—a teacher of this kind, of this character, we find not, whether we survey the past or whether we survey the present—save only the Exalted One.

6. "Inasmuch, again, as the Doctrine has been proclaimed by that Exalted One, a Doctrine for the life that now is, a Doctrine not for mere temporary gain, a Doctrine of welcome and of guidance, to be comprehended by the wise each in his own heart—a preacher of such a Doctrine so leading us on, a teacher of this kind, of this character we find not, whether we survey the past, or whether we survey the present, save only the Exalted One.

7. "'This is good; that is bad'—well has this been revealed by that Exalted One, well has he revealed that this is wrong, [223] and that is right, that this is to be followed, that to be avoided, that this is base and that noble, that this is of the Light and this of the Dark[1]. Such a Revelation of the nature of things, a teacher of this kind, of this character we find not, whether we survey the past, or whether we survey the present, save only the Exalted One.

8. "Well revealed, again, to his disciples by that Exalted One is the Way leading to Nirvana; they run one into the other, Nirvana and the Way. Even as the waters of the Ganges and the Jumna flow one into the other, and go on together united, so it is with that well-revealed Way leading to Nirvana; they run one into the other, Nirvana and the Way. A revealer of such a Way leading to Nirvana, a teacher of this kind,

---

[1] In Milinda, these contrasted distinctions are given to illustrate the exercise of sati ('minding' or 'remembering') by way of careful practice. 'Questions of King Milinda,' i. 58.

of this character we find not, whether we survey the past, or whether we survey the present, save only that Exalted One.

9. "Comrades too has this Exalted One gotten, both students only, travelling along the Way, and Arahants who have lived 'the life.' Them does he not send away, but dwells in fellowship with them whose hearts are set on one object. A teacher so dwelling, of this kind, of this character, we find not, whether we survey the past, or whether we survey the present, save only that Exalted One.

10. "Well established [1] are the gifts made [2] to that Blessed One, widely established is his fame, so much so that the nobles, methinks, continue well disposed towards him. Yet notwithstanding, that Exalted One takes sustenance with a heart unintoxicated by pride. One so living, a teacher of this kind, of this character, we find not, whether we survey the past, or whether we survey the present, save only that Exalted One.

11. [224] "The acts, again, of that Exalted One conform to his speech; his speech conforms to his acts. One who has so carried out hereby the greater and the lesser matters of the Law, a teacher of this kind, of this character, we find not, whether we survey the past, or whether we survey the present; save only that Exalted One.

12. "Crossed, too, by that Exalted One has been the sea of doubt, gone by for him is all question of the 'how' and 'why,' accomplished for him is every purpose with respect to his high resolve and the ancient rule of right. A teacher who has attained thus far, of this kind, of this character, we find not, whether we survey the past, or whether we survey the present, save only that Exalted One."

'These eight true praises, lord, of the Exalted One

---

[1] Abhinippanno lâbho.
[2] Ajjhâsayaṃ âdi-brahmacariyaṃ. Buddhaghosa says these two words are to be taken distributively, and refer to his lofty intentions and to the ethics of the Aryan Path.

did Sakka, ruler of the gods, utter before the Three-and-Thirty gods. Hereat the Three-and-Thirty gods were even more abundantly pleased, gladdened and filled with joy and happiness over the things they had heard.

13. 'Then certain gods, lord, spoke thus :—" Oh! sir, if only four supreme Buddhas might arise in the world and teach the Doctrine even as the Exalted One! That would make for the welfare of the many, for the happiness of the many, for compassion to the world, for the good and the gain and the weal of gods and men."

'And certain other gods spoke thus :—" It would suffice, sir, if there arose three supreme Buddhas in the world."

'And certain other gods spoke thus :—" It would suffice, sir, if two supreme Buddhas arose in the world . . . for the good and the gain and the weal of gods and men."

14. [225] 'Then answered Sakka, ruler of the gods to the Three-and-Thirty :—" Nowhere, gentlemen, and at no time is it possible that, in one and the same world-system, two Arahant Buddhas supreme should arise together, neither before nor after the other. This can in no wise be. Ah! gentlemen, would that this Blessed One might yet live for long years to come, free from disease and free from suffering! That would make for the welfare of the many, for the happiness of the many, for loving compassion to the universe, for the good and the gain and the weal of gods and men!"

'Then, lord, the Three-and-Thirty gods having thus deliberated and taken counsel together concerning the matter for which they were assembled and seated in the Hall of Good Counsel, with respect to that matter the Four Kings were receivers of the spoken word, the Four Great Kings were receivers of the admonition given, remaining the while in their places, not retiring[1].

---

[1] This sounds very much as if the Four Great Kings were looked upon as Recorders (in their memory, of course) of what had been

Taking the uttered word and speech, the Kings
Stood there, serene and calm, each in his place.

15. 'Then, lord, from out of the North came forth
a splendid light, and a radiance shone around, surpassing the divine glory of the gods.   Then did Sakka,
ruler of the gods, say to the dwellers in the heaven
of the Three-and-Thirty :—"According, gentlemen, to
the signs now seen, the light that ariseth, the radiance
that appeareth—will Brahmâ now be made manifest.
For this is the herald sign of the manifestation of
Brahmâ, when the light ariseth and the glory shineth.

Even by yonder signs great Brahmâ draweth nigh.
For this is Brahmâ's sign, this glorious splendour vast.

[226] 'Then, lord, the Three-and-Thirty gods sat
down again in their own places, saying :—"We will
ascertain what shall be the result of this radiance;
when we have realized it, we will go to meet him."
The Four Kings also sat down in their places, saying
the same.   And when they heard that, the Three-and-
Thirty gods were all agreed saying : " We will ascertain what will be the result of this radiance ; when we
have verified it, we will go to meet him."

16. 'When, lord, Brahmâ Sanamkumâra appears
before the Three-and-Thirty gods, he manifests himself as an individual of relatively gross substance which
he has specially created.   For Brahmâ's usual appearance is not sufficiently materialized for the scope of the
sight of the Three-and-Thirty gods.   And, lord, when
Brahmâ Sanamkumâra is manifested before these gods,
he outshines the other gods in his appearance and his
glory.   Just as a figure made of gold outshines the
human frame, so, when Brahmâ Sanamkumâra is manifested before the Three-and-Thirty gods, does he outshine the other gods in his appearance and his glory.
And when, lord, Brahmâ Sanamkumâra is manifested

---

said.   They kept the minutes of the meeting.   If so (the gods being
made in the image of men) there must have been such Recorders at
the meetings in the Mote Halls of the clans.

before the Three-and-Thirty gods, not one god in that
assembly salutes him, or rises up, or invites him to be
seated.   They all sit in silence with folded hands and
cross-legged, each thinking : ' Of whichever god Brahmâ
Sanamkumâra now desires anything, he will seat himself on that god's divan.   And that god by whom he
does so seat himself is filled with a sublime satisfaction,
a sublime happiness, [227] even as a Kshatriya king
that is just anointed and crowned, is filled with a sublime satisfaction, a sublime happiness.

17. ' Then, lord, Brahmâ Sanamkumâra, perceiving
how gratified were those Three-and-Thirty gods, uttered
his approval while invisible in these verses :—

The Three-and-Thirty, verily, both gods and lord,
    rejoice,
Tathâgata they honour and the cosmic law sublime,
Whereas they see these gods new-risen, beautiful and
    bright,
Who erst the holy life had lived, under the Happy
    One,
The Mighty Sage's hearers, who had won to higher
    truths,
Come hither; and in glory all the other gods out-
    shine.
This they behold right gladly, both lord and Thirty-
    Three,
Tathâgata they honour and the cosmic law sublime.

18. ' This, lord, was the substance of Brahmâ the
Eternal Youth's speech.   And he spoke it with a voice
of eightfold quality—a voice that was fluent, intelligible,
sweet and audible, sustained and distinct, deep and
resonant.   And whereas, lord, he made himself audible
to that assembly by his voice, the sound thereof did not
penetrate beyond the assembly.   He whose voice has
these eight qualities is said to have a Brahmâ-voice.

19. ' Then, lord, to Brahmâ the Eternal Youth the
Three-and-Thirty gods spoke thus :—

" 'Tis well, O Brahmâ ! we do rejoice at this that we
have noted.   [228] Moreover Sakka, ruler of the gods,

hath rehearsed to us eight truthful praises of that
Exalted One, and these too we have marked and do
rejoice thereat."

'Then, lord, Brahmâ the Eternal Youth spoke thus
to Sakka, ruler of the gods :—" 'Tis well, O ruler of the
gods ; we too would hear the eight truthful praises of
that Exalted One."

"So be it, O Great Brahmâ," replied Sakka. And
thereupon, beginning " Now what thinketh my lord, the
Great Brahmâ ?" [he uttered once more those eight
truthful praises of the Blessed One, §§ 21–27]¹. Hereat,
lord, Brahmâ the Eternal Youth was pleased and gladdened, and was filled with joy and happiness when he
had heard those praises.

28. [230] 'And so, lord, Brahmâ the Eternal Youth
materializing himself and becoming in appearance like
the youth Five-crest, manifested himself to the Three-
and-Thirty gods, and rising up into the air, he sat down
cross-legged in the sky. Just, lord, as easily as a strong
man might sit down cross-legged on a well-spread divan
or a smooth piece of ground, even so did Brahmâ the
Eternal Youth, rising up into the air, sit down cross-
legged in the sky. And he addressed the Three-and-
Thirty gods thus :—

29. " Now what think ye, my lord gods Thirty-and-
Three ? For how long hath the Blessed One been of
great wisdom? ²

Once upon a time there was a king named Disampati. And king Disampati's minister was a brahmin
named Govinda (the Steward) ³. And king Disampati
had a son named Renu, and Govinda had a son named
Jotipâla. And prince Renu and the young Jotipâla
and six other young nobles—these eight—were great
friends. [231] Now in the course of years Govinda

¹ §§ 5–12 repeated in the text.
² The Cy. here supplements: Himself desirous of clearing up this
problem, it is as if he went on to say, that there was nothing wonderful in that, so he tells the story.
³ It is evident from §§ 30, 31 that Govinda, literally 'Lord of the
Herds,' was a title, not a name, and means Treasurer or Steward.

died. And king Disampati mourned for him, saying:
—'Alas! just when we had devolved all our duties on
Govinda the brahmin, and were surrounded by and
giving ourselves up to the pleasures of sense, Govinda
has died!'

Then said prince Re*n*u to the king:—'Mourn not,
sire, so excessively for Govinda, the brahmin. Govinda
has a son, young Jotipâla, who is wiser than his father
was, better able to see what is profitable than his father.
Let Jotipâla administer all such affairs as were entrusted
to his father.'

'Do you think so, my boy?'

'I do, sire.'

30. Then king Disampati summoned a man and
said: 'Come you, good man, go to Master Jotipâla,
and say to him:—May good fortune attend the honourable Jotipâla! King Disampati calls for the honourable
Jotipâla. King Disampati would like to see the
honourable Jotipâla.'

'So be it, sire,' responded the man, and going to
Jotipâla he [232] repeated the message.

'Very good, sir,' responded Jotipâla, and went to
wait upon the king. And when he had come into the
king's presence, he exchanged with the king the greetings and compliments of politeness and courtesy, and
sat down on one side. Then said king Disampati to
Jotipâla:—"We would have the honourable youth
Jotipâla administer for us. Let him not refuse to do
so. I will set him in his father's place and appoint him
to the Stewardship[1]."

'So be it, sire,' replied Jotipâla in assent.

31. So king Disampati appointed Jotipâla as his
Steward, and set him in his father's place. And thus
appointed and installed, whatever matters his father
had administered, those did Jotipâla administer; and

---

[1] Govindiye abhisiñcissâmi. Literally, 'I will anoint him to
the Govinda-ship' (the Lordship over the herds). The expression
'anoint' is noteworthy. It suggests that the office was of royal rank.
But a king was of lower rank then than now.

whatever his father had not administered, those matters
did he too not administer. And whatever works his
father had accomplished, and no others, even such
works, and no others, did he too accomplish. Of him
men said:—'The brahmin is verily a Steward!
A Great Steward is verily this brahmin!' And
on this wise Jotipâla came to be called the High
Steward.

32. Now it came to pass that the Great Steward
went to those six nobles, and said to them : 'Disampati
the king is old and wasted with age, [233] full of years,
and arrived at the term of life. Who indeed can
answer for the survival of the living? When the king
dies, it will behove the king-makers to anoint Renu
the prince as king. I suggest, gentlemen, that you
wait on prince Renu, and say to him thus: 'We are
the dear, beloved, and congenial friends of our lord
Renu. We are happy when our lord is happy; unhappy when he is unhappy. Disampati, our lord
king, is old and wasted with age, full of years and
arrived at the term of life. Who indeed can answer
for the living? When the king dies, it will behove
the king-makers to anoint our lord Renu king. If
our lord Renu should gain the sovereignty, let him
divide it with us."'

33. 'So be it,' responded the six nobles, and waiting
upon prince Renu they repeated these words to him.

'Why, sirs, who besides myself ought to prosper in
this realm if it be not you? If I, sirs, shall gain the
sovereignty, I will divide it with you.'

34. [234] And it came to pass in course of time that
king Disampati died. And after his death, the king-
makers anointed Renu his son king. And he, when
he was made king, lived surrounded by and given up
to the pleasures of sense. Then the High Steward
went to those six nobles and said thus :—

'Disampati, gentlemen, is dead, and my lord Renu
lives surrounded by and given up to the pleasures of
sense. Well, gentlemen, who can say? The pleasures
of sense are intoxicating, I would suggest, gentlemen,

that you wait on king Re*n*u and say to him : " king Disampati, my lord, is dead, my lord Re*n*u is anointed king.   Does my lord remember his promise ? " '

' Very good, sir,' responded the six nobles, and going into Re*n*u's presence, they said :—

' King Disampati, sire, is dead, and my lord Re*n*u is anointed king.   Does my lord remember his promise ?'

' I do remember my promise, gentlemen.   Which of you gentlemen now is able successfully to divide this mighty earth, so broad on the north and . . . [1] on the south, into seven equal portions ?'

' Who, sire, is able if it be not the Great Steward, the brahmin ?'

35. Then king Re*n*u sent a man to the Great Steward, saying :—' Come, my good fellow, go to the Great Steward, the brahmin, and say : " The king has sent for you, my lord." ' [235] And the Great Steward was told and obeyed, and, coming into the king's presence, exchanged with him the greetings and compliments of politeness and courtesy, and sat down on one side.   Then said the king to him : ' Will you go, my lord Steward, and so divide this great earth wide on the north and . . . . on the south into seven equal portions, all . . .'

' Very good, sire,' responded the High Steward, [And this he did.]

36. And king Re*n*u's country held the central position.   As it is said :—

---

[1] Saka*t*amukka. This adjective, applied here to the earth, and at the end of the next section to the seven kingdoms, is at present quite unintelligible ; and is left untranslated. The traditional explanations differ. Samarasekara (Colombo, 1905) translates here (p. 1016) daku*n*u pasin gael mukhayak lesa*t*a, that is, ' on the south side like a waggon's mouth.' Buddhaghosa has nothing here ; but below as applied to the kingdoms he explains ' with their mouths debouching together.' Neither is satisfactory. It has been suggested that it might mean ' facing the Wain,' that is, the constellation of the Great Bear. But this is unfortunately in the North. The front opening of a bullock waggon is (now) elliptical in form.

Dantapura of the Kâlingas, and Potana for the
Assakas,
Mâhissatî for the Avantis, and Roruka in the Sovîra
land.

Mithilâ of the Videhâs, and then Campâ among the
Angas,
Lastly Benares in the Kâsi realm :—all these did the
Great Steward wisely plan.

[236] Then were those six nobles well pleased each
with his allotted gain, and at the success of his plan.
For they said :—'What we wished for, what we
desired, what we intended, what we aimed at, lo!
that is what we have gotten.' And the seven kings
were named :—

Sattabhu and Brahmadatta, Vessabhu with Bharata,
Renu and two Dhataratthas :—These are the seven
Bhâratas.[1]

Here ends the first Portion for Recitation.

---

[1] If we follow the order of the names in this no doubt very old
mnemonic doggrel, the result may be tabulated thus :—

City.	Tribe.	King.
1. Dantapura	Kâlingas	Sattabhu.
2. Potana	Assakas	Brahmadatta.
3. Mâhissatî	Avantis	Vessabhu.
4. Roruka	Sovîras	Bharata.
5. Mithilâ	Videhas	Renu.
6. Campâ	Angas	Dhataratthâ.
7. Bârânasi	Kâsis	Dhataratthâ.

This list is enough to show that the verses do not fit with the story.
Renu's kingdom is said in the text to be in the middle. No one of
these seven kingdoms is in the midst of the others. Benares would
suit that position less badly, than any other. It was probably intended therefore that Disampati and Renu were kings or chieftains in
Benares. The king Bharata of the Sovîras of J. III, 470 may be the
same as the Bharata who also appears in the table here as king of the
Sovîras. The Renu of J. IV, 444 is king of the Kurus. None of the
numerous Brahmadattas in the Jâtakas can be identified with our
Brahmadatta. Our Disampati and Renu are referred to, apparently
as kings of Benares, at Dîpavamsa III, 40.
The verses survived, but in a very corrupt state, down to the time
of the Mahâvastu (Vol. III, p. 208, ed. Senart).

37. Now those six nobles came to the High Steward and said to him :—'Just as the honourable Steward was dear, beloved and congenial as companion to Re*n*u the king, so has he been also to us a companion, dear, beloved and congenial. We would that the honourable Steward administer our affairs; we trust he will not refuse to do so.'

'Very good, sirs,' replied the Great Steward. And so he instructed those seven anointed kings in government; and he taught the mantras to seven eminent and wealthy Brahmins and to seven hundred young graduates.

38. [237] Now later on the excellent reputation of the brahmin, the High Steward, was noised abroad after this fashion :—'With his own eyes the High Steward sees Brahmâ! Face to face does the High Steward commune with Brahmâ, converse and take counsel with Him!' Then the High Steward thought: 'This flattering rumour is noised abroad about me, that I both see Brahmâ and hold converse with Him. Now I neither see Him, nor commune with Him, nor converse or take counsel with Him. But I have heard aged and venerable brahmins, teachers and pupils, say : " He who remains in meditation the four months of the rains, and practises the ecstasy of pity, *he* sees Brahmâ, communes, converses, takes counsel with Brahmâ? What if I now were to cultivate that discipline ? "'

39. So the High Steward waited on king Re*n*u, and telling him of the reputation imputed to himself, and of his wish to practise seclusion, added : 'I wish, sir, to meditate during the four months of the rains and to practise the ecstasy of pity. No one is to come near me save some one who will bring me my meals.'

'Do, honourable Steward, whatever seems to you fit.'

40. [238] And the High Steward went round to each of the six nobles, told them the same, and took his leave of them also.

41. Then he went to those seven eminent and wealthy Brahmins, and to the seven hundred graduates,

and telling them [too of the rumours and of his wish to practise seclusion], said :—' Wherefore, sirs, according as you have heard the mantras and have committed them to memory, continue to rehearse them in full, and teach them to each other. I, sirs, wish to meditate during the four months of the rains, and to practise the ecstasy of pity. No one is to come near me save some one who shall bring me my meals.'

' Do, honourable Steward, whatever seems to you fit.'

42. [**239**] Next the High Steward went to his forty wives who were all on an equality, and told them [too of the rumours and of his wish to practise ecstasy in seclusion. And they replied like the others.]

43. Then the High Steward had a new rest-house built eastward of the city, and there for the four months of the rains he meditated, rapt in the Ecstasy of Pity ; nor did any one have access to him save one who brought him his meals. But when the four rainy months were over, then verily came disappointment and anguish over him as he thought : ' Here have I heard aged and venerable brahmins, teachers and their pupils, say : " He who remains in meditation the four months of the rains, and practises the Ecstasy of Pity, he sees Brahmâ, communes, converses, and takes counsel with Brahmâ." But I see not Brahmâ, I commune not, nor converse, nor take counsel with Him.'

44. Then Brahmâ, the Eternal Youth, when in his mind he knew the thoughts [**240**] of the High Steward's mind, vanished from his heaven, and, like a strong man shooting his arm out or drawing back his out-shot arm, appeared before the High Steward. Then verily came fear, then came trembling upon the High Steward, then did the hair of his flesh stand up [1] when he saw this thing that had never been seen before. And he, full of fear and dread with stiffening hair, addressed Brahmâ the Eternal Youth in these verses :—

---

[1] See above, p. 240.

' O Vision fair, O glorious and divine!
Who art thou, lord? knowing thee not we ask,
That we may know!'
　　　　　　　　' In heaven supreme I'm known
As the Eternal Youth. All know me there.
Know me e'en thou, Govinda.'
　　　　　　　　　　' To a Brahmâ Blest
Let seat and water for the feet and sweet
Cooked cakes and drink be brought. We ask what gift
The Lord would take. Would he himself decide
The form for us [1].'
　　　　　　' Hereby we take thy gift,
And now—whether it be for good and gain
In this thy present life, or for thy weal
In that which shall be—Thou hast leave. Come, ask,
Govinda, whatsoe'er thou fain would'st have?'

45. Then the High Steward thought: 'Leave is given me by Brahmâ the Eternal Youth! What now shall I ask of him, some good thing for this life, or a future good?' [241] Then it occurred to him : ' I am an expert regarding what is profitable for this life. Even others consult me about that. What now if I were to ask Brahmâ the Eternal Youth for something of advantage in a life to come?' And he addressed the god in these verses :—

' I ask the Brahmâ, the Eternal Youth,
Him past all doubt I, doubting, ask anent
The things that others would fain know about.
Wherein proficient, in what method trained
Can mortal reach th' immortal world of Brâhm?'

---

[1] The expressions here are all elliptical, and it is not certain that the meanings supplied are quite right as the idioms agghe pucchati and aggham no karoti do not occur elsewhere. The sequence of ideas would seem to be : 'Only such and such are fit to be offered as a mark of respect to so holy a deity. But not knowing which is best, I ask. Let the Holy One make it right.' Then the deity, who wants nothing, taking the will for the deed, says he accepts; and offers a boon.

'He among men, O Brahmin, who eschews
All claims of "me" and "mine"; he in whom thought
Rises in lonely calm, in pity rapt,
Loathing all foul things, dwelling in chastity,—
Herein proficient, in such matters trained,
Mortal can reach th' immortal heav'n of Brâhm.'

46. 'What the Lord saith touching "eschewing all
claims of 'me' and 'mine'" I understand. It is to
renounce all property whether it be small or large,
and to renounce all family life, whether the circle of
one's kin be small or large, and with hair and beard
cut off and yellow robes donned, to go forth from the
home into the homeless life. Thus do I understand
this.

'What the Lord saith touching "thought rising in
lonely calm" I understand. It is when one chooses
a solitary abode—the forest, at the foot of a tree,
a mountain brae, a grotto, a rock-cavern, a cemetery,
or a heap of grass out in the open field. Thus do I
understand this [242].

'What the Lord saith touching "in pity rapt" I
understand. It is when one continues to pervade one
quarter of the horizon with a heart charged with pity,
and so the second quarter, and so the third, and so the
fourth. And thus the whole wide world, above, below,
around and everywhere does one continue to pervade
with a heart charged with pity, far-reaching, expanded,
infinite, free from wrath and ill will. Thus do I understand this.

'Only in what He saith touching "loathing the foul"
do I not understand thee, Lord.

'What mean'st thou by "foul odours among men,"
O Brahmâ? here I understand thee not.
Tell what these signify, who knowest all.
When cloaked and clogged by what is man thus foul,
Hell-doomed, and shut off from the heaven of Brâhm?'

[243] 'Anger and lies, deceit and treachery,
Selfishness, self-conceit and jealousy,

Greed, doubt, and lifting hands 'gainst fellow men,
Lusting and hate, dulness and pride of life,—
When yoked with these man is of odour foul,
Hell-doomed, and shut out from the heav'n of Brâhm.'

'As I understand the word of the Lord concerning
these "foul odours," they cannot easily be suppressed
if one live in the world. I will therefore go forth
from the home into the life of the homeless state.'

'Do, lord steward, whatever seems to you fit.'

47. Then the High Steward waited on king Re*n*u
and said to him :—'Will my lord now seek another
minister, who will administer my lord's affairs ? I wish
to leave the world for the homeless life. I am going
forth in accordance with the word of Brahmâ which I
have heard concerning foul odours. These cannot be
easily suppressed when one is living in the world.'

'King Re*n*u, lord o' the land, I here declare :—
Do thou thyself take thought for this thy realm!
I care no longer for my ministry.'

'If for thy pleasures aught there lacketh yet,
I'll make it good.   If any injure thee,
Them I'll restrain, warlord and landlord I !
Thou art my father, Steward, lo! I am thy son!
Abide with us, Govinda, leave us not.'

'Naught lack I for my pleasures, nor is there
One who doth injure me.   But I have heard
Voices unearthly.   Henceforth home holds me not.'

[244] 'What like is this Unearthly ? What did He say
To thee, that having heard thou will straightway
Forsake our house and us and all the world ?'

'Ere I had passed through this Retreat, my care
Was for due altar-rites, the sacred fire
Was kindled, strewn about with kusa-grass.
But lo! Brahmâ I saw, from Brahmâ's heav'n,
Eternal god.   I asked; he made reply;
I heard.   And now irksome is home to me.'

'Lo! I believe the words that thou hast said.
Govinda.   Having heard the Unearthly Voice.
How could it be thou should'st act otherwise?
Thee will we follow after.   Be our guide,
Our teacher!   So, like gem of purest ray,
Purg'd of all dross, translucent, without flaw,—
As pure as that we'll walk according to thy word.'

'If the honourable Steward goes forth from the home into the homeless, I too will do the like.   For whither thou goest, I will go.'

48. Then the High Steward, the brahmin, waited upon the six nobles, and said to them: 'Will my lords now seek another minister who will administer my lords' affairs?   I wish to leave the world for the homeless life.   I am going forth in accordance with the word of Brahmâ which I have heard concerning foul odours.   These cannot be easily suppressed when one is living in the world.'

Then the six nobles went aside together [245] and thus deliberated:—'These brahmin folk are greedy for money.   What if we were to gain him over through money?'   And coming to the High Steward they said:—'There is abundance of property, sir, in these seven kingdoms.   Wherefore, sir, take of it as much as seems profitable to you.'

'Enough, sirs! I have already abundant possessions, thanks to the action of my lords.   It is that luxury that I am now relinquishing in leaving the world for the homeless life, [even as I have told you].'

49. Then the six nobles went aside together, and thus deliberated: 'These brahmin folk are greedy about women.   What if we were to gain him over through women?'   And coming to the High Steward they said: 'There is, sir, in those seven kingdoms abundance of women.   Wherefore, sir, conduct away with you as many as you want.'

'Enough, sirs! I have already these forty wives equal in rank.   All of them I am forsaking in leaving the world for the homeless life, [even as I have told you].'

50. [246] 'If the honourable Steward goes forth from the home into the homeless life, we too will do the like. Whither thou goest we will go.'

'If ye would put off fleshly lusts that worldling's heart
    coerce,
Stir ye the will, wax strong, firm in the power of
    patience.
This is the Way, the Way that's Straight[1], the Way
    unto the End[2],
The Righteous Path that good men guard, to birth
    in Brahmâ's heaven.'

51. 'Wherefore, my lord Steward, wait yet seven years, and when they are over, we too will go forth from the world into the homeless life. Whither thou goest we will go.'

'Too long, my lords, are seven years! I cannot wait for my lords seven years. For who can answer for the living?[3] We must go toward the future, we must learn by wisdom[4], we must do good, we must walk in righteousness, for there is no escaping death for all that's born. Now I am going forth in accordance with the word of Brahmâ which I have heard concerning foul odours. They cannot be easily suppressed when one is living in the world.'

52. 'Well then, lord Steward, wait for us six years, . . . [or] wait five years . . . four years . . . three . . . two years . . . one year. When a year has gone by we too will leave the world for the Homeless State. Whither thou goest we will go.'

53. 'Too long, my lords, is one year. I cannot [247] wait for my lords one year. For who can answer for the living? We must go towards the future, we must learn by wisdom, we must do good, we must walk

---

[1] See S. I, 33:—'Straight is that way named.'
[2] Anuttaro, lit. having no beyond. The Cy. interprets asadiso, uttamo (unique, supreme).
[3] See above, p. 268.
[4] Mantâya. Mantâ vuccati paññâ, says Buddhaghosa. Cp. the commentary on Dhp. 363; and Anguttara II, 141-228.

in righteousness, for there is no escaping death for all that's born. Now I am going forth in accordance with the word of Brahmâ which I have heard concerning foul odours. They cannot easily be suppressed when one is living in the world.'

54. 'Well then, lord Steward, wait for us seven months . . . six months . . . five . . . four . . . three . . . two months . . . one month . . . [55] half a month . . . seven days, [248] till we have devolved our kingdoms on to our sons and brothers. When seven days are over, we will leave the world for the Homeless State. Whither thou goest we will go.'

'Seven days, my lords, is not a long time. I will wait, my lords, for seven days.'

56. Then the High Steward, the brahmin, came to those seven eminent and wealthy brahmins and to those seven hundred graduates, and said :—'Will ye now seek another teacher, sirs, who will (by repetition) teach you the mystic verses ?[1] I wish to leave the world for the homeless life. I am going forth in accordance with the word of Brahmâ which I have heard concerning foul odours. These cannot easily be suppressed when one is living in the world.'

'Let the honourable Steward not leave the world for the homeless life ! Leaving the world means little power and little gain ; to be a brahmin brings great power and great gain.'

'Speak not so, gentlemen, of leaving the world or of being a brahmin. Who for that matter has greater power or wealth than I ? I, sirs, have been hitherto as a king of kings, as Brahmâ to brahmins, as a deity[2] to householders. And this, all this, I put away in leaving the world, in accordance with the word of Brahmâ . . .' [249]

'If the lord Steward leaves the world for the Homeless State, we too will do the like. Whither thou goest, we will go.'

---

[1] Mante. See last note.

[2] Devatâ; 'like Sakka, king of gods, to all other heads of families.' Cy. The phrase might be taken to mean that Brahmâ was not a devatâ.

57. Then the High Steward, the Brahmin, went to his forty wives, all on an equality, and said :—'Will each of you, ladies, who may wish to do so, go back to her own family and seek another husband ? I wish, ladies, to leave the world for the homeless life, in accordance with the word of Brahmâ . . .'

'Thou, even thou, art the kinsman of our hearts' desire ; thou art the husband of our hearts' desire. If the lord Steward leaves the world for the Homeless State, we too will do the like. Whither thou goest, we will go.'

58. And so the High Steward, the brahmin, when those seven days were past, let his hair and beard be cut off, donned the yellow robes and went forth from his home into the Homeless State. And he having so acted, the seven kings also, anointed kshatriyas, as well as the seven eminent and wealthy brahmins and the seven hundred graduates, the forty wives all on an equality, several thousand nobles, several thousand brahmins, several thousand commoners and several young women from women's quarters, let their hair be cut, donned the yellow robes and went forth from their homes into the Homeless State. And so, escorted by this company, the High Steward, the brahmin, went a-wandering through the villages, towns, [250] and cities. And whether he arrived at village or town or city, there he became as a king to kings, as Brahmâ to brahmins, as a deity to commoners. And in those days when any one sneezed or slipped, they called out :—'Glory be to the High Steward, the brahmin ! Glory be to the Minister of Seven !'

59. Now the High Steward, the brahmin, continued to pervade each of the four quarters of the horizon with a heart charged with love . . . with pity . . . with sympathy in joy . . . with equanimity. And so the whole wide world above, below, around, and everywhere did he continue to pervade with heart charged with equanimity, far-reaching, expanded, infinite, free from wrath and ill will. And he taught to disciples the way to union with the world of Brahmâ.

60. Now all they who at that time had been the High Steward's disciples and in all points wholly understood his teaching, were after their death reborn into the blissful world of Brahmâ. They who had not in all points wholly understood his teaching, were after their death reborn into the company either of the gods who Dispose of Joys purveyed from without, or of the gods of the Heaven of Boundless Delight, or of the gods of the Heavens of Bliss, or of the Yâma gods, [251] or of the Three-and-Thirty gods, or of the gods who are the Four Kings of the Horizon. Even they who accomplished the lowest realm of all, attained to the realm of the Gandharva fairies.

Thus of all those clansmen there was not one whose renunciation proved vain or barren; in each case it bore fruit and development.'

---

61. 'Does the Exalted One remember?'

'I do remember, Five-crest. I was the High Steward of those days.[1] I taught my disciples the way to communion with the Brahmâ world. But, Five-crest, that religious life did not conduce to detachment, to passionlessness, to cessation of craving, to peace, to understanding, to insight of the higher stages of the Path, to Nirvana, but only to rebirth in the Brahmâ-world. On the other hand my religious system, Five-crest, conduces wholly and solely to detachment, to passionlessness, to cessation of craving, to peace, to understanding, to insight of the higher stages of the Path, to Nirvana. And that is the Aryan Eightfold Path, to wit, right views, right intention, right speech, right action, right livelihood, right effort, right mindfulness, right rapture.

62. 'Those of my disciples, Five-crest, who in all points wholly understand my teaching, they from the

---

[1] In spite of this express statement this legend of the High Steward does not appear in the canonical collection of Birth Stories. See Rhys Davîds's 'Buddhist India,' p. 196, for other instances.

destruction of the Deadly Taints have by and for themselves understood, realized and attained to, even in this life, freedom from taint, liberty of heart, liberty of intellect. [252] Those who do not in all points wholly understand my teaching, some of them, in that they have broken away the five Fetters belonging to the Hither Side, are reborn without parents, where they will utterly pass away, being no more liable to return to this world. And some of them, in that they have broken away three [other] Fetters, and have worn down passion and hate and dulness, become Once-Returners, who after once returning to this world shall make an end of Ill. And some of them, again, in that they have broken away those three Fetters, become Stream-Attainers, not liable to be reborn in any state of woe, but assured of attaining to the Insight. And so, Five-crest, of all, even all those persons, there is not one whose renunciation is vain or barren ; in each case it will have brought fruit and development.'

Thus spoke the Exalted One. And Five-crest of the Gandharva fairies was pleased at the word of the Exalted One, and in delight and gladness he saluted the Exalted One, and with the salutation of the right side he vanished from that place.

Here endeth the Story of the Lord High
Steward.

INTRODUCTION

TO THE

MAHÂ-SAMAYA SUTTANTA

THE method followed in this poem is nearly the same as in the two previous Suttantas, only here it is rather the minor gods,—the local deities, the personification of natural phenomena, guardian spirits, fairies, harpies, naiads, dryads, and many others—who are represented as themselves proclaiming their adherence to the new movement. Important gods are indeed incidentally mentioned; and it is perhaps not without intention that great and small are here thrown together, as if Soma and Varuna and Brahmâ were really all of the same kind as the long list of spirits and fairies in which they appear[1].

The poem is almost unreadable now. The long list of strange names awakes no interest. And it is somewhat pathetic to notice the hopeless struggle of the author to enliven his unmanageable material with a little poetry. It remains, save here and there, only doggrel still.

There are three parts to the poem. The first is the list of gods; the second the frame-work, put into the Buddha's mouth, at the beginning (after the prologue), and at the end; the third the prologue, with the verses of the four gods of the Pure Abode. The prologue has been preserved as a separate episode in the Samyutta, I, 27. The way in which the list is fitted into the frame-work in our sections 4, 5, and 6 is very confused and awkward; and the grammar of the frame-work is inconsistent with the grammar of the list. It is highly probable therefore that the list itself, and also the epilogue, had been handed down as independent works in the community before our Suttanta was composed. The frame-work may be the work of the editor.

Our list here begins in §§ 7, 8, with seven classes or groups of gods, without personal names. The personal names begin at § 9, with the four Great Kings of the four quarters; and

---

[1] So above, Vol. I, p. 17, the worship of Agni is deliberately inserted in a list of animistic hocus-pocus.

§§ 10-20 follow with ten other groups in each of which the principal personal names are given. There is another list of gods in the Âṭânâṭiya (No. 32 in the Dîgha). This other list also begins with the four Great Kings; and then adds, as a sort of afterthought or appendix, the names of forty-one gods, all mentioned one after another, without division into groups, and without any details. Our §§ 10-20 look very much like an improved and enlarged edition of the bare list in the Âṭânâṭiya. The latter is just such a mnemonic doggrel as was found useful in other cases also by the early Buddhists, who had no books, and were compelled to carry their dictionaries and works of reference in their heads. There are other instances in Pâli literature of the original mnemonic verses, and their subsequent expansion, having both been preserved.

As the contents of the two lists, and their great importance for the history of religion in India, have been discussed else-where[1], it is only necessary here to remind the reader that when these Suttantas were composed the names they con-tain were full of meaning to the people; and that the legends here told were intended to counteract the animistic delusions about them then so prevalent in the Ganges valley. They are almost the only evidence we have as yet outside the priestly books. Perhaps the most important fact to which they bear testimony is the continual change in animistic belief that went on in India. They are of especial value, as they show what those beliefs were at a particular period. We shall not be able to have a scientific history of religion in India until the absurd anachronisms of the classical Sanskrit literature have been discarded; and until we have learnt care-fully to distinguish between the divers faiths and gods which, in those books, are mixed up together, and supposed to have remained the same for many centuries on end.

---

[1] Rhys Davids's 'Buddhist India,' pp. 219-237.

[XX. MAHÂ-SAMAYA SUTTANTA.

The Great Concourse.]

1. [253] Thus have I heard. The Blessed One was once dwelling among the Sâkiyas, at Kapilavatthu in the Great Wood, together with a great band of the brethren, about five hundred of them, all being Arahants. And gods from the ten thousand world-systems oft-times assembled there that they might visit the Exalted One and the band of brethren.

2. Now to four gods of the hosts of the Pure Abodes this thought occurred :—'That Blessed One is now dwelling among the Sâkiyas, at Kapilavatthu in the Great Wood, together with a great band of the brethren, about five hundred of them, all being Arahants. And gods from the ten thousand world-systems oft-times are assembling there to see the Exalted One and his band of brethren. What if we, too, were to go into his presence, and before him were to recite each of us a poem ?'

3. Then those gods, as easily as a strong man might stretch out his arm, or draw back his out-stretched arm, [254] vanished from the Pure Abodes, and appeared before the Exalted One. There they saluted him and stood on one side. And so standing one of the gods recited to the Blessed One this verse :—

'Great is the gathering in the glade! The hosts of
    heaven together met!
We too are come unto this congress blest, and fain
    would see
       The Company Invincible.'

Then another god recited to the Exalted One this verse :—

' The brethren there, wrought up to concentration rapt,
        make straight their hearts,
Wisely, as driver keeping grip on rein, their faculties
        they guard.'

Then another god recited to the Exalted One this
verse :—

'All bars and bolts are hewn in twain for them,
The threshold is dug up.[1]
        In purity, their way they go,
Stainless, with vision clear, like well-tamed elephants.'

[255] Then the other god recited to the Exalted
One this verse :—

' Who in the Buddha refuge take, they shall not go to
        woeful doom.
When they put off this human frame they shall fill
        up the hosts in heaven.'

4. Then said the Exalted One to the brethren :—
'Oft-times, brethren, do gods from the ten world-
systems foregather to see the Tathâgata and the company of the Brethren. Whosoever, brethren, in the
past were Arahant Buddhas supreme, upon them
waited a like number of the heavenly hosts, and a like
number shall wait upon whosoever shall, in the future,
be Arahant Buddhas supreme. I will detail to you,
brethren, the names of the hosts of gods, I will publish
abroad, brethren, their names, I will teach you,
brethren, their names. Hearken hereunto and pay
heed, and I will speak.'

' Even so, lord,' responded the brethren. And the
Exalted One spake thus :—

5. 'In measured speech I will give utterance :—
        Where'er their realm, there will ye find the gods,
        But they who in the bowels of the hills
            Sit with heart throughly purged and well com-
                posed,

---

[1] ' The bars and bolts and hindering threshold stone of lust, ill-will
and stupidity,' explains Buddhaghosa.

Like to so many lions crouching still,
Are vanquishers over the creeping dread,
White-minded, pure, serene and undefiled.

[256] Seeing within Kapilavatthu's grove
Five hundred such and more, disciples all,
To them who loved his word the Master spoke :
            " Celestial hosts draw nigh !
Look to it, brethren, that ye them discern ! "
And they, hearing the Buddha's word, forthwith
Strove ardently to see.[1]

6.   And lo ! in them
Arose vision of those not born of men.
Some saw one hundred gods, ten hundred, some,
And some saw seventy thousand, others saw
Infinite multitudes thronging around.
And all their sight and seeing He Who Sees
Intuitively marked and understood.

Then to his followers who loved his Word
The Master turned and spoke :—" Celestial hosts
Draw near !   Them do ye, brethren, recognize
As I, in rhythmic speech, each in their turn
Proclaim them unto you in order due :—"

7. Seven thousand Yakkhas of our country's soil
Of wondrous gifts and powers exceeding great,
And comeliness, and splendid following [2],
Are come rejoicing to the forest glade
To see the brethren met together there.

Six thousand Yakkhas from Himâlaya,
Diverse in hue, of wondrous gifts and powers

---

[1] The connexion of the various clauses of this stanza is obscure ;
and the interpretations of the native scholars differ. We have
followed the version of the Colombo Sannaya of 1891. Samarasekhara's
translation (Col. 1905) takes the assitâ in line 1 to refer to the
Arahants. Buddhaghosa's commentary may be understood either
way. All agree in referring ñatvâ in line 5 to the Buddha.

[2] Yassassino, glossed here by Buddhaghosa as parivârasam-
pannâ, and later, in this Suttanta, by yasena samannâgatâ.

And comeliness and splendid following,
Are come rejoicing to the forest glade
To see the brethren met together there.

From Sâta's Hill three thousand Yakkhas more,
Diverse in hue, of wondrous gifts and powers
And comeliness, with splendid following,
Have come rejoicing to the forest glade
To see the brethren met together there.

Thus have I sixteen thousand Yakkhas told,
Of diverse hue, of wondrous gifts and powers
And comeliness, and splendid following,
Who come rejoicing to the forest glade
To see the brethren met together there.

8. [**257**] Five hundred more from Vessâmittâ's host,
Of diverse hue, of wondrous gifts and powers
And comeliness and splendid following,
Have come rejoicing to the forest glade
To see the brethren met together there.

Kumbhîra, too, of Râjagaha town,
Having his dwelling on Vepulla's mount,
More than a hundred thousand in his train,
This Yakkha likewise to the wood is come.

9. King Dhataratṭha rules the Eastern clime,
Lord of Gandhabbas, mighty monarch he,
With splendid following.   Sons has he too, ·
Many and strong, all after Indra named.
And these of wondrous gifts and mighty power
And comeliness and splendid following,
Have come rejoicing to the forest glade
To see the brethren met together there.

Virûḷha, ruler of the Southern clime,
Lord of Kumbaṇḍas, mighty monarch he,
With splendid following.   Sons has he too,
Many and strong, all after Indra named.
And these of wondrous gifts and mighty power
And comeliness and splendid following,
Have come rejoicing to the forest glade
To see the brethren met together there.

Virûpakkha rules o'er the Western clime,
Lord of the Nâgas, mighty monarch he,
With splendid following. Sons has he too,
Many and strong, all after Indra named.
And these, of wondrous gifts and mighty power
And comeliness and splendid following,
Have come rejoicing to the forest glade
To see the brethren met together there.

Kuvera rules over the Northern clime,
Lord of the Yakkhas, mighty monarch he,
With splendid following. Sons has he too,
Many and strong, all after Indra named.
And these, of wondrous gifts and mighty power
[258] And comeliness and splendid following,
Have come rejoicing to the forest glade
To see the brethren met together there.

So stood those four great kings within the wood
Of Kapilavatthu, on the four climes
Shedding effulgent radiance round about:
Over the East King Dhataraṭṭha shone,
To right, Virûḷhaka, westward
Virûpakkha, Kuvera o'er the North.

10. With them are come their vassals versed in craft,
Hoodwinking wizards, apt to cloak and feign :—
Mâyâ, Kuṭenḍu, Veṭenḍu, Viṭu,
Viṭucca, Candana, Râmaseṭṭha too,
Kinnughaṇḍu, Nighaṇḍu (nine in all).
Next, these Gandhabba chieftains all are come:—
Panâda, Opamañña too, and Mâtali
The driver of the gods, Cittasena
The Gandhabba, Nala, Janesabha,
Pañcasikha and Suriyavaccasâ,
Daughter of Timbarû. These princes all
And with them other chiefs, Gandhabbas too,
Are come rejoicing to the forest glade
To see the brethren met together there.

11. Now too Nâgas are come from Nabhasa,
And from Vesâli and from Tacchaka,

Kambalas, Assataras, Pâyâgas
With all their kin.   Nâgas from Yamuna,
And Dhatara*tth*a, too, with brilliant trains,
Erâvana, great among Nâga folk,
He too is come into the forest glade.

They who twice-born [1], wingèd and keen
Of sight, the heavenly Harpies who,
With violence prey on Nâga chiefs,—
Gaudy and Well-wingèd are their names—
Have flown into the wood. [259]—
The cobra kings felt quite secure.
A refuge from the dreadful birds
Buddha had made.   With gentle words
Entreating one another they,
The Harpies and their prey alike
To the Buddha as their Sanctuary come.

12. They whom the Lightning-Hand did smite,
Now dwellers in the ocean, Asuras,
Vâsava's brethren, they of wondrous gifts
And splendid train [2] :—The Kâlakañjas all
Of fearsome shape, the Dânaveghasas,
Sucitti, Vepacitti, and Pahârada—
With them came Namucî, spirit of Evil ;
And Bali's hundred sons, all of them named
After Veroca [3], having armed a host
Of warriors, hied them to their noble liege,
And Râhu said, " Good luck attend this mote
For which the brethren now have sought the
wood ! "

13. The gods of Fire and Water, Earth and Air
Are hither come ; celestial Varu*n*as

---

[1] All birds are twice-born, first from the mother's womb (when she lays the egg), and then from the egg itself.

[2] These are all born of Sujâ, Vâsava's mother, and had been driven out of heaven by ' Him-with-the-thunderbolt-in-his-hand.' The latter had been identified, at the time when this poem was composed, with Sakka.

[3] That is, their uncle Râhu.

With their attendant Varuneian sprites,
And Soma with Yaso.   Come, too, the gods
From Love and Pity born, with splendid train.
   These ten, a tenfold host in all, of hue
   Diverse, of wondrous gifts and mighty power,
   And comeliness, with splendid following,
   Are come rejoicing to the forest glade
   To see the brethren met together there.

14. Come Vish*n*u with his gods, the Sahalîs,
   The Asamas and the Yama twins [1]; the elves
   That dwell within the moon attend the Moon,
   The solar fairies too attend the Sun,
   While fragile spirits of the Clouds attend
   The Constellations; [260] Lord of the Vasus, too,
   God Sakka, Generous One of yore [2]:—
      These ten, a tenfold host in all, of hue
      Diverse, of wondrous gifts and mighty powers,
      And comeliness, with splendid following,
      Are come rejoicing to the forest glade
      To see the brethren met together there.

15. Now too are come the fairies Sahabhu,
   In flaming radiance like crests of fire:—
   The Arit*th*akas, Rojas, like azure flowers,
   With Varu*n*â and eke Sahadhammâ,
   And Accutâ is come, Anejakâ
   And Suleyya and Rucirâ are come,
   Come too Vâsavanesi deities.
      These ten, a tenfold host in all, of hue
      Diverse, of wondrous gifts and mighty powers,
      And comeliness, with splendid following,
      Are come rejoicing to the forest glade
      To see the brethren met together there.

16. Samânas, Great Samânas, sprites like men
   And sprites like Supermen, are come, the gods

[1] The Castor and Pollux of Indian mythology.
[2] This seems to come in here most strangely: but it is an epithet of Sakka expressly designed to distinguish him from Indra, the Vedic god, whose epithet was 'Destroyer of Towns,' see p. 297.

Debauched-by-sport [1] are come and those
    Debauched-
In-mind [2], fairies that haunt the Green and they
That wear the Red, they too that Pass-Over,
And the Great Passers-o'er, with splendid following.
 These ten, a tenfold host in all, of hue
 Diverse, of wondrous gifts and mighty powers,
 And comeliness, with splendid following,
 Are come rejoicing to the forest glade
 To see the brethren met together there.

17. Sukka, Aruna, Karumha fairies too,
 With Veghanasas, having at their head
 Th' Odâtagayhas, come ; Vicakkhanas,
 Sadâmattas, Harâgajas, and they
 Called the Mixed gods with splendid following ;
 Pajunna thundering is come, he who
 Pours down the rains upon the quarters four.
  These ten, a tenfold host in all, of hue
  Diverse, of wondrous gifts and mighty powers,
  And comeliness, with splendid following,
  Are come rejoicing to the forest glade
  To see the brethren met together there.

18. [261] The Khemiyas and gods from Tusita
 And Yâma heav'ns, the Katthakas and suite,
 Lambîtakas and the chief Lâma-gods,
 The Fiery spirits, and the Âsavas,
 They who rejoice in shapes they make themselves,
 And they who use creations not their own [2].
  These ten, a tenfold host in all, of hue
  Diverse, of wondrous gifts and mighty powers,
  And comeliness, with splendid following,
  Are come rejoicing to the forest glade
  To see the brethren met together there.

19. These sixty spirit hosts, of divers hues,
 According to their name and class are come,

[1] On these described in the Brahmajâla Suttanta, see Dialogues I, 3[2], 33.
[2] Nimmânarati, Paranimmita[vasavatti].

And with them others, whosoe'er they be,
Saying " Him who has outlived birth, for whom
No barrier stands, for whom the flood is crossed,
The Âsavas are not, Him shall we see,
Ferry-man o'er the flood, mighty through purity [1],
Moon that has passed beyond th' enshrouding dark."

20. Then Tissa, the Eternal Youth, and with
Him Paramatta and Subrahmâ, sons
Of the Potent One, came to the congress-wood.
Great Brahmâ, suzerain of thousand worlds
In Brâhma-heaven, has thither been reborn [2],
Mighty in power, and in shape awesome
And vast, of great renown.   Ten of his lords,
Each regnant o'er a Brahma-world, are come,
And in their midst with all his suite comes Hârita [3].

---

[1] In this word-play, Nâgo means also N'âgu, not having sin, says
the Cy.:—âgum akaranato.   So the gods, too, make bad puns!—
untranslateable ones, alas.

[2] Upapanno. Note the Buddhist care to bring even 'Great
Brahmâ' under the universal Law, 'rem inexorabilem.'

[3] The inter-dependence of the clauses, and also of the names, in
this stanza, is ambiguous.   It may hereafter become clear that the
author (or authoress) thought of Tissa and the Eternal Youth as two
distinct persons, or of the Eternal Youth and the Great Brahmâ of the
Buddha's time as one.   The grammar is against the first of these
suppositions.   But we have seen (above, p. 272, 3) that the Mahâ-
Brahmâ of Govinda's time was Sanam-kumâra, the Eternal Youth (so
also D. I, 200 compared with D. II, 209, 225); and Tissa according to
tradition (Smp. p. 296, 7) was the name of a Mahâ-Brahmâ.   Buddhaghosa explains 'the Potent One' (iddhimâ) as the Buddha; it is
much more likely to have been intended for Brahmâ, who claims
(above, p. 247) to have acquired the potency of iddhi.

This legend of the Ever-virgin Knight, Sanam-kumâra, is the Indian
counterpart of the European legend of Sir Galahad.   The oldest mention of it is in the Chândogya Upanished (Ch. VII), where the ideal
of the saintly knight teaches a typical brahmin about the highest truth
(compare Deussen's note on p. 171 of 'Sechzig Upanishads ').   In the
Nikâyas the Eternal Youth is frequently quoted as the author of a
famous verse which says that, though the knight takes precedence
among all those that trust in lineage, he that is perfect in wisdom takes
precedence over all (see above, I, 121, and M. I, 358; S. I, 153;
A. V, 326.   At S. II, 284 the verse is ascribed to the Buddha).   A
similar sentiment is ascribed to him in the Great Bhârata.   In
mediaeval literature he is said to have been one of five or seven mind-

21. To all of them thus hither come, those gods,
    Marshalled around the Lord and Great Brahmâ,
    The host of Mâra cometh up.   Lo! now
    The folly of the Murky One [1] :—[262] "Come on
    And seize and bind me these, let all be bound
    By lust! Surround on every side, and see
    Ye let not one escape, whoe'er he be!"
    Thus the Great Captain bade his swarthy host [2],
    And with his palm did smite upon the ground
    Making a horrid din, as when a storm-cloud
    Thunders and lightens, big with heavy rains.
    Then he recoiled, still raging, powerless
    Aught to effect.

22. And He-Who-Sees by insight knew all this
    And understood.   Then to his followers
    Who loved his word the Master spake: "The host
    Of Mâra comes! Brethren, beware of them!"
    And they, hearing the Buddha's word, forthwith
    Held themselves all alert.   The foe departs
    From them in whom no lust is found, nor e'er
    Upon whose bodies stirs a hair.   [Then Mâra
        spake :—]
    "All they, those victors in the fight, for whom
    All fear is past, great of renown, His followers,
    Whose fame among the folk spreads far and wide,
        Lo! now with all creation they rejoice [3]."

born sons of Brahmâ, like the Sons of the Potent One in our verse.
(For the five see the references in Wilson's 'Vishnu Purâna,' I, 38;
for the seven those in Garbe's 'Sâmkhya-philosophie,' p. 35).
Buddhaghosa has a similar tale (quoted J.R.A.S., 1894, p. 344). A later
and debased Jain version of the legend tells us at length of the love
adventures and wives of the chaste knight, with a few words at the end
on his conversion to the saintly life (Jacobi, 'Ausgewählte Erzählun-
gen in Mahârashtrî,' pp. 20–28, translated by de Blonay in 'Rev. de l'H.
des Rel.,' 1895, pp. 29–41).

[1] Kanho, for Mâra.   Cf. Kâlî, the Black Woman.
[2] Mâra is called Mahâ-seno, his army being of course senâ. The
Pâli, making no distinction between syena (hawk) and sena, it is
not impossible that a pun is here intended.
[3] We have followed the traditional interpretation in ascribing these
last four lines to Mâra. They may quite as well, or better, be a
statement by the author himself.

INTRODUCTION

TO THE

SAKKA-PAÑHA SUTTANTA.

THIS is the last of the series of mythological dialogues, and in some respects the most interesting of them all. Here we reach the culmination, in the last paragraph, in the conversion of Sakka. Though the various episodes leading up to this culmination are not all equal in literary skill to the charming story and striking verses of Five-crest, they have each of them historical value; and they lead quite naturally up to the conversion at the end.

It seems odd to talk of the conversion of a god. But what do we understand by the term god? He—it is often more correct to say she, or it—is an idea in men's minds. To the worshipper he seems immense, mysterious, unchanging, a unity. And he is, in a sense, a unity—a temporary unity of a complex of conceptions, each of them complex. To use the technical Buddhist terms a god is khanika, and samkhâra. In the same sense we can speak of a chemical compound as a unity; but to understand that unity we must know of what it is compounded. Now what are the ideas of which the unity we know under the name of Sakka is made up? Let us take them in the order of personal character, outward conditions, and titles.

Personal.

Sakka has not become free from the three deadly evils—lust, illwill, and stupidity (A. I, 144; S. I, 219).

He is not free from anxiety (S. I, 219).

He is still subject to death and rebirth (A. I, 144). As examples of this it is mentioned that Sunetta had thirty-five times been reborn as Sakka (A. IV, 105), a statement transferred to the Buddha (A. IV, 89)[1].

He comes down from heaven to confirm Uttara's teaching

---

[1] We have had another instance (above, p. 73) of a detail in Sunetta's biography being taken over into the biography of the Buddha.

that one should bear in mind and compare one's own and others' failings and attainments (A. IV, 162).

One of the shortest of the Samyuttas is devoted to Sakka. It has twenty-five short Suttas. In the first and second, Sakka praises energy (viriya). In the third he denounces timidity. In the fourth he shows forbearance to his enemy [1]. In the fifth he advocates the conquest of anger by kindness ; in the sixth kindness to animals ; in the seventh he denounces trickery even towards enemies ; and in the ninth he preaches courtesy and honour to the wise (to Rishis). In eleven it is said he acquired his position as Sakka by having observed in a former birth seven lifelong habits—support of his parents, reverence to clan elders, gentleness of speech, dislike of calumny, generosity, truth, and freedom from anger. Twelve and thirteen repeat this and explain his titles. In fourteen Sakka explains how new gods who outshine the old ones do so because they have observed the Buddha's teaching [2]. In fifteen he says that the most beautiful spot is where Arahants dwell. In sixteen he praises gifts to the Order. In seventeen he praises the Buddha, but is told he has selected the wrong attributes for praise. In eighteen to twenty he says that, whereas brahmins and nobles worship him, he himself worships good men, and Arahants. Nos. 21, 22, 24 and 25 are against anger, and 23 is against deceit.

In one passage Sakka is represented as coming down from heaven to make an inquiry about Nirvana (S. I, 201), and in another as listening, in heaven, to Moggallâna's exposition of the simplest duties of a good layman (S. IV, 269–280).

He, Sakka, is present at the death of the Buddha and utters, in verse, a simple lament very different from the thoughtful verses ascribed to Brahmâ (above, p. 175).

He proclaims a eulogy on the Buddha, in which he emphasizes eight points of comparatively simple character (above, p. 260).

These Nikâya passages are sufficient to show that Sakka was considered by the early Buddhists to be a god of high character indeed, kindly and just ; but not perfect, and not very intelligent. He has reached as far as a good layman might have reached, to the point where his conversion was immanent.

Outward conditions.

Sakka dwells in the Tâvatimsa heaven, that is, in the heaven of the thirty-three great gods of the Vedic pantheon.

---

[1] This Sutta is repeated at Samyutta IV, 201.
[2] The very words of the Sakka-pañha are here used.

This is not by any means the highest plane of being, nor is it quite the lowest. It is an essential part of the early Buddhist cosmogony (and not held by any other school in India) that there were twenty-six planes of celestial beings :—1. The Four Great Kings, guardians of the four quarters of the world. 2. The Thirty-Three. 3. The Yâma gods. 4. The Tusita gods. 5. The Nimmana-rati gods. 6. The Paranimitta-vasavatti gods[1]. Above these are the twenty worlds of Brahmâ. For practical ethical purposes the stress is laid on two planes only—the six just mentioned, which have a collective name (Kâmâvacara-devaloka), and the world of Brahmâ[2]. It is only the lower of these two that is meant when heaven (sagga) is referred to. Sakka dwells therefore in the lowest heaven but one of the lower plane.

There he dwells in the palace Victoria (Vejayanta, S. I, 235, 6). It was built by Sakka, is described at Majjhima I, 253, and is illustrated on the Bharahat Tope[3].

Dwelling in that palace he is king over all the Thirty-Three. When the gods fight the Titans (Asuras) it is under his banner, and under his orders, that they fight. But he is no absolute monarch. He is imagined in the likeness of a chieftain of a Kosala clan. The gods meet and deliberate in their Hall of Good Counsel; and Sakka, on ordinary peaceful occasions, consults with them rather than issues to them his commands. Yet in ten matters he surpasses them all—in length of life, in beauty, in happiness, in renown, and in lordship, and in the degree of his five sensations, sight, hearing, smelling, taste, and touch (A. IV, 242).

Titles.

Sakka. In its Sanskrit form, S'akra, it occurs nearly fifty times in the Vedas as an adjective qualifying gods (usually Indra). It is explained as meaning 'able, capable[4].' It is not found as a name in pre-Buddhistic literature.

Kosiya used, not in speaking of, but in speaking to Sakka, just as the family (gotta) name, not the personal name, is used

---

[1] These are often mentioned in sequence. See, for instance, above, Vol. I, pp. 280, 281.

[2] The later Mahâ-bhârata borrowed this idea, though, as Hopkins points out ('Religions of India,' 358), it is 'a view quite foreign to the teaching current elsewhere in the epic.'

[3] Cunningham, 'Stupa of Bharhut,' p. 137.

[4] For another derivation, a pretty piece of word-play, see Samyutta, I, 230.

by polite persons in addressing a man[1]. It means 'belonging to the Kuśika family,' and occurs D. II, 270; M. I, 252. It is used once in the Rig Veda of Indra, in what exact sense is not known. Have we a survival here from the time when Indra was only the god of a Kuśika clan?

Vâsava, as chief of the Vasu gods[2] (D. II, 260, 274; S. I, 223-30; SN. 384).

Purindada, 'the generous giver in former births' (S. I, 230; P. V. II, 9, 12, 13; Jât. V, 395), no doubt with ironical allusion to the epithet of Indra, Purandara, ' destroyer of cities.'

Sujampati, the husband of Sujâ (S. I, 225, 234-6; SN. 1024).

Maghavâ, because, as a man, he had once been a brahmin of that name (S. I, 230; cp. Jât. IV, 403=V, 137). This had been also, for another reason, an epithet of Indra and other gods.

Thousand-eyed (Sahassa-cakkhu, sahassakkha, S. I, 230, sahassa-netta, S. I, 226; SN. 346). This also had been used of Indra.

Yakkha. Scarcely perhaps an epithet: but it is interesting to notice that even so high a god as Sakka was considered to be a Yaksha (M. I, 252; see S. I, 206).

Inda (=Indra). This is used occasionally of the Vedic god (e.g. D. I, 244; ii. 274; SN. 310), but is applied also to Sakka himself (D. I, 221, 261, 274; SN. 316, 679, 1024). The god Indaka, of S. I, 206 and PV. II, 9, is quite another person.

Conclusions.

Now what are the conclusions which can fairly be drawn from the above facts? In the first place it is evident that Sakka and Indra are quite different conceptions. Of course Indra is also a complex conception, and not by any means only the savage ideal of a warrior, big and blustering and given to drink. But we shall not be far wrong if we say that no single item of the personal character of Sakka is identical with any point in the character of the Vedic Indra, and not one single item of the character of Indra has been reproduced in the descriptions of Sakka. Some of the epithets are the same, and are certainly borrowed, though they are explained differently in harmony with the new conception. Some of the details of the outward conditions may be, and probably are, the outgrowth of corresponding details as told of the older

---

[1] This point has been discussed above, Vol. I, pp. 193-6.
[2] Their names (ten of them) in PVA., p. 111.

god, but varied and softened in harmony with the new conception.

And further, all these mythological dialogues are *Tendenzschriften*, written with the object of persuading the Kosala clansmen that they need not be in the least afraid, for their own gods were on the side of the reformation. The storytellers who invented them have twisted the details to suit their purpose. But they will not have changed the figure of the god so much that there could be any doubt as to the god they talked of being the then popular god. To do so would have been to defeat their object. We may be sure that at the time when Buddhism arose the popular god in Kosala was already very different from Indra, so different that he was spoken of under a new name. This remains true, though he probably was a degeneration, as the brahmins would say, or a development, as their opponents would say, of the old Vedic hero-god.

We cannot be surprised to learn that the conception which appealed so strongly to a more barbarous age, and to clans when engaged in fighting their way into a new country, were found discordant, unattractive, not quite nice, in the settled and prosperous districts of Kosala, after many centuries of progress and culture. It is so with every god known to history. He seems eternal. But by the gradual accumulation of minute variations there comes a time, it may be in a few generations, it may be after the lapse of centuries, when the old name no longer fits the new ideas, the old god falls from his high estate, and a new god, with a new name, occupies the place he filled in the minds of men. Of course the priests went on repeating the old phrases about Indra. But even to the priests they had become barely intelligible. The people paid little heed to them; they followed rather other gods more up-to-date, and of their own making. And it was of these new gods that the leaders of the new movement told their new stories to point a new moral [1].

---

[1] The above is based exclusively on Nikâya evidence. It is confirmed by that of the later books given by Childers (*sui voce* Sakko).

THE QUESTIONS OF SAKKA.

1. [**263**] Thus have I heard. The Exalted One was once staying in Magadha, to the east of Râjagaha, at a brahmin village named Ambasaṇḍâ. There he resided on the Vediya mountain to the north of the village, in the cave called the cave of Indra's Sâl Tree [2]. Now at that time a longing came over Sakka, the king of the gods, to visit the Exalted One.

And this idea occurred to him :—'Where may he now be staying, the Exalted One, the Arahant, the Buddha supreme?' And Sakka saw that he was staying in Magadha at Ambasaṇḍâ, east of Râjagaha, in the cave called Indra's Sâltree Cave on the Vediya mountain to the north of the village. And seeing that, he said to the Three-and-Thirty gods:—'Gentlemen, that Exalted One is staying in Magadha, to the east of Râjagaha at a brahmin village named Ambasaṇḍâ, in the cave called Indra's Sâltree Cave, on the Vediya mountain to the north of the village. How would it be, gentlemen, if we were to go and visit the Exalted One?'

'So be it and good luck to you!' replied the Three-and-Thirty gods consenting.

---

[1] This Suttanta is quoted by name at Saṃyutta III, 13; Mahâvastu I, 350; Milinda 350; Sumaṅgala Vilâsinî I, 24 (where it is called vedalla). The last passage is repeated at Gandha Vaṃsa 57.

[2] Inda-sâla-guhâ. Buddhaghosa says there was a cave here between two overhanging rocks with a large Sâl tree at the entrance. The village community had added walls with doors and windows; and ornamented it with polished plaster scroll-work and garlands, and presented it to the Buddha. In Fâ Hian's time (Legge, p. 81) it was still inhabited. In Yüan Chwâng's time (Watters, II, 173) it was deserted. Both pilgrims were told that certain marks on the rock had been made by Sakka writing his questions (!). The Sanskritisation of the name into Indra-śaila-guhâ (Schiefner, Böhtlingk-Roth, Julien, Legge, and Beal) is a mere blunder. The name Indra enters into the names of several plants, probably merely in the sense of excellent. There is nothing to justify the idea that Indra was supposed to haunt this tree.

2. Then Sakka [made the same statement and pro-
posal to Five-crest the Gandhabba, [264] and received
the same reply] and Five-crest taking his lyre of yellow
Beluva wood, followed in attendance on Sakka, the
king of the gods.

So Sakka, the king of the gods, surrounded by the
Thirty-and-Three, and attended by Five-crest the
Gandhabba, vanished from his heaven as easily as a
strong man might shoot out his arm, or draw in his arm
outshot, and reappeared in Magadha, standing on the
Vediya mountain.

3. Now at that time the Vediya mountain was
bathed in radiance, and so was Ambasandâ, the
brahmin village,—such is the potency of the celestials
—so much so that in the villages round about folk
were saying:—'For sure the Vediya mountain is on
fire to-day, for sure the Vediya mountain is burning
to-day, for sure the Vediya mountain is in flame to-day!
Why, O why, is the Vediya mountain bathed in radiance
to-day, and Ambasandâ too the brahmins' village?'
And they were anxious and sore afraid.

4. Then said Sakka, the king of the gods, to Five-
crest the Gandhabba:—[265] 'Difficult of approach,
dear Five-crest, are Tathâgatas, to one like me, when
they are rapt in the bliss of meditation, and for that
purpose abiding in solitude. But if you were first to
gain over the Exalted One [by your music] then might
I afterwards come up and visit him, the Arahant, the
Buddha supreme.'

'So be it and good luck to you!' consented Five-
crest, and taking his lyre he went to the Indra-Sâltree-
cave. On coming there he thought:—'Thus far will
the Exalted One be neither too far from me nor too
near to me, and he will hear my voice.' And he stood
on one side, and let his lyre be heard and recited
these verses concerning the Awakened One and the
Truth, the Arahants and Love:—[1]

---

[1] This idea is found again in the Mahâ-bhârata (I, 2. 383). That
poem there claims to be artha-śâstra, dharma-śâstra, and kâma-

5. 'Lady, thy father Timbaru I greet
With honour due, O Glory-of-the-Sun![1]
In that he wrought a thing so nobly fair
As thou, O fount divine of all my joy!

Sweet as the breeze to one foredone with sweat,
Sweet as a cooling drink to one athirst,
So dear art thou, O presence radiant!
To me, dear as to Arahants the Truth.

[266] As medicine bringing ease to one that's
sick,
As food to starving man, so, lady, quench,
As with cool waters, me who am all a-flame.

E'en as an elephant with heat oppressed,
Hies him to some still pool, upon whose face
Petals and pollen of the lotus float,
So would I sink within thy bosom sweet.

E'en as an elephant fretted by hook,
Dashes unheeding curb and goad aside,
So I, crazed by the beauty of thy form,
Know not the why and wherefore of my acts.

By thee my heart is held in bonds, and all
Bent out of course; nor can I turn me back,
No more than fish, once he hath ta'en the bait.

Within thine arm embrace me, lady, me
With thy soft languid eyne embrace and hold,
O nobly fair! This I entreat of thee.

Scanty in sooth, O maid of waving locks,
Was my desire, but now it swelleth aye,
Indefinitely great, e'en as the gifts
Made by the faithful to the Arahants.

śâstra. So Windisch ('Buddha's Geburt,' 82) speaks of a group of
ideas, recurrent in Indian literature, which very happily sums up and
exhausts the matter—the Useful, the True, and the Agreeable—to
which Emancipation is sometimes added as a fourth. Our passage
here is the earliest in which such a group appears.
[1] Suriya-vaccase, the young lady's name; sunshine in prose.
See § 10 of the Mahâ-samaya.

[267] Whate'er of merit to such holy ones
I've wrought, be thou, O altogether fair,
The ripened fruit to fall therefrom to me.

Whate'er of other merit I have wrought
In the wide world, O altogether fair,
Be thou the fruit thereof to fall to me.

As the great Sâkyan Seer, through ecstasy
Rapt and intent and self-possessed, doth brood
Seeking ambrosia, even so do I
Pursue the quest of thee, O Glory-of-the-Sun!

As would that Seer rejoice, were he to win
Ineffable Enlightenment, so I
With thee made one, O fairest, were in bliss.

And if perchance a boon were granted me
By Sakka, lord of Three-and-Thirty gods,
'Tis thee I'd ask of him, lady, so strong
My love.   And for thy father, wisest maid—
Him as a sâl-tree freshly burgeoning
I worship for such peerless offspring giv'n.'

6. When Five-crest had finished the Exalted One
said to him :—' The sound of your strings, Five-crest,
so harmonizes with that of your song, and the sound
of your voice with that of the strings, that your lyre
does not too much colour your song, nor your song
too much colour your play.   Where, Five-crest, did
you learn these verses "concerning the Awakened
One and the Truth, the Arahants, and Love ? "'

' The Exalted One, lord, was once staying at
Uruvelâ, on the bank of the Nerañjarâ river, at the
foot of the Goatherd's Banyan tree [268] before he
attained to Enlightenment.   Now at that time, lord,
the lady called Bhaddâ, in appearance as Sunshine,
daughter of Timbaru, king of the Gandhabbas, was
beloved by me.   But that lady, lord, was in love with
another—Sikhaddi, son of Mâtali the charioteer.   And
since I could not get the lady by any method whatever,
I took my lyre of yellow Beluva wood, and going to
the abode of Timbaru, king of the Gandhabbas, I

played my lyre and recited these verses concerning
the Awakened One, the Truth, the Arahants and
Love :—

7. 'Lady, thy father Timbaru I greet
   With honour due, O Glory-of-the-Sun,
   In that he wrought a thing so nobly fair
   As thou, O fount divine of all my joy!

   Sweet as the breeze to one foredone with sweat,
   Sweet as a cooling drink to one athirst,
   So dear art thou, O presence radiant!
   To me, dear as to Arahants the Truth.

   As medicine bringing ease to one that's sick,
       As food to
   Starving man, so, lady, quench,
   As with cool waters, me who am a-flame.

   E'en as an elephant with heat oppressed,
   Hies him to some still pool, upon whose face
   Petals and pollen of the lotus float,
   So would I sink within thy bosom sweet.

   E'en as an elephant fretted by hook,
   Dashes unheeding curb and goad aside,
   So I, crazed by the beauty of thy form,
   Know not the why and wherefore of my acts.

   By thee my heart is held in bonds, and all
   Bent out of course; nor can I turn me back,
   No more than fish, once he hath ta'en the bait.

   Within thine arm embrace me, lady, me
   With thy soft languid eyne embrace and hold,
   O nobly fair! This I entreat of thee.

   Scanty in sooth, O maid of waving locks,
   Was my desire, but now it swelleth aye,
   Indefinitely great, e'en as the gifts
   Made by the faithful to the Arahants.

   Whate'er of merit to such holy ones
   I've wrought, be thou, O altogether fair,
   The ripened fruit to fall therefrom to me.

Whate'er of other merit I have wrought
In the wide world, O altogether fair,
Be thou the fruit thereof to fall to me.

As the great Sâkyan Seer, through ecstasy
Rapt and intent and self-possessed, doth brood
Seeking ambrosia, even so do I
Pursue the quest of thee, O Glory-of-the-Sun!

As would that Seer rejoice, were he to win
Ineffable Enlightenment, so I
With thee made one, O fairest, were in bliss.

And if perchance a boon were granted me
By Sakka, lord of Three-and-Thirty gods,
'Tis thee I'd ask of him, lady, so strong
My love. And for thy father, wisest maid—
Him as a sâl-tree freshly burgeoning
I worship for such peerless offspring giv'n.

'And when I had finished, lord, the Lady Suriya-vaccasâ said to me :—

" That Blessed One, sir, I have not seen face to face, and yet I heard of him when I went to dance at the Sudhamma Hall of the Three-and-Thirty gods [1]. Since you so extol the Blessed One, let there be a meeting between thee and me to-day. [269] So, lord, I met that lady, not on that day but afterwards." '

8. Now Sakka, the king of the gods, thought :— ' Five-crest and the Exalted One are in friendly converse.' And he called to Five-crest and said :—' Salute the Exalted One for me, dear Five-crest, and tell him :— " Sakka, lord, the ruler of the gods, with his ministers and suite, does homage at the foot of the Exalted One." [And Five-crest did so.]

' May good fortune, Five-crest, attend Sakka, ruler of gods, and his ministers and suite. For they desire happiness—those gods and men, Asuras, Nâgas, Gandhabbas, and whatever other numerous hosts there be ! '

---

[1] When Sakka pronounced his eulogy in the Mahâ-govinda, says Buddhaghosa.

On this wise do the Tathâgatas salute these dignitaries. And so saluted by the Exalted One, Sakka, the king of the gods, entered the cave of Indra's Sâl-tree, and saluting the Exalted One stood on one side. Thus did also the Three-and-Thirty gods and Five-crest the Gandhabba.

9. Now at that time in the cave the rough passages were made smooth, the narrow spaces were made wide, and in the dark cavern it became bright, such was the potency of the celestials [270]. Then said the Exalted One to Sakka :—'Wonderful is this! marvellous is this, that the venerable Kosiya, with so much to do, so much to perform, should come hither!'

'For a long time, lord, have I been desirous of coming to see the Exalted One, but I was hindered by one task and another that I had to perform for the Three-and-Thirty gods, and was not able to come. On one occasion the Exalted One was staying at Sâvatthi, in the Sa*l*ala cottage. So I went to Sâvatthi to see the Exalted One.

10. 'Now at that time, lord, the Exalted One was seated, rapt in some stage of meditation, and Bhuñjatî, wife of Vessava*n*a [1], was waiting on him, worshipping with clasped hands. Then I said to Bhuñjatî :— " Madam, do you salute the Exalted One for me, and say :—'Sakka, lord, ruler of gods, with ministers and suite, does homage at the feet of the Exalted One.'" And Bhuñjatî replied :—" 'Tis not the right time, sir, for seeing the Exalted One; he is in retreat." [271] "Well then, madam, when the Exalted One rouses himself from his meditation, salute him for me and say what I have told you." Did the lady so salute the Exalted One, lord, for me? And does the Exalted One remember what she said?'

'She did salute me, ruler of gods. I remember her words. And this too—that it was the noise of your

---

[1] That is, Kuvera, king of the North Quarter, ruler over Yakkhas. See previous Suttanta, § 9.

excellency's chariot wheels that aroused me from that meditation.'

11. 'Lord, I have heard and understood when in the presence of those gods who were reborn into the heaven of the Three-and-Thirty before Us, that when a Tathâgata, an Arahant Buddha supreme, arises in the world, the celestial hosts wax in numbers, and the Asura hosts wane. And I myself, lord, have seen and can witness that this is so. Take, lord, this case. There was, at Kapilavatthu, a daughter of the Sâkyans named Gopikâ, who trusted in the Buddha, the Dhamma and the Order, and who fulfilled the precepts. She, having abandoned a woman's thoughts and cultivated the thoughts of a man, was, at the dissolution of the body after her death, reborn to a pleasant life, into the communion of the Three-and-Thirty gods, into sonship with us. And there they knew her as " Gopaka of the sons of the gods, Gopaka of the sons of the gods." Moreover, lord, there were three bhikkhus who, having followed the religious life prescribed by the Exalted One, were reborn into a lower state among the Gandhabbas. Surrounded by and enjoying the pleasures of the five senses, they used to wait upon and minister to us. Things being so, Gopaka upbraided [272] them saying :— " Where were your ears, sirs, that ye hearkened not to the Dhamma of the Exalted One ? Here am I who being but a maiden, trusting in the Buddha, the Dhamma and the Order, and fulfilling the precepts, abandoned all my woman's thoughts and, cultivating a man's thoughts, was reborn after my death into a pleasant life, into communion with the Three-and-Thirty gods, into the sonship of Sakka, the lord of the gods, and am known as Gopaka, son of the gods. But ye, sirs, following the religious life of the Exalted One, have only been reborn into the lower state of Gandhabbas. A sad thing, indeed, is this to see, when we behold our co-religionists reborn into the inferior condition of Gandhabbas." Of those fairies, lord, thus rebuked by Gopaka, two acquired in that same lifetime

mindfulness, and therewith the heaven of the ministers
of Brahmâ. But the third fairy clave to sensuous
enjoyment.

12. GOPAKA'S VERSES.

" Disciple once of Him-Who-Sees,—
    By name they called me :—Gopikâ,—
In Buddha, Dhamma, firm my trust,
    I served the Order glad of heart.
Through this good service paid to Him
    Behold me son of Sakka, born
All glorious in the Deva-world,
    Of mighty power, and known henceforth
As Gopaka. Now saw I men
    Who, bhikkhus in a former birth,
Had won to mere Gandhabba rank.
    What! persons erst of human kind,
And followers of Gotama,—
    Supplied by us with food and drink
And tended in our own abode,—[273]
    Where were their ears that they, so blest,
Yet failed to grasp the Buddha's Law?
    The Gospel well proclaimed to all
And understood by Him-Who-Sees,
    Each for himself must comprehend.
I, serving only you, have heard
    The good words of the Noble Ones—
And now behold me reborn here,
    All glorious and powerful,
As Sakka's son in Deva-world,
    But you who served the Best of men,
And by the Highest shaped your lives,
    Have re-appeared in lowly rank,
Degraded from your due advance.
    An evil sight is this, to see
One's co-religionists sunk low,
    Where, as Gandhabba spirits, sirs,
Ye come to wait upon the gods.
    For me see! what a change is here!

From house-life as a woman, I,
   A male to-day, a god reborn,
In joys celestial take my share."

   Upbraided thus by Gopaka,
Disciple erst of Gotama,
   They in sore anguish made response :—
" Yea verily ! let us go hence
   And strive our utmost, lest we live
The slaves of others ! "   Of the three [274]
   Two bent their will unto the work,
Mindful of Gotama's behests.
   The perils in the life of sense
They saw, e'en here cleansing their heart
   And like an elephant that bursts
Each strap and rope, so they o'ercame
   The fetters and the bonds of sense,
Ties of the Evil One, so hard
   To get beyond—yea, e'en the gods,
The Three-and-Thirty, seated round
   With Indra, with Pajâpati,
Enthronèd in Sudhammâ's Hall,
   The heroes twain left far behind,
Purging all passion, ousting lust.

   At sight of them distress arose
In Vâsava, ruler of gods,
   In midst of all his retinue :—
" Lo now ! these, born to lower rank,
   Outstrip the Three-and-Thirty gods ! "
His sovereign's apprehension heard,
   Gopaka spake to Vâsava :—
" O Indra ! in the world of men
   A Buddha, called the Sâkya Sage,
Is conqueror o'er the world of sense.
   And these his children, who had lost
All conscience when they left the world,
   Through me their conscience have regained.
[275] One of the three yet dwelleth here,
   Reborn among Gandhabba folk ;
And two, on highest Wisdom bent,
   In deepest rapture scorn the gods.

Let no disciple ever doubt
  That by the kind who here abide
The Truth may yet be realized.
  All hail to Buddha who hath crossed
The flood and put an end to doubt,
  Great Conqueror and Lord of all!"

They recognized thy Truth e'en here; and they
Have onward passed and won to eminence.
'Mong Brahmâ's ministers they twain have won
A higher place than this.   And we are come,
O master, here that we too may attain
That Truth[1].   If the Exalted One should grant
Us leave, Master, we fain would question him.'

13. Then the Exalted One thought: 'For a long
time now this Sakka has lived a pure life.   Whatever
question he may ask of me will be to good purpose,
and not frivolous.   And what I shall answer, that will
he quickly understand.'   Then did the Exalted One
address these verses to Sakka, lord of gods:—

'Question me, Vâsava, whate'er thy mind desires,
And on each problem put I'll end thy doubts!'

End of the First Portion for Recitation.

---

[1] We follow the printed text.   It is more probable that pattiyâ is
the gloss.   In that case the version would be: 'For that Truth's sake,
O master, have we come.'   The full stop after visesagû is a misprint.

CHAPTER II.

1. [**276**] Thus invited, Sakka, the ruler of the gods, asked this first question of the Exalted One:—'By what fetters, sir, are they bound—gods, men, Asuras, Nâgas, Gandhabbas, and whatever other great classes of beings there be—in that they, wishing thus:—"Would that, without hatred, injury, enmity, or malignity, we might live in amity!"—do nevertheless live in enmity, hating, injuring, hostile, malign?

Such was the fashion of Sakka's first question to the Exalted One. To him the Exalted One so asked made answer:—

'By the fetters of envy and selfishness, ruler of gods, are they bound—gods, men, Asuras, Nâgas, Gandhabbas and whatever other great classes of beings there be—in that they wishing thus:—"Would that, without hatred, injury, enmity, or malignity, we might live in amity!"—do nevertheless live in enmity, hating, injuring, hostile, malign.'

Such was the fashion of the Exalted One's answer to Sakka's question. And Sakka, delighted with the Exalted One's utterance, expressed his pleasure and appreciation saying:—'That is so, Exalted One, that is so, Welcome One! I have got rid of doubt and am no longer puzzled, through hearing the answer of the Exalted One.'

2. [**277**] So Sakka, expressing pleasure and appreciation, asked a further question of the Exalted One:—'But envy and selfishness, sir,—what is the source thereof, the cause thereof? what gives birth to them? how do they come to be? What being present, are envy and selfishness also present? What being absent, are they also absent?'

'Things as dear and not dear to us, ruler of gods,—this is the source and cause of envy and selfishness, this is what gives birth to them, this is how they come to be. In the presence of what is dear or not dear, envy and selfishness come about, and in the absence of such feelings, they do not come about.'

'But what, sir, is the source, what the cause of things being dear and not dear, what gives birth to these feelings, how do they come to be? What being present, do we so feel, and what being absent, do we not so feel?'

'Desire [1], ruler of gods, is the source and cause of things being dear or not dear, this is what gives birth to such feelings, this is how they come to be. If desire be present, things become dear and not dear to us; if it be absent, things are no more felt as such.'

'But desire, sir,—what is the source and cause of that? What gives birth to it, how does it come to be? What being present, is desire present, and what being absent, is desire also absent?'

'Mental pre-occupation [2], ruler of gods,—this is the source, this is the cause of desire, this is what gives birth to desire, this is how desire comes to be. Wherewith our mind is pre-occupied, for that desire arises; if our mind is not so pre-occupied, desire is absent.'

'But what, sir, is the source and what is the cause of our mind being pre-occupied? What gives birth to such a state, how does it come to be? What being present, does our mind become pre-occupied, and what being absent, does it not?'

---

[1] Chanda. The Cy. distinguishes exegetically five kinds of chanda:—desire to seek, to gain, to enjoy, to hoard, to spend, and includes all in the present connexion with the words: 'here it is used in a sense tantamount to craving (tanhâ).'

[2] Vitakka. The Cy. does not give the Abhidhamma definition of this term (see Dh. S., § 7; 'Bud. Psy.,' p. 10: 'the disposing, fixating, focusing, applying the mind.' Cf. also 'Compendium of Buddhist Philosophy,' Appendix: vitakka, P.T.S., 1910), but gives as a parallel term vinicchaya (see above, p. 55 'lâbham paticca vinic-chayo'—'deciding respecting gain'). The word is used, according to Suttanta method, not with any fine shade of psychological meaning, but in its popular sense of μεριμνάω, 'taking thought for' (Matt. vi. 25), 'being pre-occupied about.'

'The source, ruler of gods, the cause of our becoming
pre-occupied is what we may call obsession[1]. This is
what gives birth to pre-occupation of mind, this is how
that comes about. If that obsession is present, our
mind is pre-occupied [by the idea by which we are
obsessed]; if it is absent, it is not.'

3. 'But how, sir, has that bhikkhu gone about who
has reached the path suitable for and leading to the
cessation of obsession?'

'[278] Happiness, ruler of gods, I declare to be twofold, according as it is to be followed after, or avoided.
Sorrow too I declare to be twofold, according as it is to
be followed or avoided. Equanimity too I declare to
be twofold, according as it is to be followed or avoided.

'And the distinction I have affirmed in happiness,
was drawn on these grounds:—When in following after
happiness I have perceived that bad qualities developed
and good qualities were diminished, then that kind of
happiness was to be avoided. And when, following
after happiness, I have perceived that bad qualities
were diminished and good qualities developed, then
such happiness was to be followed. Now of such happiness as is accompanied by pre-occupation and travail
of mind, and of such as is not so accompanied, the
latter is the more excellent.

'Thus, ruler of gods, when I declare happiness to be

---

[1] Papañca-saññâ (idée fixe). An exactly similar sequence of
ethical states is put elsewhere (M. I, 111, 112) into the mouth of
Mahâ Kaccâna. Buddhaghosa glosses papaña here by mattappa-
mattâkâra-pâpana, where pâpana is etymological word-play, and
mattappamatta may be rendered 'infatuation.' The infatuation is
either craving (tanhâ) in one or other of its 108 forms, or self-conceit
(mâna) in one or other of its nine forms, or speculation (ditthi) in
one or other of its sixty-two forms.

This is one of the most recurrent conceptions of the higher Buddhism,
the system of the Aryan Path (see above, Vol. I, p. 188), and is one of
the many ways in which the early Buddhists struggled to give more
precise and ethical an implication to the Indian conception of Avijjâ.
It is also one of the technical terms most frequently misunderstood.
Neumann all through the Majjhima renders it Vielheit, plurality, and
Dahlke follows him.

twofold, according as it is to be followed after, or avoided, I say so for that reason.

'Again, ruler of gods, when I declare sorrow to be twofold, according as it is to be followed after, or avoided, for what reason do I say so? When, in following after sorrow¹ I have perceived that bad qualities developed and good qualities were diminished, then that kind of sorrow was to be avoided. And when, following after sorrow, I have perceived that bad qualities were diminished and good qualities were developed, then such sorrow was to be followed after. Now of such sorrow as is accompanied by pre-occupation and travail of mind, and of such as is not so accompanied, the latter² is the more excellent. Thus, ruler of gods, when I declare sorrow to be twofold, according as it is to be followed after, or avoided, I say so for that reason.

'[279] Again, ruler of gods, when I declare equanimity to be twofold, according as it is to be followed after, or avoided, for what reason do I say so? When, in following after equanimity, I have perceived that bad qualities developed and good qualities were diminished, then that kind of equanimity was to be avoided. And when, following after equanimity, I perceived that bad qualities were diminished and good qualities were developed, then that kind of equanimity was to be followed after³. Now of such equanimity

---

¹ The two sorts of sorrow or grief are geha-sita and nekkhamma-sita, and are well paralleled by St. Paul's τοῦ κόσμου λύπη and κατὰ θεὸν λύπη (2 Cor. vii. 10). And the working of the latter: 'for that ye sorrowed after a godly sort . . . wrought in you . . . what vehement desire, yea, what zeal'—has its counterpart in Buddhaghosa's exposition, namely, that through insight into the impermanence of all sensuous satisfaction 'arouses yearning for deliverances even without beyond (anuttaresu), and that yearning leads to sorrow, when one thinks, O that I might reach that state wherein the elect (Ariyas) do dwell even now.'

² According to the Cy., 'the latter' in this and the foregoing paragraph refers especially to the state of mind reached in the second and higher stages of Jhâna, as compared with the first, which is savîtakkam savicâram.

³ For equanimity thus ethically distinguished, see M. I, 364.   The

as is accompanied by pre-occupation and travail of
mind and of such as is not so accompanied, the latter
is the more excellent. Thus, ruler of gods, when I
declare equanimity to be twofold, according as it is to
be followed after, or avoided, I say so for that reason.

'And it is on this wise that a bhikkhu, ruler of gods,
must have gone about, who has reached the path
suitable for, and leading to, the cessation of perceiving
and taking account of distractions.'

Such was the fashion of the Exalted One's answer
to Sakka's question. And Sakka, delighted with the
Exalted One's utterances, expressed his pleasure and
appreciation saying :—' That is so, Exalted One, that
is so, O Welcome One! I have got rid of doubt and
am no longer puzzled, through hearing the answer of
the Exalted One.'

4. So Sakka, expressing his pleasure and appreciation, asked a further question of the Exalted One :—
' But how, sir, has that bhikkhu gone about who has
acquired the self-restraint enjoined by the Pâtimokkha?'

' I say, ruler of gods, that behaviour in act and in
speech, as well as those things we seek after are twofold, according as they are to be followed after or
avoided. [280] And for what reason do I say so?
When, in following some mode of behaviour in act or
speech or in pursuing some quest, I have perceived that
bad qualities developed and good qualities diminished,
then such behaviour or such pursuits were to be
avoided. And when, again, I perceived as the consequence of some other mode of behaviour in act or
speech, or of some other pursuit that bad qualities were
diminished and good qualities were developed, then
that behaviour, or that pursuit, was to be followed after.
Thus when I, ruler of gods, declare that behaviour in
act, behaviour in speech, and the things we seek after
are twofold, I say so for those reasons.

Commentator (who repeats his comment in Asl. 194) describes the
former ethical indifference (upekhâ) as that of the foolish average
person, confused in mind, who has not overcome limitations or results
(of Karma), but is bound by his world of objects of sense.

[281] 'And it is on this wise, ruler of gods, that a bhikkhu must have gone about to have acquired the self-restraint enjoined by the Pâtimokkha.'

Such was the fashion of the Exalted One's answer to Sakka's question. And Sakka, delighted with the Exalted One's utterance, expressed his pleasure and appreciation saying :—' That is so, Exalted One, that is so, O Welcome One! I have got rid of doubt and am no longer puzzled, through hearing the answer of the Exalted One.'

5. So Sakka, expressing his pleasure and appreciation, asked a further question of the Exalted One :—' But how, sir, has that bhikkhu gone about who has acquired control of his faculties ?'

' I say, ruler of gods, that the objects of the senses—visible, audible, odorous, sapid, tangible and mental objects [1]—are twofold, according as they are to be followed after or avoided.'

Then said Sakka to the Exalted One :—'I, sir, understand the details of that which you have told me in outline. [282] Those sense-objects which are not to be followed are such as cause bad qualities to develop and good qualities to diminish ; and those sense-objects which have the opposite effect are to be followed after. And because I can thus understand in detail the meaning of that which the Exalted One has told me in outline, I have got rid of doubt and am no longer puzzled, now that I have heard the Exalted One's answer to my question.'

6. So Sakka, expressing his pleasure and appreciation, asked a further question of the Exalted One :—' Are all recluses and brahmins, sir, wholly of one creed, one practice, one persuasion [2], one aim ?'

---

[1] According to Buddhist psychology, these are not ideas as distinct from impressions, but are *any* presentations or objects of consciousness, whether on occasion of sense or of reflexion, *at that stage* when mind 'turns toward' the object and 'receives' it (âvajjana, sampaticchana).

[2] Ekantacchandâ, lit. of one desire, will or purpose ; but equated by the Cy. with ekaladdhikâ, of one heresy.

' No, ruler of gods, they are not.'

' But why, sir, are they not ?'

' Of many and divers elements, ruler of gods, is this world composed.   And that being so, people naturally incline to adhere to one or another of those elements ; and to whichsoever it be they, being so inclined, become strongly and tenaciously addicted, holding that "just *this* is true, the rest is foolish."   And therefore it is that recluses and brahmins are not all wholly of one creed, one practice, one persuasion, one aim.'

[283] 'Are all recluses and brahmins, sir, perfectly proficient, perfectly saved, living perfectly the best life[1], have they attained the right ideal [2]?'

' No, ruler of gods, they are not all so.'

' Why, sir, are they not all so ?'

' Those recluses and brahmins, ruler of gods, who are set free through the entire destruction of craving, only they are perfectly proficient, only they are perfectly saved, only they are living perfectly the best life and have attained the ideal.   Therefore is it that not all recluses and brahmins are perfectly proficient, perfectly saved, living perfectly the best life, and have attained the ideal [3].'

Such was the fashion of the Exalted One's answer to Sakka's question.   And Sakka, delighted with the Exalted One's utterances, expressed his pleasure and appreciation saying :—' That is so, Exalted One, that is so, O Welcome One !   I have got rid of doubt and am no longer puzzled, through hearing the answer of the Exalted One.'

7. So Sakka, expressing his pleasure at, and appre-

---

[1] Accanta-brahmacârî = 'se*tthatth*ena brahma*m* ariya-magga*m* caratîti.' Cy. 'Walking in the highest, Aryan Path.'

[2] Accanta-pariyosânâ = 'pariyosânan ti nibbâna*m*.' Cy. ' The ideal' is a free rendering, the term meaning the end, goal or climax.

[3] This paragraph is quoted as from the Sakka-pañha at Sa*m*yutta III, 13. Two unnecessary words are there added at the end of it. Buddhaghosa does not say anything on the discrepancy. The two words are either there added by mistake from Majjhima I, 251, where the phrase recurs, or stood originally in our text here.

ciation of the Exalted One's utterance, spoke thus :—
'Passion [1], lord, is disease, passion is a cancer, passion
is a dart, passion drags a man about by one rebirth and
then another, so that he finds himself now up above
now down below. Whereas other recluses and brahmins
not of your followers, lord, gave me no opportunity to
ask these questions, the Exalted One has answered for
me, instructing me at length, so that the dart of doubt
and perplexity has by the Exalted One been extracted.'

[284] 'Do you admit to us, ruler of gods, that you
have put the same questions to other recluses or
brahmins ?'

'I do, lord.'

'Then tell me, if it be not inconvenient to you, how
they answered you.'

'It is not inconvenient to me when the Exalted One
is seated to hear, or others like him.'

'Then tell, ruler of gods.'

'I went to those, lord, whom I deemed to be recluses
and brahmins, because they were dwelling in secluded
forest abodes, and I asked them those questions. Being
asked, they did not withdraw themselves, but put a
counter-question to me :—"Who is the venerable one ?"
I replied, "I, sir, am Sakka, ruler of gods." They asked
me further :—"What business has brought the venerable
ruler of gods to this place ?" Whereupon I taught
them the Dharma as I had heard and learnt it. And
they with only so much were well pleased saying :—
"We have seen Sakka, ruler of gods, and he has
answered that which we asked of him!" And actually,
instead of me becoming their disciple, they became
mine. But I, lord, am a disciple of the Exalted One,
a Stream-winner, who cannot be reborn in any state of
woe, and who has the assurance of attaining to enlightenment [2].'

---

[1] Ejâ = calana*tth*ena ta*nh*â. Cy., i.e. 'Craving, with respect to
the thrill' (e-motion, com-motion) caused by it. 'Passion' lacks
etymological coincidence with the implication of 'movement' in ejâ, but
no other term is forceful enough.

[2] Cf. Vol. I, pp. 190–2.

'Do you admit to us, ruler of gods, that you have ever before experienced such satisfaction and such happiness as you now feel?'

[285] 'Yes, lord, I do admit it.'

'And what do you admit, ruler of gods, with regard to that previous occasion?'

'In former times, lord, war had broken out between gods and asuras. Now in that fight the gods won and the asuras were defeated. Then when the battle was over, to me the conqueror the thought occurred: "The gods will henceforth enjoy not only celestial nectar but also asura-nectar." But, lord, the experiencing satisfaction and happiness such as this, which was wrought by blows and by wounds, does not conduce to detachment, nor to disinterestedness, nor to cessation, nor to peace, nor to the higher spiritual knowledge[1], nor to enlightenment, nor to Nirvana. But this satisfaction, lord, this happiness that I have experienced in hearing the Dhamma of the Exalted One, this which is not wrought by blows and by wounds does conduce to detachment, to disinterestedness, to cessation, to peace, to spiritual knowledge, to enlightenment, to Nirvana.'

8. 'What are the things present to your mind, ruler of gods, when you confess to experiencing such satisfaction and such happiness?'

'Six are the things present to my mind, lord, that I feel such satisfaction and happiness :—

'I who here merely as a god exist
Have [by my acts][2] incurred the destiny
To live again once more. Hear, sir, and know!

'This, lord, is the first meaning implied in what I said. [286]

'Deceasing from the gods I shall forsake
The life that's not of men, and straight shall go
Unerring to that womb I fain would choose.

---

[1] Abhiññâ, i.e. knowledge of that advanced (abhi-) nature, which is neither conveyed by the channels of sense, nor is occupied with sense-experience as such.

[2] Cy. aññena kammavipâkena, by another result of action.

'This, lord, is the second meaning implied in what
I said.

> 'I who have had my problems rendered clear
> And live delighting in His Word, shall then
> Live righteously, mindful and self-possessed.

'This, lord, is the third meaning implied in what
I said.

> 'And if into my life thus rightly led
> Enlightenment should come, then shall I dwell
> As one who Knows, and this shall be the end.

'This, lord, is the fourth meaning implied in what
I said.

> 'Deceasing from the human sphere, I then
> Forsake the life of men, and lo! once more
> A god I'll be, best in the Deva-world.

'This, lord, is the fifth meaning implied in what
I said.

> 'Finer than Devas are the Peerless Gods [1]
> All glorious, while my last span of life
> Shall come and go 'tis there my home will be.

[287] 'This, lord, is the sixth meaning implied in my
confession of experiencing such satisfaction and such
happiness.
'These, lord, are the six things present to my mind
that I feel such satisfaction and such happiness.'

9. 'With aspirations unfulfilled, perplexed
> And doubting, long I wandered seeking him
> Who-had-on-That-wise-Thither-Come.   Me-
> thought,
> Hermits who dwell secluded and austere
> Must sure enlightened be! To them I'll fare.
> "What must I do to win, what doing fail?"
> Thus asked they rede me naught in Path or Ways.

---

[1] Those called Akani*tth*â.

But me, forsooth, whereas they know that I
Who come, am Sakka of the gods, 'tis me
They ask, " What would'st thou that thou comest
    here ?"
Thereat to them I teach, as I have heard,
As all may hear, the Dhamma ; whereat they
Rejoicing cry, forsooth, "Vâsava have we seen !"

But since I've seen the Buddha, seen my doubts
Dispelled, now would I, all my fears allayed,
On him, the Enlightened One, adoring wait.
Him do I worship who hath drawn the dart
Of craving, him the Buddha, peerless Lord.
Hail, mighty hero ! hail, kin to the sun !
[288] E'en as by gods is Brahmâ reverenced,
Lo ! even thus to-day we worship thee.
Thou art the Enlightened One, Teacher
    Supreme
Art thou, nor in the world, with all its heav'ns
Of gods, is any found like unto thee !'

10. Then spake Sakka, ruler of gods, to Five-crest of
the Gandhabbas :—'Great has been your help to me,
dear Five-crest, in that you first placated the Exalted
One. For it was after you had first placated him, that
we were admitted to his presence to see the Exalted
One, the Arahant, Buddha Supreme. I will take the
place of father to you, and you shall be king of the
Gandhabbas, and I will give to you Bhaddâ, the Sun-
maiden, whom you have longed for.'

Then Sakka, touching the earth with his hand to
call it to witness, called aloud thrice :—

'Honour to the Exalted One, to the Arahant, to
    the Buddha Supreme !'

Now while he was speaking in this dialogue, the
stainless spotless Eye for the Truth arose in Sakka, the
ruler of the gods, to wit : 'Whatsoever thing can come
to be, that must also cease to be [1].' And this happened
also to eighty thousand of devas besides.

---

[1] See Vol. I, p. 184.

[289] Such were the questions which Sakka was invited to ask, and which were explained by the Exalted One [1]. Therefore has this dialogue the name of 'The Questions of Sakka.'

---

[1] 'Was invited' is doubtful. Sakka had not been invited to put any particular questions. Leave had been granted him generally to put any question he liked. Yet the editions printed in Siam and Ceylon read 'the invited questions put.' Buddhaghosa reads ajjhittâ. It is doubtful whether the other reading (ajjitthâ) could be properly applied to a question. In Vin. I, 113 it is applied to a person who is invited to speak. It looks here like a conjectural emendation of a *lectio difficilior*.

INTRODUCTION

TO THE

MAHÂ SATIPA*TTH*ÂNA SUTTANTA.

THE doctrine here expounded is perhaps the most important, after that of the Aryan Path, in early Buddhism; and this tract, the oldest authoritative statement of the doctrine, is still in frequent and popular use among those Buddhists who have adhered to the ancient faith.

The two doctrines are closely connected. The exposition here of mindfulness (Sati) includes that of the Path, and no exposition of the Path is complete without the inclusion of mindfulness. Whosoever neglects the fourfold practice of mindfulness he misses the Path, whosoever practises mindfulness has found the Path (Sa*m*yutta V, 179, 180, 294). The right way to the practice of mindfulness is precisely the Aryan Path (*ibid.* 183). And that practice is in turn, in one passage, called the Path to the Unconditioned (Asa*m*khata, that is, Arahantship, Nirvana, the goal of the Aryan Path).[1]

What then is this Mindfulness? This Suttanta will show. But a few observations may help the student of it. Etymologically Sati is Memory. But as happened at the rise of Buddhism to so many other expressions in common use, a new connotation was then attached to the word, a connotation that gave a new meaning to it, and renders ‘memory’ a most inadequate and misleading translation. It became the memory, recollection, calling-to-mind, being-aware-of, certain specified facts. Of these the most important was the impermanence (the coming to be as the result of a cause, and the passing away again) of all phenomena, bodily and mental. And it included the repeated application of this awareness, to each experience of life, from the ethical point of view. ‘Thus does he cultivate those qualities which ought to be practised, and not those which ought not. That is how repetition is the mark of Mindfulness,’ says Nâgasena[2], in complete accord with our Suttanta.

---

[1] Sa*m*yutta IV, 363.   [2] Questions of King Milinda, I, 59.

When Christians are told: 'Whether therefore ye eat or drink, or whatsoever ye do, do all to the glory of God,' a way is shown by which any act, however lowly, can, by the addition of a remembrance (a Sati), be surrounded by the halo of a high moral enthusiasm; and how, by the continual practice of this remembrance, a permanent improvement in character can be obtained. The Buddhist idea is similar. But the remembrance is of what we should now call natural law, not of a deity. This has been made a corner-stone of the system of ethical self-training. The corresponding corner-stone in the West is conscience; and indeed, so close is the resemblance in their effects that one scholar has chosen 'conscience' as a rendering of Sati;—wrongly, we think, as this introduces a Western idea into Buddhism. The curious notion of an internal monitor, distinct from the soul, yet speaking independently of the will of the man himself, is confined to animistic modes of thought. Buddhaghosa uses it, indeed, as a simile, to explain the connotations of Sati; but he expressly pours scorn on any idea of a separate entity.[1]

On the other hand though Sati (Smrti) does not occur in any ethical sense in pre-Buddhistic literature, it is possible that the Buddhist conception was, in one way, influenced by previous thought. Stress is laid in the Upanishad ideal on Intuition, especially as regards the relation between the soul, supposed to exist inside each human body, and the Great Soul. In the Buddhist protest against this, the doctrine of Sati, dependent not on intuition, but on grasp of actual fact, plays an important part. This opposition may have been intentional. On the other hand, the ethical value of Mindfulness (in its technical sense) would be sufficient, without any such intention, to explain the great stress laid upon it.

The following are some of the proposed translations of Sati:—

Conscience,	Spence Hardy, 'Manual,' 412.
Attention,	Spence Hardy, 'Manual,' 497.
Meditation,	Gogerly, 'Ceylon Buddhism,' 584.
"	Childers, 'Dictionary.'[2]
Memory,	Oldenberg, 'Vinaya Texts,' I, 96.
"	E. Hardy, 'Buddha,' 40.

---

[1] See Mrs. Rhys Davids's 'Buddhist Psychology,' p. 16, note 1: and note 1 above on Vol. I, p. 81.

[2] He renders kâyagatâ sati, where the word occurs in its technical sense, as 'meditation on the body.' He has other renderings for popular usage.

Contemplation,   Warren, 'Buddhism in Translations,' 353.
Insight,   Neumann, 'Majjhima,' I, 85.
Thought,   Pischel, 'Buddha,' 28.
    „   Oldenberg, 'Buddha' (English translation),
                   128.

The other word in the compound that gives the title to this
Suttanta is Pa*tth*âna—which would mean etymologically
'putting forward, setting forth.' It does not occur in pre-
Buddhistic literature. It has not been yet found in the
Nikâyas in its concrete, primary, sense; or in any connexion
except this. Buddhaghosa here paraphrases it, exegetically
only, by go*c*ara, which is the feeding-ground, resort, of an
animal. The mediaeval use of the word (in its Sanskrit form)
was in the sense of starting off, going away, departure. It is
the title of the most often quoted book in the Abhidhamma,
and there means probably Origins, Starting-points, as it gives
under twenty-four categories the pa*cc*ayas (causes) of phenomena. In one passage of a fifth-century commentator
(Jât. I, 78.[5]) the Abhidhamma Pi*t*aka as a whole is said to be
samantapa*tth*âna, 'having (or giving) the settings-on-foot,
the points of departure, of all things.' Childers gives the
word as a neuter. It is masculine throughout our Suttanta.
But he analyses the compound (*sub voce* upa*tth*âna*m*), not
into Sati + pa*tth*âna, but into Sati + upa*tth*âna. This is
a possible contraction, and Buddhaghosa gives it as an alternative explanation which he does not adopt. Had we adopted
it, the rendering of the title would have been 'The getting-
ready of Mindfulness.' Neumann renders it 'Pillars of Insight,' and Warren 'Intent Contemplations.' Neither of these
is much more than a distant cousin of the Pâli.

It is not easy at first sight to understand the choice of just
those four fields or areas (comp. pa*tth*ânâ = thânâ = go*c*arâ),
to which, in this Suttanta, 'mindfulness' is to be applied, or in
respect to which it is to be set up. We need ourselves to be
mindful, lest, in interpreting them, we follow too closely
European points of view. In trying to avoid this danger, we
do not consider our choice of terms leaves nothing to be
desired, or to be explained.

The ethical desirableness of Sati, as the instrument most
efficacious in self-mastery, lay in the steady alertness of
inward vision which it connoted, whether past or present
experience was contemplated. In discussing it, the Buddhist
was concerned, not with the outer world as such, but with the
microcosm of his subjective experience, and with the vehicles
thereof—sense and mind. These he is here represented as
considering under the fourfold aspect of—

(1) kâya, physical structure and activities.

(2) vedanâ, the emotional nature, first as bare feeling, then as having ethical implications.

(3) citta, conscious life, consciousness or intelligence, considered under ethical aspects.

(4) dhammâ, with its subdivisions—

    (a) the Five Hindrances.

    (b) the Five Groups.

    (c) the Six Spheres of Sense.

    (d) the seven Factors of Enlightenment.

    (e) the four Aryan Truths.

Now it is always difficult to make any English term co-incide with either dhamma or dhammâ. Here, as elsewhere in Buddhist diction, it is chiefly the context that must be the guide to meaning. The Suttanta is a discipline—the supreme discipline—in ethical introspection. And in Buddhist introspective analysis, dhammâ (elsewhere translatable now by 'things,' now by 'qualities') are, more especially, 'cognoscible objects.' These are related to mano (consciousness as apprehending), just as each kind of sense-object is related to one kind of sense-organ; thing-seen, for example, to sight. A cognoscible object is any presentation (German, Vorstellung), that has got beyond the stage of mere sensory re-action. It is an idea or perception in the wider sense used by Locke :— 'Whatsoever is the immediate object of perception, thought, or understanding.' But neither cognoscible object, nor presentation, is a term which lends itself with sufficient simplicity and impressiveness to ethical homily. We have therefore decided to perpetuate the Lockean 'idea.'

For the same reason we use 'thought' for citta, in preference to a term of more psychological precision; and we understand by 'thought', thinking, or knowing, or being intelligently conscious, and do not restrict the word to any special mode of cognition.

Hence we get this distinction of aspects in (3) and (4): under citta, the ever-changing ever-active continuance of consciousness, or re-acting intelligence; under dhammâ, those same activities considered objectively, as concrete states, procedure, 'content of consciousness,' as the psychologists phrase it. Under (3) we watch the agency as a whole, in its chameleon-like phases. Under (4) we take transverse cuttings, so to speak, of our subjective experience.

It is interesting to note that Buddhaghosa, explaining the inclusion, under No. 4, of the Six Senses and the fivefold Khandha doctrine, says :—'in contemplation of the body the Exalted One taught only the grasp of matter, in contemplation of feeling and consciousness, only the grasp of the immaterial. Now in order to teach grasp of matter and the immaterial mixed (rûpârûpamissakapariggaho), he' spoke of dhammâ. And again: 'grasp of the rûpa-khanda being taught by contemplation of body, and grasp of the khandhas of feeling and viññâṇa (cognition or consciousness) by contemplation of feeling and citta, He now, to teach grasp of the khandhas of perception and saṅkhâra (let us say, volition and other mental factors) went on' to speak of dhammâ.

[XXII. MAHÂ SATIPA*TTH*ÂNA SUTTANTA.

SETTING-UP OF MINDFULNESS.]

[290] Thus have I heard.

1. The Exalted One was once staying among the Kurus. Kammâssadhamma is a city of the Kuru country. There the Exalted One addressed the brethren, saying, 'Bhikkhus!' 'Reverend sir!' responded the brethren. And the Exalted One said:

The one and only path, Bhikkhus leading to the purification of beings, to passing far beyond grief and lamentation, to the dying-out of ill and misery, to the attainment of right method [1], to the realization of Nirvana, is that of the Fourfold Setting up of Mindfulness.[2]

Which are the Four? Herein [3], O bhikkhus, let a brother, as to the body, continue so to look upon the body that he remains ardent, self-possessed, and mindful, having overcome both the hankering and the dejection common in the world. And in the same way as to feelings, thoughts, and ideas, let him so look upon each, that he remains ardent, self-possessed, and mindful, having overcome both the hankering and the dejection common in the world.

---

[1] Ñâya. Practical Buddhism is summed up (Majjhima II, 182, 197) as exertion in ñâya, dhamma, and kusala (the Method, the Norm, and the Good). Ñâya is defined at Sa*m*yutta V, 388 as what comes pretty much to our method in philosophy. Above (p. 167) it is rendered System. There, in a very old verse, the Buddha says that seeking after Good he had been a pilgrim through the realm of System and Law, outside of which no victory can be won.

[2] See Introduction.

[3] The commentarial tradition sees in this word idha, the implication of 'belonging to this order or doctrine or school' (imasmi*m* sâsane), and thus an antithesis to 'ito bahiddhâ,' outside this [order] —an expression which occurs immediately after the verse mentioned in the last note.

2. [291] And how, bhikkhus, does a brother so continue to consider the body?

[1] Herein, O bhikkhus, let a brother, going into the forest, or to the roots of a tree, or to an empty chamber, sit down cross-legged, holding the body erect, and set his mindfulness alert[2].

Mindful let him inhale, mindful let him exhale. Whether he inhale a long breath, let him be conscious thereof; or whether he exhale a long breath, let him be conscious thereof. Whether he inhale a short breath, or exhale a short breath, let him be conscious thereof. Let him practise with the thought 'Conscious of my whole body will I inhale'; let him practise with the thought 'Conscious of my whole body will I exhale.' Let him practise with the thought 'I will inhale tranquillizing my bodily organism; let him practise with the thought 'I will exhale tranquillizing my bodily organism.'

Even as a skilful turner, or turner's apprentice, drawing (his string) out at length, or drawing it out short, is conscious that he is doing one or the other, so let a brother practise inhaling and exhaling.

[292] So does he, as to the body, continue to consider the body, either internally or externally, or both internally and externally. He keeps on considering how the body is something that comes to be, or again he keeps on considering how the body is something that passes away; or again he keeps on considering the coming to be with the passing away; or again, conscious that 'There is the body,' mindfulness hereof becomes thereby established, far enough for the purposes of knowledge and of self-collectedness. And he abides independent, grasping after nothing in the world

---

[1] Quoted Pa*t*isambhidâ I, 175, and 'Yogâvacara Manual,' p. 1. Each quotation gives a word for word commentary; and so does Sum. I, 210.

[2] Parimukha*m* sati*m* upa*tth*apati, literally, 'set up his memory in face of (the object of his thought). The ultimate object is throughout, as the 'Yogâvacara Manual' says, Nirvana. Examples of the subsidiary, changing, objects of thought are given in what follows.

whatever. Thus, bhikkhus, does a brother continue to regard the body.

3. And moreover, bhikkhus, a brother, when he is walking, is aware of it thus :—'I walk'; or when he is standing, or sitting, or lying down, he is aware of it. However he is disposing the body, he is aware thereof.

So does he, as to the body, continue to consider the body, either internally or externally, or both internally and externally. He keeps on considering how the body is something that comes to be, or again he keeps on considering how the body is something that passes away; or again he keeps on considering the coming to be with the passing away; or again, conscious that ' There is the body,' mindfulness hereof becomes thereby established, far enough for the purposes of knowledge and of self-collectedness. And he abides independent, grasping after nothing in the world whatever. Thus, bhikkhus, does a brother continue to regard the body.

4. And moreover, bhikkhus, a brother—whether he departs or returns, whether he looks at or looks away from, whether he has drawn in or stretched out [his limbs], whether he has donned under-robe, over-robe, or bowl, whether he is eating, drinking, chewing, reposing, or whether he is obeying the calls of nature —is aware of what he is about. In going, standing, sitting, sleeping, watching, talking, or keeping silence, he knows what he is doing.

[293] So does he, as to the body, continue to consider the body, either internally or externally, or both internally and externally. He keeps on considering how the body is something that comes to be, or again he keeps on considering how the body is something that passes away; or again he keeps on considering the coming to be with the passing away; or again, conscious that ' There is the body,' mindfulness hereof becomes thereby established, far enough for the purposes of knowledge and of self-collectedness. And he abides independent, grasping after nothing in the world whatever. Thus, bhikkhus, does a brother continue to consider the body.

5. And moreover, bhikkhus, a brother reflects upon this very body, from the soles of his feet below upward to the crown of his head, as something enclosed in skin and full of divers impurities :—' Here is in this body hair and down, nails, teeth, skin, flesh, sinews, bones, marrow, kidney, heart, liver, membranes, spleen, lungs, stomach, bowels, intestines ; excrement, bile, phlegm, pus, blood, sweat, fat, tears, serum, saliva, mucus, synovic fluid, urine.'

Just as if there were a double-mouthed sample-bag [1], bhikkhus, full of various sorts of grain, such as rice, paddy, beans, vetches, sesamum or rice husked for boiling ; and a keen-eyed man were to reflect as he poured them out :—' That's rice, that's paddy, those are beans,' and so forth.   Even so, bhikkhus, does a brother reflect upon the body, from the soles of the feet below upward to the crown of the head, as something enclosed in skin and full of divers impurities.

So does he, as to the body, continue to consider the body, either internally or externally, or both internally and externally.   He keeps on considering how the body is something that comes to be, or again he keeps on considering how the body is something that passes away ; or again he keeps on considering the coming to be with the passing away ; or again, conscious that ' There is the body,' mindfulness hereof becomes thereby established, far enough for the purposes of knowledge and of self-collectedness.   And he abides independent, grasping after nothing in the world whatever.   Thus bhikkhus, does a brother continue to regard the body.

6. [294] And moreover, bhikkhus, a brother reflects upon this very body, however it be placed or disposed, with respect to its fundamentals :—' There are in this body the four primary elements of earth, water, heat,

---

[1] Mutoli. Buddhaghosa has no explanation. But Daramiṣipola says mallak pasumbiyak, that is, a small bag, such as is used by grain merchants for keeping samples in. The particular kind meant is kept tied up with string at both ends, and either end can be opened. The word only occurs in this connexion (here, and at M. I, 57 ; III, 90).   The spelling of the word is uncertain.

and air.' Just as a cattle-butcher, or his apprentice, when he has slain an ox, displays the carcase piece-meal at the crossways as he sits, even so, bhikkhus, does a brother reflect upon this very body . . . with respect to its fundamental constituents . . .

So does he, as to the body, continue to consider the body, either internally or externally, or both internally and externally. He keeps on considering how the body is something that comes to be, or again he keeps on considering how the body is something that passes away; or again he keeps on considering the coming to be with the passing away; or again, conscious that ' There is the body,' mindfulness hereof becomes thereby established, far enough for the purposes of knowledge and of self-collectedness. And he abides independent, grasping after nothing in the world whatever. Thus bhikkhus, does a brother continue to regard the body.

7. [**295**] And moreover, bhikkhus, a brother, just as if he had seen a body abandoned in the charnel-field, dead for one, two, or three days, swollen, turning black and blue, and decomposed, applies that perception to this very body (of his own), reflecting : ' This body, too, is even so constituted, is of even such a nature, has not got beyond that (fate).'

So does he, as to the body, continue to consider the body, either internally or externally, or both internally and externally. He keeps on considering how the body is something that comes to be, or again he keeps on considering how the body is something that passes away; or again he keeps on considering the coming to be with the passing away; or again, conscious that ' There is the body,' mindfulness hereof becomes thereby established, far enough for the purposes of knowledge and of self-collectedness. And he abides independent, grasping after nothing in the world whatever. Thus bhikkhus, does a brother continue to regard the body.

8. And moreover, bhikkhus, a brother, just as if he had seen a body abandoned in the charnel-field pecked by crows, ravens, or vultures, gnawn by dogs or jackals or by various small creatures, applies that perception

to this very body (of his own), reflecting : ' This body, too, is even so constituted, is of such a nature, has not got beyond that (fate).'

[296] So does he, as to the body, continue to consider the body, either internally or externally, or both internally and externally. He keeps on considering how the body is something that comes to be, or again he keeps on considering how the body is something that passes away ; or again he keeps on considering the coming to be with the passing away ; or again, conscious that ' There is the body,' mindfulness hereof becomes thereby established, far enough for the purposes of knowledge and of self-collectedness. And he abides independent, grasping after nothing in the world whatever. Thus, bhikkhus, does a brother continue to regard the body.

9. And moreover, bhikkhus, a brother, just as if he had seen a body abandoned in the charnel-field [reduced to] a chain of bones hanging together by tendons, with flesh and blood yet about it, or stripped of flesh but yet spotted with blood ; or cleaned of both flesh and blood ; or reduced to bare bones, loosed from tendons, scattered here and there, so that the bones of a hand lie in one direction, in another the bones of a foot, in another those of a leg, in another a thigh bone, in another the pelvis, in another [297] the spinal vertebrae, in another the skull, applies that perception to this very body (of his own) reflecting : ' This body, too, is even so constituted, is of such a nature, has not got beyond that (fate).'

So does he, as to the body, continue to consider the body, either internally or externally, or both internally and externally. He keeps on considering how the body is something that comes to be, or again he keeps on considering how the body is something that passes away ; or again he keeps on considering the coming to be with the passing away ; or again, conscious that ' There is the body,' mindfulness hereof becomes thereby established, far enough for the purposes of knowledge and of self-collectedness. And he abides independent, grasping after nothing in the world whatever. Thus, bhikkhus, does a brother continue to regard the body.

10. And moreover, bhikkhus, a brother, just as if he had seen a body abandoned in the charnel-field, [reduced to] white bones the colour of a sea-shell . . . or to a mere heap of bones a year old . . . or to rotten powder, this perception does he apply to this very body (of his own) reflecting :—' This body too is even so constituted, is of such a nature, has not got beyond that (fate).'

So does he, as to the body, continue to consider the body, either internally or externally, or both internally and externally. He keeps on considering how the body is something that comes to be, or again he keeps on considering how the body is something that passes away; or again he keeps on considering the coming to be with the passing away ; or again, conscious that ' There is the body,' [298] and mindfulness hereof becomes thereby established, far enough for the purposes of knowledge and of self-collectedness. And he abides independent, grasping after nothing in the world whatever. Thus, bhikkhus, does a brother, as to the body, continue to consider the body.

11. And how, bhikkhus, does a brother, as to the feelings, continue to consider the feelings ?

Herein, O bhikkhus, is a brother when affected by a feeling of pleasure, aware of it, reflecting : ' I feel a pleasurable feeling.' So, too, is he aware when affected by a painful feeling, or by a neutral feeling, or by a pleasant or painful or neutral feeling concerning material things, or by a pleasant or painful or neutral feeling concerning spiritual things.

So does he, as to the feelings, continue to consider feeling, both internally and externally, or internally and externally together. He keeps on considering how the feelings are something that comes to be, or again he keeps on considering how the feelings are something that passes away, or he [299] keeps on considering their coming to be with their passing away. Or again, with the consciousness : ' There is feeling,'

mindfulness thereof becomes thereby established far
enough for the purposes of knowledge and of self-
collectedness. And he abides independent, grasping
after nothing in the world whatever. Thus, bhikkhus,
does a brother, with respect to the feelings, continue
to consider feeling.

12. And how, bhikkhus, does a brother, as to thought,
continue to consider thought [1]?

Herein, O bhikkhus, a brother, if his thought be
lustful, is aware that it is so, or if his thought be free
from lust, is aware that it is so; or if his thought be
full of hate, or free from hate, or dull, or intelligent,
or attentive, or distrait, or exalted, or not exalted, or
mediocre, or ideal, or composed, or discomposed, or
liberated, or bound, he is aware in each case that his
thought is so, reflecting : 'My thought is lustful,' and
so on.

So does he, as to thought, continue to consider
thought, internally or externally, or internally and
externally together. He keeps on considering how
thought is something that comes to be, or again he
keeps on considering how a thought is something that
passes away, or again he ever considers its coming to
be and passing away together. Or again, with the
consciousness : 'There is a thought,' mindfulness
thereof becomes thereby established, [300] far enough
for the purposes of knowledge and of self-possession.
And he abides independent, grasping after nothing in
the world whatever. Thus, bhikkhus, does a brother,
with respect to thought, continue to consider thought.

13. And how, bhikkhus, does a brother, as to ideas [2],
continue to consider ideas ?

Herein, O bhikkhus, a brother, as to ideas, continues

---

[1] Citta. The reader is reminded that 'thought' is used here for
citta in the widest sense possible to that term, such as is intended
when, in the Christian tradition, it is made to complement the 'word
and deed' of the Epistles. And as such it is 'thinking' rather than
'what is thought,' that should be understood.

[2] Dhammâ. See Introduction.

to consider ideas from the point of view of the Five Hindrances [1].

And how, bhikkhus, does a brother, as to ideas, continue to consider ideas relating to the Five Hindrances [1]?

Herein, O bhikkhus, a brother, when within him is sensuous desire, is aware of it, reflecting: 'I have within me sensuous desire.' Or again, when within him is no sensuous desire, he is aware of this. And he knows of the uprising of such desire unfelt before, knows too of his putting aside that uprisen sensuous desire, knows too of the non-arising in future of that banished sensuous desire.

[The paragraph is repeated [301] of ill-will, sloth and torpor, flurry and worry, and doubt.]

So does he, as to ideas, continue to consider them, both internally or externally, or internally and externally together. He ever considers how an idea is a thing that comes to be, again he ever considers how an idea is a thing that passes away, or he ever considers their coming to be with their passing away; or again, with the consciousness: 'There is such and such an idea,' mindfulness thereof is thereby established, far enough for purposes of knowledge and of self-possession. And he abides independent, grasping after nothing in the world whatever. Thus, bhikkhus, does a brother, with respect to dispositions, continue to consider dispositions in the case of the Five Hindrances.

14. And moreover, bhikkhus, a brother, as to ideas, continues to consider these from the point of view of the Five Skandhas of Grasping. And how, bhikkhus, does he so consider them?

Herein, O bhikkhus, a brother reflects: 'Such is material form, such is its genesis, such its passing away; such is feeling—perception—the mental activities—such is cognition, its genesis, its passing away.

So does he, as to dispositions, continue to consider them, ... [302] ...

---

[1] Literally, 'in the Five Hindrances.'

15.˙And moreover, bhikkhus, a brother, as to ideas, continues to consider ideas from the point of view of the Six Internal and External Spheres of Sense. And how does he do this?

Herein, O bhikkhus, a brother is aware of the organ of sight, is aware of the objects of sight, and any Fetter which arises on account of them both—of that, too, is he aware; and how there comes an uprising of a Fetter not arisen before—of that, too, is he aware; and how there comes a putting-aside of a Fetter that has arisen —of that, too, is he aware; and how in the future there shall arise no Fetter that has been put aside—of that, too, is he aware.

And so, too, with respect to the organ of hearing and sounds, to the organ of smell and odours, to the organ of taste and tastes, to the organ of touch and tangibles, to the sensorium and images, he is aware of the sense and of the object, of any Fetter which arises on account of both, of how there comes an uprising of a Fetter not arisen before, of how there comes a putting-aside of a Fetter that has arisen, and of how in the future there shall arise no Fetter that has been put aside.

So does he, as to ideas, continue to consider ideas, from the point of view of the Six Internal and External Spheres of Sense. [303]

16. And moreover, bhikkhus, a brother, as to ideas, continues to consider ideas, with respect to the Seven Factors of Enlightenment. And how does he do this?

Herein, O bhikkhus, a brother, if there be present to him subjectively mindfulness as a factor of enlightenment, is aware that it is present. Or if it be absent, he is subjectively aware of its absence. And how there comes an uprising of such mindfulness not hitherto uprisen—of that, too, is he aware; and how there comes a full development of such mindfulness when it has arisen—of that too is he aware. And so too with respect to the other subjective factors of enlightenment:—search the truth, energy, joy, serenity, rapture, equanimity—he is aware if they are subjectively present, or absent, and he is aware of how there comes an uprising of any factor not hitherto uprisen, and of how there comes a full development of such factors when it has arisen.

So does he, as to ideas, continue to consider ideas from the point of view of the Seven Factors of Enlightenment. [304]

17. And moreover, bhikkhus, a brother, as to ideas, continues to consider ideas from the point of view of the Four Aryan Truths. And how does he do this?

Herein, O bhikkhus, a brother at the thought: ' This is Ill!' is aware of it as it really is;—at the thought: 'This is the coming to be of Ill!' is aware of it as it really is;—at the thought: 'This is the cessation of Ill!' is aware of it as it really is;—at the thought: 'This is the way leading to the cessation of Ill!' is aware of it as it really is.

18[1]. [305] And what, bhikkhus, is the Aryan truth [regarding] Ill?

Birth is painful, old age is painful[2], death is painful, grief, lamentation, suffering, misery and despair are painful, painful is it not to get what is wished for, in

---

[1] What follows (down to the line and space on p. 345) is not found in the Majjhima recension of the Satipaṭṭhâna (M. I, 55 ff.). Except for this the two recensions agree, and ours here is doubtless called the Mahâ-satipaṭṭhâna, precisely because, to that extent, it is longer. That would show that when that title was first used the Majjhima recension was already known. It would not follow that the Dîgha is younger than the Majjhima; they may have been edited at the same time from older material.

The Dîgha addition is interesting as containing a fragment of Old Commentary (as old as the texts) of which other fragments are found in the Nikâyas, and also in the Vinaya.

The Vibhanga (99–106) quotes this Dîgha addition verbatim.

[2] Many MSS. and the Colombo edition of 1876 add 'disease is painful.' But this is not mentioned in the word-for-word commentary that follows. It is probably transferred as a gloss from the Saṃyutta recension of the Four Truths (S. V, 421) which differs slightly from that of the repeaters of the Dîgha (the Dîgha-bhânakâ).

a word, the Five Groups that arise from Grasping are
connected with pain [1].

And what, bhikkhus, is birth ?   Birth is the production, the outcome [2], the rising up in a new form, the
appearance of the Groups, the acquisition of sense-
spheres, by this or that being in this or that class of
beings.   This is what is called birth.

And what, bhikkhus, is growing old [3] ?   Growing
old is the decay, the decrepitude, the breaking-up, the
hoariness, the wrinkled state, the shrinkage of life's
span, the collapse [4] of the sense-faculties of this or that
being in this or that class of beings.   This is what is
called growing old.

And what, bhikkhus, is dying ?

Dying is the fall (out of any state), the dropping
out of it, the dissolution, the disappearance, the death,
the dying, the accomplishment of the life-term, the
breaking up of the Groups, the laying down of the
body of this or that being in this or that class of
beings.   This is called dying.

And what, bhikkhus, is grief ?

Grieving is the state of woe, heart ache, and afflic-
tion.   The inward grief, the hidden wretchedness, of
one who is visited by some calamity or other, of one
who is smitten by some kind of ill. [306] This is
what is called grief.

And what, bhikkhus, is lamenting ?

---

[1] Pañc' upâdânakkhandhâ. The Groups are the five groups
of material and mental qualities that form, in combination brought
about by grasping, an individual.   One might, therefore, express this
central thought of the first Aryan truth in modern Western language
by saying that pain is involved in individuality—a most pregnant and
far reaching suggestion.   The rest of the Truth is merely a statement
of facts universally admitted.

[2] Sañjâti only found elsewhere as yet Dîgha I, 227, where it
means the produce arising out of an estate and accruing to the
landlord.

[3] Cf. Dh. S. and Bud. Psy. on rûpassa jaratâ (§ 644).

[4] Paripâka, which in all other passages means maturity, must here
mean over-ripeness, loss of power through having reached their full
vigour and begun to give out.

Lamenting is the act and the state of mourning, lamentation, deploring, of one who is visited by some calamity or other, of one who is smitten by some kind of ill.   This is what is called lamenting.

And what, bhikkhus, is suffering?

Suffering is bodily ill, bodily pain, ill that is born of bodily contact, the being bodily affected by what is painful.   This is what is called suffering.

And what, bhikkhus, is misery?

Misery is mental ill, mental pain, ill that is born of mental contact, the being mentally affected by what is painful.   This is what is called misery.

And what, bhikkhus, is despair?

Despair is the act and state of dejection, of despondency, of one who is visited by some calamity or other, of one who is smitten by some kind of ill.   This is what is called despair.

[307] And what, bhikkhus, is the ill of not getting what is wished for?

In beings subject to birth the wish arises:—'Ah! if only we were not subject to birth, if only we could avoid being born!'   But this is not to be got by wishing. This is the ill of not getting what is wished for.   So too in the case of growing old, falling ill, dying, grieving, lamenting, suffering, being in misery and in despair, in being subject to these the wish arises:—'Ah! if only we were not subject to this one or that one of those things! If only we could avoid them!'   But this cannot be had for the wishing.   This again is the ill of not getting what is wished for.

And what, bhikkhus, is 'in a word the Five Groups that arise from Grasping'?   These are the Groups of material form, of feeling, of perception, of dispositions, and of cognition that arise from grasping.   This is what is called 'in a word the Five Groups that arise from Grasping are associated with Ill.'

This, bhikkhus, is the Aryan Truth regarding Ill.

19. [308] And what, bhikkhus, is the Aryan Truth concerning the coming to be of Ill?

Even this Craving, potent for rebirth, that is accom-

panied by lust and self-indulgence, seeking satisfaction
now here now there, to wit, the craving for the life of
sense, the craving for becoming (renewed life), and the
craving for not becoming (for no rebirth) [1].

Now this Craving, bhikkhus, where does it take its
rise, where does it have its dwelling? In those
material things of this world which are dear to us,
which are pleasant. There does Craving take its rise,
there does it dwell.

What things in this world are dear, what things are
pleasant? The sense of sight, the sense of hearing, the
senses of smell, taste, touch and imagination—these are
the things in this world that are dear, that are pleasant.
There does Craving take its rise, there does it dwell.

Things seen, things heard, things smelt, tasted,
tangible, things in memory recalled—these are the
things in this world that are dear, that are pleasant.
There does Craving take its rise, there does it dwell.

The thoughts that arise through sight, the thoughts
that arise through hearing, the thoughts that arise
through smell, taste, touch and imagination—these are
the things in this world that are dear, that are pleasant.
There does Craving take its rise, there does it dwell.

The stimulus of visual sense, the stimulus of auditory
sense, the stimulus of the senses of smell, taste, touch
and imagination—these are the things in this world
that are dear, that are pleasant. [309] There does
Craving take its rise, there does it dwell.

Feeling that is born of the stimulus of the visual
sense, feeling that is born of the stimulus of the

---

[1] Vibhava. This word usually means power, prosperity, success—
the prefix vi being used as an intensitive particle. In this particular
connexion the traditional interpretation takes the prefix in a negative
sense, and paraphrases the word by 'the absence of becoming
(bhava).' This view is apparently supported by some Nikâya
passages (S. III, 57; It. no. 49), and by the Dhamma Sa*m*ganî 1314.
But it may be derived from them; and it is odd that the word should
have been found nowhere else in that sense. It is quite possible that
the original sense was the usual one. At Dhp. 282 it seems to mean
decline in wisdom.

auditory sense, feeling that is born of the stimulus of the senses of smell, taste, touch and feeling born of imagination—these are the things in this world that are dear, that are pleasant.   There does Craving take its rise, there does it dwell.

The perceiving of things visible, the perceiving of things audible, the perceiving of things odorous, sapid, tangible, of things in memory recalled—these are the things in this world that are dear, that are pleasant. There does Craving take its rise, there does it dwell.

Intentions concerned with things visible, intentions concerned with things audible, intentions concerned with things odorous, sapid, that may be smelt, tasted, touched, tangible, with things in memory recalled—these are the things in this world that are dear, that are pleasant.   There does Craving take its rise, there does it dwell.

Craving for things visible, craving for things audible, craving for things that may be smelt, tasted, touched, for things in memory recalled—these are the things in this world that are dear, that are pleasant.   There does Craving take its rise, there does it dwell.

Pre-occupation about things seen, pre-occupation about things heard, pre-occupation about things smelt, tasted, tangible, about things in memory recalled— these are the things in this world that are dear, that are pleasant.   There does Craving take its rise, there does it dwell.

Deliberating about things seen, deliberating about things heard, deliberating about things smelt, tasted, tangible, about things in memory recalled—these are the things in this world that are dear, that are pleasant. And there does Craving take its rise, there does it dwell.

[310] This, bhikkhus, is what is called the Aryan Truth concerning the coming to be of Ill.

20. And what, bhikkhus, is the Aryan Truth concerning the cessation of Ill ?

The utter cessation of and disenchantment about that very Craving, giving it up, renouncing it, emancipation from it, detachment from it.

But now this Craving, bhikkhus, where, in being put away, is it put away; where, in ceasing, does it cease? In those material things of this world which are dear to us, which are pleasant—there may this Craving be put away, there does it cease.

What things in this world are dear, what things are pleasant? The sense of sight, the sense of hearing, the senses of smell, taste, touch and imagination—these are the things in this world that are dear, that are pleasant. Here may this Craving be put away, here does it cease.

Things seen, things heard, things smelt, tasted, tangible, things in memory recalled—these are the things in this world that are dear, that are pleasant. Here may this Craving be put away, here does it cease.

The thoughts that arise through sight, the thoughts that arise through hearing, the thoughts that arise through smell, taste, touch and imagination—these are the things in this world that are dear, that are pleasant. Here may this Craving be put away, here does it cease.

The stimulus of visual sense, the stimulus of auditory sense, the stimulus of the senses of smell, taste, touch and imagination—these are the things in this world that are dear, that are pleasant. [311] Here may this Craving be put away, here does it cease.

Feeling that is born of the stimulus of the visual sense, feeling that is born of the stimulus of the auditory sense, feeling that is born of the stimulus of the senses of smell, taste, touch and feeling born of imagination—these are the things in this world that are dear, that are pleasant. Here may this Craving be put away, here does it cease.

The perceiving of things visible, the perceiving of things audible, the perceiving of things odorous, sapid, tangible, of things in memory recalled—these are the things in this world that are dear, that are pleasant. Here may this Craving be put away, here does it cease.

Intentions concerned with things visible, intentions concerned with things audible, intentions concerned with things odorous, sapid, that may be smelt, tasted,

touched, tangible, with things in memory recalled—these
are the things in this world that are dear, that are
pleasant. Here may this Craving be put away, here
does it cease.

Craving for things visible, craving for things audible,
craving for things that may be smelt, tasted, touched,
for things in memory recalled—these are the things in
this world that are dear, that are pleasant. Here
may this Craving be put away, here does it cease.

Pre-occupation about things seen, pre-occupation
about things heard, pre-occupation about things smelt,
tasted, tangible, about things in memory recalled—
these are the things in this world that are dear, that
are pleasant. Here may this Craving be put away,
here does it cease.

Deliberating about things seen, deliberating about
things heard, deliberating about things smelt, tasted,
tangible, about things in memory recalled—these are
the things in this world that are dear, that are pleasant.
Here may Craving be put away, here does it cease.

This, bhikkhus, is what is called the Aryan Truth
concerning the cessation of Ill.

21. And what, bhikkhus, is the Aryan Truth concerning the Way that leads to the Cessation of Ill?

This is that Aryan Eightfold Path, to wit, right
view, right aspiration, right speech, right doing, right
livelihood, right effort, right mindfulness, right rapture.

And what, bhikkhus, is right view? [312]

Knowledge, bhikkhus, about Ill, knowledge about
the coming to be of Ill, knowledge about the cessation
of Ill, knowledge about the Way that leads to the
cessation of Ill. This is what is called right view.

And what, bhikkhus, is right aspiration?

The aspiration towards renunciation[1], the aspiration

---

[1] Nekkhamma. Burnouf ('Lotus,' 334) derives this word from
nis+karma; Oldenberg ('Vinaya Texts,' I, 104) from nis+kâma,
and Childers (*sub voce*) from nis+kramya. These three deri-
vations would give the meaning respectively as having no Karma,
being devoid of lust, and going forth from home. Daramiśipola
explains it here as meaning either the second or the third. No doubt

towards benevolence, the aspiration towards kindness. This is what is called right aspiration.

And what, bhikkhus, is right speech?

Abstaining from lying, slander, abuse and idle talk. This is what is called right speech.

And what, bhikkhus, is right doing?

Abstaining from taking life, from taking what is not given, from carnal indulgence. This is what is called right doing.

And what, bhikkhus, is right livelihood?

Herein, O bhikkhus, the Aryan disciple having put away wrong livelihood, supports himself by right livelihood.

And what, bhikkhus, is right effort?

Herein, O bhikkhus, a brother makes effort in bringing forth will that evil and bad states that have not arisen within him may not arise, to that end he stirs up energy, he grips and forces his mind. That he may put away evil and bad states that have arisen within him he puts forth will, he makes effort, he stirs up energy, he grips and forces his mind. That good states which have not arisen may arise he puts forth will, he makes effort, he stirs up energy, he grips and forces his mind. That good states which have arisen may persist, may not grow blurred, may multiply, grow abundant, develop and come to perfection, he puts forth will, he makes effort, he stirs up energy, he grips and forces his mind. This is what is called right effort.

And what, bhikkhus, is right mindfulness? [313]

Herein, O bhikkhus, a brother, as to the body, continues so to look upon the body, that he remains ardent,

---

Oldenberg is right as to the derivation. But Darami/ipola is also right if we take his note as exegetical, not philological. The fact is that the derivation had been, from very early times, forgotten or confused; and the connotation of the word was renunciation generally, with special reference to these two kinds. It never had anything to do with Karma.

The three aspirations of our paragraph here recur at Samyutta II, 152, and on p. 151 nekkhamma is replaced by kâma. See also It. no. 72, and M. I, 114.

self-possessed and mindful, having overcome both the
hankering and the dejection common in the world.
And in the same way as to feelings, thoughts and ideas,
he so looks upon each, that he remains ardent, self-
possessed and mindful, having overcome the hankering
and the dejection that is common in the world. This
is what is called right mindfulness.

And what, bhikkhus, is right rapture?

Herein, O bhikkhus, a brother, aloof from sensuous
appetites, aloof from evil ideas, enters into and abides
in the First Jhâna, wherein there is cogitation and
deliberation, which is born of solitude and is full of
joy and ease. Suppressing cogitation and deliberation,
he enters into and abides in the Second Jhâna, which
is self-evoked, born of concentration, full of joy and
ease, in that, set free from cogitation and deliberation,
the mind grows calm and sure, dwelling on high. And
further, disenchanted with joy, he abides calmly contemplative while, mindful and self-possessed, he feels in
his body that ease whereof Aryans declare 'He that
is calmly contemplative and aware, he dwelleth at
ease.' So does he enter into and abide in the Third
Jhâna. And further, by putting aside ease and by
putting aside mal-aise, by the passing away of the
happiness and of the melancholy he used to feel, he
enters into and abides in the Fourth Jhâna, rapture of
utter purity of mindfulness and equanimity, wherein
neither ease is felt nor any ill. This is what is called
right rapture.

This, bhikkhus, is the Aryan Truth concerning the
Way leading to the cessation of Ill. [**314**]

So does he, with respect to ideas continue to consider ideas, both internally, or externally, or internally
and externally together. He ever considers how ideas
are something that comes to be, again he ever considers how they are something that passes away, or
again he ever considers their coming to be with their
passing away; or again with the consciousness 'There
are ideas,' mindfulness thereof is thereby established,

far enough for purposes of knowledge and of self-possession. And he abides independent, grasping after nothing in the world whatever. Thus, bhikkhus, does a brother, with respect to ideas, continue to consider ideas with respect to the Four Aryan Truths.

22. Bhikkhus! whoso shall thus practise these Four Applications of Mindfulness for seven years, in him one or two kinds of fruition may be looked for:— either in this present life The Knowledge [1], or, if there be yet residuum for rebirth, the state of him who returns no more. Or, not to speak of seven years, bhikkhus, whoso shall thus practise these Four for six years, for five only, for four only, for three only, for two only, for one year only, in him one or two kinds of fruition may be looked for: either in this present life The Knowledge, or, if there be yet residuum for rebirth, the state of him who returns no more. Or not to speak of one year, bhikkhus, whoso shall thus practise these Four for six months, or for five months, for four only, or three, or two, or one month only, [315] or half a month only, in him one or two kinds of fruition may be looked for: either in this present life The Knowledge, or, if there be yet residuum for rebirth, the state of him who returns no more. Or not to speak of half a month, bhikkhus, whoso shall thus practise these Four for seven days, in him one of two kinds of fruition may be looked for: either in this present life The Knowledge, or if there be yet residuum for rebirth, the state of him who returns no more. It was on account of this that that was said which was said (at the beginning) 'The one and only path, bhikkhus, leading to the purification of beings, to passing far beyond grief and lamentation, to the dying out of ill and misery, to the attainment of right method, to the realization of Nirvana, is that of the Four-fold Setting-up of Starting.

Thus spake the Exalted One. Pleased were the brethren, delighting in that which was spoken by the Exalted One.

---

[1] Aññâ; one of the many epithets of Arahantship.

INTRODUCTION

TO THE

PÂYÂSI SUTTANTA.

THIS Dialogue is one of the few which refer to events that took place in the Community after the Buddha's death. We hear from Dhammapâla (in his commentary on the 'Vimâna Vatthu,' p. 297) that the Dialogue was believed, when he wrote (that is, at Kâñcipura in South India in the fifth century) to have taken place after the erection of the cairns (thûpas) over the ashes of the Teacher. He does not say how long after; and the length of the interval is not very important, for all the Dialogues were put together more than fifty years at least after the Buddha's death[1]. The difference is only this, that whereas the Dialogues in which the principal part is ascribed to the Buddha himself may well, and very often undoubtedly do, contain material much older than the date of the redaction of the Dîgha, this Suttanta (and that is also true of the few others that fall into the same category) may not. The difference is not great.

In this particular case we find nothing fresh in the Suttanta. The climax, led up to at the end, shows us a messenger from the gods coming down from heaven to teach the doctrine of generosity (dâna) by laymen. We have discussed above in the Introduction to the 'Mahâ-govinda Suttanta' (p. 254) the reasons which induced ancient authors to bring down a divinity from heaven to support any particular opinion. Why was it done here? It seems scarcely necessary.

True, the doctrine does not occupy a very high position in the earliest documents. It does not appear at all in the thirty-seven points (afterwards called the Bodhi-pakkhiya-dhammâ) in which the Buddha, just before his death, summed up his teaching[2].

---

[1] See the general Introduction to the 'Dialogues,' I, 19.

[2] See above, pp. 128–30. The Wings of Wisdom are really only thirty, not thirty-seven, as seven of them are repeated. So there was plenty of room, had it been wanted, for charity. The Aryan Path is in the list. But the Path, though open to laymen and lay-women, contains no mention of dâna.

It does not appear in the Dhammapada, an anthology of verses current in the Community on twenty-six subjects which the makers of the anthology held of most importance. There is a miscellaneous section into which verses on charity might well have been introduced, had it been considered a point of equal value with the rest ; but it is not there. It is the first and lowest in the list of the ten Pâramitâs, the virtues necessary to the attainment of Buddhahood [1]. But this list is a late one, and is not found in the Four Nikâyas, or even in the Vinaya.

On the other hand there are several incidental references to giving in charity, and always by way of approval, in the Dialogues and the Samyutta. And in the Anguttara (which contains a good deal more of the milk for babes than the other three of the great Nikâyas) [2] there is a special Dâna Vagga with seven short Suttas on the subject, and six or seven more are scattered through the work [3].

It is clear therefore, though this particular virtue is ranked after the thirty Wings of Wisdom, that it is accorded, in the earliest Buddhism, a very respectable place. Nevertheless at this particular juncture, when the death of their Master had weakened the prestige of the Order, it is quite possible that the brethren, finding their numbers in excess of the sources of income and support, should have found it advisable to invoke the help of a *deus ex machina* to set the discrepancy right.

The rest of the Suttanta throws some light on the reputation in which Kassapa, the Boy-Wanderer, was held by his fellows. As becomes a flowery speaker (citra-kathî) he is lavish in illustration, and tells a number of stories, some of them quite good, and all of them bearing more or less relation (usually less) to the particular point in dispute. They are sufficient, however, to throw dust into the eyes of Pâyâsi, whose arguments, futile as they are, do not depend so exclusively on analogy, that most misleading of guides.

---

[1] The scholastics, by dividing each of the ten into three (see Childers, *sub voce*), have brought the number up to thirty, the same as the real number of the more ancient Wings of Wisdom, to which this later list is meant as a counterblast or rival.

[2] Compare Mrs. Rhys Davids's remarks in the Introduction to vol. VI.

[3] See Miss Hunt's 'Indexes,' under Dâna.

[XXIII. PÂYÂSI SUTTANTA.

REBIRTH AND KARMA.]

[316] Thus have I heard.

1. The venerable Kumâra Kassapa [1] was once walking on tour in Kosala together with a great company of bhikkhus, to the number of about five hundred, and coming to the Kosalese city named Setavyâ, he there abode. And there the venerable Kumâra Kassapa dwelt to the north of Setavyâ, in the Simsapâ-tree Grove. Now at that time the chieftain Pâyâsi was residing at Setavyâ, a spot teeming with life, with much grass-land and wood-land, with water and corn, on a royal domain granted him by King Pasenadi of Kosala, as a royal gift, with power over it as if he were the king [2].

2. Now at that time there came over Pâyâsi an evil view of things to this effect :—' Neither is there any other world, nor are there beings reborn otherwise than from parents, nor is there fruit or result of deeds well done or ill done.'

[317] Now the brahmins and householders of Setavyâ heard the news :—' They say that the wanderer Master Kassapa, disciple of the wanderer Gotama, walking on tour with a great company of bhikkhus, to the number of about five hundred, has arrived at Setavyâ and is staying there to the north of the town, in the

---

[1] The touching story of his birth is told in the Introductory Story to the twelfth Jâtaka, translated in Rhys Davids's 'Buddhist Birth Stories,' pp. 199 ff. He was declared by the Buddha to be the best of the preachers in the Order (A. I, 24). Kumâra was a nickname, 'The Boy' (because he was ordained so young), which distinguished him from the other Kassapas in the Order, and clung to him even in advanced years. It was the more appropriate, as kumâra means a boy of good family, a young gentleman, a master; and Kassapa, the son of a clansman, had been brought up at Pasenadi's court.

[2] See Vol. I, p. 108, note 1.

Si*m*sapâ-tree Grove. Now regarding that Master
Kassapa, such is the excellent reputation that has been
raised abroad :—' Wise and expert is he, abounding in
knowledge and learning, eloquent and excellent in
discourse, venerable too and an Arahant. And good is
it to interview Arahants like him.' Then the brahmins
and householders of Setavyâ, coming out from the town
in companies and bands from each district so that they
could be counted [1], went by the north gate, to the
Si*m*sapâ-tree Grove.

3. Now at that time Pâyâsi, the chieftain, had gone
apart to the upper terrace of his house for siesta. And
seeing the people thus go by he said to his doorkeeper:—
' Why are the people of Setavyâ going forth like this
towards the Si*m*sapâ-tree Grove ? ' [318] Then the
doorkeeper told him the news. And he said :—' Then,
good doorkeeper, go to the brahmins and householders
of Setavyâ and say to them :—" Pâyâsi, sirs, bids you
wait ; he will come himself to see the Wanderer
Master Kassapa." That Boy Kassapa will be winning over at the outset those foolish and inexpert
brahmins and householders of Setavyâ to think :—
" There is both another world and there are beings
who are born not of parents, and there is fruit, and
result of deeds well done and ill done." But, my good
doorkeeper, these three things do not exist.'

' Even so, sir,' said the doorkeeper, and carried out
his master's bidding.

4. So Pâyâsi, the chieftain, surrounded by the brahmins and householders of Setavyâ, came to the Si*m*sapâ-
tree Grove, and finding the venerable Kassapa,
exchanged with him the greetings and compliments of
politeness and courtesy, and took his seat on one side.
[319] And as to the brahmins and householders of
Setavyâ, some of them bowed before the venerable
Kassapa and took their seats on one side ; some of
them exchanged with him the greetings and compliments of politeness and courtesy and then took their

---

[1] The expression is somewhat ambiguous. See the note on I, 145.

seats on one side; some of them saluted him with joined hands and took their seats on one side; some of them called out their name and family and did likewise, some of them took their seats on one side in silence.

5. And when he was seated Pâyâsi spoke thus to the venerable Master Kassapa :—

'I, Master Kassapa, am of this opinion, of these views :—Neither is there another world, nor are there beings reborn not of parents, nor is there fruit or result of deeds well done or ill done.'

'I, Prince, have neither seen or heard of any one holding such a view, such an opinion. How then can you declare, as you do, that "there neither is another world, nor rebirth as inheritor of the highest heavens, nor fruit or result of deeds well-done or ill-done"? Wherefore, Prince, I will cross-question you herein, and do you reply in what way you may approve. What think you, yon moon and sun, are they in this world or in another world, are they divine or human?'

'This moon and sun, Master Kassapa, are in another world, not in this, they are gods, not human.'

'Then, Prince, let this be taken as evidence that there is both another world, and rebirth as inheritor of the highest heavens, and fruit and result of deeds done well or ill.'

6. 'Even though Master Kassapa says thus, it still appears to me that not one of these things exists.'

'Have you, Prince, any proof to establish that they do not exist?'

[320] 'I have, Master Kassapa.'

'As how?'

'Here it is, Master Kassapa. I have had friends, companions, relatives, men of the same blood as myself, who have taken life, committed thefts, or fornication, have uttered lying, slanderous, abusive, gossiping speech, have been covetous, of malign thoughts, of evil opinions. They anon have fallen ill of mortal suffering and disease. When I had understood that they would not recover from that illness, I have gone to them and

said :—" According to the views and opinion held, sirs,
by certain wanderers and brahmins, they who break
the precepts of morality, when the body breaks up
after death, are reborn into the Waste, the Woeful Way,
the Fallen Place, the Pit.   Now you, sirs, have broken
those precepts.   If what those reverent wanderers and
brahmins say is true, this, sirs, will be your fate.   If
these things should befall you, sirs, come to me and
tell me, saying :—' There is another world, there is
rebirth not of parents, there is fruit and result of deeds
well-done and ill-done.'   You, sirs, are for me trustworthy and reliable, and what you say you have seen,
will be even so, just as if I myself had seen it."   They
have consented to do this, saying, " Very good,"
[321] but they have neither come themselves, nor
dispatched a messenger.   Now this, Master Kassapa,
is evidence for me that there is neither another world,
nor rebirth not by human parents, nor fruit or result
of deeds well done and ill.'

7. ' Well then, prince, I will yet ask you this, and do
you answer even as you think fit.   What think you ?
Take the case of men who have taken a felon red-
handed and bring him up saying :—" My lord, this felon
was caught in the act ; inflict what penalty you wish."
He replies :—" Well then, sirs, bind this man securely,
his arms behind him, with a strong cord ; shave his
head ; lead him around, to the sound of a sharp drum,
from street to street, from cross-road to cross-road, and
out at the southern gate ; there, south of the town in
the place of execution, cut off his head."   They, assent-
ing with " Very good," proceed to carry out these
orders, and, in the place of execution, make him sit
down.   Now would the felon gain permission of this
sort from his executioners: " Let my masters, the
executioners, wait till I have visited my friends and
advisers, my kinsmen by blood, in this or that village
or town, and come back" ?   [322] Or would the
executioners cut off the head of this vain talker ?'

'They would not grant the permission, Master
Kassapa ; they would cut off his head.'

'But this felon, prince, is human and cannot get leave from human executioners. How much less then would your friends and relatives, after death, in the Pit, gain permission from the keepers of the Pit, saying:—" Let my masters, the Pit-keepers, wait till we have gone and told the chieftain Pâyâsi, that there is both another world and rebirth other than of parents, and fruit and result of deeds well-done and ill ?" Be this exposition a proof to you, Prince, that these things exist.'

8. 'Even though Master Kassapa says thus, it still appears to me that not one of these things exists.'

'Have you, prince, any further proof to establish that they do not exist ?'

'I have, Master Kassapa.'

'As how ?'

[323] 'Here it is, Master Kassapa. I have had friends and companions, kinsmen, men of the same blood as myself, who have abstained from taking life, from committing thefts, or fornication, from lying, slandering, rude, or frivolous speech, who have not coveted, or had malign thoughts or evil opinions. They anon have fallen ill of mortal suffering and disease. When I had understood that they would not recover from that illness, I have gone to them and said : " According, sirs, to the views and opinions held by some Wanderers and Brahmins, they who keep the precepts of morality, when the body breaks up, are after death reborn into the bright and happy world. Now you, sirs, have kept those precepts. If what those reverend samaṇas and brahmins say is true, this, sirs, will be your fate. If these things should befall you, sirs, when you have been there reborn, come to me and let me know that there is both another world, rebirth other than of parents, and fruit and result of deeds well-done and ill-done. You, sirs, are for me trustworthy and reliable, and what you say you have seen, will be even so, just as if I myself had seen it." They have consented to do this, saying " Very good " ; but they have not come and let me know, nor have

they dispatched a messenger. Now this again, Master Kassapa, is evidence to me that [**324**] there is neither another world, nor rebirth other than of parentage, nor fruit and result of deeds well-done and ill-done.'

9. 'Well then, Prince, I will make you a simile, for by a simile some intelligent persons will recognize the meaning of what is said. Just as if a man were plunged head-under in a pit of mire. And you were to order men saying :—"Well now, masters, pull the man out of that pit." They, saying "Very good," were to comply and pull him out. You were then to say to them :— "Well now, masters, brush the mire smearing him from off his body with split bamboo [1]." And they were to obey you. And you were to say to them :— "Well now, masters, shampoo this man's body a treble massage with yellow shampoo powder." And they were to do so. And you were to say to them :—" Now, masters, rub him with oil, and bathe him three times using fine chunam." And they were to do so. And you were to say to them :—" Well, masters, now dress his hair [2]." And they were to do so. [**325**] And you were to say to them :—" Now, masters, deck him with a costly garland and costly unguent and costly garments." And they were to do so. And you were to say to them :—" Well, masters, take him up on to the palace and amuse him with the pleasures of the five senses." And they were to do so. Now what think you, O chieftain ? Would this man, well bathed, well anointed, shaved and combed, dressed, wreathed and adorned, clad in clean raiment, taken to the upper palace, and indulging in, surrounded by, treated to, the five pleasures of sense, be desirous of being plunged once more into that pit of mire ?'

'No indeed, Master Kassapa.'

---

[1] No doubt a sort of brush made of split bamboo.

[2] How elaborate were the coiffures used by men at this date may be seen from the illustration in Rhys Davids's 'Buddhist India,' p. 97.

' And why ? '

' Foul, Master Kassapa, is a pit of mire, foul and counted as such, stinking, disgusting, repulsive, and counted as such.'

' Even so, Prince, are human beings in the eyes of the gods, foul and counted as such, stinking, disgusting, repulsive, and counted as such.   The smell of man offends the gods a hundred leagues away.   What then ? Shall your friends and companions, your kinsmen and connexions who, having kept the precepts, are reborn into the bright and happy place, come and bring you word that there is another world, that there is rebirth other than by parentage, [326] that there is fruit and result of deeds well-done and ill-done ?   Let this exposition, chieftain, be evidence to you that these things exist.'

10. ' Even though Master Kassapa says so, it still appears to me that not one of these things exists.'

' Have you any further evidence, prince ? ' . . .

' I have, Master Kassapa.'

' As how ? '

' Here it is, Master Kassapa.   I have had friends, companions, kinsmen, men of the same blood as myself, who kept the precepts, abstaining from taking life ; from taking what was not given, from inchastity, lying speech and strong intoxicating liquors.   They anon have fallen mortally ill ; and I, having told them how some samaṇas and brahmins say that, after such a life, one would be reborn in the communion of the Three-and-Thirty Gods, have asked them, if they were so reborn, to come and let me know that there was another world, birth other than of parents, and fruit and result of deeds well-done and ill-done.   [327] They have promised to do so, but they have neither come and told me, nor sent a messenger.   This, Master Kassapa, is evidence to me that not one of those things exists.'

11. ' Well then, Prince, I will reply by asking you something, and do you answer as you think fit.   That which, humanly speaking, is a century, this to the

Three-and-Thirty Gods is one night and day. Of
such a night thirty nights are the month—of such a
month twelve months are the year—of such a year
the celestial thousand years are the life-span of the
Three-and-Thirty Gods. Those of whom you now
speak will have attained rebirth into the communion
of these Gods. If it should occur to them thus :—
"Let us for two or three days indulge ourselves, surrounded by and steeped in the five pleasures of sense,
and thereafter let us go and tell the chieftain Pâyâsi
that there is another world, rebirth other than of
parents, and fruit and result of deeds well-done and
ill-done"—would they then have come to you, and
told you so?'

'Certainly not, Master Kassapa ; for we should have
been dead long before. But who lets Master Kassapa
know all these things :—that there are Three-and-
Thirty Gods, or that the Three-and-Thirty Gods live
so many years? We do not believe him when he says
these things.' [328]

'That, Prince, is just as if there were a man born
blind who could not see objects as dark or bright, as
blue, yellow, red or brown ; who could not see things
as smooth or rough, nor the stars, nor moon, nor sun.
And he were to say :—" There are none of these things,
nor any one capable of seeing them. I don't know
them, I don't see them ; therefore they don't exist."
Would one so speaking, speak rightly, Prince?'

'Not so, Master Kassapa. The visual objects of
which you speak do exist, and so does the faculty of
seeing them. [329] To say "I don't know them, I
don't see them ; therefore they don't exist" : that would
not be speaking rightly.'

'But even so, methinks, do you, Prince, talk like
the blind man in my parable when you say :—" But
who lets Master Kassapa know that there are Three-
and-Thirty Gods, or that the Three-and-Thirty Gods
live so many years? We do not believe him when he
says these things." For, Prince, the other world is not,
as you imagine, to be regarded with this fleshly eye.

Those Wanderers and Brahmins who haunt the lonely
and remote recesses of the forest, where noise, where
sound there hardly is, they there abiding strenuous,
ardent, aloof, purify the eye divine; they by that purified eye divine, passing the vision of men, see both
this world and that other world, and beings reborn not
of parents.   In this way, Prince, is the other world to
be seen; and not, even as you imagine, by this fleshly
eye.   Let this be a proof to you that there is another
world, that there are beings reborn not of parents,
that there is fruit and result of deeds well-done and
ill-done.'

12. 'Even though Master Kassapa says so, [330]
yet it still appears to me that not one of these things
exists.'

'Have you any further evidence, Prince?'

'I have, Master Kassapa.'

'As how?'

'Here it is, Master Kassapa.   I see Wanderers and
Brahmins moral and of virtuous dispositions, fond of
life, averse from dying, fond of happiness, shrinking
from sorrow.   Then I think, Master Kassapa:—"If
these good Wanderers and Brahmins were to know
this—'When once we are dead we shall be better off'
—then these good men would take poison, or stab
themselves, or put an end to themselves by hanging,
or throw themselves from precipices.   And it is because
they do not know that, once dead, they will be better
off, that they are fond of life, averse from dying, fond
of happiness, disinclined for sorrow.   This, Master
Kassapa, is for me evidence that there is no other
world, no beings reborn otherwise than of parents, no
fruit and no result of deeds well and ill-done.'

13. 'Well then, Prince, I will make you a simile,
for by way of a simile some wise men discern the
meaning of what is spoken.   Once upon a time, Prince,
there was a brahmin who had two wives.   By one he
had a son, ten or twelve years of age; the other was
pregnant and near her time.   Then the brahmin
died.   Now the boy said to his mother's co-wife:—

"Whatever treasure there is, lady, or grain, or silver, or gold, all that is mine. [331] There is nothing here for you whatever ; make over to me, lady, the heritage of my father ! " Then the brahminee made answer to him :—" Wait, my lad, till my child is born. If 'twill be a boy, one portion shall be his ; if a girl, she shall wait on you."

'But the boy reiterated his claim again and yet again. Then the brahminee, taking a sword, entered an inner room and ripped up her belly, saying :—" If I can only find out whether 'tis a boy or a girl." Thus did she destroy both her own life and her unborn infant, and her wealth also, through the foolish and thoughtless way in which, seeking a heritage, she met with ruin and disaster. Even so you, Prince, foolish and thoughtless that you are, will meet with ruin and disaster by seeking without wisdom for another world. [332] Moral and virtuous Wanderers and Brahmins do not force maturity on that which is unripe ; they, being wise, wait for that maturity. The virtuous have need of their life. In proportion to the length of time such men abide here, is the abundant merit that they produce and accomplish for the welfare of many, for the happiness of many, out of compassion for the world, for the advantage, the welfare, the happiness of gods and men. Let this then be a proof to you, Prince, that there is another world, that there is rebirth other than of parentage, that there is fruit and result of deeds well and ill-done.'

14. 'Even though Master Kassapa says so, it still appears to me that not one of these things exists.'

'Have you further evidence, Prince ? '

'I have, Master Kassapa.'

'As how, Prince ? '

'Here it is, Master Kassapa. Take the case of men who having taken a felon red-handed bring him up, saying :—" This felon, my lord, was caught in the act. Inflict on him what penalty you wish." And I should say :—" Well then, my masters, throw this man alive into a jar ; close the mouth of it and cover it

over with wet leather, put over that a thick cement
of moist clay, put it on to a furnace and kindle a fire."
[333] They saying "Very good" would obey me and ...
kindle a fire. When we knew that the man was dead,
we should take down the jar, unbind and open the
mouth, and quickly observe it, with the idea :—" Perhaps we may see the soul of him coming out!" We
don't see the soul of him coming out! This, master
Kassapa, is for me evidence that there neither is
another world, nor rebirth other than by parentage,
nor fruit or result of deeds well or ill-done.'

15. 'Well then, Prince, I will in reply ask you something, and do you answer as you may please. Do you
not admit, Prince, that, when you are taking siesta,
you see dreams of enjoyment in garden, grove, country,
or lake side?'

'I do admit it, Master Kassapa.'

'Are you at that time watched over by attendant
women—hunchbacks and dwarfs, and maidens[1] and
girls?'

'That is so, Master Kassapa.'

'Do they see your soul entering or leaving you?'

[334] 'Not so, Master Kassapa.'

'So they who are living do not see the soul of you
who are living entering or leaving you (when you
dream). How then will you see the soul of a dead
person entering or leaving him? Let this be a proof
to you, Prince, that those things do exist.'

16. 'Even though Master Kassapa says so, it still
appears to me that not one of those things exists.'

'Have you any further evidence, Prince?'

'I have, Master Kassapa.'

'As how?'

'Take the case, Master Kassapa, of men taking a felon
red-handed, and bringing him up saying :—" My lord,
we caught this felon in the act. Inflict what penalty

---

[1] Velâmikâ, 'very young and childish,' says Buddhaghosa here.
Above, p. 231, it seems to be a clan name, but used in a similar
connexion.

you wish." And I say:—"Well then, my masters,
take this man and weigh him alive; then strangle him
with a bowstring and weigh him again." And they do
so. While he lives, he is more buoyant, supple, wieldy.
When he is dead, he is weightier, stiffer, unwieldier.
This, Master Kassapa, is evidence for me that there is
neither another world, nor rebirth other than by human
parentage, nor fruit nor result of deeds well-done or
ill-done.'

17. 'Well now, Prince, I will give you a simile [**335**],
for by way of a simile some wise men discern the meaning of what is said. It is just as if, Prince, a man
were to weigh in a balance a ball of iron that had been
heated all day, and was burning and glowing with heat;
and were to weigh it later on in a balance when it was
cool and quenched. When would that ball of iron be
lighter, softer and more plastic? When it was burning and glowing with heat, or when it was cool and
quenched?'

'When, Master Kassapa, that ball of iron, with its
lambent and gaseous concomitants, is burning and
glowing with heat, then it is lighter, softer, more plastic,
but when, without those lambent and gaseous concomitants, it is cool and quenched, it is then heavier, more
rigid, less plastic.'

'Even so, Prince, when this body has its concomitants
of life, heat and intelligence, then it is lighter, softer
and more plastic. But when it lacks those three
concomitants, then it is heavier, more rigid, less plastic.

'Let this, Prince, be a proof to you that there is both
another world, rebirth other than of parents, and fruit
and result of deeds well and ill-done.'

18. 'Even though Master Kassapa says this, it still
appears to me that not one of those things exists.'

'Have you any further evidence, Prince?'

'I have, Master Kassapa.'

'What might that be like?'

'Take the case, Master Kassapa, of the men taking
a felon red-handed and bringing him up, saying:—"My
lord, this felon was caught in the act. [**336**] Inflict on

him what penalty you wish." And I say:—"Well, my masters, kill this man by stripping off cuticle and skin and flesh and sinews and bones and marrow." They do so. And when he is half dead, I say:—"Lay him on his back, and perhaps we may see the soul of him pass out." And they do so, but we see the passing of no soul. Then I say:—"Well then, lay him bent over . . . on his side . . . on the other side . . . stand him up . . . stand him on his head . . . smite him with your hand . . . with clods . . . on this side . . . on that side . . . all over; perhaps we may see the soul of him pass out." And they do so, but we see the passing of no soul. He has sight and there are forms, but the organ does not perceive them; he has hearing and there are sounds, but the organ does not perceive them; he has smell and there are odours, [**337**] but the organ does not perceive them, he has a tongue and there are tastes, but the organ does not perceive them; he has a body and there are tangibles, but the organ does not perceive them. This, Master Kassapa, is for me evidence that there is neither another world, nor rebirth other than of parents, nor fruit or result of deeds well or ill-done.'

19. 'Well then, Prince, I will give you a simile, for by way of a simile some wise men discern the meaning of what is said. Once upon a time, Prince, a certain trumpeter, taking his trumpet of chank-shell, travelled to the folk on the border. When he came to a certain village, he stood in its midst and blew thrice on his trumpet, then laying it on the ground sat down beside it. Now, Prince, those border folk thought:—"Whose is this sound so charming, so lovely, so sweet, so constraining, so enervating?" Coming together they asked the trumpeter. "This, my masters, is what men call a trumpet, the sound whereof is so charming, so lovely, so sweet, so constraining, so enervating." They laid the trumpet on its back and said:—"Speak, master trumpet! speak, master trumpet!" No sound did the trumpet make. They laid the trumpet curving downward, on this side, on that side, they stood it upright,

they stood it topsy turvy, they struck it with their hands, with a clod, with a stick, with a sword, on one side, on the other, on every side, saying :—" Speak, master trumpet ! speak, master trumpet ! " [**338**] Then, Prince, the trumpeter thought :—" How silly are these border born men ! Why will they seek so senselessly for the trumpet's sound ? " And while they looked on, he took his trumpet, blew thrice upon it and, taking it with him, went away. Then, Prince, those border born men thought thus :—" When forsooth there was with that trumpet a man, and an effort, and air, that same trumpet made sounds. But when there was with it neither man, nor effort, nor air, that same trumpet made no sounds." Even so, Prince, when this body has its concomitants of life, heat and intelligence, then it goes about and comes back, it stands and sits and lies down, it sees forms with the eye, hears sounds with the ear, smells odours with the smell, tastes tastes with the tongue, touches the tangible with the body, cognizes things with the mind. But when it lacks those three concomitants, it can do none of these things. Let this, Prince, be to you a proof that there both is another world, rebirth other than of parents, and fruit and result of deeds well and ill-done.'

20. ' Even though Master Kassapa says this, [**339**] it still appears to me that there is neither another world, nor rebirth other than of parents, nor fruit or result of deeds well or ill-done.'

' Have you any further evidence, Prince ? '

' I have, Master Kassapa.'

' What may that be like ? '

' Take the case, Master Kassapa, of men who have taken a felon red-handed and bring him up, saying :— " My lord, we caught this felon in the act ; inflict on him what penalty you wish." And I say :—" Well, my masters, flay this man alive, perchance we may see the soul of him passing out." They do so, but no passing of the soul of him do we see. And in cutting out his integument, and his flesh, and his nerves, and breaking his bones and extracting the marrow thereof, still no

soul of him do we see.   This, Master Kassapa, is for me
evidence that there is neither another world, nor rebirth
other than of parents, nor fruit or result of deeds well
or ill-done.'

21. 'Well now, Prince, I will give you a simile, for
it is by way of a simile that some intelligent men discern
the meaning of what is spoken.   Once upon a time,
Prince, a fire-worshipping Jaṭila was dwelling in a leaf-
hut in a woodland spot.   Now the people of a certain
country-side migrated.   And their leader, after spend-
ing one night near the Jaṭila's hermitage, went away.
[340] Then the Jaṭila thought :—" If I were to go to
that leader's camp, I might perhaps get something
useful."   And rising up betimes he came to the leader's
camp, and there he saw, abandoned and lying on its
back a little baby.   And when he saw it he thought :—
" It is not fit that I should let a human being die while
I look on.   What if I were to carry this baby to my
hermitage, and foster, tend, and rear it ? "   So he
carried the baby to his hermitage, and fostered, tended,
and reared it.   When the boy had attained the age of
ten or twelve years, it happened that the Jaṭila had
something or other to do in the country-side.   So he
said to the boy :—" I want to go to the country-side, my
lad ; keep up the fire ; do not let it go out.   If it should
go out, here is a hatchet, here are sticks, here is the fire
drill, so that if you do let the fire out, you can rekindle
it again."   And having thus instructed the boy, the
Jaṭila went off to the country-side.   Intent upon his
play, the boy let the fire out.   Then he thought :—
" Father told me, ' Tend the fire, my lad ; let it not go
out.   If it should go out, here is a hatchet, here are
sticks, here is the fire drill, so that if you do let the fire
out, you can rekindle it again.'   What if I were now
to do so ? "   [341] Then the boy chopped the fire drill
with the hatchet, thinking :—" Perhaps that's how I
shall get fire."   No fire got he.   He split the fire drill
in twain, in three, four, five, ten, a hundred pieces, he
made it into piecemeal, he then pounded it in a mortar,
and winnowed it in the wind, thinking that so he might

perhaps get fire. No fire got he. Then the Ja*t*ila, having accomplished his business, came back to his own hermitage and said to the boy:—" Why, child, you have let the fire out!" "Father, the fire went out because I was busy at my game. Then I thought of what you had told me, and I set about rekindling it. And I chopped the fire drill with the hatchet to get fire, but no fire came. And I went on till I had smashed the fire drill into atoms, pounded it in a mortar and winnowed it in the wind, but I never got any fire!" Then the Ja*t*ila thought :—" How silly, how unintelligent is the lad! Why will he be seeking fire in this senseless manner?" And while the boy looked on, he took a fire drill, and making fire said to him :—[342] " This is how to make fire, my lad. One doesn't try to get it as you, so silly and unintelligent, were trying." Even so, Prince, have you, silly and unintelligent, sought after another world. Renounce, Prince, this evil set of opinions. Let them not involve you for long in bale and sorrow!'

22. 'Even though Master Kassapa says this, I still cannot bring myself to renounce this evil set of opinions. King Pasenadi the Kosalan knows me, and so do foreign kings, as holding to the creed and the opinion that there is neither another world nor rebirth other than of parents, nor fruit or result of deeds well and ill-done. If I, Master Kassapa, renounce these opinions, people will say of me :—" How silly is Prince Pâyâsi, how unintelligent, how badly he grasps anything!" In wrath thereat will I keep to it. In guile will I keep to it. In self-respect will I keep to it!'

23. 'Well then, Prince, I will give you a simile; for it is by way of a simile that some intelligent men discern the meaning of what has been said. Once upon a time, Prince, a great caravan of a thousand carts was going from the East country into the West country. Wherever it went, it consumed swiftly straw, wood, water and verdure. Now in that caravan were two caravan leaders, each commanding one half of the carts. [343] And this occurred to them :—

' " This is a great caravan, one of a thousand carts.
Wherever we go, we consume everything. What if
we were to divide this caravan into two, five hundred
carts in each."

'So they divided that caravan into two equal
portions. Then one of the leaders collected large
quantities of straw, wood and water, and started [his
carts]. On the second or third march the leader saw
a swarthy red-eyed man coming from the opposite
direction, armed with a quiver, wearing a lotus wreath,
his garments and hair wet, and driving a chariot drawn
by asses, its wheel splashed with mud. When he saw
this man he said :—" Whence come you, Sir ? "

' " From such and such a district "

'" Whither go you ? "

'" To such and such a district."

' " Has there, Sir, been any great fall of rain recently
in the jungle ? "

'" Yes indeed, Sir, there has been a great rain in
the jungle just in front, the roads are well watered,
there is much grass and wood and water. [344] Throw
away the grass and wood and water, Sir, you have
already got ; with light-laden carts you will go quite
quickly ; do not tire your teams."

' Then the leader told his carters what the man had
said, and bade them throw away their provender and
wood, that the caravan might travel more quickly.

' " So be it, sir," the carters replied, and did so. But
at their first camp they saw no grass or wood or water,
nor at the second, third, fourth, fifth, sixth or seventh
camp. So they all met with ruin and disaster. And
then that fiend, the yakkha, devoured all the men and
the cattle in that caravan, leaving only the bones
behind.

' When the second caravan leader knew that the
other caravan had got well on its way, he took in large
supplies of grass and wood and water and set out.
And he too met a swarthy red-eyed man, [345] and
exchanged with him the same remarks, and was also
bidden to throw away his provender.

'Then that leader said to his carters: "This man, sirs, says that there has recently been much rain in the jungle, that the roads are watered, and there is plenty of grass and wood and water. And he advises us to throw away our provender, so that, with lightened carts we may travel quicker and not weary our teams. But this man, sirs, is not a friend of ours, nor a kinsman, nor of our blood. Why should we act as if we trusted him? Our stock of provender is not to be thrown away; let the caravan proceed with the goods we brought; let us not part with what we have."

'"So be it, sir," agreed the carters, and went on with the stock they had loaded. And at seven successive camping places they saw no grass or wood or water; [**346**] but they saw the other caravan that had come to grief. And they saw the skeletons of the men and cattle devoured by that yakkha fiend.

'Then the caravan leader said to the carters: "That caravan, my masters, met with ruin and disaster, through having that silly caravan leader for its guide. Well then, let us leave here such of our wares as are of little value, and take from that caravan such wares as are of great value. "So be it, master," replied the carters, and made the transfer, and passed safely through the jungle, through having this wise caravan leader for their guide.[1]

'Even so you, Prince, silly and unintelligent, will meet with ruin and disaster in that you seek so senselessly after another world, even like that former caravan leader. They who fancy that they can believe whatever they hear, will meet with ruin and disaster, even like those carters. Renounce, Prince, this evil set of opinions; renounce them, I say! Let them not involve you long in bale and sorrow!'

24. 'Even though Master Kassapa says this, I still

---

[1] This story has been turned into a Jâtaka by identifying the hero as the Buddha in a previous birth, and has been made the first story in the collection afterwards put together as the Jâtaka Book. It is one of twelve stories in that book found in the older texts. See 'Buddhist India,' p. 195.

cannot bring myself to renounce this evil set of opinions. King Pasenadi the Kosalan knows me, and so do foreign kings, as holding to the creed and the opinion [347] that there is neither another world, nor rebirth other than of parents by human parentage, nor fruit or result of deeds well and ill-done. If I, master Kassapa, renounce these opinions people will say of me : " How silly is prince Pâyâsi, how unintelligent, how badly he grasps any-thing !" In wrath thereat will I keep to it. In guile will I keep to it. In self-respect will I keep to it !'

25. 'Well then, Prince, I will give you a simile, for it is by way of a simile that some intelligent men discern the meaning of what has been said. Once upon a time, Prince, a certain swineherd was going from his own village to another village. There he saw a heap of dry dung thrown away. Seeing it he thought :—"That's a lot of dry dung thrown away which will feed my pigs. What if I were to carry it away ?" So he spread out his cloak and collecting the dry dung tied it into a bundle and lifting it on to his head went on. In the after-part of his journey there fell a heavy shower of rain out of season. He, splashed with muck to his nail-tips, bearing his oozing, dripping dung-burden, went on his way. And men seeing him said :—" Gramercy, you must be mad, you must be out of your senses ! How can you tote along that oozing, dripping load of dung, splashed with muck to your nail-tips ? " " It's you that are mad, you that are out of your senses ; by this my pigs will get food." [348] Even so, methinks, Prince, do you talk, like this dung-carrying simile. Renounce, Prince, this evil set of opinions, renounce them, I say ! Let them not be long a cause of bale and sorrow to you.'

26. ' Even though Master Kassapa says this, I cannot bring myself to renounce this evil set of opinions. King Pasenadi the Kosalan knows me, and so do foreign kings, as holding to the creed and the opinion that there is neither another world, nor rebirth other than of parents by human parentage, nor fruit or result of deeds well or ill-done. If I, Master Kassapa, renounce these opinions, people will say of me :—" How silly is Prince Pâyâsi, how

unintelligent, how bad is his grasp of things!" In anger
thereat will I keep to it. In guile will I keep to it. In
self-respect will I keep to it!'

27. 'Well then, Prince, I will give you a simile, for it
is by way of a simile that some intelligent men discern
the meaning of what is said. Once upon a time, Prince,
two gamesters were playing with dice. One gamester
swallowed as it came each adverse die. The other
gamester saw him do this and said:—"Look here, friend,
you've won outright; give me the dice; I will make
a votive offering of them." " Good, friend," said the
other, and handed over the dice. Then the second
gamester smeared over the dice with poison, and proposed to the former :—" Come along, friend, let's play."
" Good, friend," replied the other. Again, therefore,
they played, and again that gamester swallowed each
adverse die. [349] The second gamester saw him doing
so and said :—

> The man knows not the swallowed die
> With sharpest burning is smeared o'er.
> Swallow, you false cheat, swallow now!
> Bitter the hour at hand for you![1]

'Even like the simile of the gamester, Prince, methinks
is what you say. Renounce, Prince, this evil set of
opinions, renounce them, I say! Let them not be long
a source of bale and sorrow to you!'

28. 'Even though Master Kassapa says this, I still
cannot bring myself to renounce this evil set of opinions.
King Pasenadi the Kosalan knows me, and so do foreign

---

[1] This story is also in the Jâtaka Book, I, 380. The *modus
operandi* of the cheat is rendered obscure by our ignorance of the
game played. Lüders in his 'Würfelspiel der alten Inder' has
shown that the dice were seeds of a tree called the Vibhîtaka, and
that the usual game was probably to throw a number of seeds on
a board, having previously fixed on a certain number. The seeds
fell some upright, some on their sides. Only the upright ones
counted. If they were less than the agreed number it was a draw; if
equal the thrower won and threw again; if more he lost, and lost the
throw. An extra seed was called the kali, 'the unlucky die.' This
the cheat seems to have managed to pick up, and swallow.

kings, as holding to the creed and the opinion that
there is neither another world, nor rebirth other
than of parents, nor fruit or result of deeds well or
ill-done. If I, Master Kassapa, renounce these opinions,
people will say : " How silly is Prince Pâyâsi, how unintelligent, how bad is his grasp of things ! " In wrath
thereat will I keep to it. In guile will I keep to it. In
self-respect will I keep to it.'

29. 'Well then, Prince, I will give you a simile, for it
is by way of a simile that some intelligent men discern
the meaning of what is said. Once upon a time, Prince,
a certain country-side migrated. And one man said
to his crony :—" Let's go friend, to that country-side ;
perhaps we may come upon some treasure." " Good,
friend," assented the other. And they came to where,
in that country-side, there was a certain village street.
[350] There they saw a heap of hemp thrown away.
Then one said to the other : " Here's a heap of hemp :
do you make some into a bundle, I'll do the same and
we'll carry it away." The other consented, and they
did so.

'Bearing this burden they went on to another village
street. There they saw a heap of hempen thread
thrown away, and one said to the other :—" This heap
of hempen thread thrown away is just the thing we
want hemp for. Well then, friend, you throw away
your load of hemp, I'll throw away mine, and we'll take
away each a load of hempen thread." " I've brought
this load of hemp a long way, friend, and it's well tied
up—that's enough for me ; you choose for yourself."
So the former changed his load for one of hempen
thread.

'Then they came to another village street. There
they saw a heap of hempen cloths. And the one
said to the other :—" This heap of hempen cloths is
just the thing we want hemp for, or hempen thread
for. Well then, friend, do you throw away your load
of hemp, I'll throw away my load of hempen thread,
and we'll each take a load of hempen cloth." " I've
brought this load of hemp a long way, friend, and it's

well tied up—that's enough for me; you choose for yourself." So the former changed his load for one of hempen cloth.

'Then they came to another village street. There they saw a heap of flax; and to another where they saw linen thread; and to another where they saw linen cloth. And at each place the one crony made a change for the better, the other retained his hemp. [351] Further they saw cotton-down, cotton thread and calico; and the same thing happened. Further they saw iron, copper, tin, lead, silver, gold. So that in the end the one crony had a load of gold, the other of hemp.

'So they came to their own village. There the crony who brought a load of hemp pleased neither his parents, nor his own family, nor his friends, and won neither pleasure or happiness. [352] But the other with his load of gold both gave and won pleasure.

'Even like the simile of the load of hemp, methinks Prince, is what you say. Renounce, Prince, this evil set of opinions, renounce them, I say! Let them not be long a source of bale and sorrow to you.'

30. 'With Master Kassapa's first simile I was pleased, I was charmed; moreover I wanted to hear his ready wit in questions, for I regarded Master Kassapa as one who was to be opposed. It is wonderful, Master Kassapa, it is marvellous! just as if one were to set up what has been upset, or were to reveal that which has been hidden away, or were to point out the road to the bewildered, or were to bring a lamp into the darkness, so that they that have eyes may see—even so has the truth been declared in many a figure by Master Kassapa. And I, even I, betake myself for refuge to Gotama the Exalted One, to the Doctrine and to the Brotherhood. May Master Kassapa accept me as a disciple, as one who from this day forth as long as life endures, has taken him as his guide. And I should like, Master Kassapa, to offer a great sacrifice. Let Master Kassapa instruct me herein that it may bring me long welfare and happiness.'

31. 'At the sort of sacrifice, Prince, where oxen are

slain, or goats, or fowls and pigs, or divers creatures
are put an end to; [353] and those that take part in
the sacrifice have wrong views, wrong intention, wrong
speech, wrong action, wrong livelihood, wrong endeavour, wrong mindfulness, wrong rapture, such a
sacrifice, Prince, is neither of great fruitfulness nor of
great profit, nor of great renown, nor of widespread
effect [1].   It is just as if a farmer, Prince, were to enter
a wood taking with him plough and seed, and were
there, in an untilled tract, in unfavourable soil, among
unuprooted stumps, to plant seeds that were broken,
rotten, spoilt by wind and heat, out of season, not in
good condition, and the god were not to give good
rain in due season. Would those seeds attain to
growth, increase and expansion, or would the farmer
get abundant returns ? '

'No indeed, Master Kassapa.'

'So is it, Prince, with that sort of sacrifice.   But
where, Prince, neither oxen are slain, nor goats, nor
fowls and pigs, nor are divers creatures put an end to,
and those that partake of the sacrifice have right
views, right intention, right speech, right action, right
livelihood, right endeavour, right mindfulness, right
rapture, such a sacrifice is of great fruitfulness, of great
profit, of great renown, of widespread effect.   It is
just as if a farmer, Prince, were to enter a wood,
taking with him plough and seed, and were there, in
a well-tilled tract, in favourable soil well cleared of
stumps, [354] to plant seed that was unbroken, free
from mildew, unspoilt by wind or heat, in season and
in good condition, and the god were to give good rain
in due season.   Would those seeds grow, increase, expand, and would the farmer get abundant returns ? '

'He would indeed, Master Kassapa.'

'So is it, Prince, with that sort of sacrifice, where ...
no creatures are put to death, and those that take part

---

[1] So of the sacrifice intended by the Very Reverend Sir Gold-stick
Sharp-tooth in the Kû*adanta.   See especially above, I, 163.

therein are of high character. Such a sacrifice is of great fruitfulness, profit, renown and widespread effect.'

32. Then Prince Pâyâsi instituted a gift to Wanderers and Brahmins, the poor, wayfarers, beggars and petitioners. In that gift such food was given as gruel and scraps of food, and coarse robes with ball-fringes [1]. And at that gift a young brahmin named Uttara was passed over [2]. When the largesse had been distributed he mocked, saying : ' By this largesse I have met Prince Pâyâsi in this world, but how about the next?[3]' [355] Pâyâsi heard of this, and sent word to Uttara asking him if it was true that he was saying this ?

' Yes, sir,' replied Uttara.

' But why have you been saying this, my dear Uttara ? Do not we who are seeking merit look for result from giving ? '

' In your gift, sir, such food as gruel and broken meats are given which you, sir, would not touch with your foot, much less eat; also coarse ball-fringed robes which you, sir, would not deign to use as carpets, much less to wear. You, sir, are pleasant and dear to us; how are we to associate what is pleasant and dear with what is unpleasant?'

' Well then, my dear Uttara, do you arrange that such food shall be given as I eat, and such garments be given as I wear.'

' Very good, sir,' replied Uttara, and did so [4].

---

[1] To keep the robes down.

[2] Vyâva/o. This became almost a technical term in connexion with largesse. It is literally 'hindered'; but when the things to be given were too limited as compared with the number of applicants, some had to be passed over. They were dâna-vyâva/â 'hindered at the largesse' (Jât. III, 129). Compare D. II, 141; Sum. I, 296; Jât. I, 89; VVA. 298. But here perhaps it may simply mean 'objected to the largesse.'

[3] Literally ' do not associate (with him) in the next.' The gibe intended must be very nearly as we have rendered. But both the reading of the text and the grammatical construction are doubtful. The word we have rendered 'mocked' (uddissati) has only been found here. Perhaps it means 'showed (the matter) up,' which comes to much the same as to point the finger of mockery.

[4] Apparently at his own cost.

[356] Now prince Pâyâsi, inasmuch as he had bestowed his gift without thoroughness, not with his own
hands, without due thought, as something discarded,
was, after his death, reborn into the communion of the
Four Great Kings[1], in the empty mansion of the
Acacia. But the youth Uttara, who had objected to
that gift and had bestowed his gift thoroughly, with
his own hands, with due thought, not as something
discarded, was, after his death, reborn in a bright and
happy world, into the communion of the Three-and-
Thirty Gods.

33. Now at that time the venerable Gavampati[2]
used frequently to go for siesta to the empty mansion
of the Acacia. And Pâyâsi, now one of the gods, came
up to him and, saluting him, stood on one side. To
him so standing the venerable Gavampati said :—'Who
art thou, friend?'

'I, sir, am prince Pâyâsi.'

'Wert thou not once of the opinion that there was
no other world, no rebirth other than of parents, no
fruit or result of deeds well or ill-done?'

[357] 'I was indeed, sir, but through his reverence
Kumâra Kassapa I detached myself from that evil set
of opinions.'

'But the youth Uttara, who objected to thy gift,
friend, whereunto has he been reborn?'

'He, Sir, having objected to my gift, and having
himself bestowed a gift thoroughly, with his own hands,
with due thought, not as something discarded, has,
since he died, been reborn in the bright and happy
world, into the communion of the Three-and-Thirty
Gods. I, sir, inasmuch as I bestowed my gift without
thoroughness, not with my own hand, without due
thought, as something discarded, was after my death

---

[1] The guardian spirits of the four quarters. See the Introduction
to the Mahâ-samaya Suttanta.

[2] He had been the son of a merchant at Benares; and had been
received into the Order by the Buddha at the very beginning of his
career as a teacher (Vin. I, 19). This legend supposes him, still a
man, going for meditation to the lower heavens.

reborn into the communion of the Four Great Kings, in the empty mansion of Acacia. Wherefore, Gavampati, Sir, go thou into the world of men and tell them :—" Give ye your gifts with thoroughness, with your own hands, with due thought, and give not as if ye were discarding somewhat. For so did not prince Pâyâsi; and he after his death was reborn into the communion of the Four Great Kings, in the empty mansion of the Acacia. But the youth Uttara, who bestowed his gifts in the right way, was after his death reborn in the bright and happy world, into the communion of the Three-and-Thirty Gods." '

34. So the venerable Gavampati came back to the world of men, and there told these things.

The Pâyâsi Dialogue is ended.

INDEX I.

PRINCIPAL SUBJECTS AND PROPER NAMES.

Vessabhu, one of the six previous Buddhas, 6, 7.
Vessâmitta, god, 287.
Vessavana, a god, 241, 251, 259, 305.
Vetendu, god, 288.
Vetha-dîpa, brahmin of, 188.
Vicakkhana fairies, 291.
Vihâra, in old texts a room, not a monastery, 4, 106, 157.
Vipassi, a former Buddha, 6 ff.; people's derivation of the name, 17.
Virûlhaka, a guardian spirit, 241, 259, 287.
Virûpakkha, god of the West quarter, 259, 288.
Vishnu, 290.
Visions, the four; aged, diseased, dead man, and a wanderer, 18 ff. See Eye.
Vissakamma, architect to the gods, 212.
Viru, and Virucca, gods, 288.

Voice, the ideal kind of, 16.

Wanderer, described, 22.
Weighing a dead man, 360.
Welfare, conditions of, for clansmen and Wanderers, 80 ff.
Wheel, the mystic, behaviour of, 202–204.
Wheel, Lord of the, king of the Golden Age, 13, 155, 157.
Wings of Wisdom, the thirty-seven, 128, 129.
Wisdom Tree, 23, 33, 113.
Women, 98, 102, 154, 160, 163, 206, 276, 279, 306.
World, the next, messenger from, 352–355.

Yama, twins, 290.
Yasa, a god, 290.

Zarathustra, 1.

INDEX II.

PALI WORDS DISCUSSED.